SHAPING TOMORROW'S LAW

Human Rights and European Law

SHAPING TOMORROW'S LAW

Human Rights and European Law

Building New Legal Orders

VOLUME I

MARY ARDEN
Lady Justice of Appeal

OXFORD
UNIVERSITY PRESS

OXFORD
UNIVERSITY PRESS

Great Clarendon Street, Oxford, OX2 6DP,
United Kingdom

Oxford University Press is a department of the University of Oxford.
It furthers the University's objective of excellence in research, scholarship,
and education by publishing worldwide. Oxford is a registered trade mark of
Oxford University Press in the UK and in certain other countries

First Edition published in 2015

Impression: 1

Published in the United States of America by Oxford University Press
198 Madison Avenue, New York, NY 10016, United States of America

British Library Cataloguing in Publication Data

Data available

Library of Congress Control Number: 2014946125

ISBN 978–0–19–872857–3

Printed and bound by
CPI Group (UK) Ltd, Croydon, CR0 4YY

Contents

Preface by The Lord Chief Justice of England and Wales

The 1990s saw the beginning of a period of unprecedented legislative change in our law, including the passing of the Human Rights Act 1998 and the devolution of legislative and executive powers to Northern Ireland, Scotland and Wales; this was followed by the coming into force of the Lisbon Treaty reshaping the EU. These changes reflected broader changes in society, the economy, and technology. During the same period, Lady Justice Arden was appointed to the High Court and then to the Court of Appeal of England and Wales.

Although cases which come before the courts have provided an opportunity to develop the common law to reflect these changes, the scale of the changes has necessitated a broader consideration which looks beyond the day to day business of judging. Lady Justice Arden describes this in several different ways, including 'work that is preliminary to judging...by looking at the subject in the round' and 'thinking outside the box'. As she rightly points out judges bring to all their work the values which are part of their experience and personality. Her broad education, her studies at Cambridge and Harvard, her chairmanship of the Law Commission, her work as Head of International Judicial Relations, and her tireless journeying to different jurisdictions (to mention but a small part of her experience) have enabled her to analyse the issues that must be faced, to suggest innovative solutions and to see them carried into practice.

One clear example is dialogue. In its long history of development the common law has frequently been enriched by ideas gleaned through dialogue with other legal systems. However, the relationship that the national courts of Europe now have with the supranational courts at Luxembourg and Strasbourg has necessitated a dialogue where much more than the exchange of ideas is required. That new dialogue Lady Justice Arden pioneered, initiated, and continues to develop. In her 2014 Neill Lecture (Chapter 20) her proposals include the issue of provisional judgments by a supranational court when it made a significant development of the law so that the national courts could comment on the development.

A second example is her clear analysis of the concepts of proportionality and subsidiarity. Her 2012 King's College Lecture (Chapter 4) is a fascinating exposition of how proportionality has been adopted into the common law and how it might be developed further.

A third is her pertinent examination of the role of the UK Supreme Court in a state without a written constitution. Although she makes plain it has a leadership role in setting out the way in which the law should develop by selecting cases that will enable it to set the law in a new direction, she questions what principles should guide the Court, where should the limits lie, and what should be the province of the elected legislature. Consistent with her overall scholarship, she urges that much more be learnt about the ways that the other supreme courts perform their modern role before the United Kingdom decides what role it wishes its Supreme Court to follow.

This first Volume of papers covers her approach to the field of European and Human Rights law. The authority with which Lady Justice Arden speaks on these topics is underlined by the contributions from Dame Sian Elias, Chief Justice of New Zealand, Bernard Stirn and Matthias Gyomar of the French Conseil d'Etat, and Professor Dr Andreas Voßkuhle, President of the Federal Constitutional Court of Germany.

We are indeed fortunate to be able to have so readily to hand this first Volume of papers which illuminate not only the way in which the common law has developed within the UK over the past 20 or so years, but to have so many pointers and ideas for its future development. I warmly commend it to a wide readership.

The Rt Hon Lord Thomas of Cwmgiedd,
The Lord Chief Justice of England and Wales

Acknowledgements

I would like to thank my senior colleagues, especially the Lord Chief Justice of England and Wales, The Lord Thomas of Cwmgiedd, who has kindly written the Preface, and the Master of the Rolls, Lord Dyson, for their support in completing this project. I would also like to thank the distinguished contributors to this Volume from other jurisdictions. They are in order: The Rt Hon Dame Sian Elias DBE, the Chief Justice of New Zealand; Bernard Stirn and Matthias Gyomar, members of the French Conseil d'Etat; and Prof Dr Andreas Voßkuhle, President of the Federal Constitutional Court of Germany. Their insights give much food for thought. I have in addition gained much from discussions with my judicial colleagues and also with judicial friends and counterparts in many jurisdictions, such as Judge Paul Mahoney and The Rt Hon Sir Francis Jacobs, and with many members of the academic and practising professions across the world. They have all played their part. So, too, have some of my non-lawyer friends, such as Alison Donaldson, who have generously given of their time to listen to my ideas about the law and shared their wisdom with me. I am deeply grateful to them all. Last, but certainly not least, I owe a deep debt of gratitude to all my family, particularly my husband, Jonathan Mance, and my friends, for their support. The faults remain my own.

Lady Justice Arden
Member of the Court of Appeal
for England and Wales

1 September 2014
Royal Courts of Justice

Note on references to the law of England and Wales
I refer in the main to English law but this should be read as meaning the law of England and Wales.

Why This Collection?

The traditional image of judges is as anonymous authority figures responsible for deciding cases, but this is slowly changing. Today, judges give more lectures and write more articles than they have done in the past. (Until the late twentieth century, judges were not encouraged to give speeches at all.) In addition, the public has come to know judges from the work which they do apart from writing judgments—such as sitting on inquiries, giving evidence in Parliament, and so on. This means that there is a growing interest in what judges have to say out of court. And there are times when the approach of a judge matters, because that judge has to decide some novel point of law, and the ideas that individual judges express out of court may give a strong clue as to their thinking. Furthermore, legal ideas are often of wide public interest, especially when they reflect social or other change.

The period since my appointment as a High Court judge in 1993 has been one of great change in law and society: globalization, Europeanization, and human rights legislation, as well as social, institutional, and constitutional developments. As senior judges, we cannot speak about party political matters, but we do regularly try to work out how changes in society affect the work of the courts and the administration of justice. Some of these changes are reflected in the lectures and articles which I have written during my judicial career. In the main, I have used writing as an opportunity to pursue new approaches or ideas that I would like to see adopted in the law. I have sought to bring to bear on the subject my academic background as well as my experience both as a judge and law reformer. The stimulus for any new approach or idea will usually come from some work that I have done judicially. The choice of subjects is thus eclectic and as varied as my caseload.

My own principal areas of interest include the law of the European Union (EU) and human rights. This first Volume brings together my writings in that area. It tracks the course of legal thinking in the wake of the decision to introduce European human rights into domestic law by the Human Rights Act 1998. It is the evolution of those ideas which is important because they demonstrate how much change has taken place and must yet take place. The second Volume will deal with more domestic but equally pressing matters, such as law in a changing society and improving and interpreting legislation.

Each Section in Volume I begins with a brief contribution by a distinguished legal figure giving their perspective on the subjects discussed. I also include my own short frontispiece to each Section which provides some context about the relevant issues.

The Sections in this Volume interlock. Although it was not obvious to me when I originally wrote the papers included in this book, they chart the impact of the system of human rights and EU law in the UK since the Human Rights Act came into force in 2000.

Section A is the starting point of this great journey. When the Human Rights Act 1998 was enacted, giving the courts power to enforce rights guaranteed by the European Convention on Human Rights (the Convention),[1] the judges had to master new methods of legal analysis and understand new concepts. The chapters in Section A deal with some of the overall effects and the most significant new concepts and methodological changes involved in absorbing European ideas on human rights into domestic law.

Section B deals with some of the more far-reaching repercussions of the Human Rights Act 1998 and EU law on our own law. Many areas of law underwent some change when the Human Rights Act 1998 came into force. My work focuses on the two particular areas where the changes raised questions about how best to balance competing interests: the protection of private information or privacy, and the determination of the rights of suspected terrorists.

Section C deals with the constitutional changes brought about by EU law and human rights. The position here is still fluid. The main issue is the relationship between the national courts and the two supranational courts in Europe, the Court of Justice of the European Union in Luxembourg (the Luxembourg Court) and the European Court of Human Rights in Strasbourg (the Strasbourg Court). This has been a very contentious issue over the last few years in the United Kingdom, where politicians frequently express the view that the Strasbourg Court has exceeded its function and trespassed on questions which the democratically elected institutions should decide. There are some calls for the United Kingdom to withdraw from the Convention. Similar points of view have been expressed in other contracting states.

Each of the two supranational courts has a different relationship with the national courts. It should also be noted that EU law is automatically binding on the national legal systems of the member states; whereas in the case of Strasbourg jurisprudence, there is some scope for variation in implementation. But, even in the former case, there is a debate about the scope of the powers conferred on the European Union by the EU Treaties and thus on the remit of EU law. The debate about these relationships started, in my experience, at the relatively lowly level of the steps which the supranational courts take to make it easier for national courts to follow their case law and to make the system of supranational adjudication more effective. I particularly promoted the idea of dialogue between the national and supranational courts to provide a forum for these ideas. Courts have developed that dialogue and it has been constructive. This has evolved into dialogue of a different kind, namely expressions of differences of view between national and

---

[1] The Convention rights incorporated by the Human Rights Act 1998 and the principal provisions of that Act are set out in the Appendix, together with Arts 1 and 13 of the Convention. These Articles were not incorporated by the 1998 Act but are referred to in the text.

supranational courts as to the bounds of the legitimate exercise of their respective powers.

The debate about the relationships between national courts and supranational courts is ongoing and expanding its ground. The case law of each of the supranational courts creates a legal order which is distinct and separate from any national legal order. So the debate is shaping legal orders and forging the constitutional position of the supranational courts. The end is not yet in sight: it is not yet clear what the shape of those legal orders will be. There are at least three possible outcomes: integration, disintegration, or a more equal partnership between national and supranational courts.

It is evident that complex legal ideas do not simply emerge from the ether fully-fledged, but take time to develop. It is easy to forget what went before, but we have to recall the past in order to assess how far we have come. I have therefore deliberately not updated or amended the lectures, which should be read as at the dates they were first given or published.[2] However, the frontispieces at the beginning of each Section give a flavour of how issues have evolved over time.

If anyone were to ask me why he or she should read the two Volumes in this collection, I would answer that they shed light on how one judge at least thinks about the task of interpreting and developing the law in the face of the enormous changes which have taken place in law and society. Readers can reach their own views on the topics discussed but I hope that they will be struck by the range of ideas in the law that judges think about, and note that the approach taken is not flashy, but instead it is realistic, carefully researched, and measured.

This book refers to some of the cases I have decided in my career but they are not its focus. Judges do not generally discuss their decisions after they have been delivered. As former Chief Justice Murray Gleeson of Australia once put it, you cannot write your judgment twice. It is for another court to interpret it. A judge cannot add to or detract from what he or she has decided in a judgment by some comment in a lecture given or article written out of court. If this happened, it would undermine the certainty of what has been decided in the recorded judgment.

This book is therefore about what I would regard as work preliminary to judging. Writing articles and giving speeches provides an opportunity to look at a subject in the round, without the constraints of a particular case. But, sooner or later, the skills or knowledge learnt become relevant to an actual judgment. If there is an issue before me as to whether an idea I have expressed in a lecture or article represents the law, I have to decide that issue in the light of the parties' arguments at the time.

I hope the ideas discussed will be relevant and stimulating for a variety of readers. These include, first, people with an interest in the legal world, whether judges, practitioners, or politicians and members of Parliament; second, other people who are concerned about the law; and, third, members of those groups currently under-represented in the judiciary (which is predominantly white and male) who are considering whether to aim for a judicial career.

---

[2] There is inevitably some overlap between the papers as ideas develop.

A career with an international outlook

It may be clear by now that one of the major themes in my particular career is the international perspective. I have always regarded it as extremely important to gain new perspectives by comparing the law in my own country with that of other jurisdictions, or by looking at whole new areas of law that have been developed elsewhere to resolve problems that we have not yet had to face. Insights can be obtained by studying comparative law in textbooks and journals or by visiting foreign courts and judiciaries, attending conferences and receiving visits from overseas judges and academics. By learning how issues are dealt with abroad we can do our job better at home.

My career has given me ample opportunity to draw such comparisons. Since 2005 I have been the Judge in charge, now Head, of International Judicial Relations for England and Wales. The post had not previously existed but was created in anticipation of the separation of the judiciary of England and Wales from the legislature and executive brought about by the Constitutional Reform Act 2005. As a separate institution, the judiciary had to conduct its own foreign policy and I became, so to speak, its foreign secretary. My responsibility was, where appropriate, to facilitate relations with other judiciaries and to receive visits from them in London. This led me to having particular responsibility for relations with the two European supranational courts, the Luxembourg Court and the Strasbourg Court. For instance, I set up a regular series of meetings between the UK judiciary and the judges of these courts. There are many benefits to the judiciary from engagement with other jurisdictions. There are often points of mutual interest. Moreover, not only can we learn from other legal systems. On occasions, we can also influence them.

Going further back in time, some of my interest in international judicial relations and comparative law may have its origins in my experiences while growing up. I spent my childhood in Liverpool, a major seaport looking westwards away from continental Europe towards Ireland and the Americas. The city has a rich cultural heritage: Welsh, Chinese, Polish, Caribbean, and so on. It is also socially diverse, with large numbers of poor and unemployed. When I was growing up, it had been a rich and vibrant seaport but was for various reasons in decline. Geographically, Liverpool is very close to Wales, and thus I spent many holidays in areas of outstanding natural beauty, getting to know some of the ways of the Welsh community.

School life also gave me a taste for the world beyond Britain. I had many friends whose parents and families lived in far-flung parts of the former British Empire, particularly Africa. I grew up hearing stories about life in these interesting places and felt that I wanted to know more about them. From school I went to Girton College, Cambridge. This gave me further opportunities to meet people from other parts of the world, as well as an excellent grounding in the law.

The Cuban missile crisis occurred while I was at school, and we discussed among ourselves what difference this might make for our futures and our hopes in life.

Our greatest fear was war and the thought that we, like our parents before us, would lose siblings and fathers in the conflict. In the event, it was not this crisis, but President Kennedy's assassination, that had a major effect on my life. Following that tragic event, the City of London raised large sums of money for education, which were put into the Kennedy Memorial Trust. My good fortune was to receive a scholarship from the Trust to study for another master's degree, following my undergraduate years and master's degree at Cambridge, this time at Harvard Law School in Boston, Massachusetts in 1970. That opportunity made a profound difference to the way I saw the role of the law in society. It also changed my perception that our own law would always produce a perfect answer. It was, moreover, a great honour and encouragement to receive an award in memory of one of the most progressive and charismatic leaders of his time.

While at Harvard Law School, I attended seminars by the best known scholars of their generation, including Professors Lon Fuller, Jack Dawson, James Chadbourn, Louis Loss, and Sam Thorne. Professor Fuller followed in the tradition of the 'American realists', the twentieth century movement of scholars in the United States. This was highly influential on the study of law in the United States and it placed significantly greater emphasis on how the law should be developed and applied to meet prevailing social conditions than on the study of past case law. In addition, in the 1960s there was tremendous activity in the field of civil rights. It was not until 1965 that African Americans were put on an equal footing for voting, and the process of integration was ongoing while I was there. There was an intense debate about freedom. There were also many demonstrations about civil rights and the war in Vietnam. Perhaps what we saw in the United States was the early development of a protest democracy in support of human rights. I had not seen the like in the United Kingdom.

We increasingly have to know about developments in other parts of the world and this is as true in the law as anywhere else. I hope this book contributes to a deeper understanding of human rights and European law.

SECTION A

MASTERING A NEW SYSTEM

Section A starts with the features of the 'Convention system', that is, the legal order operated by the Strasbourg Court, which most impressed me while I was there in 1999 before the Human Rights Act 1998 was implemented. There is an overall assessment of the first decade of the 1998 Act and an explanation of the important new concepts which human rights and EU law introduced into domestic law, such as proportionality and subsidiarity. It becomes clear that a robust approach is required when interpreting statutes related to human rights in EU law, and that the roots of the qualified rights[1] go back to nineteenth century liberalism.

---

[1] That is, those rights, such as that of freedom of expression, with which the state may, under the express provisions of the Convention, interfere.

Preface by The Rt Hon Dame Sian Elias, DBE PC, Chief Justice of New Zealand

When I started practising law in the courts of New Zealand in the late 1960s, human rights hardly featured. They were something invoked overseas, not at home. The law of the United Kingdom, to which we looked for most ideas, was similarly barren. And if some of us, like the author of these essays, returned from graduate study in the United States fizzing with ideas about civil rights and equality for women, we soon subsided. It was a time when courts were deeply suspicious of social or political context and often indifferent to administrative injustice in result, unless it was demonstrated to be perverse or irrational. Into that world came the New Zealand Bill of Rights Act 1990, a statute which then had no equivalent elsewhere. It preserved the decencies of Parliamentary sovereignty. Its principal author described it as 'a set of navigation lights' for legislators, administrators, and judges. Its most significant provision was a strong direction to judges that legislation was to be interpreted to give effect to the rights identified. Although some, including Lord Cooke of Thorndon, saw the transformative potential of the Act, the more generally-held view was that the legislation built on existing law and was 'evolutionary'. The legal system was not well-prepared for the change. More than twenty years later, some of the more difficult questions about human rights are only just beginning to emerge.

Today, in confronting the issues thrown up by human rights, we are fortunate to have the context of the very similar Human Rights Act enacted in 1998 in the United Kingdom, and the case law and scholarly thinking it has generated. The United Kingdom engagement with human rights has also brought greater accessibility for outsiders to the rich and developed European jurisprudence on human rights, helpfully translated for those with common law habits. The benefit of comparison and exchange in such matters is not confined to legal systems which have adopted statutory bills of rights (which now include the State of Victoria and the Australian Capital Territory). The treatment of human rights does not differ greatly in countries in which such standards constitute fundamental law, as they do in most Commonwealth jurisdictions. So linkages and connections in thought help all jurisdictions in domestic cases and spread a culture of rights in which, under the influence of international obligations and international legal orders, greater congruence is inevitable. Comparison is both steadying and, at times, salutary. The publication in accessible form in this collection of a selection of the works of one of the more thoughtful and knowledgeable commentators on comparative human rights law, and the new methodology and thinking it requires, is a welcome spur to the hard thinking which is required if human rights are to be fit for purpose.

Statutory statements of rights occupy space rightly described as 'constitutional'. Many, especially those at the business end of law, who share the British constitutional tradition, did not have much occasion before the advent of human rights statements to think about constitutional values. Sleep-walking through the human rights transformation is not the path taken by Mary Arden. She is concerned in her writings to get her thinking in order, in advance. She suggests that human rights require us to alter the way we think about the position of the individual in relation to the state and are changing the way we think about law. In addition, as Mary Arden points out, they force us to think about democracy, because the justification for qualification or limitation of rights is grounded on what is acceptable in a free and democratic society.

Since all are interested in human rights and their impact on society and democracy, the judiciary has a special responsibility to make judgments accessible. The statutory expression of rights provides organizing principles which have democratic legitimacy. They need to be conscientiously applied in patient exposition. A 'law is law' formalism will not convince. And because the most important role of statements of rights is in developing a constitutional culture of respect and observance, judges will do real disservice to rights if they do not convince when applying human rights in actual cases.

Human rights need to be assessed in a wide context, which has implications for judicial selection, education, and method. Sweeping conclusions need to be justified. This requires flexible and sophisticated application of proportionality analysis (it is instructive here to look closely at the methodology adopted by the Luxembourg and Strasbourg Courts).

Domestic traditions too must be respected. They provide the legitimacy of their own and safe methodology (the common law way). They also prompt questions about whether international standards provide a foundation upon which domestic responses to human rights can develop.

The values of human rights are well supported by the values of the common law and are illuminated by the ideas of British thinkers, as Mary Arden illustrates in relation to positive notions of liberty (the site of much contemporary contest about privacy). Because human rights are not static and turn on cultural and ethical insight, litigation about rights raises questions about our attitude to precedent, evidence of 'legislative fact', and statutory interpretation. Their application raises consequential questions for domestic law such as whether a finding of proportionality is one of fact or law.

Finally, the 'new boundaries' to law provided by human rights spread beyond direct application. Mary Arden suggests that human rights jurisprudence may yet become a 'crowbar' which will open up private law (the branch of law that deals with the rights and duties of private individuals and the relations between them) for invigoration.[2] In raising and addressing hard questions such as these, comparative law provides both a spark to the imagination and a reality check. And the comparative law analysis undertaken in this collection is peppered with well-chosen illustrations from European and United Kingdom case law.

This illuminating collection is written by a judge and law reformer, a close observer of the human rights phenomenon, and someone who is intensely interested in how this fits within the architecture of the law and law's 'inner morality'.

The Rt Hon Dame Sian Elias,
Chief Justice of New Zealand

---

[2] See the Conclusion of Chapter 2, *Building a Better Society.*

PART I

IMPLEMENTING HUMAN RIGHTS

Undoubtedly the most important challenge that has faced the judiciary during my time so far as a judge has been the incorporation of human rights into domestic law by the Human Rights Act 1998. This legislation called for new knowledge and skills on the part of judges. It brought in its train some of the most difficult problems in particular fields such as terrorism and media law, and it required judges to engage with some new concepts, in particular proportionality (in other words, the principle that state or other action has to be proportionate). The problems are ongoing and the concepts are still in their early stages of development.

People often ask why in this country we need to have human rights. After all, it is said, the common law has over the centuries protected the rights of individuals to an unprecedented extent. My answer is that human rights represent values of a modern democratic and plural society governed by the rule of law. Human rights are often about the protection which such a society gives to a minority against the will of the majority. Therefore, they will sometimes be about, or be perceived as being about, giving rights to unpopular elements in society (suspected terrorists, for example) at the expense of the majority.

In addition to the rights that are given by our common law, the human rights that apply in the United Kingdom today are those set out in the European Convention on Human Rights, which dates from 1950. This Convention set up the European Court of Human Rights in Strasbourg, which is the court that authoritatively interprets the Convention.

The United Kingdom chose to adopt these rights in its domestic legal order rather than to establish some new statement of rights of its own. The United Kingdom is a member of an international organization of European states known as the Council of Europe, and the states that are members of the Council of Europe agree to abide by the Convention. Furthermore, UK lawyers were very influential when the Convention was drafted and thus many values of the common law find their reflection in the Convention. Today, events have moved on and there is a serious debate as to whether the United Kingdom should have its own bill of rights and what that bill of rights might contain. (Such a bill of rights would be adopted by statute rather than an international instrument and might contain or build on the rights in the Convention.) There is also a debate as to whether the United Kingdom should remain a party to the Convention. But these are political issues and not matters in which judges are directly involved.

When I was at university in the late 1960s, law schools did not teach human rights jurisprudence created by the European Court of Human Rights. The result was that judges such as myself were without the basic university training in human rights that law students would get today. So, when the Human Rights Bill was first introduced into Parliament, I arranged to take leave of absence and spend time working in the European Court of Human Rights. This gave me an invaluable insight into the way that the Court worked and the content of its case law. Knowledge of the way the Strasbourg Court works is important for UK lawyers and judges, given that it is the authoritative court for interpreting the Convention. Moreover, the responsibility for giving effect to Convention rights is shared by that court and the various courts in the states that are party to the Convention. In due course, judges were given extensive training in human rights before the Human Rights Act 1998 came into force and I became one of the judges who instructed other judges.

Early experiences in Strasbourg

In the paper on which Chapter 1 is based, *Common Law in the Age of Human Rights*, I wrote about the way in which the European Court of Human Rights carries out its role. Much of what I then said remains valid, although the number of Convention states has increased from 43 to 47 in the meantime. In addition, as a result of the work of the United Kingdom during its recent presidency of the Council of Europe, there have been a number of reforms to the procedure of the European Court of Human Rights. And since 2000, there has also been a considerable increase in the judicial dialogue between the different European jurisdictions (a subject I take up in Section C).

Chapter 2, *Building a Better Society*, deals with the impact which the Human Rights Act 1998 had on judicial review of executive action (which is used when the court's jurisdiction to review a decision of a public body for lawfulness, rationality or fairness is invoked). As a result of the Human Rights Act 1998, the onus of proof in judicial review proceedings shifts to the government to justify any interference with a Convention right. In addition, the governmental action has to be 'proportionate'. I deal with proportionality in more detail in Part II, but the basic idea is that the state should interfere with a person's rights only to the extent that the needs of the community require it to do so. This is a more intense level of scrutiny of governmental action than applies in cases not involving human rights issues. (In such cases, where it is said that the decision of a minister or public body was unreasonable, the applicant must surmount the high hurdle of showing that the decision was one which no reasonable decision-maker, properly instructed as to the law and the facts, could reasonably have made.[1])

---

[1] This is known as the *Wednesbury* test after the decision of the Court of Appeal in *Associated Pictures Houses v Wednesbury Corporation* [1948] 1 KB 223, in which Lord Greene MR laid down this test.

Historical and philosophical context

The third chapter of this Part, Chapter 3, *On Liberty*, was written in honour of Lord Bingham of Cornhill, to whom much of the development of the case law is due. In it, I sought to show the origins of the Convention rights in the liberal philosophy in the United Kingdom of the nineteenth century, which was itself a product of liberal thought in Europe at that time. In addition, as mentioned, English lawyers were substantially responsible for its drafting. These points are worth remembering at a time when there is a serious debate as to whether the United Kingdom should remain a party to the Convention.

1

Common Law in the Age of Human Rights

This chapter is based on the Holdsworth Lecture 2000: Presidential address of
The Rt Hon Lady Justice Arden DBE.*

Introduction

On 2 October 2000 the principal provisions of the Human Rights Act 1998 came
into effect in England and Wales. After that date the courts[1] must not act in a way
which is incompatible with the rights secured by the European Convention on
Human Rights and must take into account the jurisprudence (that is, case law) of
the European Court of Human Rights. This change is sometimes said to threaten
to bring about a sea change in the common law. Journalists point to the experience
in Scotland where, in less than a year since the Convention became part of the law
of Scotland as respects acts of the Scottish Executive, there have been several
hundred cases raising points under the Convention. Under the title 'A judicial
iceberg that threatens our rulers', Magnus Linklater wrote in *The Times* on 16
March 2000 about the notion that the European Convention on Human Rights
would challenge the traditional supremacy of Parliament in the following terms:

The speed with which that has been demonstrated in Scotland has caught lawyers and civil
servants by surprise. More than 300 cases have already been brought under the European
Convention, and not just on minor points of law. One of them contested the rights of
temporary sheriffs, routinely drafted in by the Government to speed up the courts, to hear
cases. The Lord Advocate, who selects them, is a political appointee, and that, under article
6 of the Convention,[2] which defines the right to a fair trial, is not independent enough.

The whole system is having to be scrapped and a new body set up to introduce the necessary
element of objectivity. Scotland's widely admired Children's Panel system, which deals with
offending behaviour by young people, could be overturned because its members too are
appointed by government.

---

* This chapter is reproduced here with the kind permission of the Holdsworth Club, Faculty of Law
in the University of Birmingham.

[1] References to 'the courts' in this paper are to the courts of England and Wales.

[2] The Convention rights incorporated by the Human Rights Act 1998 and the principal provisions
of that Act are set out in the Appendix.

Even the conviction of motorists for drink-driving is having to be reconsidered. A landmark judgment handed down by Lord Rodger, Scotland's senior judge, overturned the conviction of a woman who had been asked under Section 172 of the Road Traffic Act to identify her car. She was freed because, according to the Convention, her admission deprived her of her right to silence[3]. The judge accepted that the implications of the case were 'momentous', and since the Act is a British one, it will need attention at Westminster as well as the Crown Office in Edinburgh.

. . . It is hard to see where it will end. The rights of organisations like the British Medical Council, the Law Society or even the Stock Exchange, to determine if a member should be disbarred and deprived of his livelihood, could well be challenged.

. . .

The legal department of the Scottish Executive is pondering the prospect of having to pay out millions of pounds in compensation to Scotland's fish-farming industry as a result of the European Convention. In May 1998, infectious salmon anaemia was diagnosed on the West Coast of Scotland. The disease occurs naturally in the North Atlantic and they have lived with it in Norway for years. But Scottish ministers, perhaps panicked by the BSE crisis, said that all stock must be destroyed on any farm where the disease was detected. Millions of healthy fish have been killed, several businesses face financial disaster, and *no compensation has been offered.* Instead a £9 million aid package has been proposed to help fish farms to restart—nothing like the huge cost, perhaps £100 million, of full legal restitution.

A Scottish minister, desperate to hold the line, has argued that the Government was not required 'to pay compensation for naturally occurring events'. He is likely to have to eat those words along with a stiff dose of the Convention's first protocol. As the former Lord Chancellor, Lord Mackay of Clashfern, observed: ' . . . the destruction of private property, such as salmon stocks reared for commercial purposes . . . in the absence of a scheme to pay compensation, is on the face of it, a violation of an owner's rights.'

I suspect that this principle will also apply to the Scottish Executive's Land Reform Act, which envisages giving local communities the right to bid for and buy large estates, thus effectively reducing the value of those properties; under the Convention a seller might be entitled to claim that his rights were being infringed and to apply, at the very least, for compensation.

Even the present Lord Chancellor may find his position challenged. Last month Lord Irvine of Lairg testily dismissed a case where a conviction in Guernsey was overturned under the convention because the judge held both political and judicial roles. He claimed it was a local issue confined to the Channel Islands, which did not affect him. But there will be other cases to come, and no one, not even Lord Chancellors, are above European law. It is, as I say, a sizeable iceberg. Lord Irvine should remember the *Titanic.*

The tone of this article is not untypical of the media's reaction to the news of the commencement of the Human Rights Act 1998. A certain amount of anxiety about the future is understandable but in some parts of the media the anxiety has been translated into antagonism or even xenophobia. We take a certain insular pride in our legal system, and express doubts as to whether there could be any substance in any claim for breach of human rights in this country.

---

[3] The Privy Council has since allowed an appeal against this decision: *Brown v Stott* [2003] 1 AC 681.

In this paper I propose to examine not the Strasbourg jurisprudence but rather the features of that Court which make it such a remarkable institution and then look at the possible impact of the Human Rights Act 1998 on our common law.

My visit to the European Court of Human Rights

In March 2000 I spent a month as a study visitor in the European Court of Human Rights and this enabled me to attend hearings, meet some of the judges, read files and research cases, and so on. I had rarely met human rights when I was in practice and I do not recall that a course on human rights was offered as an option in my university when I was a student. I have never appeared as counsel in Strasbourg, an admission that will soon date me as there seem to be numerous members of English Bar appearing there now—and the standard of their advocacy is the subject of many admiring comments. Thus, when the Human Rights Act 1998 became law, I felt that I had a large hole in my legal understanding which needed filling in depth before I could express as an authoritative and well-informed a view as I should wish to do. This should not be seen as any criticism of the education that has been made available to judges by the Judicial Studies Board ('JSB').[4] The JSB has engaged in a programme of training courses for all full-time and part-time judges in England and Wales. I was told that the United Kingdom has taken more steps than any other country to train its judges in the jurisprudence of the Convention. No doubt there are good reasons as a matter of judicial administration for doing this, but it is a significant achievement of the JSB for which we can be very grateful. Nonetheless, I felt that, to be reasonably at home with this vast new body of jurisprudence, I would have to devote some time to private research and study and the European Court of Human Rights was generous enough to make it possible for me to do this at the Court and this, of course, was far the best place to be for this purpose. It must seem to many of my colleagues a curious subject for a Chancery judge to research, but my experience prior to being appointed to the Chancery Bench and during three years at the Law Commission brought me in to contact with a far wider area of the law than is seen in the Chancery Division. Furthermore, the first case which arose in the domestic courts in Ireland concerning the Convention was not a criminal case but a planning case concerning Art 1 of the First Protocol.[5] Moreover, it is in the sphere of property rights that very substantial just satisfaction has been ordered. Accordingly, I had no doubt that the experience would be a useful one.

And so it turned out. My month in the European Court of Human Rights was a very valuable experience, and it gave me a vast insight into the work of the Court and the pressures upon it and the factors that shape its approach. I went in the knowledge that some people have misgivings about the role of the European Court of Human Rights, but as time went on and my understanding of the Court and its work grew I found that many of my fears were dispelled.

---

[4] Now the Judicial College.
[5] *Pine Valley Developments Ltd v Ireland* (1991) 14 EHRR 319.

The European Court of Human Rights as an institution of the Council of Europe

The European Court of Human Rights is not a familiar institution to many British lawyers, and to understand its jurisprudence it is necessary, I think, to have a fairly clear picture in one's mind of the institution that one is talking about. A startling fact is that there are now some 800 million people who are entitled to bring claims in the European Court of Human Rights. There are some courts that serve a wider population—for instance, the Supreme Court of India serves a population of over 1 billion—but there cannot be many courts whose jurisdictions include people from such diverse cultures or such large populations.

First, let us consider its role as an institution of the Council of Europe. The Council of Europe was set up in May 1949 by Belgium, Denmark, France, Ireland, Italy, Luxembourg, the Netherlands, Norway, Sweden, and the United Kingdom. While the aim of the Common Market was economic, the aim of the Council of Europe was to achieve greater unity between its members for the purpose of safeguarding and realizing the ideals which were their common heritage. One of the means by which this was to be achieved was by the maintenance of fundamental rights and freedoms. The Council of Europe now has 43 members.[6] Its overriding aims are a free and plural society, the rule of law, and human rights. Every member of the Council of Europe must sign the European Convention on Human Rights. Every signatory to European Convention on Human Rights may appoint a judge to the European Court of Human Rights.

Under Art 20(1), judges must be of high moral character and must either possess the qualifications required for appointment to high judicial office or be *jurisconsults* of recognized competence. They are elected by the Parliamentary Assembly of the Council of Europe by a majority of votes from a list of three candidates nominated by the High Contracting Parties.[7] The Committee of Ministers of the Council of Europe has passed certain resolutions about the appointment of judges to the Court. There must be a balance between the numbers of those who were already judges, those who were practitioners, those who were academics, and those who held some public office such as that of ambassador or minister of justice. There is also a recommendation that member states should, so far as possible, ensure participation of men and women 'in an equitable proportion' in the institutions of the Council of Europe.[8] Once appointed, judges do not represent the state by which they were nominated but sit in their own right. They are, of course, required to be independent. They must take an oath of office. The Secretariat carries out the task of writing judgments of the Court (other than separate or dissenting opinions) and this too helps ensure uniformity of standards and approach.

---

[6] Following the accession of Armenia and Azerbaijan on 25 January 2001. (As at 1 September 2014, there are 47 states which are parties to the Convention.)

[7] Article 22(1).

[8] Recommendation of the Committee of Ministers No R (81) 6, 30 April 1981.

What then is the function of the European Court of Human Rights? It was never intended to be a standing supreme court for the member states. It was simply intended to provide a mechanism, if one was needed, to ensure that violations did not take place or if they took place that there was just compensation and that the member states took steps to ensure that the violation was not repeated. This is known as the process of execution of the Court's judgments. The process of execution is handled by the Committee of Ministers of the Council of Europe. So, for instance, following *T and V v UK*[9] there are negotiations with the British government about the relinquishment by the Home Secretary of his powers to alter the tariff set by judges for those with life sentences. There has been legislation in the United Kingdom following a ruling of the Court to prohibit corporal punishment in UK state schools, and there has been legislation in Northern Ireland to decriminalize homosexual conduct. In the same way, when, as appears not to be infrequent, Turkey is found liable for the actions of its security forces against the civilian forces in south-western Turkey, there are negotiations at the political level to ensure that these actions are stopped. This, hopefully, will be the peaceful way in which the maltreatment of ethnic minorities in Europe will be solved in the years to come, thus avoiding any need for military intervention. Every case which the European Court of Human Rights decides is referred to the Committee of Ministers for execution and the Committee of Ministers meets six monthly and receives reports on the state of progress on the execution of judgments by the Contracting state involved. Sometimes execution is a short matter, for example where it involves the payment of a small sum of money, but sometimes execution can take many years. But the enforcement of judgments is an important factor in maintaining the credibility of the Court. Some of the jurisprudence of the Court leads to measures which affect several contracting states and not just the contracting state which was a party to the proceedings, for example the recommendation on the re-examination or reopening of certain cases at domestic level following judgments of the European Court of Human Rights.[10]

It follows from this scheme that it is a deliberate object of the structure that there should be, to a certain extent, a level of uniform minimum level of observance of human rights within the members of the Council of Europe. Now we may not always think that it is necessary. For instance, the continental European approach to the separation of powers is considerably more purist than our own. Thus, for instance, it may be difficult sometimes for those trained in that approach to comprehend that I (like other judges) spent three years of my career as a sitting judge as the full-time Chairman of the Law Commission, a non-departmental public body having close connections with the executive. It also has close connections with the judiciary, who give views on provisional recommendations or proposals that the Law Commission may make. The fact that there is a High Court judge as Chairman gives, I think, added force to its recommendations, but it is in a minor way a muddying of the waters between the judiciary and the executive

---

[9] (2000) 30 EHRR 121.   [10] Recommendation R (2000) 2, 19 January 2000.

branch of government. As a result the United Kingdom may find that the European Court of Human Rights interprets the Convention requirement for independence of the judiciary in a way which is inconsistent with some practices in the United Kingdom. Change which we did not seek may be one of the prices to pay for adhering to the European Convention on Human Rights.

The Convention covers the basic civil, criminal, and political rights. The original rights have already been extended, for instance in the field of property and education. They may be extended further by means of the 12th Protocol, which is now open for signature, so as to include a self-standing right of equality. Other rights may follow, such as the right of a woman to decide whether to have children, due process in regard to matters which are neither civil nor criminal matters for the purposes of Art 6, such as immigration,[11] the right to political asylum, and so on. These would be controversial areas, and may only be developed slowly, since changes to the Convention must receive a large measure of support, if not unanimity, from the contracting parties.

The European Court of Human Rights has also been criticized as being an inappropriate body to lay down human rights for a developed democracy such as our own. But the fact is that the United Kingdom ratified the Convention as long ago as 1950. All that has happened in the Human Rights Act 1998 is that English courts are given powers to rule on Convention rights. The European Court of Human Rights has had that power even in applications from the United Kingdom for some considerable time. The next point that must be made is that it has been the good fortune of the post-war generation in Western Europe that there has been no war there. The institutions of the Council of Europe have made a major contribution to the maintenance of peace in the post-War period.

I will mention some of the other institutions of the Council of Europe. The Directorate of Human Rights has many functions. It is engaged in assisting in the implementation of a number of treaties, including the European Convention on Human Rights and the Convention for the Prevention of Torture. When a new member is admitted to the Council of Europe, it signs the treaty setting up the Council of Europe and the Convention. Before it ratifies the Convention, the Directorate assists the country in question to carry out a study to see the extent to which its laws comply with the European Convention on Human Rights. The country will then make changes to its laws as necessary. The Directorate also carries out programmes of awareness in human rights and judicial training. In addition, it advises the Committee of Ministers on the implementation of judgments, that is, it considers whether any other reforms are necessary apart from the payment of any damages which the Court has ordered. It has committees on racism, the media, and gender equality. There is also now a Human Rights Commissioner of the Council of Europe.

Prior to 1 November 1998 there were two separate organs: the European Commission on Human Rights and the European Court of Human Rights.

---

[11] cf *Maaouia v France* (2001) 33 EHRR 42.

There is now only one Court, with as many judges as contracting states. The judges are divided into four sections and each section has a committee of three judges. Seventeen of the judges constitute the 'Grand Chamber'. Hearings before the European Court of Human Rights are much shorter, with fixed time limits being rigorously applied. After the advocates have made their addresses the judges ask questions if they wish and then retire to consider their judgment. There will generally be seven or more judges, which is more than in any English court.

One might pause to compare the European Court of Justice in Luxembourg. This is undoubtedly a supranational court in relation to Community law and definitely sees its role as such. It is therefore a very different type of institution. The European Court of Justice in general applies the jurisprudence of the European Court of Human Rights, although it is not bound by it. There is a proposal that the member states of the European Union should adopt a separate charter of human rights for community law. There is a risk that this will be a divisive move, and create a situation in which there are two courts who hand down possibly conflicting judgments on the subject of human rights.

Summary of procedure

The proceedings are initiated by an application. This is assigned to a section and then registered. If it is not apparently defective, it is referred to a Chamber of Judges who will decide whether or not it is admissible. If it is defective, it will be referred to a committee who may by unanimous vote declare an application to be inadmissible or strike out an application.

If the case is referred to a Chamber, a rapporteur is appointed to examine the case and to make a report to the Chamber. The rapporteur's identity and his or her report are not made known to the parties.

If there is a serious question of interpretation of the Convention or where there is serious risk of departing from existing case law, the Chamber can decide to refer the case to a Grand Chamber. When this happens either party can object within one month of notification.

Chamber decisions on admissibility are taken on a majority vote and contain reasons, which must be made public. Admissibility decisions handed down by chambers are a valuable source of Strasbourg jurisprudence. When a case is decided by a Chamber or the Grand Chamber, there must always be the national judge of the respondent state. Cases may be held to be partially inadmissible. The Court retains an inherent power to reopen a question of admissibility.

Once a case has been held to be admissible the Court may decide to go on a fact-finding mission. In this event, it sends a small number of judges to the country concerned to hear witnesses. This has been done on several occasions in Turkish cases.

More about the judges

There are currently forty-one judges of the European Court of Human Rights.[12] The judges can be divided into different groups in a number of different ways. First, there are the geographical differences: some come from Western Europe, such as France, Germany, and the Netherlands, and some come from countries that were formerly countries behind the Iron Curtain, such as Hungary and Bulgaria. These countries of the old East bloc now have new constitutions which incorporate guarantees as to human rights, often by reference to those in the European Convention on Human Rights. That is the first division. Then there are differences in age and gender. It is a young court—about a quarter of the judges are below the current average age for a High Court Judge and about 20 per cent of the judges are women, which, of course, is well above twice the proportion of women in the higher judiciary (High Court, Court of Appeal, and House of Lords) here. Then there is the difference between the judges in terms of their qualifications for the post of judge of the European Court of Human Rights. Nine of them were members of the European Commission on Human Rights. Some thirteen were already judges, of whom several were members of the old Court of Human Rights. Another ten or so have spent most of their careers as academic lawyers, often in private or public international law. Of the remainder some six were formerly politicians, ambassadors, or prosecutors, and a further five were practising lawyers.

An obvious difference between the judges is that some of them have wide practical experience of judging. Some of them have wide practical experience of human rights through the Commission or the old Court of Human Rights. Others are academic lawyers. Their contribution is important, though one of the many challenges for a court such as this must surely be to maintain a balance between the academic and practical. The academic input is also necessary to maintain the high standard of legal result.

But the greatest difference between the judges must surely be their legal traditions. Take, for instance, Albania. This country was ruled by the Turks until 1913 and then had kings and democratic government until it was taken over by the communists after the Second World War. In 1992 it underwent a peaceful change to democracy. It has little legal tradition of its own. It borrowed law from Russia and from Italy in fields where it did not have law of its own. It must be very difficult sometimes for a judge from such a country to understand the problems that affect the developed Western world. Yet one of the great values of the Court must surely be to enable countries from the old East bloc to benefit from the standards in human rights that apply in other countries of Europe: this is one of the ways in

---

[12] This number of permanent judges is fixed according to the number of the states which are parties to the Convention and has therefore increased since this paper was written to take account of the accession of new contracting parties since 2000. There are also ad hoc judges, who are appointed for specific purposes or cases, who are not included in this number. Details of the current permanent judges' background and gender can be found on the Strasbourg Court's website, <http://www.echr.coe.int>.

which they can catch up on democracy. Yet this also poses a problem for the Court: to secure the support and participation from judges from these traditions while at the same time producing results which command respect and support in other European countries. It is a major challenge to collegiate judging. In such a court, it is desirable, so far as possible, to produce a common view. There is a risk that in so doing some points cannot be pursued, or must be expressed in a way that is not very precise, or that several grounds for a decision must be given. But the opinion of the Court must be the stronger when it is the view of all the judges rather than just some. In this respect, I appreciate that the position of the European Court of Human Rights may be different from that of other courts, but it is a difference with a reason, and one I think that is helpful to bear in mind when studying the judgments.

The legal tradition from which judges come is likely to be a material factor. Continental Europeans are accustomed to judges declaring the law in short judgments, like tablets of stone, and to reading the doctrine contained in writings of scholars. The Soviet system does not have a case law system, but from time to time the settled practice is codified in guidelines to judges. It is only the common law countries that have training in how to manipulate case law, which is where the jurisprudence of the European Court of Human Rights is now to be found. On the other hand, common lawyers are less accustomed to identifying and developing principles, and concentrate on the facts to a greater extent than judges from civil law countries.

With all these differences, it is truly remarkable that the Court presents such a consistent corpus of jurisprudence as it does. This is all the more so when one considers that the Court sits in sections and not just as a single Court.

Access to the Court's jurisprudence

There are two aspects to this question. There is the practical matter of researching the case law. The second question is how to read the judgments.

Speaking for myself, I sometimes find that the language in which the judgments are expressed difficult to follow. But we are really in no position to complain. The jurisprudence of the Strasbourg Court is now case law. We are equipped by training to be able to deal with this. Most other legal traditions do not operate by means of case law but primarily have codes. Lawyers trained in these traditions have less experience of manipulating case law. Second, at least we have the advantage that English is one of the official languages of the Court. Think of the difficulties for lawyers and judges in Moldova, Georgia, Estonia, and other countries who may not even have the reports in their own language. English lawyers are really in a privileged position. Third, judgments of the Court are divided into parts: the procedure before the Court, the facts including the domestic law background, and then the evaluation by the Court and the disposition of the case. So it is easy to navigate in these judgments, particularly electronically.

I do not intend to deal with the subject of law reporting in detail. Needless to say there are several series of reports. The Court has its own series of reports: it decides which merit reporting, and the registrar of the section to whom the case was allocated will prepare a note of the principal findings which is the 'headnote'. The judgments are not always easy reading. Sometimes cases are decided on their own particular facts and it is difficult to define or to draw the boundaries around the principle which they illustrate. As I have said, because the judgment may seek to represent the reasoning and approach of more than one judge, it may be expressed in broad general terms or contain several grounds for the decision.

In the past, decisions have been reported in both French and English. In future, some decisions may be reported only in one language. If so, it will be necessary to search for and read decisions in both languages. As I have already observed, decisions on admissibility may contain a considerable amount of valuable jurisprudence which is not to be found in judgments on the merits. Many of these decisions can be accessed via the Court's electronic database, HUDOC, which is on the Court's website.

Judicial Statistics

The European Court of Human Rights receives a staggering number of cases. In 2000, some 10,486 new applications were registered. In the same period some 7,852 applications were disposed of by judgment or were the subject of an admissibility decision or striking off (for example, because a friendly settlement had been reached). So, on the assumption that the number of new cases will remain the same, the backlog of cases will increase by at least 2,634 cases per year. As at the end of 2000, the outstanding backlog of cases was approximately 14,265 and the number of new cases registered in 2000 exceeded the number of new cases registered in 1999 by 2,090.[13] The Court aims to deal with both admissibility and judgment in a case in an average period of three years. In 2000, 626 new cases from the United Kingdom were registered, an increase of 195 over the previous year. This puts the United Kingdom in seventh place after Russia, France, Italy, Poland, Turkey, and Ukraine. But it is likely that the number of cases from the United Kingdom will decline after the implementation of the Human Rights Act 1998 as more and more applicants have their Convention rights protected by our domestic courts.

Apart from registered cases there are also a large number of provisional files on cases. It is said that the Court receives some 650 letters per day.

It is clear that the Court has a major problem of case overload. With the enlargement of the Council of Europe there is a risk that, unless some change occurs, the number of applications will before long overwhelm the Court. As matters stand it must accept every case that comes to it: no case requires leave.

---

[13] The figures in this paragraph are taken from the Court's *Survey of Activities 2000*, published in January 2001.

The Court may conclude that the case is inadmissible but even this preliminary stage can be a resource-intensive process.

There is a large number of cases from Italy about the excessive length of legal proceedings. From Turkey, there is a large number of cases about attacks on the Kurdish civilians in south-east Turkey. From Russia, there are cases about the non-payment of claims, for example for salary, and about the non-enforcement of judgments obtained against central or local government. However, many of these are inadmissible because they relate to events before Russia became a signatory to the Convention.

The Convention and the common law

The Convention was, of course, drafted with the help of experts including lawyers from the Foreign Office or former legal advisers. It was ratified as a treaty. In other contracting states the act of ratification meant that it automatically became part of the country's domestic law. This is not, of course, the case in the United Kingdom. The view was taken that the Convention did not need to be incorporated into English law as it was the same as the common law. But the European Court of Human Rights developed its jurisprudence and so, inevitably, the common law and the Convention have ceased to be consistent in some respects. There were several attempts to incorporate it, culminating in the Human Rights Act 1998.

Main provisions of the Human Rights Act 1998

This is a convenient moment to give a short account of the Human Rights Act 1998. The purpose of the Act is 'to give further effect to the rights and freedoms guaranteed under the European Convention on Human Rights' in the United Kingdom.[14] The Act does not therefore incorporate the Convention as such into domestic law. The Government's intention was 'to bring rights *home*', that is, to enable people to enforce their Convention rights against the state in the British courts without 'having to incur the delays and expense which are involved in taking the case' to the European Court of Human Rights. The Government expressed the hope that 'enabling courts in the United Kingdom to rule on the application of the Convention will also help to influence the development of case law on the Convention by the European Court of Human Rights on the basis of familiarity with our laws and customs'.

The Act starts by defining 'the Convention rights'. The Convention rights for the purposes of the Act are those listed in s 1. These omit, for example, Art 13 of the Convention. It was considered unnecessary to include this Article on the ground that English law would itself provide sufficient remedies. But there may be

---

[14] This summary deals only with the position in England and Wales, and not that in Scotland or Northern Ireland.

occasions when English law does not provide a remedy (for example, if the powers of the court are limited by a statute which is not compatible with the Convention, as to which see the discussion of s 3, below).

Section 2 of the Act requires a court when determining any question which arises in connection with a Convention right to take account of the jurisprudence of the European Commission of Human Rights and the European Court of Human Rights. This is a new duty. But it does not mean that the courts are bound to follow the jurisprudence of the European Court of Human Rights. They may, for instance, set higher standards, so long as this does not infringe the Convention rights of another person. It has been said that the jurisprudence of the Commission and the European Court of Human Rights is to be treated as a floor and not a ceiling.

Section 3 requires an English court so far as possible to interpret legislation (whenever enacted) so that it is in conformity with Convention rights. This new duty goes further than the existing law, under which there is a presumption that Parliament intended to comply with its treaty obligations. That is only a presumption and it has to take its place alongside a number of other canons of construction. The new duty enables the court to develop new principles giving guidance as to when it is possible to construe legislation so as to comply with Convention rights, so that Convention rights are given priority over the need to adhere to the literal meaning of the provision. But this does not empower the court to 'rewrite' legislation. Nor does it empower the court to strike down primary legislation, that is, legislation enacted by Parliament as opposed to secondary legislation made under powers conferred by Parliament.

If the court cannot interpret primary legislation so that it conforms to the Convention, it can (if it is one of the higher courts) make a declaration of incompatibility (s 4). There are two consequences of this. First, in the case before it, the court must apply the legislation as it stands (and it will not be able to give effect to the Convention). Second, the Government may use a streamlined procedure to introduce an amendment to make the legislation conform to the Convention (s 10). Thus Parliamentary sovereignty is preserved.

Section 6 provides that it is unlawful for public authorities to act in a manner which is incompatible with Convention rights. So if a department of state wishes to exercise a discretionary power, it must do so in conformity with the Convention. The Act does not define 'public authority'. However s 6 states that the court is a public authority. It too has a duty not to act incompatibly with the Convention. This clearly means that the court must apply Arts 5, 6, and 7 of the Convention. It is also clear that in litigation involving a public authority the court must enforce the Convention rights given to the other party, who will thus be able to rely on the Convention. Again, however, Parliamentary sovereignty is preserved because the new duty does not apply to an act if the public authority could not have acted differently because of primary legislation (s 6(2)(a)). I will return to s 6 later.

Section 7 gives a remedy against public authorities if they act incompatibly with the Convention. For this purpose the applicant must be a victim for the purpose of the Convention (s 7(3), (7)). The court may grant such remedy as it thinks appropriate (s 8(1)). In deciding whether to award damages, and if so how much, the court must take into account the jurisprudence of the European Court of Human Rights on just satisfaction (8(4)). The Law Commission and the Scottish Law Commission have published a review of the jurisprudence of the European Court of Human Rights in this area.[15]

Section 12 contains some additional provisions about freedom of expression. It was introduced because the Press was concerned about applications for injunctions without notice and the possibility that the courts would make immediate (though temporary) orders preventing publication on the grounds that there was a serious issue to be tried as to whether publication would violate Art 8. This might prevent the press from publishing the information at a time that is particularly important. There are a number of bodies in the United Kingdom which promote standards of reporting and have codes of practice, such as the Press Complaints Commission. The effect of s 12 is that the court may not grant an injunction which might limit the right to freedom of expression in the absence of the defendant unless the circumstances are exceptional. Moreover the court must be satisfied that the applicant is likely to establish that the publication should not be allowed, and in addition it must have regard to any relevant privacy code as well as, of course, the public interest in publication.

Section 19 provides for statements of compatibility with the Convention to be attached to Government bills when they are introduced in Parliament. As I understand it, the Delegated Powers Committee has ensured that a similar certificate will be attached to all secondary legislation.

Implications of the Human Rights Act for the common law

The first observation that I should like to make will be an obvious one. The effect of giving effect to Convention rights is to make the European Court of Human Rights a supranational court whose decisions will receive great weight in the courts of the United Kingdom. There will, in effect, be a presumption that they should be followed and good reason will be needed before departing from Strasbourg juris-prudence in future. The change that will come about will be much more sudden and far-reaching than the effect of the reception of Roman law into English law. Holdsworth described that in the following terms:

We have received Roman law; but we have received it in small homeopathic doses, at different periods and as and when required. It has acted as a tonic to our native legal system . . .[16]

Likewise, we have received Commonwealth and American cases and indeed most recently cases from France and Germany. In all those cases the authority has been

---

[15] The Law Commission and the Scottish Law Commission, *Damages under the Human Rights Act 1998* (Law Com No 266 and Scots Law Com No 180, 2000).

[16] WS Holdsworth, *A History of English Law* (3rd edn, Methuen, 1945) volume IV, p 293.

persuasive. Strasbourg jurisprudence, on the other hand, will have to be researched and considered, and unless there is good reason not to do so, the courts are likely to apply to it.

My second observation is that the Human Rights Act 1998 will lead to common law being developed 'in the shadow of' the Convention. The courts will naturally prefer to reach a result that is compatible with Convention rights by applying the common law, which is indigenous. If the court finds that the particular right in question is a common law right, it can enforce the same right as between individuals without invoking the Convention. This involves using the Convention right as establishing a norm, and using it to enrich the common law and as a prompt to develop the common law in this way. Reliance on common law rights has the great advantage that it remains open to the courts, in theory at least, to find that the common law right has features or restrictions which are not the same as those found in the Strasbourg jurisprudence. Exceptionally, this might be a useful reserve power for the courts to have. Furthermore, the human rights jurisprudence will be more effectively integrated if it is interwoven with the common law in this way. If this route is taken, it may well be desirable for the court where possible to refer to the Strasbourg jurisprudence. If it does so it will provide assistance not merely to the appellate courts but also to the European Court of Human Rights in due course should an application be made to that Court, based on a breach of some positive obligation to intervene to protect one individual against another.

Third, it is likely that there will be changes in domestic public law. For instance, the level of scrutiny evolved by our courts in judicial review in cases where it is alleged that the decision was unreasonable is known as the *Wednesbury* principle.[17] Under that principle, the courts in general grant judicial review of a decision only where no decision-maker, properly directing himself as to the relevant law and acting reasonably, could have reached that decision. If the decision fails to meet this test, it may be set aside. Where Convention rights are in issue the courts will have to apply a different level of review, namely whether any restriction on a Convention right had a legitimate aim and was proportionate. This assessment involves looking at the substance of the decision and entails a lesser degree of deference to the conclusion of the decision-maker. Where all these changes in public law may lead is another question. They are potentially capable of leading to a change in the constitutional relationship between the courts, the legislature, and the executive. However, in my view the courts can be relied on to move slowly and carefully, as they are well practised at doing in the fields of state responsibility and other fields. As Lord Diplock said, the common law develops incrementally. It is unlikely that that fundamental characteristic, which is so important to the stability of society, will change overnight.

Fourth, another area of the common law which may be subject to the impact of the Convention is in private litigation where English law does not conform to the

---

[17] Following the decision of the Court of Appeal in *Associated Picture Houses v Wednesbury Corporation* [1948] 1 KB 223.

Convention. This depends on the effect of s 6. This might turn out to be one of the most difficult sections in the Act for civil courts because it is not clear whether, and if so, to what extent, the court must enforce the Convention if the parties are both private citizens. Often the common law is in line with the Convention or it can be developed in a way which is compatible with the Convention. In those circumstances this question does not matter. Where, however, this is not the situation, for example because English law does not regard the violation as a wrong which gives rise to a remedy, the effect of s 6 is unclear. There is a dispute between commentators as to whether the courts who are themselves public authorities are bound to create a remedy even in disputes between two parties where there has been a breach of a Convention right. Indeed, it may be very strange to a lay person if a person whose Convention right of privacy has been infringed by both the BBC and an independent television company could claim compensation from the former but not the latter. At this stage we meet an interface between the common law and the Strasbourg jurisprudence. The European Convention on Human Rights has no application to inter-individual disputes.[18] For the Strasbourg Court to find that a violation of a Convention right has occurred, it must find that the liability of the respondent state has been engaged. If private disputes arise in the English courts, the British government will not be a party.

The better view seems to be that the court has a duty to give a remedy only where the Convention has been held by the European Court of Human Rights to impose a positive obligation on the state *and* there is already a cause of action in English law. A positive obligation is one imposed on the state to take steps to protect individuals. It may therefore require the state to protect one individual against another. It is not altogether clear when the Convention imposes a positive obligation but it seems that it will do so where the right aims primarily to uphold the rights of the individual as opposed to a shared democratic right and where but for the inaction of the state the damage would not have occurred. Positive obligations have been held to exist under Arts 2, 3, 4, 8, 9, 10, and 11. Thus, for example, positive obligations have been held to exist under Art 3, where a violation was found because the state had not taken steps to prevent a child from receiving corporal punishment.[19]

To recap, the Human Rights Act provides that it is unlawful for any public authority to act in breach of Convention rights, and to this end the Act creates a new tort so that a victim may claim compensation if a public authority acts in breach of this section. There are limitations to this remedy, particularly as regards who may claim compensation and the amount of it. However, the creation of this new remedy means that in many cases there is no need to find a remedy under the common law for a breach of Convention rights.

[18] *The Swedish Engine Drivers' Union v Sweden* (1976) 1 EHRR 230.
[19] *Campbell and Cosans v UK* (1982) 4 EHRR 186.

Conclusions

I have of, course, to be realistic about the difficulties for common lawyers in Strasbourg. The common law can be difficult to follow and the structure of a common law legal system is quite different from that of civil law systems. Our trial process is in many respects quite different—take, for example, the jury. The common law has traditionally had different priorities. It has, for instance, devoted great energies to the protection of various forms of property. Abstract statements of principle tend to be rare. As Bernard Shaw says in *St Joan*, 'the thick fogs of England do not breed philosophers'. There is always a risk that the system of the common law will not be understood in a supranational court, but there are safeguards to prevent this happening, including the requirement for a national judge. So I remain optimistic about the future of the common law.

There is bound to be some change, and a re-focusing of our traditional approach, in areas such as criminal procedure, (to a lesser extent) civil procedure, family law, and in the field of freedom of expression, such as defamation. It is perhaps tempting to think, however, that, in areas such as criminal law and evidence, if there were points to be taken they would have been taken already, but this may well be over-optimistic.

There are bound to be decisions of the European Court of Human Rights which require changes which we do not want. That must be so for other countries as well. At the end of the day the United Kingdom has to take the rough with the smooth. It is all a question in the end of what we are achieving by giving effect to the European Convention on Human Rights in United Kingdom law. As I endeavoured to show at the outset of this paper, the Convention has wider implications for the development of the whole of Europe. It is one of the means by which the countries which are not advanced democracies like our own can raise their standards. The benefit for us and our successors is the increased prospect for peace and stability of Europe.

Before very long it will become second nature to us to check our law for human rights points in the same way that we instinctively apply the fundamental principle of the rule of law to all we do. In the meantime we should ensure a smooth transition from the old order to the new, moving carefully and with full consideration, so far as possible in a way that secures public confidence and support. That is an especial responsibility in the immediate period following commencement of the Human Rights Act 1998. However, on a wider front, given our experience of the common law method, and the enthusiasm of lawyers, scholars, and judges in analysing and reconstructing the law, I venture to think that, now we have the opportunity, we shall make a worthy contribution to that great and unique corpus of jurisprudence which has been created by the European Court of Human Rights and its predecessors in Strasbourg.

2

Building a Better Society

This chapter is based on the Keynote Address given at the JUSTICE 10th Annual Human Rights Law Conference, 21 October 2008.*

Introduction

I will begin this paper with a few thoughts about the first ten years after the Human Rights Act 1998 was enacted. I will then make and develop my overarching point, which is that the effect of the European Convention on Human Rights (the 'Convention') has been to alter the way we think about the position of the individual in relation to the state. Where human rights are engaged, the Human Rights Act 1998 means that we now focus on the rights of the individual rather than those of the majority. I will suggest that this has changed the way we think about democracy, and should stimulate more discussion about the meaning of the requirement in the Convention that a restriction on a right be 'necessary in a democratic society'.

I will then identify four of the consequences which flow from this refocusing:

(1) The Human Rights Act 1998 has changed the way we think of democracy.

(2) We need to think about the institutions of our democracy to ensure that they are appropriate to the needs of the human rights era.

(3) Questions of human rights can no longer be decided in isolation from developments in human rights jurisprudence in other parts of the world.

(4) Human rights jurisprudence will more and more infuse the common law and will be one of the major ways in which it is developed in this jurisdiction in the next ten years.

Some thoughts about the first ten years of the Human Rights Act

The Human Rights Act was enacted in 1998, which was my final year as Chair of the Law Commission of England and Wales. It was not brought into force until

* 'Building on 10 years of the Human Rights Act' was published in the *JUSTICE Journal* (2008), vol 5, no 2, pp 23–26. It is reproduced here with the kind permission of JUSTICE.

2 October 2000—co-incidentally the day on which I became a member of the Court of Appeal of England and Wales.

In the course of the bill's passage through Parliament, there was much enthusiasm for the new legislation and, in the period leading up to its commencement, there was a great deal of preparation, particularly by civil servants in Whitehall and by the Judicial Studies Board. I took a little time out myself, and I had the privilege of spending a month at the European Court of Human Rights. In that time, I learnt at first hand the sheer scale and variety of that Court's work and the way in which it worked.

Perhaps the first point that an English lawyer notices about the Convention is the open-textured way in which Convention rights are expressed. We are now very familiar with them, but we should not forget that they are enunciating broad statements of principle and setting standards, and that we need to respond to them on that level and not in the way that we would approach an ordinary statute. Let us not forget that the Convention encapsulates standards and values, and that it is a living instrument whose meaning may change over time. As Kirby J of the High Court of Australia has said, if you construe a constitution as if it were a last will and testament, that is what it will become.[1] It is, I suggest, important to keep this point in mind and to avoid getting distracted from the substance of the rights by intricacies in the case law.

I also sat as an ad hoc judge in the European Court of Human Rights on two cases. One of them, *Z v United Kingdom*,[2] was of great importance to the common law of negligence. It made it clear that there was no violation of Art 6 of the Convention if the domestic court held that there was no duty of care owed, in that case by a public authority to a citizen. The other case, *TP and KM v United Kingdom*,[3] is less well known but it is also important. It established that, where human rights are engaged, there has to be a system, through the courts or otherwise, for investigating the complaint and where appropriate providing redress. This follows from Art 13 of the Convention. This holding operates in certain circumstances to counterbalance the situation if the court holds as a matter of domestic law that there is no breach of the duty of care. (Since the Human Rights Act 1998, a remedy for violation of human rights has been provided by ss 6 and 7 in cases where those sections apply.)

For me, sitting in Strasbourg was an illuminating experience. It does not always come through in the judgments but the judges often bring very different experiences to bear from those of the judges in the United Kingdom. Review by a supranational court can in appropriate cases be a salutary experience.

At the time of the enactment of the Human Rights Act 1998, there was concern in the United Kingdom about the impact of the Act on the resources of public

---

[1] The Hon Justice Michael Kirby AC CMG, Justice of the High Court of Australia, *Judicial Activism*, Hamlyn Lectures, 2003 (Sweet & Maxwell, 2004), 40.
[2] (Application 29392/95) (2001) 34 EHRR 97, [2001] 2 FCR 246.
[3] (Application 28945/95) (2001) 34 EHRR 42, [2001] 2 FCR 289.

institutions. There was likewise a great concern that the integration of human rights jurisprudence would cause difficulty; in the end it did not cause a constitutional crisis. Great credit must be given to the Appellate Committee of the House of Lords for this smooth transition. The fact that members of the Appellate Committee sit also on the Privy Council may well have something to do with this, as cases in the Privy Council frequently raise constitutional questions. Constitutional issues require considerable judgment and sensitivity to the environment in which they are given.

During the course of a visit to courts in France, I saw a memorial to the seventeenth century French statesman, Mazarin. One of the figures in that memorial is that of the goddess of Prudence. She is holding a mirror so that she can see over her shoulder and backwards into history. One of the strengths of our common law tradition is its methodology. It builds on what has gone before. In this way it ensures so far as possible that, if there is change, the transition is smooth and occurs in a way that is consistent with the traditions of our society. For my part, I consider that the common law has had an important role in securing change and stability in our law over many centuries and it is a tradition of which we should be very proud. It has enabled the judges in an appropriate case to move the law on in accordance with social conditions and needs.

At the same time, there are limits to the role of the courts. There are other ways in which the rights guaranteed by the Convention can be enforced. There are, of course, pressure groups like JUSTICE, and they have a very valuable role to play. I would like to express my particular admiration for the work JUSTICE has done over the last year. Human rights can also be enforced through the normal processes of law reform, including projects conducted by the Law Commission. In *Van Colle v Chief Constable of Hertfordshire Police*,[4] in which JUSTICE made a joint intervention with MIND and INQUEST, Lord Phillips, now the Senior Law Lord, held:

[102] The issues of policy raised by this appeal are not readily resolved by a court of law. It is not easy to evaluate the extent to which the existence of a common law duty of care in relation to protecting members of the public against criminal injury would in fact impact adversely on the performance by the police of their duties. I am inclined to think that this is an area where the law can better be determined by Parliament than by the courts. For this reason I have been pleased to observe that the Law Commission has just published a Consultation Paper No 187 on '*Administrative Redress: Public Bodies and the Citizen*' that directly addresses the issues raised by this appeal.

Leaving issues to Parliament is not always the answer but there is more reason to do so where there is a Law Commission project on foot or a recent Law Commission report. One of the most difficult questions for a judge is when to leave an issue to Parliament. Similar difficulties can arise in determining the relative institutional competence of the courts and other institutions, but this exercise does not discharge

---

4 [2008] UKHL 50, [2009] 1 AC 225.

the court from its responsibility to review the acts of a public authority at the appropriate level.

The structure of the Human Rights Act 1998 is probably unique in the world. In it, there are limitations on the enforcement of human rights. Declarations of incompatibility can only be made in the higher courts, but it does not appear that this restriction has given rise to any serious difficulty. There are other limitations. If a declaration of incompatibility is made, it is not binding on the parties to that case. There is also no right to compensation if a public authority has acted pursuant to statute in violating human rights. Those restrictions are more controversial, but are consistent with Parliamentary sovereignty. It is still necessary in these cases, and in cases caught by the transitional provisions in the Human Rights Act 1998, for the parties affected to apply to the Strasbourg Court. With these qualifications, however, the Human Rights Act 1998 has been widely welcomed as a means of giving protection to Convention rights in domestic law. Moreover, some problems arise not out of the structure of the Human Rights Act 1998 but out of the way litigation is funded. It is an internationally known fact that the costs of proceedings in England are considerable, and any discussion of bringing rights home not just to our shores, but to the average citizen's living room, has to solve this problem as well.

The first ten years of the Human Rights Act 1998 has seen a large number of landmark cases under the Act. I can do no more than single out one case that bears on the overall point that I want to make about this time: the *'Belmarsh* case'.[5] It concerned suspected terrorists who were aliens and who could not be departed because of fears for their safety in the country to which they would be returned. They were held in indefinite executive detention in Belmarsh prison.

By its decision the House of Lords, in exercise of its powers conferred by the Human Rights Act 1998, quashed the Human Rights (Designated Derogation) Order 2001,[6] and made a declaration that s 23 of the Anti-terrorism Crime and Security Act 2001 (providing for detention without trial) was incompatible with Arts 5 and 14 of the Convention. The first issue arose from Art 15 of the Convention and it concerned the question whether the government were right in saying that circumstances had arisen entitling the United Kingdom to derogate from the Convention under Art 15. Article 15 provides that '[i]n time of war or other public emergency threatening the life of the nation any High Contracting Party may take measures derogating from its obligations under this Convention to the extent strictly required by the exigencies of the situation . . . '. Specifically, the question was whether a state of emergency had arisen for the purposes of Art 15. The House of Lords (by a majority) rejected the detainees' arguments on this point. The House was prepared to attach great weight to the judgment of the Secretary of State and Parliament on the issue whether there was a public emergency threatening the life of the nation.

The second issue was whether the provisions of the 2001 Act relating to detention violated Convention rights only 'to the extent strictly required by the

[5] *A and others v Secretary of State for the Home Department* [2004] UKHL 56, [2005] 2 AC 68.
[6] SI 2001/3644.

exigencies of the situation' for the purposes of Art 15. Here, the detainees' arguments focused on the fact that the powers of detention related only to foreign nationals who could not be deported. It could not be said that foreign nationals were the only threat; and if they were a threat, they could under the 2001 Act go abroad and carry on their activities from abroad. They could be detained even if the threat that they presented was not as members of Al-Qaeda but of some other organization altogether which had not been responsible for the state of emergency justifying the derogation. The House of Lords (by a majority) accepted these arguments: in a word, s 23 was irrational. The power of detention did not prevent any person who was content to return to his own country from doing so and carrying on terrorist activities from there.

The third issue was whether the powers of preventive detention discriminated unjustifiably between non-UK nationals and UK nationals, who could not be detained on suspicion. The House held that there was unjustified discrimination. The power of detention did not prevent United Kingdom nationals from carrying on terrorist activities because they could not be detained under this power.

I have called the *Belmarsh* case a landmark case. It was the first major challenge to the enforcement of human rights in the courts. The field was the highly charged one of terrorism. Nonetheless the House did not shrink from reaffirming the values in the Convention and enforcing Convention rights. It demonstrated that it was part of the courts' role to give content and teeth to human rights.

A crucial change—my overarching point

What I have called my 'overarching' point is that the Human Rights Act 1998 has focused attention on the individual in relation to the state. That is quite different from the position that prevailed before the Human Rights Act 1998 and has changed the way in which we think about democracy. The *Belmarsh* case is indeed an example of this refocusing and that case could not, of course, have been decided the way it was before the Human Rights Act 1998. I need to develop this point.

This point can be developed by reference to the ideas in John Stuart Mill's famous essay, *On Liberty*.[7] In this essay, John Stuart Mill put forward the idea that the individual should be allowed the greatest freedom unless it could be shown that his actions would harm others. This is called the 'harm principle'. Mill wrote:

That principle is, that the sole end for which mankind are warranted, individually or collectively, in interfering with the liberty of action of any of their number, is self-protection.

---

[7] JS Mill, *On Liberty* (2nd edn, London: John W. Parker & Son, 1859). Available online: <http://www.bartleby.com/130>.

That the only purpose for which power can be rightfully exercised over any member of the civilised community, against his will, is to prevent harm to others. His own good, either physical or moral, is not a sufficient warrant.

An individual was entitled to act without restriction unless his conduct concerned others:

To justify [compulsion], the conduct from which it is desired to deter him, must be calculated to produce evil to someone else. The only part of the conduct of anyone, for which he is amenable to society, is that which concerns others. In the part which merely concerns himself, his independence is, of right, absolute. Over himself, over his own body and mind, the individual is sovereign.

Mill also develops the argument that each individual has a right to liberty of self-development. Again this is subject to the rights of others. He says in *On Liberty*:

In proportion to the development of his individuality, each person becomes more valuable to himself, and is therefore capable of being more valuable to others.

The more that individuals develop themselves, the more they and society would benefit.

The harm principle is not uncontroversial or easy to apply. But it throws light on the effect of the Convention.

The Convention distinguishes between absolute rights and qualified rights. Absolute rights include the right to life and the prohibition on torture. The court cannot interfere with absolute rights, nor can the state. Qualified rights include the right to respect for private and family life, freedom of thought, conscience, and religion and so on. These rights are said to be qualified because the state can interfere with them in limited circumstances. (The right to property is a form of qualified right, but the state is allowed greater latitude to interfere with this right than with the rights conferred by Arts 8 to 11, and so in the interests of simplicity I leave that right out of account for the purposes of this discussion.)

If the individual complains that his human rights have been infringed, then the court has to ask if the right is an absolute one or a qualified one. If it is an absolute right, no one can interfere with it and the individual's right must prevail.

If the right is a qualified one, such as the right to freedom of expression and freedom to manifest one's religion, the right is not unlimited, but it is still not open to the state simply to interfere with it as it chooses.

It must meet the requirements of the Convention. It must show, in accordance with the express requirements of the Convention, that the interference is prescribed by law, necessary in a democratic society, and proportionate. In order to show that the interference is proportionate, the state must show a pressing social need.

As with Mill's harm principle, the state must justify its interference with the individual's freedom to act as he determines. The Convention reaches in this respect the same broad result as Mill's harm principle.

We can contrast this with judicial review where no human rights are involved. A decision made by the state that is within the law is not set aside unless it is perverse. Moreover, and this is an important point in practice, the onus of showing that it is perverse lies on the individual seeking to establish that it is perverse and not on the state. This would not meet Mill's harm principle.

As it seems to me, one of the greatest achievements of human rights has been to refocus the law on the rights of the individual. Either his rights cannot be abridged, or, if the state can interfere with them, the onus has shifted to the state to show that any interference with the right is essential and not just one which could be classed as not being perverse.

I began by saying that there are some consequences that flow from this refocusing. I now turn to these consequences.

First, the Human Rights Act 1998 has changed the way we think about democracy.

It used to be enough to speak of democracy as requiring that each person had one vote and all that that entails. However, with the refocusing of the law on the individual where human rights are engaged, we can see that, equally importantly, democracy also consists of a complex interplay between majority and minority rights. In this way, the Human Rights Act 1998 has changed the way we think about democracy.

Indeed, one of the by-products of the Convention is that when it comes to the qualified rights we are expressly directed to think about democracy. The question of what democracy means and requires must now be considered in more depth as part of the legal issue of determining whether the state was entitled to interfere with the right in question.

There is some guidance in the authorities as to what is necessary in a democratic society. Baroness Hale has held that democracy is founded on the principle that each individual has equal value. Lord Hoffmann has referred to equality before the law as one of the building blocks of a democracy. In a case concerning the limits of the procedural duty to hold an investigation under Art 2 of the Convention, I held that the interests of a democracy did not require that there should be an investigation into questions of the allocation of resources, which was a question for the executive and Parliament, and that approach was approved by the House of Lords.[8]

Much more thought, however, could usefully now be given to what is meant by 'necessary in a democratic society'. Interestingly, the European Court of Human Rights has said relatively little about the meaning of democracy in this context. I think that there is probably a good reason for this, namely that the term needs to be understood in the context of the particular member state. It is therefore something that we should expect to be free to decide for ourselves.

Second, we need to think about the institutions of our democracy to ensure that they are appropriate to the needs of the human rights era.

The Victorians built great buildings like the Royal Courts of Justice. They did so on a breathtaking scale. They planned for a society in which public institutions would play an important part.

---

[8] See *R (Scholes) v Secretary of State for the Home Department* [2006] EWCA Civ 1343, (2007) 93 BMLR 136 at [83] approved by Lord Bingham in *R (Gentle and another) v Prime Minister and others* [2008] UKHL 20, [2008] 1 AC 1356 at [9].

In the twenty-first century, we have to build institutions for the future. They are institutions of a different kind. They are the institutions necessary to ensure the success of individual rights. Society has to protect a liberal democracy from within and from those forces within society that would if accepted diminish its liberal values.

To recognize protect and enhance human rights, the state has to have the correct fabric of laws and institutions which are fit for the task.

In fact, we are on the eve of an important institutional change in our legal system. Under a year from now the work of the Appellate Committee of the House of Lords will be transferred to the new Supreme Court of the United Kingdom. This represents a unique opportunity for setting up an apex court for the twenty-first century. It will of course have the same powers, and only the same powers, as the existing Appellate Committee of the House of Lords. Nonetheless the institution of the Supreme Court is the start of a new chapter. There are many issues to be considered.

One of those is the selection of cases: for example, should the court take on different cases or should it have different criteria, for instance, for cases which raise issues of a constitutional nature?

Another issue to be considered is the form of judgments. This may seem a very narrow and technical area, but it is, in fact, all about the way in which courts communicate with the public. Things have changed radically in the last fifty years. The public is no longer simply content to be told *what* the law is. They want to know *why* it is. This is particularly the case with human rights. The judgment, at whatever level it is given, must be clearly reasoned and speak to the issues. When the court is dealing with an issue of a person's human or constitutional rights, the audience is not just the parties and practitioners. It is also the general public, because when, for instance, there is a significant question of human rights, many members of the public will be interested or involved.

I would expect that, if the Supreme Court evolves, it will only do so slowly, in the way that institutions have evolved throughout our history. I cannot say whether or how it will evolve or how long it will take to evolve, but let me illustrate how courts evolve by taking the example of the Conseil Constitutionnel, or Constitutional Council, in France. I choose this example because I have been to the Conseil Constitutionnel and thus can speak with the benefit of my researches. It is, I think, of some considerable interest to JUSTICE in view of its report, *A British Bill of Rights: informing the debate*.[9]

The Conseil Constitutionnel was set up in 1958 to monitor disputes arising from elections, and also the boundary between Parliament and the executive. The President or the Prime Minister or the Speaker of the French Parliament or a specified number of members of Parliament can ask the Conseil Constitutionnel, after a statute is passed by the Parliament but before it is brought into force, to consider whether the statute is in accordance with the Constitution. The Conseil

---

[9] JUSTICE Constitution Committee, 2007.

Constitutionnel is not a court in the ordinary sense. Its membership is drawn not simply from judges. Its members include distinguished persons from other walks of life. In the form in which it was originally set up, the Conseil Constitutionnel was not unlike, as it seems to me, a select committee of the House of Lords. It heard evidence from those it chose to call as witnesses.

The Conseil Constitutionnel produced decisions on issues of constitutionality. In due course, the Conseil Constitutionnel held that it could consider the question of constitutionality by reference not only to the actual provisions of the Constitution but also by reference to documents referred to in the recitals to the Constitution. This included the far-reaching *Declaration of the Rights of Man 1789* and also the preamble to the previous constitution of 1946 setting out socio-economic rights. Later, the Conseil Constitutionnel went further still and held that it could assess whether a legislative proposal was constitutional by reference to general principles to be found in legislation passed by Parliament in the period 1789 to 1946.

Finally, in July 2008 the French Parliament adopted a law which enables either the Conseil d'Etat or the Cour de Cassation to refer to the Conseil Constitutionnel a question of constitutionality arising in the course of litigation. This is a major change. When this amendment comes into force, the Conseil Constitutionnel will perform not only an anterior review of legislation when requested to do so by Parliament but also a posterior review of legislation when an issue arises as to its constitutionality in litigation. In either case, it will be able to annul the law if it considers it to be unconstitutional in the sense that I have described. In some ways, this development is comparable to the right given by the Human Rights Act 1998 to an individual citizen to challenge a law on the ground that it is incompatible with human rights. But it goes much further than the Human Rights Act 1998 did. It enables the citizen to argue that primary legislation is unconstitutional and to seek an order that it be set aside.

No doubt the Parliament of the United Kingdom, if it were ever so minded, could likewise give an individual the right to challenge legislation on the grounds that it is not in conformity with the fundamental principles of the common law. Until that happens the individual citizen must look to Community law, the Convention, and (to the extent that it is available) the common law to protect his rights, though such protection will not, save in the case of Community law, avail against primary legislation. It is for others to say whether that position is anomalous, but it is the law of the land. The like position in French law has apparently proved unsustainable in the longer term.

We shall have to see how the Conseil Constitutionnel evolves in the future. I do not suggest that there will be a parallel development in the United Kingdom but the Conseil Constitutionnel illustrates how institutions can change and evolve as circumstances require. In making this point, I have no specific institutions in the United Kingdom in mind but am simply re-affirming the importance of having appropriate institutions and the need for vigilance here.

Third, questions of human rights can no longer be decided in isolation from developments in other parts of the world.

When questions of human or constitutional rights arise, the judicial system in the United Kingdom can no longer operate in complete isolation from what is going on in the rest of the world. Courts must be mindful of the experience in other countries and take what we can from them. Accordingly, I have always strongly supported meetings of judges from different jurisdictions. Personal contacts are extremely important. It enables ideas to be exchanged and networks to be built up.

I also support the study of comparative human rights and constitutional law as this will enrich our understanding of human rights and constitutional rights in our own jurisdiction and enable us better to resolve new cases as they arise.

Fourth, human rights jurisprudence will more and more infuse the common law and be one of the major ways in which it is developed in this jurisdiction in the next ten years.

Over the centuries, judges have been responsible for developing the common law. The common law has enabled the law to adapt incrementally and thus in a way which encourages change commensurate with stability as social conditions require. It may be that more change is required and from time to time the Law Commissions make recommendations for change, or Parliament itself makes a change in the law. But there are still whole swathes of law that are common law and for which judges are responsible. Their role is crucial. They are at the heart of the system for human rights.

Building up human rights jurisprudence is, in some respects, the same type of task as developing the common law, though there may be new priorities, including a need for communication and transparency.

Human rights require that regard be had not just to legal rules but also to the wider context in which the rules operate. Law is, as is sometimes said, a discourse on other discourses. In the field of human rights, we are all discovering that law has new boundaries: the limits are not now the same as we always thought they were. So there may need to be a dialogue, not in the formal sense, but in the sense of an awareness between the law and other disciplines, so that so far as possible decisions are taken on the basis of the best information available.

This country is rightly proud of its common law tradition. The common law has contributed much to human rights and will continue to do so. But the traffic goes both ways. Over the decade to come, human rights jurisprudence may well become a crowbar for opening up and reinvigorating the common law in aspects of private law. Indeed, in some areas it has already done so. Human rights jurisprudence may also be used as a reason for changing the *Wednesbury* test in judicial review to one of proportionality. The existence of the new system for the protection of human rights can occasionally be used as a reason for restricting the development of the common law, as it was in *Van Colle*. However, it is likely that it will more often be used as a means of putting the common law on a more openly principled basis and bringing it up to date. Certainly that has been my experience in the Court of Appeal in the last few years.

Conclusions

So the overarching idea that I have discussed here is this.

The Human Rights Act 1998 made a profound difference to the work of the courts in its first ten years and I have no doubt that it will continue to affect what we do and how we think in the years ahead.

The Human Rights Act 1998 focused attention on the individual and the onus has changed from the individual to the state to justify any interference with his human rights in those cases where some interference is permitted. That is quite different from the position that prevailed before the Human Rights Act and still prevails in judicial review where human rights are not engaged. The Human Rights Act changed our understanding of democracy. We can now clearly see that democracy is also a complex interplay between majority and minority rights. Lawyers could usefully consider what it means to be 'necessary in a democratic society'.

There are important consequences from this, including the following:

(1) The Human Rights Act 1998 has changed the way we think about democracy.

(2) We need to think about the institutions of our democracy to ensure that they are appropriate to the needs of the human rights era.

(3) We need to be mindful of the experience in other countries and take what we can from them.

(4) Human rights jurisprudence will more and more infuse the common law and be one of the major ways in which it is developed in this jurisdiction in the next ten years. Human rights jurisprudence will reinvigorate the common law.

In conclusion, the first ten years of the Human Rights Act 1998 were very important and productive but there is still much to be done.

3

On Liberty

This chapter was originally written for a Liber Amicorum, a volume in honour of Lord Bingham of Cornhill.*

Introduction

This short paper is an opportunity to celebrate the work of a great judge, Lord Bingham. It brings together some thoughts about his unique contribution to the development of human rights in this country. I focus on one very small part of Lord Bingham's work but on a part that I regard as of great importance to all who value the law in this jurisdiction. From there, I go on to draw some parallels between human rights jurisprudence and the philosophy of John Stuart Mill, as expressed in his famous essay, *On Liberty*.[1] My object is to show that, as one would expect, one of the foundations of human rights jurisprudence is philosophical thinking on the nature of freedom in society.

Time to incorporate

It is well known that, although lawyers from the United Kingdom played a major part in the drafting of the European Convention on Human Rights (the 'Convention'), Parliament did not incorporate it into English domestic law until it passed the Human Rights Act in 1998. However, there was an important turning point some five years previously when Lord Bingham, then Sir Thomas Bingham MR, threw his considerable intellectual weight behind incorporation into domestic law in a lecture which argued in vigorous terms that the Convention should be incorporated.

The lecture was entitled 'The European Convention on Human Rights: time to incorporate'.[2] In this lecture, Lord Bingham emphasized the centrality to both

---

* Mary Arden, 'On Liberty and the European Convention on Human Rights' in Mads Andenas and Duncan Fairgrieve, *Tom Bingham and the Transformation of the Law: A Liber Amicorum* (Oxford University Press, 2009).

[1] JS Mill, *On Liberty* (2nd edn, London: John W. Parker & Son, 1859). Available online: <http://www.bartleby.com/130>.

[2] (1993) 109 LQR 390–400.

democracy and the judicial function of protecting the individual against the state. Under traditional constitutional theory, Parliament protected the rights of the citizen. However, there had been important changes in the way the constitutional arrangement worked. For example, the power of the executive had grown considerably. This had led to the increase in judicial review. However, the doctrine of Parliamentary sovereignty left the protection of individual rights in an unsatisfactory position. Lord Bingham suggested that:

... a government intent on implementing a programme may overlook the human rights aspects of its policies, and ..., if a government of more sinister intent were to gain power, we should be defenceless. There would not, certainly, be much the judges could do about it.

Lord Bingham added:

So anyone who sees Parliament as a reliable guardian of human rights in practice is, I suggest, guilty of wishful thinking.

He referred to the 'increasingly heterogeneous nature of our society and the increasingly assertive stance of minorities'. He referred to the 'general lessening of deference to authority, a growing unwillingness to accept the say-so of the teacher, a local government officer or the man from the ministry'.

Lord Bingham predicted a growing number of cases in which prevailing practice, perhaps of very long standing, will be said to infringe the human rights of some smaller group or some individual. He concluded:

As it stands, courts are not well-fitted to mediate in these situations.

From this standpoint, Lord Bingham went on to declare that the Convention offered a clear improvement on the then position. He drew on the work in this field of Anthony Lester QC (now Lord Lester of Herne Hill).[3]

Lord Bingham observed that incorporation of the Convention was 'at first blush, ... a simple and obvious way' of protecting the rights of minorities. He cogently observed that, whenever the United Kingdom was found to have acted in violation of Convention rights, the government had taken steps to cure the default and pay compensation.

Lord Bingham reviewed the arguments both for and against incorporation. He may have seen some force in the argument that incorporation could politicize the judiciary and lead to the decisions of the court trumping the power of Parliament because he proceeded on the basis that incorporation would not give the judges power to strike down legislation but rather that it would enable them to interpret legislation in accordance with the Convention, in accordance with the express will of Parliament as a result of having incorporated the Convention. Foreshadowing his later contribution to the debate on Parliamentary sovereignty, Lord Bingham expressed the view that 'in the scarcely imagined case of an express abrogation or derogation by Parliament, the judges would give effect to that provision also'.

---

[3] It is not possible within the scope of this paper to pay tribute to the monumental work of Lord Lester in this field, but for many years he actively promoted the idea of incorporation.

It was Lord Bingham's view that, while the Convention could not be entrenched, in practical terms it was inconceivable that a government would want to derogate from Convention obligations. He noted the argument that judges could become the subject of damaging controversy when deciding Convention issues but observed that there was no evidence that this had occurred elsewhere. Lord Bingham considered, but strongly disavowed, the suggestion that it was not appropriate for judges to decide questions about the relations between an individual and society. It was illogical to allow these decisions to be taken by the Strasbourg Court, but not in the first instance by judges of the United Kingdom. Moreover, judges were already involved in scrutinizing the decisions of ministers through the process of judicial review. The common law had not always provided the degree of protection conferred by the Convention. Although the Convention had been drafted in the 1950s, the argument that the Convention was in some way dated was ill founded, because of the evolutive[4] nature of Convention jurisprudence. He noted that the Court of Justice recognized principles of Convention jurisprudence, and in that way the United Kingdom became bound to apply the Convention to Community law. Lord Bingham noted that incorporation had the support of Lord Slynn of Hadley, an eminent one-time Advocate General and later a judge of the Court of Justice and member of the Appellate Committee of the House of Lords.

The final paragraph of the lecture was written in those magisterial tones which we now so strongly associate with the judgments of Lord Bingham:

> I end on a downbeat note. It would be naïve to suppose that incorporation of the Convention would usher in the new Jerusalem. As on the morrow of a general election, however glamorous the promises of the campaign, the world would not at once feel very different. But the change would over time stifle the insidious and damaging belief that it is necessary to go abroad to obtain justice. It would restore this country to its former place as an international standard bearer of liberty and justice. It would help to reinvigorate the faith, which our eighteenth and nineteenth century forebears would not for an instant have doubted, that these were fields in which Britain was the world's teacher, not its pupil. And it would enable the judges more effectively to honour their ancient and sacred undertaking to do right to all manner of people after the laws and usages of this realm, without fear or favour, affection or ill will.

The use of the word 'downbeat' in the first sentence of this passage is perhaps a little Delphic, but as I read it Lord Bingham was drawing an allusion with the first beat of a grand overture, rather than using the word in its colloquial sense suggesting a pessimistic tone. The 'forebears' to whom he referred may have included the great English philosophers such as John Locke and John Stuart Mill, as well as eminent judges.

A most impressive feature of the lecture is, however, the marshalling of cogent arguments so that they became in legal terms unanswerable. Furthermore, the support for the Convention from such a senior and well-respected member of the

---

[4] The Strasbourg Court's approach to interpretation is called 'evolutive' because under its jurisprudence the Convention is a living instrument which it must interpret in the light of modern day conditions.

judiciary was highly influential and changed the thinking of many lawyers in this country. A whole generation of lawyers, whose first studies in the law would probably not have included human rights, and some of whom might then have confused the European Court of Human Rights with the Court of Justice sitting in Luxembourg, began to take an interest in the issue. It was characteristic of Lord Bingham to speak in forthright terms on an issue of high constitutional importance. Its importance in that context cannot be overstated. The fact that he threw his powerful intellectual weight behind it must surely have been one of the factors that led to the incorporation into domestic law of the Convention by the Human Rights Act 1998.[5] The Act was not brought into force immediately, so that judges and others had time to become adjusted to the implications of the Act. In 2000, Lord Bingham, who had been appointed Lord Chief Justice in 1996, retired from that office and became the senior Lord of Appeal in Ordinary just four months before the Human Rights Act 1998 came into force.

Building a human rights jurisprudence

After he became senior Law Lord, Lord Bingham was instrumental in making the Convention part of the waft and weave of English law. All his speeches repay careful study, but I would make a brief reference to two decisions which bear on the theme of this paper. The first is *R (Pretty) v Director of Public Prosecutions*.[6] In this case, the appellant suffered from a progressive and degenerative terminal illness. She wanted to control the timing and manner of her death but she could not do so without the assistance of her husband because of her illness. She requested an assurance from the Director of Public Prosecutions that her husband would not be prosecuted for the offence of assisting her to commit suicide contrary to s 2 of the Suicide Act 1961. She claimed that she had a right under the Convention to commit suicide with assistance. The Director of Public Prosecutions refused to give her any undertaking. The appellant relied on Arts 2, 3, 8, 9, and 14 of the Convention. Article 8 guarantees respect for a person's private life. Mrs Pretty's case under Art 8 was that this Article gave her a right to self-determination and that there had to be serious reasons to justify interference with an intimate part of her private life. However, on that particular issue Lord Bingham held:

Article 8 is expressed in terms directed to protection of personal autonomy while individuals were living their lives, and there is nothing to suggest that the article has reference to the choice to live no longer.[7]

The other members of the House agreed with Lord Bingham. The case subsequently went to the European Court of Human Rights, which took the unusual step of setting out the whole of Lord Bingham's judgment within its judgment. On

---

[5] The Convention rights incorporated by the Human Rights Act 1998 and the principal provisions of that Act are set out in the Appendix.

[6] [2001] UKHL 61, [2002] 1 AC 800.   [7] At [23].

the specific issue of Art 8, it was not prepared to hold that there was no interference with her private life for the purpose of Art 8. However, it held that the interference was within the state's margin of appreciation,[8] and justified because of the risk of abuse of the claimed right, which meant that the ban on assisted suicide was not disproportionate. It found that there was no violation of any Article of the Convention.

The second case to which I would briefly refer is *A v Secretary of State for the Home Department*,[9] known as the '*Belmarsh* case'. This concerned the right to liberty of persons who were suspected terrorists who had been detained indefinitely under certificates issued by the Home Secretary under s 23 of the Anti-terrorism, Crime and Security Act 2001. The House quashed an order derogating from the Convention on the grounds that the requirements for derogation had not been fulfilled. The House also held that s 23 of the 2001 Act was incompatible with the Convention. I have considered this landmark case in depth elsewhere.[10] For present purposes, I draw attention to the powerful statement of the importance of the right to personal freedom in Lord Bingham's speech:

[36]   In urging the fundamental importance of the right to personal freedom, as the sixth step in their proportionality argument, the appellants were able to draw on the long libertarian tradition of English law, dating back to chapter 39 of Magna Carta 1215, given effect in the ancient remedy of habeas corpus, declared in the Petition of Right 1628, upheld in a series of landmark decisions down the centuries and embodied in the substance and procedure of the law to our own day. Recent statements, not in themselves remarkable, may be found in *In re S-C (Mental Patient: Habeas Corpus)* [1996] QB 599, 603 and *In re Wasfi Suleman Mahmod* [1995] Imm A R 311, 314. In its treatment of article 5 of the European Convention, the European Court also has recognised the prime importance of personal freedom. In *Kurt v Turkey* (1998) 27 EHRR 373, para 122, it referred to 'the fundamental importance of the guarantees contained in article 5 for securing the right of individuals in a democracy to be free from arbitrary detention at the hands of the authorities' and to the need to interpret narrowly any exception to 'a most basic guarantee of individual freedom'. In *Garcia Alva v Germany* (2001) 37 EHRR 335, para 39, it referred to 'the dramatic impact of deprivation of liberty on the fundamental rights of the person concerned'. The authors of the 'Siracusa Principles', although acknowledging that the protection against arbitrary detention (article 9 of the ICCPR) might be limited if strictly required by the exigencies of an emergency situation (article 4), were none the less of the opinion that some rights could never be denied in any conceivable emergency and, in particular (para 70 (b)), 'no person shall be detained for an indefinite period of time, whether detained pending judicial investigation or trial or detained without charge...'

This is a timeless reminder of the fundamental nature of the right to liberty of the person.

---

[8] For an explanation of this term, see Glossary and also Chapter 4, *Proportionality: The Way Ahead?*, and Chapter 20, *An English Judge in Europe.*
[9] [2004] UKHL 56, [2005] 2 AC 68.
[10] 'Human Rights in an Age of Terrorism' (2005) 121 LQR 604.

John Stuart Mill—a little about the man and his place in history

Mill lived from 1806 to 1873. From a very early age, he was educated by his father to be a utilitarian after the philosopher, Jeremy Bentham. The details of his extraordinary education can be found in Mill's autobiography.[11] But Mill used his intense early education to go beyond the utilitarian thinking on which his father had brought him up. In his early twenties, he went through a personal crisis which he describes in his autobiography. He overcame that crisis and went on to revise utilitarian philosophy. His theory focused on the importance of the individuality and autonomy of individual members of society. He wrote several works, of which *On Liberty* is probably the best known.[12]

Mill wrote *On Liberty* in 1859 in memory of Harriet Taylor, his long-time confidante, who, after her first husband's death, became his wife. She died in 1858. In 1865, Mill became a member of Parliament. He campaigned unsuccessfully for women to be given the vote in Parliamentary elections. However, in his time as an MP, a bill giving women the right to vote in municipal elections passed through the House of Commons unopposed in June 1869. Mill helped to bring about the passing of the Married Women's Property Act 1870, which gave women the right to hold property in their own name after matrimony. It has been said that by the beginning of the twentieth century, Mill had come to displace Locke as the guardian of liberty.[13] I do not, of course, suggest that Mill was the only philosopher who has had any influence on the Convention but he may well have been one of the philosophers who had the greatest influence on it.

On Liberty—the basic themes

Much had been written about Mill's short but powerful essay, *On Liberty*. In his recent biography of Mill,[14] Richard Reeves wrote that:

Few will doubt the status of *On Liberty* as a masterpiece; and as a panegyric of individual liberty and the nobility of a self-governed life it remains unsurpassed.[15]

Mill's work had an immense effect on Victorian thought and continues to have a great influence today. Reeves describes *On Liberty* as an intellectual hand grenade rolled into the reading rooms of all the best clubs.[16]

---

[11] JS Mill, *Autobiography* (1873).
[12] JS Mill, *On Liberty* (2nd edn, London: John W. Parker & Son, 1859). Available online: <http://www.bartleby.com/130>.
[13] AW Brian Simpson, *Human Rights and the End of Empire: Britain and the Genesis of the European Convention* (Oxford University Press, 2004), 22.
[14] Richard Reeves, *John Stuart Mill: Victorian Firebrand* (Atlantic Books, 2007).
[15] Reeves, *John Stuart Mill: Victorian Firebrand*, 263.
[16] Reeves, *John Stuart Mill: Victorian Firebrand*, 296.

There are two particular arguments in *On Liberty* that are of interest in relation to the Convention. They are intertwined with each other. The first argument is known as 'the harm principle'. Mill wrote that the object of the essay was to assert this principle as one which should govern all control exerted by society over an individual whether by controlling him physically or by 'the moral coercion of public opinion'. He famously wrote that:

That principle is, that the sole end for which mankind are warranted, individually or collectively, in interfering with the liberty of action of any of their number, is self-protection. That the only purpose for which power can be rightfully exercised over any member of the civilised community, against his will, is to prevent harm to others. His own good, either physical or moral, is not a sufficient warrant.

An individual was entitled to act without restriction unless his conduct concerned others:

To justify [compulsion], the conduct from which it is desired to deter him, must be calculated to produce evil to someone else. The only part of the conduct of any one, for which he is amenable to society, is that which concerns others. In the part which merely concerns himself, his independence is, of right, absolute. Over himself, over his own body and mind, the individual is sovereign.

Another argument which Mill develops in his essay is that each individual has a right to liberty of self-development. Again this is subject to the rights of others. He says in *On Liberty*:

It is not by wearing down into uniformity all that is individual in themselves, but by cultivating it and calling it forth, within the limits imposed by the rights and interests of others, that human beings become a noble and beautiful object of contemplation; and as the works partake the character of those who do them, by the same process human life also becomes rich, diversified and animating, furnishing more abundant aliment to high thoughts and elevating feelings, and strengthening the tie which binds every individual to the race, by making the race infinitely better worth belonging to. In proportion to the development of his individuality, each person becomes more valuable to himself, and is therefore capable of being more valuable to others. There is a greater fullness of life about his own existence, and when there is more life in the units there is more in the mass which is composed of them ... it is only the cultivation of individuality which produces, or can produce, well developed human beings.

The more that individuals developed themselves, the more they and society would benefit.

In drawing a line between liberty of self-development and harm to others, Mill was talking about what might be called today the individual's need for private space or privacy, as opposed to the public space that the state or other members of society can enter. Both arguments share an underlying belief that people should be allowed to act in accordance with their own beliefs. This is not simply liberty in a political sense of freedom from state interference but liberty in a much wider, personal sense. Liberty should be allowed to individuals as far as possible. That is not to say that there are no limits on the right of an individual to cause harm to himself. Mill recognized for example that a man should not be free to sell himself into slavery: 'The principle of freedom cannot require that the person be free not to be free.'

Liberty in this wider sense used by Mill is an essential element of a plural society which enjoys freedom under the law. Liberty in this sense is consistent with, for example, diversity of religious practices, and it facilitates and mandates toleration of them. This is important because religious and cultural differences often pose challenges for societies which, like that of the United Kingdom, are increasingly heterogeneous. This point was one of the points which Lord Bingham noted in his lecture. But toleration of difference comes to an end if it leads to violence or other harm. Moreover, as Passayat J of the Supreme Court of India said, a religion which teaches violence 'strikes at the very root of an orderly society'.[17]

There are many questions that Mill's arguments leave unanswered or that are not worked out. For instance, many aspects of the concept of 'harm' are unclear. Does it for example include harm of which the victim is unaware? One might be tempted to answer that question in the negative, but the question whether harm takes place may well depend on the type of harm. It is thus possible to envisage examples of harm where knowledge of it is irrelevant to an invasion of another's rights (such as the inclusion of erroneous information about an individual in his personnel file, thus adversely affecting his promotion prospects in his employment). There can be differences of view as to what constitutes harm. Smoking in public places is now illegal, but there were those who argued that smoking caused no harm to others because of the heavy taxes which smokers pay on the purchase of cigarettes, which are said to outweigh the cost to the National Health Service of illnesses caused by smoking.

So far as the right to liberty of self-development is concerned, this is open to objection that individuals cannot simply live in isolation from others. As John Donne wrote, no man is an island entire of itself.[18] In the modern world, governments often claim the right to regulate the conduct of individuals which only harms themselves. Moreover, the right to liberty of self-development assumes that that is what most individuals want and what will bring them greatest satisfaction. That is not always the case, and Mill's argument has been described as elitist. Although Mill was a campaigner for women's rights and many other causes, he does not enter into the problems that arise from the problem that some individuals are unable to exercise their right of liberty of self-development for lack of resources. Mill does not argue that resources should be redistributed so that everyone is able effectively to exercise their right of liberty to self-development: without resources, liberty, like justice, may be said to be open to everyone like the Ritz Hotel.[19] The right to liberty of self-development might mean that a person should not, for instance, have the right to medical help if he chose to harm himself. Some people are in a weak position, and some are in a strong position: if the weak are to be

---

[17] *Zahira Habibulla H Sheik v Gujurat* 2004 (4) SCC 158 (the 'Best Bakery case').

[18] J Donne, *Devotions on Emergent Occasions*, Meditation XVII.

[19] Meaning, the reverse, namely that it is effectively not so open because of the high costs of litigation and the costs-shifting rule.

protected, the state must sometimes interfere with the freedom of action of the strong. A person who suffers from an addiction may need help to throw off his addiction: it is not clear whether he should be treated like the person who agrees to sell himself into slavery. These are some of the issues that *On Liberty* does not address or resolve.

In the twentieth century, Isaiah Berlin went on to draw a distinction between negative liberty and positive liberty.[20] Negative liberty is freedom from interference, such as freedom to ride a bicycle without a helmet. He regarded positive liberty as freedom to achieve one's potential. Berlin argued that democracy must confer both sorts of liberty on its citizens. The arguments advanced in this essay are important. There are similarities between this analysis and the arguments in *On Liberty*.

The Convention and *On Liberty*

Interestingly, the word 'liberty' is only used in the Convention in one place, namely Art 5, which guarantees the right to liberty and security of person. Lawyers tend to think of liberty in terms of physical liberty and that is the sense in which the word 'liberty' is used in the European Convention on Human Rights. The word 'freedom' is the word used by the Convention to denote liberty, in the wide sense used by Mill. Thus, for example, the fourth preamble to the Convention states that the signatories reaffirm 'their profound belief in those fundamental freedoms which are the foundation of justice and peace in the world and best maintained on the one hand by an effective political democracy and on the other by a common understanding and observance of human rights on which they depend'. Article 1 states that the parties to the Convention agree to secure within their jurisdiction the rights and freedoms defined in the Convention. Article 9 guarantees the right to freedom of thought, conscience, and religion. Article 10 guarantees the right to freedom of expression and Art 11 guarantees the right to freedom of peaceful assembly and to freedom of association with others. Article 17 states that Convention rights do not imply the right to engage in any activity aimed at the destruction of the rights and freedoms set out in the Convention. Thus the Convention uses the word 'freedom' as freedom from control by others and the state. This is the sense in which Mill has principally used the term 'liberty' in his essay.

Mill stressed the importance of the individual. This idea is consistent with the Convention, which confers a series of rights on each individual member of society being a person who is entitled to rights. The individual, and not the state, assumes the centre stage.

Mill tells us that the core idea in *On Liberty* is what has become known as the harm principle. He describes a very generalized right of liberty, which is always

---

[20] Isaiah Berlin, *Two Concepts of Liberty* republished in Henry Hardy (ed), *Liberty* (Oxford University Press, 2002).

subject to a limitation if harm is caused to third parties. There is a direct parallel here with the Convention. Although the Convention does not create a general right of liberty, it creates a number of separate rights. Some of them are what are known as 'qualified' rights, such as the right to freedom of expression in Art 10:

(1) Everyone has the right to freedom of expression. This right shall include freedom to hold opinions and to receive and impart information and ideas without interference by public authority and regardless of frontiers. This Article shall not prevent States from requiring the licensing of broadcasting, television or cinema enterprises.

(2) The exercise of these freedoms, since it carries with it duties and responsibilities, may be subject to such formalities, conditions, restrictions or penalties as are prescribed by law and are necessary in a democratic society, in the interests of national security, territorial integrity or public safety, for the prevention of disorder or crime, for the protection of health or morals, for the protection of the reputation or rights of others, for preventing the disclosure of information received in confidence, or for maintaining the authority and impartiality of the judiciary.

Qualified rights are designed to give the individual the maximum private space in which to exercise his freedom but his freedom ends when the limitation is applicable. As can be seen from Art 10(2), this can broadly be described as the point at which harm to others begins. So, instead of creating a general right of liberty, the Convention may be said to create a number of specific rights of liberty, which like Mill's concept of liberty, are subject to limitation where harm to others occurs. Mill's concept of harm is a very general concept. The Convention concretizes harm in terms of the types of harm specified in the limitations on Convention rights, for example in Art 10(2).

Not all rights are qualified rights. For instance, Art 3 guarantees the right not to be subjected to inhuman or degrading treatment. This right is not subject to any qualification. Under the Convention, this right is of such importance that a violation cannot be justified. Thus a violation cannot for instance be justified on the grounds that it is necessary for the purpose of preventing crime, which may cause harm to others.

The parallels between *On Liberty* and the Convention do not end there. The right to liberty of self-development appears to find its reflection in the jurisprudence of the Strasbourg Court under Art 8. This, too, is a qualified right. It provides:

(1) Everyone has the right to respect for his private and family life, his home and his correspondence.

(2) There shall be no interference by a public authority with the exercise of this right except such as is in accordance with the law and is necessary in a democratic society in the interests of national security, public safety or the economic well-being of the country, for the prevention of disorder or crime, for the protection of health or morals, or for the protection of the rights and freedoms of others.

The concept of respect for private life is a wide one. One of the leading cases is *Bensaid v United Kingdom.*[21] In this case the Strasbourg Court emphasized the

---

[21] (Application No 44599/98) [2001] ECHR 82.

width of this concept and did so in language redolent of Mill's right to liberty of self-development:

47. Private life is a broad term not susceptible to exhaustive definition. The Court has already held that elements such as gender identification, name and sexual orientation and sexual life are important elements of the personal sphere protected by Article 8 (see e.g. the *B v France* judgment of 25 March 1992, Series A No. 232-C, para 63; the *Burghartz v Switzerland* judgment of 22 February 1994, Series A No. 280-B, para 24; the *Dudgeon v the United Kingdom* judgment of 22 October 1991, Series A No. 45, para 41, and the *Laskey, Jaggard and Brown v the United Kingdom* judgment of 19 February 1997, *Reports* 1997-1, para 36). Mental health must also be regarded as a crucial part of private life associated with the aspect of moral integrity. Article 8 protects a right to identity and personal development, and the right to establish and develop relationships with other human beings and the outside world (see e.g. *Burghartz v Switzerland*, Comm. Report, [. . .], para 47; *Friedl v Austria*, Series A No. 305-B, Comm Report, para 45). The preservation of mental stability is in that context an indispensable precondition to effective enjoyment of the right to respect for private life.

In *R (Razgar) v Secretary of State for the Home Department*,[22] Lord Walker rightly warned that the language of the last two sentences of this paragraph must be treated with care. He said:

This language is wide and imprecise and it must in my opinion be treated with some caution. There is no general human right to good physical and mental health any more than there is a human right to expect (rather than to pursue) happiness.[23]

Nonetheless, the parallel between the Convention jurisprudence, with its reference to the protection of a right to personal development, and the right to liberty of self-development expressed in *On Liberty,* are striking.

As I have already indicated, Mill did not deal with a number of issues to which his idea of liberty gave rise. Mill never had to tackle the question of proportionality. But he would no doubt have approved of the idea of proportionality in the sense of requiring a minimum interference with human rights. Mill did not have to deal with the conflicts that arise in cases under Art 1 of the First Protocol to the Convention between the right of individual members of society to property and the right of the state to take away the property for the good of the community. Here the state has a large margin of appreciation, and the level of protection guaranteed by the Convention for the individual is comparatively low.[24]

Conclusions

For all its imprecision and imperfections Mill's essay *On Liberty* has within it a fundamental truth about the importance of the individual and the value of human life in its fullest sense, which is also at the heart of the Convention. I would not say

---

[22] [2004] UKHL 27, [2004] 2 AC 368.   [23] At [34].
[24] See, for example, *James v United Kingdom* (Application No 8793/79) [1986] ECHR 2.

that Mill was the only philosopher whose thinking reflects Convention values. I would not say that his thinking always reflects Convention values. It is sufficient for the purposes of this paper that he is one such philosopher and that some parallels can be found between his work and Convention jurisprudence. This may not seem a wholly surprising conclusion, but it is one which enables the reader to see the Convention, its structure, jurisprudence, and achievement in a new and different light and from a different perspective.

Mill's *On Liberty* does not, of course, provide anything approaching a comprehensive insight into the Convention. Nor could it do so, as it is not itself a hard-edged analysis of liberty. However, Mill's work underscores the role of the Convention as an instrument of a liberal society.

A half-forgotten statue of John Stuart Mill, with his finely-chiselled face looking to the horizon, stands in Temple Place, just outside the Middle Temple on the edge of legal London. Lord Bingham must often have walked past it on his way to and from the Temple. Perhaps Mill's writing provided some inspiration for his work. We shall remember Lord Bingham for many achievements, not least that of being the senior Law Lord when the Human Rights Act 1998 was brought into force. He was also very much in favour of the institution of a Supreme Court of the United Kingdom, which opened after his retirement. The institution of the Supreme Court is another major development in the justice system of this country that owes much to Lord Bingham.

Indeed, the brief survey of Mill's work in this paper suggests that the new justices of the Supreme Court could do worse than to ask for the statue of John Stuart Mill to be moved outside the new Supreme Court building. It would remind the justices, and those who visit the new Supreme Court as litigants or otherwise, of the meaning of liberty in its fullest sense and the importance of the concept of liberty to a society which places value on the individual and his or her self-realization.

PART II

UNDERSTANDING PROPORTIONALITY AND SUBSIDIARITY

Proportionality and subsidiarity are concepts used in EU law and the case law of the European Court of Human Rights. They are not, however, indigenous principles of the common law of England and Wales. To apply EU law and European human rights jurisprudence correctly, it is necessary to analyse these concepts—hence the chapters in this Part.

In Chapter 4, *Proportionality: The Way Ahead?* I explore the concept of proportionality through the different lenses of the two European supranational courts. This gives a different perspective from our own case law. Our courts do not, in general, use the same techniques as are adopted in EU or Convention case law, as will become clear through the examples I give of cases in which our courts have applied proportionality. It is apparent that the decision by a court as to whether a measure is a proportionate interference with (say) a Convention right can be the deciding factor as to whether a new policy measure (such as a measure to reduce the number of sham marriages conducted to obtain favourable immigration status) can be adopted.

Proportionality and subsidiarity are linked concepts: both are ways of restricting the effect of a decision or rule. When national courts use these concepts (and generally they use proportionality rather than subsidiarity), they are one of the tests used to define the limits of legitimate state interference with individual rights. When they are used by the European supranational courts, on the other hand, they may also reflect those courts' view of their proper role. When those courts apply proportionality, for instance, they may leave the final decision to the national courts.

In Chapter 5, *Subsidiarity and Decentralization*, I explain that subsidiarity will need to be developed in the future to permit contracting states to implement decisions taken at the supranational level in a way appropriate for their national culture and context. Subsidiarity is also a means of achieving a greater level of participation in public affairs (because people tend to participate more in public affairs if they affect their own community) and therefore pursuing the aims of a democratic society. It is, however, easier for member states than central powers, such as the institutions of the EU, to see the merits of subsidiarity, since it is often simpler to impose a single rule across the EU than to allow regional differences. The discussion in this chapter will continue to be relevant as the balance between subsidiarity and centralization is worked out in multi-level situations such as the EU, especially now that the Luxembourg Court is developing fundamental rights.

The final chapter in this Part is Chapter 6, *Press, Privacy, and Proportionality: the Impact of Proportionality on Judicial Review*. Here I trace an area of law which may develop in response to the experience of our courts in using Strasbourg jurisprudence and applying EU law. I start by discussing the test of unreasonableness. This is used as a general test in judicial review when an individual takes legal proceedings to challenge the actions of the state. I argue that it should be replaced by a test of proportionality, which is commonly applied in EU law and Strasbourg case law. Recent developments in the field of press regulation and the Strasbourg jurisprudence on reconciling the press's right to freedom of expression and an individual's right to privacy show the usefulness of the concept of proportionality.

I conclude by adding that the courts should make this change over time. However, I consider that they will need first to develop a varying approach. There will be cases where the courts will need to give more weight to the judgment of the decision-maker than in other cases. This may be because of the constitutional allocation of powers between Parliament and the executive on the one hand, and the courts on the other.

4

Proportionality: The Way Ahead?

This chapter is based on a speech given on 12 November 2012 at King's College London as the Annual Address of the United Kingdom Association for European Law (UKAEL).*

No-one can possibly quarrel with the basic idea of proportionality as a legal concept. Simply put, the proportionality principle for the purposes of this paper means that no state or official or institution can interfere with an individual's rights under the European Convention on Human Rights (the 'Convention') or under EU law, unless it shows that the interference with those rights is justified.[1] The logic of the proportionality principle is impeccable. Its attraction is irresistible.

Indeed, proportionality is so logical that one would expect it to be found in the common law. But in fact it is not derived from the common law or from any UK statute. One writer not so many years ago commented that he could only find one piece of case law about proportionality, which was a dictum of Lord Diplock, describing proportionality as meaning '[i]n plain English, "you must not use a steam hammer to crack a nut, if a nutcracker would do"'.[2]

Today, lawyers and judges in England and Wales[3] have to understand proportionality primarily because it is part and parcel of the jurisprudence of the European Court of Human Rights (the 'Strasbourg Court') and of the jurisprudence of the Court of Justice of the European Union (the 'Luxembourg Court').[4] My starting point in this paper, therefore, is to examine the nature of that jurisprudence and show the differences of approach between the two European supranational courts. We shall find that the concept has its complexities and that it is not as simple as it looks.

---

* First published in [2013] PL 498. It is reproduced here with the kind permission of the Publisher.

[1] The proportionality principle also applies in other fields of law outside the scope of this paper, such as international law. I shall restrict my examples to civil law, but proportionality also has important implications in criminal law. For an absorbing account of proportionality, see Aaron Barak, *Proportionality* (Cambridge, 2011).

[2] *R v Goldstein* [1983] 1 WLR 151, 155B.

[3] References in this paper to England should be read as including references to Wales, even though Wales is not expressly mentioned, and cognate expressions should be treated accordingly.

[4] Proportionality is today also applied by the common law and statute law in certain other situations, mainly by extension of the principles derived from the jurisprudence of the Strasbourg and Luxembourg Courts, but this paper is not concerned with those situations.

When I have explained those differences, I will take a look at the way those differences have been reflected in the domestic legal order in four cases where the courts are grappling with 'multi-level judging': that is, they are aiming either to make English law (in the case of human rights) compatible with the Convention or (where EU law is invoked) to make it conform with EU law in accordance with the UK's Treaty obligations. I will use these cases to throw further light on the nature of the proportionality principle and the problems it brings.

I shall next address the difference between that form of unreasonableness which English lawyers call '*Wednesbury* unreasonableness' and proportionality. *Wednesbury* unreasonableness is the usual test for judicial review of administrative action in English law in the absence of illegality or procedural impropriety.

In the final part of this paper I will get out my crystal ball: I will turn to look at the way ahead. I hope that, by that stage, I will have convinced you that there are aspects of proportionality that need to be addressed at the highest level in the United Kingdom. In addition, there is a further issue to be addressed at that level as well. For some years, there had been a call for the test of unreasonableness to be replaced. Those making this call often also suggest that proportionality should be used instead of unreasonableness. For instance, Lord Diplock, in *Council for Civil Service Unions v Minister for the Civil Service*,[5] contemplated the possibility of:

… the … adoption in the future of the principle of 'proportionality' which is recognised in the administrative law of several of our fellow members of the European Economic Community …

So I will turn to explain the source of the pros and cons of that idea before drawing the threads together and leaving you with some parting thoughts of my own in order that you can—judge for yourself!

A historical diversion

Before we begin the hard work, I propose to start with a little historical diversion. It will enable us to identify what I will call the 'badges' of proportionality.

I have already said that proportionality is not a common law concept. (The common law tends to like bright-line rules, whereas proportionality requires evaluation.) However, one can say that proportionality is a very ancient concept. Precisely how ancient is a matter of debate as academics have for years disputed its precise origin. It may be as old as Hammurabi[6] (of 'an eye for an eye and a tooth for a tooth' fame). For our purposes, it is sufficient to note its origin in the administrative law in Prussia at the end of the nineteenth century. It started as a principle of necessity applied to policing. In a notable case, *Kreuzberg*,[7] the Prussian Supreme Administrative Court developed the notion that the state required special

---

[5] [1985] AC 374, at 410E.
[6] The Code of Hammurabi, a Babylonian code, dates from about 1772 BC.
[7] 14 June 1882, Pr OVG, 29, 253.

permission in order to interfere with a citizen's civil liberties. The police sought to rely on a specific provision of the law empowering the police to adopt such measures 'as are necessary for the maintenance of public order'. The Court held that, to test this reliance, it had to examine whether the police measures exceeded in intensity what was required by the pursued objective. This principle evolved into a proportionality principle. In due course, proportionality became a constitutional principle, so that the legislature was also bound by it.

The German Federal Constitutional Court, which was established after World War II, adopted and developed the proportionality principle. It had three elements:

(1) *Suitability*: the measure should be suitable for the purpose of facilitating or achieving the desired objective.

(2) *Necessity*: the measure should be necessary (and, at this stage, I am not going to say anything about *how far* it had to be necessary).

(3) *Fair balance*: the measure should not be disproportionate to the restriction which it involved.

The Federal Constitutional Court applies the proportionality principle as a generalized head of review for administrative action, and so the proportionality principle plays a key role in administrative law in Germany. The Federal Constitutional Court has, for instance, held that the police cannot enforce an absolute ban and must allow exceptions from measures when it is not absolutely necessary to have a blanket rule.

Likewise the Federal Constitutional Court uses proportionality in cases in which there are conflicts between individual rights. These rights may not be qualified to a further extent than is necessary to reconcile them.[8]

Even today there is nothing about proportionality in the German Basic Law.

The badges of proportionality

I am now ready to identify the 'badges' of proportionality, which it is helpful to keep in mind when examining proportionality. As we have seen, they are suitability, necessity, and fair balance. Courts have also held that there is a prior question, namely whether the desired objective of the act or measure was a legitimate aim. It is important to identify the legitimate aim in order to assess the suitability of the act or measure. This is not always treated as a separate test as it is implicit in suitability. Absence of a legitimate aim is likely to be a knock-out point.

With my historical diversion ended, I now return to my main theme. What I want to do is to show what we can learn by approaching proportionality not through our own cases but by looking in a broad way at the Strasbourg and

---

[8] See Southern, *Tax Law Developments—the movement from private law to public law*, paper given at Queen Mary, University of London, 12 October 2012; see also Schwarze, *European Administrative Law Developments* (Sweet & Maxwell, 2006). I am also indebted to Hugh Mercer QC for bringing this work to my attention.

Luxembourg jurisprudence from which it is derived. I turn first to the Strasbourg jurisprudence.

Strasbourg jurisprudence—a focus on fair balance

The Convention, like the administrative law of Prussia, makes no reference to proportionality by that name. It has, however, been adopted as a general concept of Strasbourg jurisprudence.

Some rights, like Art 8(1) (right to respect for private and family life), are expressly qualified by such matters as the rights of others. Thus Art 8(2) prohibits any interference by a public authority with the exercise of this right unless the interference 'is in accordance with the law and . . . necessary in a democratic society in the interests of national security, public safety or the economic well-being of the country, for the prevention of disorder or crime, for the protection of health or morals, or for the protection of the rights and freedoms of others'.[9]

It is well-established that, when the Strasbourg Court is required to determine whether an interference with private life is necessary for one of the purposes permitted by Art 8(2), it is not enough that the interference is for one of the specified purposes. It must also be a proportionate means of achieving that aim.

Not every Article in the Convention is qualified by an express provision for interference. Article 6, for instance, which guarantees the right of access to court makes no reference to any permitted restriction on that right. However, the Strasbourg Court will in appropriate circumstances treat such a restriction as implied.

In order to reach a view as to whether something is *necessary* in a democratic society for one of the specified reasons, and therefore proportionate, the interests of the individual have to be *balanced* with the rights of others or of the rest of the community. The word 'necessary' can be read as implying that the rights of the individual can only be interfered with when this is strictly necessary and no more than is absolutely necessary. However, this is not how that expression works in practice. In some situations, the Strasbourg Court will take the view that the national authorities are better placed to assess whether the interference is necessary when the interests of the individual are balanced with those of the community. The decision is then said to be within the 'margin of appreciation' of the contracting state.

A good example of the margin of appreciation being applied to what is necessary in a democratic society is the controversial decision of the Strasbourg Court in *Otto-Preminger-Institut v Austria*.[10] In that case the applicant managed a private cinema and the cinema wished to show an anti-religious film containing what the Court described as 'provocative portrayals of objects of religious veneration'. The film was a distinctly minority interest: one of the problems was that it was to be shown in the

---

[9] The Convention rights are set out in the Appendix.
[10] (Application No 13470/87) [1994] ECHR 26.

staunchly Roman Catholic area of the Tyrol. The Austrian authorities considered that the film was distasteful and would lead to disturbances. A court order was made for the seizure and destruction of the film.

The applicant complained that this was a violation of the Institut's freedom of expression. The right to freedom of expression contained in Art 10 of the Convention is, like Art 8, a qualified right. The qualification is, so far as material, the same as that in Art 8(2). By a majority of 6:3, the Strasbourg Court rejected the applicant's case and held that there had been no violation of Art 10.

The majority relied on the margin of appreciation and held that there was no violation. Their reasoning was that the right of the Institut to freedom of expression had to be balanced against the rights of others in Austria, under Art 9 of the Convention (freedom of thought, conscience, and religion), to respect for their religious feelings. The majority accepted that the right to freedom of expression was applicable to ideas that shock or disturb. However, there was also an obligation to avoid, so far as possible, expressions that were gratuitously offensive to others. Any prevention of improper attacks on objects of religious veneration had to be proportionate to the legitimate aim to be pursued. In the opinion of the majority, since religion had different significance in the various contracting states, the national authorities were best able to determine whether an outright ban was necessary in the interests of society. The position would, therefore, have been different if there had been consensus among the contracting states, for example that this sort of film should not be banned.

The majority gave no guidance as to how the national authorities were expected to carry out their task.

The judgment of the minority is, to my mind, more instructive. In essence, the minority rejected the idea that the ban fell within the margin of appreciation of the national authorities, and took the view that, since there were less restrictive measures available for dealing with the showing of the film, the ban was not proportionate.

The minority's process of reasoning is important. Unlike the majority, the minority proceeded on the basis that, to carry out the proportionality exercise, it was not sufficient simply to conclude that two Convention rights were in conflict. The minority made an assessment of the importance of each right. They pointed out that freedom of expression was a fundamental feature of a democratic society and added: 'There is no point in guaranteeing this freedom only as long as it is used in accordance with accepted opinion.'

They held that Art 10(2), permitting an interference with freedom of expression, had to be narrowly interpreted. Accordingly, the state's margin of appreciation under this provision could not be a wide one. A state could legitimately set limits to the public expression of abusive attacks on the reputation of a religious group. Moreover, 'tolerance works both ways': those seeking to exercise freedom of expression had to limit the offence they might cause.

Then the minority subjected the facts to critical examination. They held that any measures to restrict the exercise of the right to freedom of expression had to be *proportionate*. A complete ban could only be justified if the behaviour of those seeking to exercise their freedom of expression led to a high level of abuse. It was also necessary to weigh up the interference with each right having regard to the particular circumstances under consideration. On the facts of the case, the minority concluded that, as there could only be a small, paying audience in an 'art cinema', the film should not have been subjected to an outright ban.

Otto-Preminger-Institut is a striking case. There are a number of points that I want to draw out of it:

- *The minority judgment tells us how the proportionality exercise in Strasbourg jurisprudence works.* It consists of two separate steps:
  1. *Qualitative assessment*: The minority carried out a qualitative assessment of each of the rights in issue. They determined that the right to freedom of expression had great weight and accordingly they rejected a solution that gave it no weight. Any risk that the restrictions on exhibiting the film would not be adequate to prevent public disorder was thus outweighed by the value placed on the applicant's right to freedom of expression.
  2. *Application to the specific facts*: The minority examined the facts closely to see whether the two rights could be reconciled. This shows that striking the balance in an individual case does not end with the theoretical exercise involved in a qualitative assessment but involves a practical application of that assessment to the actual facts of the case.
- *The majority's judgment throws light on factors which tend to support the appropriateness in any case of the margin of appreciation.* The decision to leave a matter to the margin of appreciation of the national authorities depends of course on an assessment of the circumstances of the case. Where the particular issue thrown up by those circumstances is one on which views in the contracting states may legitimately differ, such as the protection of religious feelings, the Strasbourg Court generally allows a wide margin of appreciation. If, however, the problem is in an area where there is a common value shared by all the contracting states, for example the protection of journalistic sources from disclosure, the Strasbourg Court is *unlikely* to find that there is any margin of appreciation.
- *Treatment of the 'necessity' badge of proportionality*: Neither the majority nor the minority makes any reference at all to 'no more than necessary' or 'least intrusive means' or strict necessity as a criterion of proportionality. In Strasbourg jurisprudence, least intrusive means is a factor to be weighed in the balance, but it is not insisted on in every case. This is a point to bear in mind when we consider the more structured test in EU law. The flexibility in Strasbourg jurisprudence is consistent with the subsidiary role of the Strasbourg Court: it is well-established that primary responsibility for giving effect to Convention rights rests with the contracting states.
- *Modern trend is to give guidance to the national court*: The minority's rejection of the margin of appreciation is consistent with the more recent trend in Strasbourg cases to lay down criteria that the national courts must consider,

and then to say that, provided that they do so, it would require a strong case for the Strasbourg Court to interfere.[11]

Luxembourg jurisprudence on proportionality—a structured approach

The Luxembourg Court has borrowed the proportionality principle principally from the German Federal Constitutional Court. Again, the principle is not expressly set out in the EU treaties.

The proportionality principle is used when testing the legitimacy of a departure from one of the fundamental rights vouchsafed by EU law, such as the right to freedom of movement of goods and services, and it is applied in a structured way. To be proportionate, the departure must be suitable and necessary for the purpose of achieving the legitimate aim. As a corollary of the requirement for necessity, it must *in general* be shown that the departure is the least intrusive means of interfering with the freedom in question. Even if this test of necessity is met, the court must still go on to balance the right against the departure and be satisfied that the interference is appropriate on the facts of the case. The final step is that of balancing. This step is to be carried out by a court.

However, the Luxembourg Court does not, in my view, always carry out the necessity test or the suitability test itself, or do so to the maximum intensity. In certain cases, such as those where the impugned measure is a national measure directed at public health or national security, the Luxembourg Court is content to find that a measure is suitable and necessary if it is not manifestly unsuitable, or 'not manifestly inappropriate', as it is put.[12] This 'not manifestly inappropriate' test does not, of course, protect the state if what it is doing, under the cloak of the proportionality test, actually amounts to achieving some quite different objective from its stated legitimate aim.

The proportionality principle in Luxembourg jurisprudence is thus flexible. As I have said elsewhere,[13] the Luxembourg Court recognizes the diversity of regulatory systems and national values within the EU. For instance, not all member states will seek to protect public health in the same way. EU law allows for that choice to be made by the national legislature, not free from EU control but with a much less intensive level of scrutiny than under a strict test of proportionality. This is admirable judicial restraint.

Judicial restraint is further demonstrated by those cases in which the Luxembourg Court does not carry out the proportionality exercise itself but leaves it to the

---

[11] See, for example, *Axel Springer AG v Germany* (Application No 39954/08) [2012] EMLR 15; (2012) 55 EHRR 6 at para 88.

[12] See, for example, *R v Minster of Agriculture, Fisheries and Food, ex parte Fedesa Europeene de la Sante Animale (Fedesa)* (Case C-331/88) [1990] ECR 1–4023, and *Campus Oil v Ministry for Industry and Energy* (Case C-72/83) [1984] ECR 2727.

[13] In *R (Sinclair Collis Ltd) v Secretary of Health* [2011] EWCA Civ 437, [2012] QB 394 at [127].

national court to define whether the circumstances are sufficient to exclude the application of a fundamental freedom. This has occurred in the context of national security and criminal penalties[14] and in the context of the public policy exception from the fundamental freedoms: see, for example, *Omega Spielhallen- und Automatenaufstellungs-GmbH v Oberbürgermeisterin der Bundesstadt Bonn*,[15] (which concerned a decision of the German courts as to the constitutionality of an act of the Bonn police authority). In those circumstances, the Luxembourg Court may or may not provide guidelines for the national court.

As Lord Bingham CJ said in *R v Secretary of State for Health, ex parte Eastside Cheese Co*[16] the extent of the flexibility allowed by the Luxembourg Court depends on the nature of the case. There are, moreover, in my view, not just two points, but many points, on the spectrum.[17] Moreover, the Luxembourg Court would generally apply a higher level of intensity of review to an act of a national institution than to that of an EU institution. However, this is not always the case. The Luxembourg Court has recognized in the field of public policy, as applied to distasteful recreational games and to gaming, that national cultures and attitudes on such matters differ; that there is no need for EU law to require uniformity on these matters; and that the proper body to decide these matters is the relevant national institution: see (in the case of recreational games) the *Omega* case[18] and (in the case of gaming) *Sporting Exchange Ltd v Minister van Justitie*.[19]

I know that others have rejected my view on the existence of the 'not manifestly inappropriate' test, notably my distinguished colleague, Laws LJ. The Inner House of the Court of Session[20] has held that this lower test applies only to measures of EU institutions or national measures implementing EU law.[21] Again, this is contrary to the view that I have expressed judicially.[22] This is not the place to pursue that difference. The question whether the 'not manifestly inappropriate' test applies in EU law, and if it does, its scope is important and it is clearly one which the Supreme Court should now address.

The judicial difference of view on the 'not manifestly inappropriate' test illumines another important point. The Luxembourg jurisprudence on proportionality can be confusing. For instance, sometimes the words 'necessary' and 'suitable' may be used interchangeably.[23] It is as well to bear that in mind when studying the case

---

[14] See, eg *Ministre des Finances v Richardt* (Case C-367/89) [1991] ECR I-4621 at para 24.
[15] (Case C-36/02) [2004] ECR I-9609.
[16] [1999] 3 CMLR 123, [1999] EULR 968 at para 48.
[17] [1999] 3 CMLR 123, [1999] EULR 968 at para 48.
[18] *Omega* (Case C-36/02) [2004] ECR I-9609 at para 130.
[19] (Case C-203/08) [2010] CMLR 41.
[20] See the Opinion of the Court delivered by the Lord Justice Clerk (Lord Carloway) in *Sinclair Collis Ltd v the Lord Advocate* [2012] CSIH 80, [2013] SCLR 49.
[21] cf *Sinclair Collis Ltd* [2011] EWCA Civ 437 at [129].
[22] See *Sinclair Collis* [2011] EWCA Civ 437.
[23] See, for example, *Rosengren v Riksåklagaren* (Case C-170/04) [2007] ECR 1–4071, where the Luxembourg Court speaks of a public health measure not being 'necessary in order to achieve the declared objective', a clear reference on the facts of the case to the badge of suitability rather than that of necessity. The Luxembourg Court held that the protection of child health was a legitimate aim but that the total prohibition on imports of alcoholic beverages into Sweden was disproportionate because it

law. Common lawyers often have difficulty with Luxembourg case law, in any event, because of the Luxembourg Court's style of judgment writing: propositions are sometimes set out and repeated without full explanation or necessary qualification, in the manner of tablets of stone—but that is an issue for another day.

If I am right that there are different levels of intensity of review in EU law, then there must be at least a constitutional question whether, when judges of the national system are applying the proportionality principle in EU law, they should apply any different level of intensity than the Luxembourg Court would do. That may be a particularly acute question when the issue before the court is one of the legitimacy under EU law of an enactment of Parliament. This question is analogous to the question whether the courts should treat Strasbourg jurisprudence as a ceiling or a floor.[24]

In undertaking the proportionality exercise, there is a range of factors that can be taken into account. They include the nature of the decision-maker, but go far beyond this. The subject matter of the decision is clearly relevant: does it relate to policy or strategy, or is it about the implementation of a policy decision, which has already been taken? If it is a policy decision, does the decision fall into one of the areas that are generally left to member states, such as national security, domestic economic policy, or public health?

Sometimes a government decides to introduce a measure on its view of the scientific, or other technical, evidence in a novel situation where its accuracy is not clear. The Luxembourg jurisprudence provides guidance on this. In these situations, the Luxembourg Court applies a 'precautionary principle'. It leaves it to the decision-maker to decide which facts or opinions to act on and will not in the ordinary course seek to determine for itself whether the government is right in the view that it has formed. Under the precautionary principle, where there is uncertainty as to the existence or extent of risks to human health, the institution may take protective measures without having to wait until the reality and seriousness of those risks become fully apparent.[25] It must, however, provide the court with a risk assessment.

This brief survey serves to show that proportionality is not a simple judicial tool. Rather it is a highly sophisticated tool. It provides the flexibility to enable courts to use it in a way which reflects their own constitutional tradition of judicial restraint. The basic position, however, is that the Luxembourg Court tends to apply a more structured test than Strasbourg.

Proportionality in the domestic legal order

I now turn to consider four cases in which our domestic courts have sought to apply the proportionality principle while grappling with what I called 'multi-level

---

barred all imports to the benefit of the state monopoly for the supply of alcohol. There was evidence that the age restrictions would be difficult to use effectively.

[24] See *R v Horncastle* [2009] UKSC 14, [2010] 2 AC 373.

[25] See *R v Minister for Agriculture, Fisheries and Food ex parte National Farmers Union and others* (Case C-354/195) [1998] 1 CMLR 195.

judging', that is, they are determining domestic law is compatible with the Convention, or whether it is in conformity with the rights conferred by EU law or applying either Strasbourg or Luxembourg jurisprudence. The first case involved primary legislation which the lower court had declared to be incompatible with the Convention. In the next two cases the court was asked to strike down secondary legislation and, in a third case, to declare primary legislation incompatible. In the last case, the Supreme Court achieved compatibility with the Convention by means of statutory interpretation.

(1) *R (F (A child)) v Home Secretary*

In *R (F (A child)) v Home Secretary*[26] the appellants were offenders who had been sentenced for sexual offences of sufficient gravity to be subject by primary legislation to having to notify their address and provide certain personal information to the police for an indefinite period of time. They applied for judicial review on the basis that the notification requirements constituted a disproportionate interference with their Art 8 rights. The Supreme Court held that, in the absence of a right of review, the measure could not be justified. There had been no research on whether it would be possible to distinguish those who posed no significant risk of reoffending. In those circumstances, the Supreme Court did not consider that the situation was within the precautionary principle. As Lord Phillips, with whom the other members of the Supreme Court agreed, explained:

[56] No evidence has been placed before this court or the courts below that demonstrate that it is not possible to identify from among those convicted of serious offences, at any stage in their lives, some at least who pose no significant risk of reoffending. It is equally true that no evidence has been adduced that demonstrates that this is possible. This may well be because the necessary research has not been carried out to enable firm conclusions to be drawn on this topic. If uncertainty exists can this render proportionate the imposition of notification requirements for life without review under the precautionary principle? I do not believe that it can.

[57] I have referred earlier to a number of situations in which the degree of risk of reoffending has to be assessed in relation to sexual offenders. I think that it is obvious that there must be some circumstances in which an appropriate tribunal could reliably conclude that the risk of an individual carrying out a further sexual offence can be discounted to the extent that continuance of notification requirements is unjustified. As the courts below have observed, it is open to the legislature to impose an appropriately high threshold for review. Registration systems for sexual offenders are not uncommon in other jurisdictions. Those acting for the first respondent have drawn attention to registration requirements for sexual offenders in France, Ireland, the seven Australian States, Canada, South Africa and the United States. Almost all of these have provisions for review. This does not suggest that the review exercise is not practicable.

In the light of the approach taken by the minority in *Otto-Preminger-Institut* to an absolute ban, the result in this case is not surprising. However, it led to a furious

---

[26] [2010] UKSC 17, [2011] 1 AC 331.

reaction from politicians. In due course, however, the law was changed so that offenders had a right of review.

For my purposes, this case is particularly interesting because of the evidence on which it turned. The Supreme Court examined Parliamentary material, such as the committee debates, for background information to explain why the Act contained no right to a review of the notification requirements. It found none. Had it found an explanation, it would no doubt have taken it into account.

(2) *R (Aguilar Quila) v Secretary of State for Home Department*

In *R (Aguilar Quila) v Secretary of State for Home Department*[27] the question for determination by the Supreme Court was the proportionality of a measure raising, from 18 to 21 years, the age at which a foreign national married to a British citizen could apply for a marriage visa so that he or she could enter the UK for the purpose of living with their spouse and the age at which their spouse could sponsor them for this purpose. Similar provision applied to civic partners, and proposed spouses and civil partners. The Secretary of State had a discretion to grant the visa outside the measure, but only in compassionate or exceptional circumstances.

The purpose of the measure was to deter forced marriages. The raising of the ages was explicitly permitted by an EU Directive (although not one binding on the United Kingdom) for the purposes of promoting social integration and of reducing the number of forced marriages. Several other member states had in consequence raised the age for both parties to 21 years.

A Parliamentary select committee had urged the government to undertake research to establish whether raising the age would deter forced marriages, but the Secretary of State did not implement this recommendation. The Secretary of State issued a consultation document but the responses were said to be almost equally divided on the question whether raising the ages would deter forced marriages.

The issue of proportionality arose on the Secretary of State's argument that the measure fell within Art 8(2). (The Secretary of State also argued unsuccessfully that Art 8 was not engaged, but I am not concerned with that issue.) Raising the ages obviously interfered with the right to marry of persons who were not parties to a forced marriage. On the other hand, there was some evidence that, if the ages were raised, there would be fewer forced marriages since there would be more time to reflect.

The Supreme Court held, by a majority, that the measure was not proportionate. The majority applied all four badges of proportionality, including the requirement for the interference to be no more than necessary to enable the aim of the measure to be achieved. The majority declined to give weight to the judgment of the Secretary of State. Nor, in their judgment, could weight be given to the approval of the measure by Parliament as Parliament had limited scope to propose

---

[27] [2011] UKSC 45, [2012] AC 621.

amendments to immigration rules. The majority concluded that the Secretary of State had no 'robust' evidence that raising the age would deter forced marriages.

A further select committee report had become available by the time of the appeal to the Supreme Court. It found that a number of persons had been assisted to resist forced marriage by the new measure. However, no actual number was given and the select committee had clearly received evidence to the contrary, that is, that the measure had had no impact on the number of forced marriages.

Lord Wilson, giving the leading judgment, concluded that the number of forced marriages deterred by raising the age was highly debatable and that it was vastly exceeded by the number of unforced marriages which it obstructed. The Secretary of State had not addressed that imbalance. Even if it had been correct to say that the scale of the imbalance was a matter for the judgment of the Secretary of State, rather than for the court, it was not a judgment which on the evidence before the court the Secretary of State had ever made. She had therefore failed to establish that the amendment was no more than necessary to accomplish the legitimate aim, or that it struck a fair balance between the rights of the parties to *unforced* marriages and the interests of the community in preventing forced marriages.

Lady Hale delivered a concurring judgment. Lord Phillips and Lord Clarke agreed with the judgments of both Lord Wilson and Lady Hale.

Lord Brown entered a powerful note of dissent. He took the view that the balance of the evidence in the more recent report of the Parliamentary select committee was in favour of raising the ages. He also referred to comparative material from other EU countries supporting the change. He considered that there was sufficient evidence that raising the ages was widely regarded as helping to prevent forced marriages.[28] He concluded that 'unless demonstrably wrong, the judgment [as to the deterrent effect of the measure and the effect on unforced marriages] should be rather for government than for the courts'.[29] He considered that the value to be attached to deterring *forced* marriages as opposed to deferring *unforced* marriages should be left to elected politicians, not judges. He considered that the courts could give appropriate weight to the judgment of the minister on the measure.[30]

In the result, the measure was set aside, and in due course the Secretary of State abandoned the idea of raising the age for marriage visas.

For my purposes, this case raises some interesting points:

- This was another case in which the Supreme Court had to make a proportionality assessment on imperfect material.
- At one level it might be thought that the measure was unsupportable because it was *ineffective* to achieve the desired aim. But the position was not that the measure was shown to be ineffective but rather that it was *not* shown to be *effective* in terms of hard numbers of forced marriages prevented. There was somewhat understandably a dearth of hard numbers. There was rudimentary information that showed, for instance, that the total number of marriage visas

---

[28] *Aguilar Quila* at [90].   [29] *Aguilar Quila* at [91].   [30] *Aguilar Quila* at [91].

sought in the age group of 18 to 21 years was small—some 3,940 in 2006 and 1,945 in 2007—and that the rate of forced marriage was highest in the 17–20 years age group. Nonetheless, there was, as Lord Brown pointed out, the EU Directive already mentioned, which had specifically permitted the age to be raised to 21 years to assist in the prevention of forced marriages, and the fact that some other member states had already raised the ages. This must have been some evidence that the raising of the age had an appropriate effect.

- In the circumstances, the majority made no detailed qualitative judgment of the interests of the community in preventing forced marriages or of the interests of parties to unforced marriages. The effects on the latter had not been researched and were regarded as 'colossal'. As Lord Brown pointed out, that qualitative assessment would have required value judgments to be made on social issues, such as the value of preventing a forced marriage.

- The most striking point in this case, however, is that the majority did not consider that it was open to them to give weight to the Secretary of State's judgment on the value of the measure. Lord Brown took the contrary view, exposing a significant point of difference in law between the majority and minority judgments. This can only be resolved now by the Supreme Court. The point is significant because, unless some variation in the level of intensity, or depth, of judicial review is developed domestically, as the Luxembourg Court has developed it for the purposes of EU law, it may be very difficult for measures of social or healthcare reform to be implemented, even on an experimental basis for a short period of time. In that event, the effect of the proportionality principle for the future may be that it prevents governments from making decisions that do not meet the template of proportionality. On that basis, the proportionality principle will have ushered in a constitutional change of a profound kind. There can be no doubt that the Luxembourg Court has introduced varying levels of intensity of review at the least in relation to acts of the EU institutions.

(3) *R (Sinclair Collis Ltd) v Secretary of State for Health*

R (Sinclair Collis Ltd) v Secretary of State for Health[31] was a decision of the Court of Appeal about proportionality in EU law. It also concerned a social and healthcare measure, namely a measure to reduce under-age smoking. The principal issue was whether a legislative ban on tobacco vending machines ('TVMs') was a disproportionate interference with economic rights guaranteed by the Treaty on the Functioning of the European Union. Again the evidence about what would happen in the future was imperfect, and there was an issue as to the level of intensity of review to be applied to the decision of the Secretary of State to introduce the measure.

The ban was imposed by secondary legislation. By s 3A of the Children and Young Persons (Protection from Tobacco) Act 1991, as amended by the Health

---

[31] [2011] EWCA Civ 437, [2012] QB 394.

Act 2009, the Secretary of State was empowered to make regulations prohibiting the sale of tobacco from TVMs. The regulations had to be laid before Parliament under the procedure known as the affirmative resolution procedure. The Secretary of State exercised that power in the Protection from Tobacco (Sales from Vending Machines) (England) Regulations 2010.[32] Regulation 2(1) provided that, on coming into force, 'the sale of tobacco from an automatic machine is prohibited'. TVMs were mostly imported from other EU member states.

The owners of the machines contended that reg 2(1) was disproportionate. They adduced evidence of the substantial cost to them of the measure. They argued that the Secretary of State should have adopted one of the other policy options considered to reduce smoking, in particular the fitting of the vending machines with age restriction mechanisms ('ARMs') which meant that a person could not use a TVM until his age had been verified. They wanted to have a voluntary code for using ARMs on the machines, instead of a ban.

At first instance, the Administrative Court (Sir Anthony May PQBD) dismissed the application for judicial review on the grounds that the Secretary of State in adopting the Regulations was implementing the will of Parliament, and was therefore entitled to a very broad margin of discretion. Further, the measures adopted by the Secretary of State were not manifestly unreasonable or inappropriate.

The Court of Appeal, by a majority (Lord Neuberger MR and myself) upheld the decision of Administrative Court, and held that the outright ban imposed by s 2(1) of the Regulations was proportionate to the legitimate public health aim of reducing the sale of tobacco to young people. It is to be noted that the deterrent effect of banning TVMs on under-age smoking was not capable of proof. The appellants argued that the effect would be minimal as under-age smokers would turn to illicit sources of supply, and also that the ARMs would be as effective as a total ban. The majority did not accept these arguments. In particular, the majority considered that, if TVMs were banned, it was open to the Secretary of State to conclude that there would be less under-age smoking, as that source of supply had been stopped.

In addition, I held that the proportionality principle applied with varying intensity depending on the nature of the case. The appropriate standard to be applied to the issue of public health in this case was that the act would only be disproportionate if it was manifestly inappropriate.

There was a subsidiary issue as to the identity of the decision-maker and the effect on the proportionality exercise of this being the minister, and not Parliament. Lord Neuberger MR held that reg 2(1) must be taken to be the decision of the Secretary of State. The fact that this was a decision pursuant to powers conferred by Parliament entitled the decision to a broader margin of appreciation than a decision not pursuant to Parliamentary powers. Nevertheless that margin of appreciation was not as broad as the respect to be accorded to Parliamentary action.

---

[32] Protection from Tobacco (Sales from Vending Machine) (England) Regulations 2010 (SI 2010/864).

I took a different approach. I held that, while, in general, the margin of appreciation applying to regulations issued by the Secretary of State would be less broad than that applying to enactments by Parliament, in this case, the question of the breadth of the margin was to be answered taking into account all the relevant factors. In that case, among such factors were the overlapping responsibilities of the Secretary of State and Parliament for public health, and it followed that they were entitled to the same margin of appreciation.

Laws LJ, dissenting, held that, regardless of the margin of appreciation applied to the decision-maker, the standards of proportionality applied without dilution. Therefore, even though the Secretary of State was entitled to a broad margin of appreciation, the failure to consider or to adopt the less restrictive alternative failed the requirements of the doctrine of proportionality.

On the subsidiary question in *Sinclair Collis* of the identity of the decision-maker, the Lord Justice Clerk (Lord Carloway), delivering the Opinion of the Inner House of the Court of Session in a subsequent similar case in Scotland, usefully put the issue in the context of devolution. He observed that the legality of a measure for the purposes of EU law ought not to depend on whether it is primary or secondary legislation, or the legislation of the Westminster Parliament or of a devolved legislature, or some person or body with authority delegated to it by the Westminster Parliament or a devolved legislature.[33] I would add that devolution is a matter for the internal constitutional arrangements of the UK.[34]

Sinclair Collis was an important case, and it illustrates potential differences of approach in the domestic courts when dealing with the proportionality principle in EU law.

(4) *Manchester City Council v Pinnock*

Manchester City Council v Pinnock[35] is important for the purposes of this paper because in it we see the Supreme Court, like the majority in *Otto-Preminger-Institut*, granting a margin of appreciation to the decision-maker. However, in this case, unlike *Otto-Preminger-Institut*, it was given on the basis that it could be displaced.

This case concerned an order for possession of residential premises let by a local authority to a tenant under a form of tenancy known as a demoted tenancy, a form of tenancy that confers very little security on the tenant. It was virtually the last in a sequence of cases in which the House of Lords and then the Supreme Court had had to consider whether domestic possession proceedings were Convention-compliant.

---

[33] *Sinclair Collis Ltd v The Lord Advocate* at [60].
[34] See *R (Horvath) v Secretary of State for the Environment, Food & Rural Affairs* (Case C-428/07) [2009] ECR 1–6355.
[35] [2010] UKSC 45, [2011] 2 AC 104.

By statute, the court has to make an order for possession in the case of a demoted tenancy in certain specified circumstances. The question for the Supreme Court was whether there would be a violation of Arts 6 and 8 of the Convention if the court were to make a possession order as directed by statute in this case, or indeed in any other case, in favour of a local authority without considering and, where appropriate, giving effect to the tenant's rights under the Convention under a procedure which enabled the court to make findings of fact. Traditional judicial review was available but would not meet the requirements of the Convention. The tenant's right under Art 8 of the Convention included the right to respect for his home.

The Supreme Court held that a possession order would engage the tenant's Art 8 right and so, to be Convention-compliant, the court would have to go on to consider whether it was proportionate nonetheless to make the possession order. It was not sufficient merely to consider whether grounds were shown for judicial review of the local authority's decision to seek a possession order. The Supreme Court concluded that the statutory provisions in question could be interpreted to allow the proportionality exercise to be undertaken by the county court judge hearing the possession proceedings instituted by the local authority.

However, the Strasbourg Court had made it clear that, if the tenant had no contractual or statutory right to remain in possession, it would only be in an exceptional case that it would be proportionate not to make a possession order. Accordingly, the Supreme Court held that, if the tenant sought to rely on Art 8, the county court judge should first decide whether there was any case to be investigated. The county court judge should in addition proceed on the basis that the local authority was acting in accordance with its statutory duties to manage and allocate its housing stock, and that this presumption should only be displaced by cogent evidence to the contrary.

The point of this case for my purposes is that the Supreme Court ruled that the proportionality exercise had to be conducted on the basis that, in general, weight would be given to the decision of the local authority to seek an order for possession. In other words, the court would have to treat the local authority's decision as within its area of discretionary judgment until the contrary was shown. This, therefore, is an instance of a UK court introducing a margin of appreciation at the domestic level, and according weight to a non-judicial body.

What problem areas do the cases reveal about the proportionality principle?

I have already made the point that there are important issues of law in the area of proportionality that need resolution at the Supreme Court level. I will now mention a number of other points that the discussion so far throws up. I will deal with these points under two topic headings.

Relationship between the court and the decision-maker

(1) Law and politics

R (F (A child)) v Home Secretary shows that the proportionality review can lead to confrontation with the legislature. It can bring the courts close to that borderline between the law and politics where judges have to take care (and I am not of course suggesting that they did not do so in this case). The first point then is that proportionality can intensify judicial scrutiny of administrative or legislative acts, and calls for judicial restraint in appropriate circumstances. We often say that in the law context is everything. That is no doubt true, but, in the world of public law, the dividing line between law and politics is also everything, or at least is ever-present. It calls for vigilance.

(2) Value judgments

Proportionality requires value judgments to be made, and to be made explicitly, by courts. The *Aguilar Quila* case is an example of this. What is required in balancing is weighing up the values to be attributed to different rights. It is not about counting heads. Where it is difficult to predict the effect of a particular course of action in the future, one answer may be to apply a lower intensity of review and leave the matter to the decision-maker if that is satisfied.

(3) A domestic margin of appreciation

The *Pinnock* case shows that, under the Convention, there is room for a margin of appreciation to be given to the decision-maker; in that case, the decision-maker was the local authority. Again, in this context, there is in my view scope for subtle variation in the intensity of review.

Technical points:

(1) Evidential problems

The *Sinclair Collis* case shows (among other things) the difficulty of making evidential judgments in the course of the proportionality exercise. The material may be unsatisfactory in ways not covered by the precautionary principle. A common law court may here be at a distinct disadvantage as compared with a civil law court: the latter is likely to find it easier to direct a party to serve any additional evidence which it requires. In some cases, the courts may have a choice: either to decide that the measure is disproportionate or to find that the proportionality test is not satisfied, so as to leave it to the government to decide whether to provide better evidence next time or to abandon the measure.

This is a larger issue than I have time to deal with since it involves 'polycentric' adjudication.[36]

It is tempting to conclude that a determination of proportionality is only as good as the evidence adduced in the particular case. That must necessarily be so, and it necessarily places limits on the proportionality exercise.

(2) Precedent

The question arises whether a decision that a measure is disproportionate binds a later court. This needs detailed consideration, but at first blush it would not seem that a later court ought to be bound by a prior decision that a measure was, or was not, shown to be proportionate, if new evidence is adduced. If that is correct, it means that in this context too the determination of proportionality may only be as good as the evidence adduced in the particular case.

(3) Procedural proportionality?

In *Aguilar Quila*, the Supreme Court decided against the Secretary of State on an alternative 'procedural' ground, namely that the Secretary of State had not formed the appropriate judgments on issues involved in the measure, and therefore had failed to take all the relevant considerations into account. The dissenting judgment of Lord Justice Laws in *Sinclair Collis* (the tobacco vending machine case) can also be read as developing a form of procedural proportionality review: if there is a point which the minister has not on the evidence considered, the case should be remitted to him or her for further consideration. That may in some situations be the best solution in any given case, but for my own part, if, at least, the context is purely domestic, I would prefer to use conventional judicial review principles rather than to introduce a further qualification into proportionality.

(4) Interested third parties

In the *Aguilar Quila* case the court had the benefit of representations from interested third parties. Where a measure is challenged there will obviously be cases where this is very desirable because of the potentially wide effect of the decision on the proportionality exercise. This is a point that practitioners might usefully bear in mind.

(5) Law or fact?

The question whether an appeal against a finding that a measure or step was proportionate or not involves a question of fact or law remains to be fully worked out. That could have important practical consequences for parties.

---

[36] See, generally, Lon L Fuller, 'The Forms and Limits of Adjudication' (1978) 92 Harv L Rev 353.

(6) Material before the decision-maker

It is not clear whether in the proportionality exercise the court is restricted to the information that was before the decision-maker.[37] Since the court is making its own assessment, there would appear to be no reason in principle why it should not consider other material as well, but there may be exceptions to this.

Proportionality as compared with unreasonableness

Before I move to my final section, I need to make the point, which will be very familiar, that, in the purely domestic context, the usual test for judicial review of administrative action where there is no illegality or procedural irregularity alleged is unreasonableness, known as '*Wednesbury* unreasonableness'. That means that the court does not intervene and set aside an administrative decision unless it is perverse.[38] The House of Lords has held that the *Wednesbury* unreasonableness test does not apply to the violation of a Convention right.[39] In fact it adopted the three-part test laid out by the Privy Council in *De Freitas v Permanent Minister of Agriculture, Fisheries, Land and Housing*[40] for violations of constitutional rights, namely, that the legislative objective must be sufficiently important to justify limiting the constitutional right, the measures in question must be rationally connected to the legislative objective, and the means used to impair the right or freedom must be no more than is necessary to accomplish the objective. Subsequently, in *Huang v the Secretary of State*,[41] a fourth requirement was added for Art 8 cases, namely that the measure must achieve a fair balance between the interests of the individuals affected and the wider community. It was of course the four-part test established in this case that the Supreme Court applied in *Aguilar Quila*.

In *Daly*, Lord Steyn observed that there was a material difference between proportionality and unreasonableness. In particular proportionality required a closer scrutiny of the act in question. Nonetheless the court was not required to undertake a 'merits' review.

While *Wednesbury* continues to be the usual test for judicial review in 'non-rights' cases, there are one or two categories of case where proportionality is applied, such as where disciplinary sanctions are imposed. This would include exclusion of a child from school.

---

[37] In *Aguilar Quila*, however, the Supreme Court took account of Parliamentary material not available to the decision-maker when the measure was introduced.

[38] That is, 'so unreasonable that no reasonable authority could ever come to it' per Lord Greene MR in *Associated Picture Houses Ltd v Wednesbury Corporation* [1948] 1 KB 223 at 229 to 230.

[39] On the application of *R (Daly) v Home Secretary* [2001] UKHL 26, [2001] 2 AC 532.

[40] [1999] 1 AC 69.

[41] [2007] UKHL 11, [2007] 2 AC 167.

Proportionality—the way ahead?

Now it is time for me to get out my crystal ball and consider the way ahead. I hope that I have demonstrated that there are some important legal issues for determination: the way ahead for the most significant of those issues is at Supreme Court level. But in this final section, I want to touch on another debate. This also needs to be resolved, if it is to be resolved, at that level.[42]

I started this paper by praising the logic of proportionality. It is, as we have seen, a general principle of EU law and of Strasbourg jurisprudence. In those circumstances, so goes the argument, there is much to be said for aligning *the generalized head of judicial review* in English law with that of proportionality.

A notable protagonist of the view that *Wednesbury* unreasonableness ought to be replaced by proportionality is Professor Paul Craig.[43] I would not presume to summarize all his arguments but certain arguments seem to me to be prominent. Professor Craig points to other important advantages of proportionality, namely that it requires reasoned justification and shifts the onus of showing that the decision was proportionate on to the decision-maker. Professor Craig argues that *Wednesbury* unreasonableness is an unclear test, that it involves a less detailed inquiry than proportionality and that on occasions *Wednesbury* unreasonableness is incoherent and insufficiently analytical. Proportionality is a more structured test that facilitates more accountability. Professor Craig accepts that the adoption of proportionality as a generalized head of review would still leave a number of other grounds for judicial review in place, such as interference with legitimate expectations and the question whether the decision-maker had taken the relevant considerations into account.

The issue that Professor Craig has raised is of great importance and it deserves to be considered widely and deeply. Unless a lower intensity of review is adopted, as for instance in EU law in relation to particular situations, the level of scrutiny involved in the proportionality exercise is generally higher than that demanded by *Wednesbury* unreasonableness. As I have said, it appears that the adoption of proportionality as a generalized head of review can now only be decided at the level of the Supreme Court.[44] Some people thought that the Supreme Court might deal with it in *Aguilar Quila* but that did not happen. So where do we stand on this argument?

---

[42] See *R (Association of British Civilian Internees (Far East Region)) v the Secretary of State for Defence* [2003] EWCA Civ 473, [2003] QB 1397.

[43] See, for example, Paul Craig, 'Proportionality, Rationality and Review' [2010] NZLR 265; cf Michael Taggart, 'Proportionality, Deference, *Wednesbury*' [2008] NZLR 423, and Tom Hickman, 'Problems and Proportionality' [2010] NZLR 303.

[44] *R (Association of British Civilian Internees (Far East Region)) v the Secretary of State for Defence* [2003] EWCA Civ 473.

Drawing the threads together

The question of whether proportionality should replace *Wednesbury* is an issue which I said that I would like to leave you to consider and to judge for yourself.

In my view, there is much in principle to be said for the more disciplined and transparent analysis imposed by proportionality. On the other hand, you have in the course of this paper heard about the problem areas of proportionality, how it involves the attribution of values, how from time to time it calls for judicial restraint and the difficulties in forming a view on the evidence in some situations in a purely adversarial environment. Certainly there is a strong argument that *Wednesbury* unreasonableness speaks to a bygone age, but the points I have just made would call for a cautious approach, and one that should be developed on an incremental basis.

I am not going to express a concluded view. I will instead end by making the suggestion that there is something to take away today in a point made by Lord Cooke of Thorndon in *Daly*. In a pithy judgment, he criticized *Wednesbury* unreasonableness and spoke in terms of a sliding scale:

32 ... I think that the day will come when it will be more widely recognised that *Associated Provincial Picture Houses Ltd v Wednesbury Corpn* [1948] 1 KB 223 was an unfortunately retrogressive decision in English administrative law, in so far as it suggested that there are degrees of unreasonableness and that only a very extreme degree can bring an administrative decision within the legitimate scope of judicial invalidation. The depth of judicial review and the deference due to administrative discretion vary with the subject matter. It may well be, however, that the law can never be satisfied in any administrative field merely by a finding that the decision under review is not capricious or absurd.

His insight was, I think, this. The options open to the law are not *Wednesbury* or no *Wednesbury*: there are plenty of points in between. In addition more than one point can be chosen: it may be that different issues may require a subtly different approach, and there is room for this. Indeed, I would suggest that we can take a leaf out of the book of the Strasbourg Court and of the Luxembourg Court by approaching proportionality as a sophisticated and flexible judicial tool. We can adapt our domestic law to modern conditions by developing legal concepts in an equally creative way.

5

Subsidiarity and Decentralization

This chapter is based on an unpublished paper originally delivered in 2013 for a judicial–academic meeting in Paris.

Subsidiarity is a more developed principle in Strasbourg jurisprudence than it is in EU law. In Strasbourg case law, it is commonly called the doctrine of the 'margin of appreciation'.

The Strasbourg Court uses the doctrine of the margin of appreciation when it decides to leave national institutions to decide how to implement a Convention right in particular circumstances, rather than decide itself how the right applies. Literally, the phrase means that the decision properly falls within the remit of a national institution. The national institution must then choose how to implement the right. Its choice is subject to the overall supervision of the Strasbourg Court if it does not follow Convention principles, for example because it is arbitrary.

One situation where the Strasbourg Court might decide that a national institution should determine how to implement a right in particular circumstances is where there are legitimate cultural or other differences between states affecting the implementation of that right. These differences often exist, and mean that supranational human rights courts are likely to have to develop some concept like the margin of appreciation.

The Luxembourg Court is mostly concerned with references for preliminary rulings from national courts. When it gives a preliminary ruling, it is empowered to decide only questions of EU law. So it must leave it to the national court in any event to decide how to apply a particular EU measure to the facts.

However, there are at least two reasons why the Luxembourg Court might have to develop a margin of appreciation of its own. First, more and more, and particularly since the members of the EU ratified the Lisbon Treaty which adopts the Charter of Fundamental Rights and Freedoms, the Luxembourg Court has to decide questions of fundamental rights. Formerly, it might simply have followed Strasbourg jurisprudence.[1] Second, since the Maastricht Treaty, the constitutional principles of EU law have included a principle of 'subsidiarity'. This is now to be found in Art 5 of the Treaty on European Union (TEU).

---

[1] As, for example, in *Roquette Frères SA v Directeur Générale de la Concurrence, de la Consommation et de la Répression des Fraudes* (Case 94/00) [2002] ECR I-09011, [2003] All ER (EC) 920 at para 29.

The key provision on subsidiarity is Art 5(3). This lays down two conditions. It states that the Union shall, in areas which do not fall within its exclusive competence:

... act only if and insofar as the objectives of the proposed action

[(i)] cannot be sufficiently achieved by Member States, either at central level or at regional and local level, but

[(ii)] can rather, by reason of the scale or effects of the proposed action, be better achieved at Union level.

Both these conditions have to be given effect. The second condition, if interpreted literally, would largely deprive subsidiarity of any effect. It has therefore to be given a narrow meaning which reflects the greater value given to subsidiarity as a result of its inclusion in the TEU.

Article 5 is supplemented by EU Protocol (2) to the TEU on the application of the principles of subsidiarity and proportionality. This Protocol provides a mechanism for monitoring subsidiarity. The Commission must, for example, consult widely about any proposed measure and provide information to show how it complies with the principle of subsidiarity. In this way, no doubt the principle is intended to be self-policing. Under Art 8, the Luxembourg Court has jurisdiction to decide disputes when there is a complaint by a national parliament that an EU measure contravenes the principle.

There is an issue whether subsidiarity could be used more generally by the Luxembourg Court to avoid all member states being required to make the same decision on some matter on which they might properly wish to differ. If it could be shown that there is no good reason why all member states should have to make the same decision, then it might be useful and in accordance with the expectations of the member states that some concept of subsidiarity should apply. Subsidiarity is fundamentally a principle designed to achieve greater participation in public affairs and to ensure greater economic and regulatory efficiency.

A wider principle?

Up to present time, at least, there have been very few cases where the Luxembourg Court has expressly invoked the principle of subsidiarity.[2] This may be because the principle has been perceived as having a substantial political content, but on the

---

[2] Recent examples include *Telefónica and Telefónica de España v Commission* (Case T-336/07) 29 March 2012, where the Luxembourg Court rejected the complaint that a fine imposed by the EU Commission for unfair price tariffs infringed the principle of subsidiarity; *Luxembourg v European Parliament and Council of the EU* (Case C-176/09) 12 May 2011, where the Luxembourg Court rejected a complaint that a legislative measure infringed the principle; and *The Queen on the application of Vodafone Ltd and others v Secretary of State for Business, Enterprise and Regulatory Reform* (Case C-58/08) [2010] ECR I-4999, where the Luxembourg Court held that a EU measure to standardize wholesale and retail mobile telephone charges could reasonably be considered to comply with the principle of subsidiarity because there could then be a single regulatory authority.

other hand it is not exclusively political. There are some signs that a wider view is being taken.

For example, where there is an issue of public policy, the Luxembourg Court may leave this to the member state to decide: see for example *Omega Spielhallen- und Automatenaufstellungs-GmbH v Oberbürgermeisterin der Bundesstadt Bonn*[3] (Germany could prohibit the provision of facilities for playing violent games even though those games were not prohibited in the United Kingdom). Moreover, as in the *Omega* case, the Luxembourg Court recognizes that there are different constitutional traditions in the member states.

Another example of subsidiarity in the Luxembourg Court's case law concerns the United Kingdom's system of devolution. Devolution works in the same way as subsidiarity because the central Parliament devolves power to the different devolved legislatures. The Luxembourg Court recognized the importance of devolution in its decision in *R (Horvath) v Secretary of State for the Environment*,[4] a reference for a preliminary ruling from England and Wales. The Court held that the principle of non-discrimination in EU law was not infringed when the devolved legislatures of the United Kingdom implemented European legislation in different ways. The Court held that this would not be discriminatory for European law purposes. This decision is respectful of the constitutional situation in the United Kingdom and, of course, in other member states with similar constitutional arrangements.

The UK courts have applied the principle of subsidiarity within the domestic legal order in at least two situations.

The first situation is that of interpreting the powers of the devolved legislatures. In one case,[5] the Supreme Court gave a purposive interpretation to the powers of the Welsh Assembly so that it could enact legislation to remove the need for the Secretary of State in the UK government under Westminster legislation to confirm bye laws as part of new Welsh legislation. The intention was to streamline the making of bye laws in Wales under devolved powers. The Supreme Court relied on a provision in the devolved powers for making consequential amendments to the powers of the Secretary of State.

In an example of the second situation,[6] a minister of the central government and a local authority disagreed about whether to delay implementation of a scheme to turn local schools into non-selective entry schools. The local authority sought to use its local administrative powers. The courts construed the minister's power of intervention restrictively so that he could not intervene in matters best left to the local authority. The House of Lords held that the minister could only intervene and compel immediate implementation if the local authority acted irrationally. The local authority had on the evidence responded to what local residents wanted and could not be said to have acted irrationally.

---

[3] (Case C-36/02) [2004] ECR I-9609.   [4] (Case C-428/07) [2009] ECR I-6355.
[5] *Local Government Byelaws (Wales) Bill 2012 (a reference by the Attorney General)* [2012] UKSC 53.
[6] *Secretary of State for Education and Science v Tameside Metropolitan Borough Council* [1977] AC 1014.

Pressure from national courts for subsidiarity

Subsidiarity is not just a movement from the top downwards: there is also pressure from the lower levels upwards to have subsidiarity, as shown in the following two examples.

National courts tend to interpret 'escape clauses' in favour of national law

National courts are hardly likely to rule against their own constitutional values. This is potentially an inherent limitation on the implementation of EU measures that might have to be recognized in judicial decision-making.

An example may be taken from Italy in a case under the Rome II regulation.[7] That regulation deals with the identification of the proper law for non-contractual obligations. Rome II provides that the scope and extent of damage shall generally be governed by the law of the place where the damage occurs. There are escape clauses for situations where the case is more closely connected with some other law and for situations where it is contrary to a court's public policy to apply the law of the place where the damage occurs.

In a case concerning an Italian citizen killed in Austria,[8] the Italian Supreme Court of Cassation ruled that Italian law applied so that the family members living in Italy could bring claims for their loss. The essential reason was that it was an aspect of the constitutional protection of the rights of the individual under Italian law that those family members should receive full compensation. Austrian law did not allow bereavement damages. The Italian court was able to use the public policy exception so as to be able to apply its own law.

Kompetenz Kompetenz

The German Federal Constitutional Court has been foremost in discussing the question when a court of a member state of the EU may determine an issue related to some provision of EU law, and the term *Kompetenz Kompetenz* has become an accepted shorthand for the learning on this question. It involves consideration of whether the national or supranational court has competence to determine the particular issue.

EU law is carefully incorporated into UK law. Even so, there are limits to the EU legislation that may be incorporated into domestic law. The principal limit on such legislation is that the relevant institutions of the European Union must be

---

[7] Regulation (EC) No 864/2007 of 11 July 2007 on the law applicable to non-contractual obligations.

[8] *Wiener Staedtische Versicherung AG, Liguria Ass.ni. S.p.A. and others v B and others*, Supreme Court of Cassation, Third Civil Division, 22 August 2013, no 19405, President Giuseppe Maria Berruti, Rapporteur Enzo Vincenti, in *CED Cassazione*, 2013.

empowered to make the measure in question under the treaties which the member states have signed.

The question whether there are further limits has never been decided. However, there are cases that throw light on this question. For example, in a case in 2003,[9] Mr McWhirter and Mr Gouriet objected to the ratification by the UK Government of the Nice Treaty, on the grounds that it ceded sovereignty to the European Union and violated basic English constitutional rights, going back to Magna Carta. The Court of Appeal of England and Wales did not find that the allegations were proved, but left open two questions, first what would happen if there was a challenge regarding whether an action of the European Union was within the Treaties and, second, whether there could be European legislation which was in breach of fundamental rights given by our domestic law. That pattern has been repeated in other cases.[10] Because we have no written constitution, the limits could probably not be as extensive as those that are available in jurisdictions with written constitutions.

Importance of subsidiarity: ensuring greater accountability

In truth, devolution is the latest step in a long sequence of changes in the United Kingdom's constitutional arrangements in relation to the location of state power. (One of the advantages of not having a fully written constitution is that we can change our constitutional arrangements more frequently.)

Originally, the sovereign represented the state. Absolute monarchy gave way to constitutional monarchy, and the state became the Queen or King in Parliament. More recently, the state came to be associated with the duly elected government of the day.

Historically, under the common law, it was not possible to hold the state liable in tort for wrongs to the citizens (that position continued until 1947), but today judicial review is exacting. The judges have developed far-reaching principles of judicial review.

There are still differences between public and private law. The remedies in public law are discretionary. There is little disclosure of documents, and there are rarely monetary remedies (although the state is now often liable in tort as if it were a private citizen). Because we have no written constitutional rights, the common law of judicial review does not rely on any superior written constitutional rights of the individual for holding the state to account.

---

[9] *McWhirter and Gouriet v Secretary of State for Foreign and Commonwealth Affairs* [2003] EWCA Civ 384.
[10] See notably the judgment of Laws LJ in *Thoburn v Sunderland City Council* [2002] EWHC 195 (Admin), [2003] QB 151 (Divisional Court) (often called the 'metric martyrs case'); see also in particular the judgments of Lord Neuberger and Lord Mance in *R (HS2 Action Alliance Ltd) v Secretary of State for Transport and other appeals* [2014] UKSC 3, [2014] 1 WLR 324 at [207].

In 1973, the United Kingdom entered the European Union, and in respect of the powers conferred on the European Union, the institutions of the European Union became to that extent 'the state'.

The subsequent development of the devolution arrangements goes in the opposite direction from this. Under devolution, the state is re-conceptualized, for some purposes at least, as the national government of the particular part of the United Kingdom. Power is decentralized so that the citizen has a more direct relationship with the state, and thus a greater chance to participate in it and influence it.

Lessons for Europe from devolution?

Every time there is a shift in the location of state power, as there is with subsidiarity, there is an opportunity to think about the rights and responsibilities of the citizen to the state and of the state to the citizen, as well as the functions that are properly state functions rather than private functions. That opportunity was taken when the devolution arrangements were established in the United Kingdom because considerable provision was made for ensuring the accountability of the devolved institutions. Great care was given to fashioning the controls to which the devolved institutions should be subject.

There may be lessons here for Europe. Far fewer mechanisms exist to scrutinize the growth in 'state power' residing in the EU legal order. The culture in the United Kingdom is to seek to hold those who exercise state power to account. This perspective may help explain the popular or political difficulties that the United Kingdom has with the EU legal order, and its sense of caution in relation to the expanding powers of the Union.

So the devolution model may also assist in showing how the structures of power in the European institutions could be developed to ensure that there is a closer relationship between the state and the citizen.

In short, the concept of subsidiarity provides an opportunity to think more deeply about what exactly the relationship in legal terms should be between state power and the citizen, and the European vision on that issue.

Conclusions

Subsidiarity needs to be developed as a principle of EU law in the same way that proportionality has been developed. The examples given above show that analogies can be drawn with other aspects of EU law. Subsidiarity could now be treated as an organizing principle.

The legal content of the principle needs to be worked out. So does the role of the Luxembourg Court, for example under Art 8 of EU Protocol No 2 to the TEU. The Luxembourg Court may also be called on to scrutinize statements made in EU measures about compliance with the principle of subsidiarity pursuant to Art 5, applying the principles of review developed in EU administrative law. The

Luxembourg Court may also need to develop special techniques to deal with the challenges of subsidiarity, and also to redefine its role.

Subsidiarity is too important a principle not to be developed. It needs to be applied on a consistent basis to achieve greater accountability of state and EU power to the European citizen.

6

Press, Privacy, and Proportionality

This chapter is based on the Robin Cooke Memorial Lecture 2013, given at Victoria University of Wellington, New Zealand.

Judges bring to their work the values which are part of their experience and personality. When they are developing the law, these qualities shine out. Part of their value system may be a belief that adherence to tradition leads to stability in society, and that well-established legal concepts should be preserved from change unless a strong case is shown. Or they may think that it is important to move with the times or to make more effective guarantees of equality in society. The weight that judges give to these values may be the factor which subconsciously determines how they decide a point which could be decided one way or another. I suspect that Lord Cooke's approach was from time to time somewhat different from that of his colleagues because of the weight he personally attached to the need for change and to keep the law up to date. It means that his judgments and views will continue to have meaning for the development of the law for many years to come.

Lord Cooke's approach was one of accepting difference and recognizing change in society. Moreover, he also seemed to dislike hard rules and to prefer to dwell in the fields of judicial discretion so characteristic of public law.

Lord Cooke made an enormous contribution to modern legal thought in many areas, but I wish to focus on his contribution to the development of the general test for judicial review. As we shall see shortly, he expressed some powerful and pithy views on this subject.

For over fifty years, the courts have (in the absence of some specific ground of review such as unlawfulness) adopted as a general test for judicial review of administrative action the test of unreasonableness. In general, unreasonableness means that the decision under challenge must be outside 'the range of reasonable decisions open to the decision-maker'.[1] This high level of unreasonableness is known as '*Wednesbury* unreasonableness' after the case in which this test was first established.[2] As Lord Bingham explains in his important work on *The Rule of Law*, this test creates a high hurdle for applicants.[3]

---

[1] *Boddington v British Transport Police* [1999] 2 AC 143, 175 (HL).
[2] The case was *Associated Provincial Picture Houses v Wednesbury Corpn* [1948] 1 KB 223.
[3] Tom Bingham, *The Rule of Law* (Allen Lane, 2010).

The issue I shall consider in this paper is whether the *Wednesbury* approach should now be revised or even replaced. The principal candidate to replace it would be the doctrine of proportionality, and that is the alternative candidate on which I shall focus.

Proportionality is an approach most usually associated with civil law systems and also, by extension, by the two European supranational courts, the Court of Justice of the European Union in Luxembourg (the 'Luxembourg Court') and the European Court of Human Rights in Strasbourg (the 'Strasbourg Court').[4]

The Luxembourg Court, for instance, uses this approach to test the legality of action in terms of powers conferred by EU law. It follows that courts in the United Kingdom have to use this test when they consider the legality of acts done under EU law. Likewise, the courts in the United Kingdom have to apply the doctrine of proportionality if an applicant contends that administrative action wrongly interferes with a fundamental right which EU law has conferred on him, such as the right to freedom of movement.

The Strasbourg Court also makes much use of proportionality. Certain of the rights guaranteed by the European Convention on Human Rights (the 'Convention') are limited rights. As under the New Zealand Bill of Rights, there are rights that a state can limit. For instance, under the Convention, a state can limit the right to freedom of expression under Art 10 of the Convention by reference to the reputation or rights of others.[5] Proportionality is one of the requirements that any limitation must satisfy. There must be a reasonable relationship of proportionality between the limitation and the end to be achieved by the limitation so that the state does not impose a restriction on freedom of speech that is excessive.

What does proportionality involve? In general, it involves a highly structured approach as follows. The court must identify whether the restriction is prescribed by law and has a legitimate aim. Absence of a legitimate aim is likely to be a knock-out point. The court must also be satisfied that the act is suitable and necessary to achieve its aim. Then it has to be satisfied that a fair balance has been struck between the rule or decision in question and the right with which it interferes.

A useful (if light-hearted) way of remembering what proportionality is all about is to think of it as the 'Goldilocks' doctrine. In the fairy tale, Goldilocks finds three bowls of porridge. One was too hot, and one was too cold, but one was just right! So, with proportionality, the intrusion into a person's human rights involved in state action must be not too much. It must be 'just right'.

I am now in a position to set out Lord Cooke's important views. They are to be found in *R (Daly) v Secretary of State for the Home Department*.[6] Lord Cooke spoke in terms of a sliding scale:

---

[4] See, generally, my description of proportionality in 'Proportionality: The Way Ahead?' [2013] PL 498. (Reproduced as Chapter 4 in this Volume.)

[5] The Convention rights incorporated by the Human Rights Act 1998 and the principal provisions of that Act are set out in the Appendix.

[6] [2001] UKHL 26, [2001] 2 AC 532.

[32] . . . I think that the day will come when it will be more widely recognised that *Associated Provincial Picture Houses Ltd v Wednesbury Corpn* [1948] 1 KB 223 was an unfortunately retrogressive decision in English administrative law, in so far as it suggested that there are degrees of unreasonableness and that only a very extreme degree can bring an administrative decision within the legitimate scope of judicial invalidation. The depth of judicial review and the deference due to administrative discretion vary with the subject matter. It may well be, however, that the law can never be satisfied in any administrative field merely by a finding that the decision under review is not capricious or absurd.

Lord Cooke's observations are very enlightened and far-reaching. As I see it, Lord Cooke was here making three important points. First, *Wednesbury* unreasonableness is retrogressive if it means that a very high degree of unreasonableness is required. Second, in judicial review, the intensity of the required judicial scrutiny is case-sensitive. Third, merely to test for absurdity or capriciousness can never be an adequate level of judicial scrutiny.

Lord Cooke's views have remained topical. Scholars in the New Zealand Law Review have recently discussed the question whether the *Wednesbury* test should be replaced with a proportionality test.[7] The High Court of Australia has inched closer towards proportionality in some of its recent decisions.[8] In France, the Conseil d'Etat has modified its general test of unreasonableness for judicial review in favour of a proportionality test.[9] EU law is likely to have been one of the influences in this change.

For England and Wales, it is now only the Supreme Court which can decide whether to adopt proportionality as a general test for judicial review in place of the *Wednesbury* test. The Court of Appeal of England and Wales has held that, in that jurisdiction, that question can now only be resolved at the highest level.[10]

What I propose to do in this paper is to illustrate how proportionality works in practice by looking at the subject of press regulation. I make a detour into that subject because it is receiving enormous media attention in the United Kingdom at the present time. I shall look to see how proportionality has been applied in the context of controlling the activities of the press. The events which have caused the current problems in the United Kingdom may not occur further afield, but the underlying issue is one of press freedom, and how, if at all, to regulate that must be a matter of concern in any democracy.

Regulation of the press came to the forefront of public attention in the United Kingdom in 2011. The immediate cause was allegations of 'phone-hacking'. This was a new phenomenon. The allegations were that certain elements of the press were publishing material based on information illicitly obtained by listening to voice messages left on the recipient's mobile telephone, if that was not password-protected. The recipient was often a celebrity. There had earlier been allegations of

---

[7] See, for example, Taggart, 'Proportionality, Deference, Wednesbury' [2008] NZLR 423.

[8] See, for example, *Lange v Australian Broadcasting Corporation* (1997) 189 CLR 520, 561–2; *Monis v The Queen, Droudis v The Queen* [2013] HCA 4 at [278]–[346] per Crennan, Kiefel, and Bell JJ.

[9] See, for example, CE 28-3-1997, *Autoroute du Chablais*, Rec 120.

[10] *R (Association of British Civilian Internees (Far East Region)) v Secretary of State for Defence* [2003] EWCA Civ 473, [2003] QB 1397. The highest level at that time was the House of Lords but is now the Supreme Court. In fact, however, the House of Lords refused permission to appeal in that case.

what was thought to be isolated incidents of phone-hacking, and one or two journalists had been tried for, or convicted of, a criminal offence.

What changed in 2011 was the discovery that the *News of the World* had in 2002 hacked into the voice message box of the mobile phone of a young murder victim called Milly Dowler. The information obtained had led the newspaper to publish leads that turned out to be false. The *News of the World* was also thought to have deleted a message, thus giving her family the false hope that she was still alive. The public greeted the revelation of what had been done with utter revulsion.

Prime Minister David Cameron then announced that an inquiry would be set up and that it would be in two parts. The first part would be into the culture, practices, and ethics of the press. The second part of the inquiry would be into the extent of the unlawful or improper conduct at the *News of the World*. That second part has not yet started and there is some doubt whether it ever will. There is plenty of information coming out of the various police operations that are being conducted.

The first part of the inquiry covered newspapers (whether printed or online) but excluded broadcasters and any forms of social media.[11] The inquiry extended to the relationship between the press and politicians and the press and the police, as well as into the effectiveness of the current policy and regulatory framework, notably for data protection.

My colleague, Lord Justice Leveson was appointed to conduct this inquiry. There have been many inquiries into privacy and press freedom over the years. On the last occasion, the government warned the press that they were living in 'the last chance saloon'.[12] But no-one twenty years ago could have seen the immediate cause of the current crisis, namely phone-hacking. Phone-hacking occurred in an environment where there was strong competition between tabloid newspapers to deliver scoops on celebrities, combined with a lack of strong regulatory or ethical constraints.

The remit of such an inquiry was 'almost breathtaking in its width'. So Lord Justice Leveson was careful to scope it, taking into consideration the timeframe and costs, ensuring that the industry was fully engaged in the process and taking account, perhaps most importantly, of the interests of the public. In that respect, he provided the public with information as to the framework of the law and regulation of the press, ensured that it had access to the evidence, and allowed the public to feed in its views. He also split the terms of reference into four modules: 'the Press and the Public, the Press and the Police, the Press and the

---

[11] The Leveson Inquiry Report, *An Inquiry into the Culture, Practices and Ethics of the Press* (TSO, 2012), Part A: The Inquiry, p 11, para 1.7. This is where notably the Leveson inquiry differs significantly from the important and recent review by the New Zealand Law Commission, *The News Media meets 'New Media': Rights, Responsibilities and Regulation in the Digital Age* (NZLC R128, 2013). This focuses essentially on the impact of social media on the existing regulatory and legal system, including the possible extension of the regulatory system to new forms of media and the adequacy of the legal protections against breaches through social media.

[12] Cabinet Minister David Mellor famously stated that the press were 'drinking in the last chance saloon' at the time of the inquiries into press standards led by Sir David Calcutt in the early 1990s.

Politicians and, finally, the Future'.[13] The first three aimed to provide the platform for focused evidence gathering broadly dealing with the topic in question. The fourth was not intended to be free-standing but rather Lord Justice Leveson challenged witnesses to provide their proposals for the future. The final 2,000 page report, after setting out the importance of public interest, addresses these modules in order.

The wealth of evidence produced to the inquiry became an international and national phenomenon. There was evidence about victims. There was evidence of general harassment as where celebrities had been pursued down the street. There was also much more serious evidence which revulsed public opinion, such as the hounding of Chris Jefferies, an eccentric landlord of a murdered woman. He was never charged with her murder and someone else later admitted that he had committed the crime. The newspapers were found guilty of contempt of court for an action which might, had Mr Jefferies been charged, have caused people not to come forward on his behalf.

There was also the case of the daughter of a famous actor, who had died. She had been reduced to begging to obtain money to feed her drugs habit. There was a tip off from the police that she was begging outside an underground station in London. A *News of the World* reporter found her and propositioned her (without actually calling on her services) took photos of her and did a scoop on her. This exposé was said to be one of the factors that led to her committing suicide. The reporter accepted that he might have gone too far in his story about her, but said that it did not stop people buying the paper. That might suggest that sales of newspapers should be the acid test of whether press intrusion into a person's private life was permissible.

That incident showed the involvement of the police. The inquiry pointed out that there had been too close a relationship between the police and the press and again between politicians and the press. That issue is outside the scope of this paper.

Lord Justice Leveson issued his final report in November 2012. His analysis of the issues was simple and clear. There had been a significant amount of phone-hacking and other harassment. There was no effective system of regulation. The Press Complaints Commission ('the PCC'), the body set up by the industry (with some prominent exceptions), was not independent. It did not act as an independent regulator. The PCC did not set any standards.

Lord Justice Leveson's preference was for a new voluntary self-regulatory system that had 'statutory underpinning'. He considered that there had to be incentives created by statute for the publishers to join the new organization. He proposed a new costs remedy: if a non-participating member was found liable in civil proceedings for publishing material about a person's private life without justification, the court had a power to award costs against the publisher on a different scale from that applying to members of the new organization because the new speedy remedy for resolving disputes to be provided by the new regulator was not used. In addition,

---

[13] See the Leveson Inquiry Report, pp 12–13, paras 1.9–1.15.

Lord Justice Leveson recommended that exemplary damages should be available in these circumstances, and that the courts should be able to take into account that the defendant had not taken or followed advice from the new self-regulatory body.

Lord Justice Leveson also considered that the new body should have responsibility to improve the code of conduct and be prepared to offer advice in advance if asked for it. He recommended that a self-regulatory body be set up with a proper system for the members of its board to be appointed independently by five specially nominated commissioners.

The Leveson recommendations were very well received by the public and by many politicians. However, the Prime Minister did not agree with the statutory underpinning that Lord Justice Leveson regarded as essential. He unequivocally rejected the proposals for the statutory underpinning, stating that it would 'cross the Rubicon of writing elements of press regulation into the law of the land'.[14] A political debate ensued. Leaders of the Labour and Liberal Democrat parties, together with representatives of the victims of the scandal, supported the recommendations made by Lord Justice Leveson, whereas the press generally sided with the Prime Minister.

The drama was heightened in November 2012 when the House of Lords amended a Defamation Bill then before Parliament on a private member's amendment so as to include the statutory underpinning recommended by Lord Justice Leveson. The government threatened to drop the Defamation Bill unless the amendments were dropped. The members who supported these amendments simply announced that, if that happened, they would seek to insert them into another bill.

In January 2013, the government put forward the idea that, to minimize any risk of political interference, a new body formed by Royal Charter approved by the Privy Council would be the new press regulator and that its functions would broadly follow those recommended by Lord Justice Leveson. This became a cross-party proposal. The amendments to the Defamation Bill to empower the courts to award costs and exemplary damages against publishers who did not participate in a recognized regulatory system were dropped. That Bill became law on 25 April 2013.

The government put forward amendments to the Crime and Courts Bill 2013 to provide new powers for the courts to award costs and exemplary damages against publishers who were not members of a regulator of relevant publishers recognized by a body established by Royal Charter. The Crime and Courts Bill became law on the same date as the Defamation Bill.

In October 2013 the Privy Council rejected the proposal, advanced by some parts of the press, for a body formed by Royal Charter with a constitution that would be preferred by those parts of the press. Subsequently the Privy Council approved a body proposed by the government with cross-party support. The way is now clear for the new body set up by Royal Charter to create a new press regulator. However, the press will be able to decide whether to join this or some other body that they may establish. If they fail to join the approved regulator, they run the risk of awards of costs and exemplary damages under the Crime and Courts Act 2013.

[14] 'Leveson report: what happened next—Q&A', *The Guardian*, 12 February 2013; 'Leveson report: David Cameron refuses to "cross Rubicon" and write press law', *The Guardian*, 29 November 2012.

This detour into the aftermath of the Leveson inquiry graphically illustrates how much the press fears government interference in the distribution of news and comment. The new regulator will have power, no doubt, to impose substantial fines. It is accepted that those fines will have to be proportionate. Proportionality is now a familiar concept in the context of fines imposed by regulatory bodies and causes no surprise.

However, what is sometimes forgotten is that the press has for many years been subject to some well-honed case law of the Strasbourg Court. The Convention guarantees not just freedom of expression but also respect for private and family life, the home and correspondence.[15] The rights guaranteed by Arts 8 and 10 often appear to conflict, and the Strasbourg Court resolves this conflict by applying proportionality.

The Strasbourg Court has articulated its reasoning on proportionality with great clarity through this case law, thus providing a valuable insight into how proportionality works. A leading case is *Axel Springer AG v Germany*,[16] in which the Strasbourg Court brought together its jurisprudence in this field.

This case concerned the arrest of a well known German actor ('X') on drugs charges 'of medium seriousness'. He had been arrested at a beer festival for possession of a small quantity of cocaine. *Bild*, a German newspaper with national circulation, wished to publish a story giving details of the arrest. The national courts restrained the newspaper from doing so. Among other factors, the national courts took into account that X had not taken any drug in public, and that only a small quantity of cocaine was involved.

The Strasbourg Court observed that:

96. ... the articles in question concern the arrest and conviction of the actor X, that is, public judicial facts that may be considered to present a degree of general interest. The public do, in principle, have an interest in being informed—and in being able to inform themselves—about criminal proceedings, whilst strictly observing the presumption of innocence ... That interest will vary in degree, however, as it may evolve during the course of the proceedings—from the time of the arrest—according to a number of different factors, such as the degree to which the person concerned is known, the circumstances of the case and any further developments arising during the proceedings.

The Strasbourg Court found that the principal issue was whether there had been a fair balance between the rights of the parties and whether the restraint on publication was necessary to protect the rights of X. The Strasbourg Court came to a different conclusion from the national courts. It produced a valuable list of the criteria to be applied when balancing the right of an individual under Art 8 against that of the press under Art 10. The principal criteria were the following:

(1) *Whether the report contributed to a debate on a matter of public interest*: This is an essential pre-condition to any interference with a person's right to respect for their private life.

---

[15] Article 8 of the Convention.   [16] [2012] ECHR 227.

(2) *How well known the subject was*: It would for instance be a relevant consideration whether the subject was a private person and whether they had previously discussed their private life with the press.

(3) *Photographs*: The Strasbourg Court warned against the use of photographs purely to satisfy readers' curiosity.

(4) *Method of obtaining the information and its veracity*: There must be an adequate factual basis for the report. It may not therefore be enough, for example, simply to have read the story on *Twitter*. Publication may not be justified if the report is only based on (say) confidential material removed from someone's dustbin, or improperly obtained from a public official, such as a policeman.

(5) *Content, form, and consequences of publication*: Did the report, for instance, appear in a local or national newspaper?

(6) *Severity of any sanction imposed*: It might be relevant to take into account any other sanction imposed by law.

Applying these criteria, the Strasbourg Court came to a different conclusion from the national courts and held that the restraint on publication violated Art 10. Their reasoning was detailed, and what follows is only a summary. The information in the report was capable of contributing to the debate in a democratic society. The public were entitled to know about criminal proceedings.[17] The newspaper had acted responsibly in publishing details of the arrest. The newspaper's reporter had witnessed the arrest. It was particularly significant that the press officer at the public prosecutor's office had confirmed the nature of the arrest.[18] The newspaper did not pass any comment on the information; it merely published it. The Strasbourg Court held that the fact that one article 'contained certain expressions which, to all intents and purposes, were designed to attract the public's attention cannot in itself raise an issue under the Court's case law'.[19] The actor had previously discussed his private life in interviews, though the Strasbourg Court noted that this does not deprive a person of all protection.[20] As the actor was well known, he could be regarded as a public figure.[21]

In this decision, the Strasbourg Court applied proportionality to a case between two private citizens and not to administrative action by the state in relation to a citizen. The methodology of proportionality is the same in both cases.

However, there are very considerable differences in methodology between traditional *Wednesbury* review and proportionality review. The two forms of review have different objectives. The *Wednesbury* test is directed at seeing that the decision is made within the law, whereas the proportionality test is directed to seeing that the ends of the administrative decision justify the means that are being used to attain those ends.

---

[17] Confusingly, however, the Strasbourg Court continued to refer to the actor as 'X'.
[18] *Axel Springer*, paras 102 to 107.   [19] *Axel Springer*, para 108.
[20] *Axel Springer*, para 101.   [21] *Axel Springer*, paras 97 to 100.

It follows that, in proportionality review, the courts are much more involved in the issue between the parties than in *Wednesbury* review. Proportionality review is more engaged with the substance of the dispute and requires a deep analysis of the evidence. So we see the Strasbourg Court rolling up its sleeves, as it were, in *Axel Springer* and getting into some fine detail about whether the publication should be permitted.

The Strasbourg Court reaches its own view as to whether the restriction on publication is justified. It does not merely ask whether the decision fell within 'the range of reasonable decisions open to the decision-maker'.

The Strasbourg Court also disagreed with the national courts in Germany. They had conducted a thorough review of proportionality but struck the balance between the two rights of the parties by prohibiting publication.[22] It is particularly remarkable that the Strasbourg Court was prepared to disagree with the national courts because its jurisdiction is not as a further appeal court: it exercises merely a supervisory jurisdiction in relation to the application of Convention rights.

Nonetheless, in general, proportionality review does enable the court to allow appropriate margin of discretion for the subject matter and for type of decision-maker. For instance, if the decision relates to national security, or to scientific or other matters requiring the exercise of judgment that the decision-maker is likely to be better placed to make than the court, the court makes an appropriate allowance for this.[23]

All this leads me back to the issue confronted by Lord Cooke in his observations in *Daly*, which I set out near the start of this paper. We can concretize the issue by reference to the developments in the field of press regulation that I have described. If the new press regulator were to reach a decision on whether a publication by the press was justified and there was an application for judicial review, the question would arise whether the court should apply the test of unreasonableness established by the *Wednesbury* case, or some other test.

In fact, *Wednesbury* has been developed in recent years so that it is now much more flexible. For example, when the administrative action in issue involves an interference with a Convention right, the court does not ask whether the action was perverse on the straightforward application of the *Wednesbury* case. It is established that the court must be satisfied that the interference was justified. The court may well permit the decision-maker a discretionary area for his decision but it is smaller than that conventionally allowed by the *Wednesbury* test.[24]

This flexibility is very welcome but it may also make the operation of judicial review more uncertain. And the default rule is always the original *Wednesbury* test.

---

[22] The national courts prohibited publication of both the article/text and the photographs. The newspaper did not contend that its rights had been violated by the prohibition on the publication of the photographs so that the Strasbourg Court did not have to consider that issue separately.

[23] See, for example, *R v Ministry of Agriculture, Fisheries and Food ex parte Federation Européene law Sante Animale (FEDESA)* (Case C-331/88) [1990] ECR I-4023, and *Campus Oil v Ministry for Industry and Energy* (Case C-72/83) [1984] ECR 2727.

[24] See, for example, *R v Ministry of Defence ex parte Smith* [1996] QB 517.

Recent developments of the law have not created a new rule, but rather a number of exceptions to the old rule.

On the other hand, the proportionality review carried out by both the Strasbourg Court and the Luxembourg Court has a number of advantages. In particular, the test is logical, principled, and structured. It places great weight on the articulation of the court's reasons for its conclusions. A test of this kind is likely to produce a more consistent and coherent body of case law.

Proportionality review is also directed to the more relevant question, namely whether the decision strikes the right balance, rather than whether the decision was perverse. Going back to the example of judicial review of the press regulator, it would be easier to explain to the public and the media the reasons for interference or non-interference if there was a detailed analysis of the kind required by a proportionality review.

The *Wednesbury* test is, moreover, less conducive to the aim of raising standards of decision-making because the answer does not engage with the reasoning behind the administrative action. On that it is relatively uninformative.

Furthermore, proportionality shifts the onus of proof from the individual who can establish a breach of a Convention right, or a right protected by EU law, onto the state, which has to justify any interference with the individual's rights on the basis of proportionality. This makes proportionality a more powerful instrument of review than mere *Wednesbury* unreasonableness.

In addition, the courts of England and Wales are in any event applying the test of proportionality in other areas, such as EU law and human rights. They are thus building up skills in this area. It would enhance the consistency of English law if the courts had just one general test for judicial review, whether or not the case involved an issue of EU law or human rights. It would increase the influence of English law in Europe if our courts were able to make a contribution to the law on proportionality review based on their domestic experience. Greater use of proportionality might well make it easier for English law to absorb changes required by EU law.

However, these are not the only issues. The heart of the matter is that any move from one generalized test for judicial review to another must respect the constitutional position of the judiciary on the one hand and that of the legislature and executive on the other. It would be tempting to conclude from the idea of the separation of powers that the role of the courts in any jurisdiction should be considered separately from the roles of the other branches of the constitution. Before modifying any general test for judicial review, however, the courts must look at judicial review as part of the constitutional system.

The defining feature of the constitutional position of England and Wales[25] is that Parliament is sovereign and there is no system of constitutional review of legislation by judges at common law. The courts do not consider the legality of legislation in terms of rights conferred by a written constitution. Parliament is sovereign in making decisions on matters that fall within legislative policy. In this

---

[25] References to English law are to be read as references to the law of England and Wales even though I have not referred to both parts of the United Kingdom on each occasion.

respect, the content, culture, and traditions of the law of England and Wales are different from many of those jurisdictions that use proportionality as a generalized test of judicial review.

Parliament is to be regarded as sovereign even though, when it comes to finding out what legislation means and whether the decision is lawful, Parliament is not sovereign, but rather is bound by what the courts say. If it disagrees with the courts' interpretation, however, it can change the law.

Similar points apply in relation to international treaties and conventions. Parliament makes the decision whether to render them binding in the domestic sphere. However, Parliament will not be the body empowered to make an authoritative interpretation of the treaty or convention. That matter will be for an international court or the national courts. Parliament may not be able to change that meaning: that depends on the terms of the international instrument.

The constitutional position must be taken into account when decisions of ministers carrying out the legislative policy decided on by Parliament are the subject of judicial review.

The judiciary's functions, however, are now accepted to include a proper element of judicial review of administrative action. Even so, a generalized test of judicial review must not make it impossible for the other arms of the constitution to carry out their roles.

Would that be the inevitable result of proportionality? If proportionality means that any interference with an individual's rights must be strictly necessary for the purpose of achieving a particular aim, the choice that a government has today as to the manner of implementing its policies may be heavily circumscribed. Suppose, for example, that the government decides not to tax a particular form of benefit in kind. Under the *Wednesbury* test it is difficult to challenge this decision. However, if there was a test of proportionality which imposed a test of strict necessity, then a taxpayer may be able to object that that means that some employees benefit unfairly and that other benefits ought also not to be taxed.

However, it would in my view be wrong to conclude that proportionality needs to intrude upon proper executive decision-making. The proportionality test is a highly sophisticated tool for controlling the latitude to be given to the state, or an emanation of the state, over an individual. There is no reason why in the context of domestic judicial review the courts should not be able to work out variations in the level of intensity of review so that the test becomes case-sensitive.

I will give an example to explain what I mean by this. One objection to proportionality is that there are areas, like national security and foreign relations, where the courts traditionally allow a decision-maker a wide margin for discretionary judgment, and give weight to the decision-maker's special access to expert information. In these cases, the decision is likely to be based on matters of judgment or prediction from that information that are incapable of proof on a balance of probabilities in the usual way.

My own response is that these situations do not cause any difficulty under a proportionality test. In the context of applying the proportionality test to human rights, the Strasbourg Court gives a margin of discretionary judgment in these areas and therefore there should be no difficulty in national courts doing the same. Indeed, the Court of Appeal of England and Wales has done so in relation to national security in the context of freedom of speech when upholding the Secretary of State's decision to refuse entry to a non-national, seeking to enter the United Kingdom for the purposes of exercising the right to freedom of speech, on security grounds. It did so even though the refusal of entry amounted in effect to a denial of the right to the person seeking entry and denial of the right of the persons who wished to hear that person speak within the jurisdiction.[26]

Similarly, the Luxembourg Court has identified areas where it will respect the decision of the EU institution or the member state, and not enquire whether the interference with individual rights is strictly necessary. These include national security again, and other matters, such as public health decisions and decisions as to whether matters are contrary to public policy. In effect, the lower level of review which we would apply using the *Wednesbury* test is applied in these areas. There is no reason why the English courts should not similarly decide to apply the proportionality test with varying degrees of intensity.

Thus the imperative for national courts who are contemplating adopting proportionality in domestic law is to formulate an approach to the intensity of review which is appropriate to their constitutional system. A government might wish to introduce a new policy, for example in a matter of social policy. In the nature of things, the question whether the policy will work involves an element of prediction and judgment which may be incapable of proof in the usual way. Here again, the court would have to establish the appropriate level of intensity of review consistent with the constitutional role of the court in judicial review. The difficulties of proportionality are therefore manageable.

Proportionality is capable of being a more intensive, or, as it is sometimes put, 'muscular' review of administrative action than the *Wednesbury* test. However, and this is an important point, it remains a technique for reviewing a decision which has been taken. It is not about substituting the court's decision for that of the decision-maker. In addition, it preserves flexibility for the judiciary to develop the test on a case-by-case basis. It neither is nor need be an inflexible test. In particular, the courts will have to decide on the right level of intensity of review for the decision under review. There is no one right answer. Like Goldilocks, they will have to decide which level of review is 'just right', neither too much nor too little.

My own view is that it is inevitable that judicial review in England and Wales will move towards a generalized test of proportionality.[27] What may be holding the law back at the present time is a lack of understanding about the nuanced way in which proportionality can be operated. This understanding can be obtained from comparative law sources. As always, comparative law—the study of other systems of

---

[26] *R (Farrakhan) v Home Secretary* [2002] EWCA Civ 606, [2002] QB 1391.
[27] I should make it clear that I may reach different conclusions from those expressed in this paper if the matter arises judicially, when I would decide the issue on the basis of the cases then presented.

law—can demonstrate a wide field of experience from which courts in other jurisdictions can draw inspiration.

The end position is that there was much wisdom and foresight in what Lord Cooke had to say in *Daly*, which I set out at the start of this paper. His observations demonstrate great perceptiveness and foresight. They may have been briefly expressed, but, as I see it, time will serve to confirm the accuracy of his assessment. From little acorns mighty oaks do grow!

PART III

INTERPRETING LEGISLATION— NEW APPROACHES EMERGE

Section 3 of the Human Rights Act 1998[1] requires legislation to be read and interpreted, so far as possible, in a way that is compatible with Convention rights. It is a half-way house: the courts do not have power to strike down a provision of an Act of Parliament which is not Convention-compliant. Only the duty to interpret was given to the courts, as that would preserve Parliamentary sovereignty. So, if Parliament wished to depart from the Convention rights, it could as a matter of domestic law do so. The Human Rights Act 1998 is not therefore different from any other Act of Parliament in that respect. But Parliament did impose an important duty on the courts to interpret legislation, if they could, in such a way that Convention rights would prevail, unless Parliament had made it clear that this was not to happen.

Section 3 was virtually unprecedented in the United Kingdom. The usual method of statutory interpretation is to winnow out the meaning of a statute by looking at the language used in its context and in the light of what Parliament intended to achieve. The role of judges in conventional statutory interpretation is thus subordinate to Parliament: the courts must give effect to the will of Parliament. Judges usually adopt a 'purposive' approach to interpretation; namely, when there is doubt as to what Parliament intended, they try to find the meaning consistent with the language that most closely gives effect to what they find to be the purpose of the legislation.

There have been some exceptions. The Judicial Committee of the Privy Council (the final appeal court mainly for a number of present and former Commonwealth countries)[2] developed a different approach to statutory interpretation when construing fundamental rights conferred by constitutions.[3] Its jurisprudence places great weight on ensuring that these fundamental rights are effective, and formed one of the stepping stones to the bold approach to interpretation which the courts

---

[1] Section 3(1) is set out in full in the Appendix.
[2] Justices of the Supreme Court sit regularly on the Judicial Committee of the Privy Council, as did their predecessors, the members of the Appellate Committee of the House of Lords.
[3] See M Arden, 'Modernising Legislation' [1998] PL 65.

must now adopt under the Human Rights Act 1998. Another stepping stone was the principle, developed in relation to international law, that, where Parliament enacted legislation to fulfil some international obligation, the court should interpret the legislation (unless Parliament had clearly indicated otherwise) so that it fully met that obligation.

Section 3 means that the court must interpret legislation, so far as it can, to give effect to Convention rights even if that is not the meaning that it would have reached under the usual principles of interpretation. In addition, the obligation applies even if Parliament enacted the legislation before the Human Rights Act 1998 was passed.

In Chapter 7, *The Interpretation of UK Domestic Legislation in the Light of the European Convention on Human Rights Jurisprudence*, I set out a detailed study of the case law showing the generous interpretation which the courts had given to their new powers under the Human Rights Act 1998, s 3. Some people now take the view that this approach to interpretation has gone too far, and it maybe that in the future the Supreme Court will so decide.

As a result of that paper, I was able, in my judicial capacity, to apply the case law derived from s 3 of the Human Rights Act 1998 to the interpretation of domestic legislation that was intended to implement EU legislation, even though s 3 did not apply in that situation and the interpretation of such legislation was governed by the European Communities Act, passed in 1972. My judgment was one of the first authoritative judgments enunciating this principle of interpretation.[4]

In Chapter 8, *The Changing Judicial Role: Human Rights, Community Law, and the Intention of Parliament*, I provide a new analysis, distinguishing two models of statutory interpretation: an 'agency model' and a 'dynamic model'. The first model reflects the conventional approach to statutory interpretation and the fact that the courts are primarily bound to give effect to the intention of Parliament. This applies to purely domestic legislation, not concerned with either human rights or EU legislation. The dynamic model applies to legislation that affects human rights or is designed to implement EU legislation: here the court, if it can, has to find a meaning compatible with EU law or human rights. One of the problems which it may face is that EU law or human rights jurisprudence may have moved on since the statute was enacted.

Chapter 9, *Statutory Interpretation and Human Rights*, is based on a lecture given to the Commonwealth Association of Legislative Counsel, who draft statutes in their respective jurisdictions.[5] The aim of this lecture was to explore some of the different ways in which courts across the world approach legislation when human rights are in issue. This paper is a reminder that in solving problems of statutory interpretation and human rights in the common law world we can look for inspiration to jurisdictions outside Europe.

---

[4] *HMRC v IDT Credit Card Services Ireland Ltd* [2007] EWCA Civ 29, [2007] STC 1252.
[5] The version included in this Volume omits the sections discussing the Human Rights Act 1998 which have been covered in earlier chapters.

7

The Interpretation of UK Domestic Legislation in the Light of the European Convention on Human Rights Jurisprudence

This chapter is based on an article which appeared in 2004.*

How does human rights jurisprudence affect statutory interpretation in the United Kingdom? Unlike countries such as Canada, the United Kingdom has no modern 'home grown' charter of rights. However, the United Kingdom is a contracting party to the European Convention on Human Rights, to which I will refer as the 'Convention'. The European Court of Human Rights, referred to below as the 'Strasbourg Court', is the court ultimately responsible for interpreting the Convention. In this paper, I consider how Convention jurisprudence, that is, the case law of the Strasbourg Court and now the courts of the United Kingdom on Convention rights, affects statutory interpretation in the United Kingdom. It will be seen that, because of s 3 of the Human Rights Act 1998, Convention jurisprudence now has an important and direct role to play in statutory interpretation.[1]

The Convention and the Human Rights Act 1998

The Convention confers a large number of important rights, including the right to life, the right to liberty and security, and so on. The United Kingdom became a signatory to the Convention many years ago, but Parliament did not incorporate it into domestic law until 1998, when the Human Rights Act was passed. So the Convention was not, prior to that Act, directly relevant to statutory interpretation. It could not be a source of rights or obligations and, unless a statute was ambiguous, it could not be used for the purposes of statutory interpretation.[2] However, the Human Rights Act 1998 gives effect in UK domestic law to the rights contained in

---

* First published in (2004) 25 *Statute Law Review* 165. It is reproduced here with the kind permission of the Publisher.

[1] The Convention rights incorporated by the Human Rights Act 1998 and the principal provisions of that Act are set out in the Appendix.

[2] *R v Secretary of State for the Home Department ex p Brind* [1991] AC 696.

the Convention. For the first time, Convention rights can be enforced in our domestic courts instead of solely by exercising the right of individual petition to the Strasbourg Court. In determining questions as to Convention rights, UK courts may take into account the case law of the Strasbourg Court (and its predecessor bodies) but they are not bound to follow it.[3]

However, one of the underlying principles of the Human Rights Act 1998 is that Parliamentary sovereignty is preserved. The courts are accordingly not given any power to strike down statutes which infringe Convention rights. If the courts had such a power, they would always have a trump card. Their interpretation of the law and of what was incompatible with the Convention would always prevail. Accordingly, instead of giving the courts power to strike down statutes, two different techniques have been employed. As to the first, s 3 of the Human Rights Act 1998 has imposed on the courts an obligation so far as possible to interpret legislation, whenever passed, in a manner compatible with Convention rights.[4] I will look in detail at s 3 in this paper.

The second technique is the declaration of incompatibility. If the courts cannot construe a statute compatible with the Convention, under s 4 of the Human Rights Act 1998[5] they may make a declaration of incompatibility. However this has only limited effect because s 4(6) provides:

(6) A declaration under this section ('a declaration of incompatibility')—

(a) does not affect the validity, continuing operation or enforcement of the provision in respect of which it is given; and

(b) is not binding on the parties to the proceedings in which it is made.

The scheme of the Human Rights Act 1998 therefore leaves it open to Parliament to enact legislation which violates Convention rights if it chooses to do so. To make that clear, Parliament might in such a case specifically state that legislation applies notwithstanding any violation of any Convention right. The courts could not then interpret the statute in a manner compatible with the Convention, but they would be left with the option of making a declaration of incompatibility. Although they may make a declaration of incompatibility in such a case, they need not do so. The declaration of incompatibility has been described as a 'booby prize'. It cannot alter the result in the case in question. It merely provides a means of communicating to Parliament the courts' view that the legislation violates the Convention.

Section 3(1) of the Human Rights Act 1998

The interpretative obligation imposed on the courts by s 3(1) of the 1998 Act has a very respectable genealogy. In *Garland v British Rail Engineering Ltd*,[6] where the

---

[3] Human Rights Act 1998, s 2.
[4] Section 3 of the Human Rights Act 1998 is set out in full in the Appendix.
[5] Section 4 of the Human Rights Act 1998 is set out in the Appendix.
[6] [1983] 2 AC 751, 771.

issue was whether domestic legislation was incompatible with European Community legislation, Lord Diplock stated that:

> ... it is a principle of construction of United Kingdom statutes, now too well established to call for citation of authority, that the words of a statute passed after the Treaty has been signed and dealing with the subject matter of an international obligation of the United Kingdom, are to be construed, if they are reasonably capable of bearing such a meaning, as intended to carry out the obligation and not to be inconsistent with it.

This observation was made with respect to international treaties generally. The words in s 3(1) of the 1998 Act 'so far as it is possible to do so' are just a simpler way of saying 'if they are reasonably capable of bearing such a meaning' (the words used by Lord Diplock).

It is also well established that in relation to constitutional instruments, the court should adopt a generous and purposive construction. Thus, for example, in *Ministry of Health v Fisher*[7] Lord Wilberforce said that constitutional instruments:

> ... call for a generous interpretation of wording avoiding what has been called 'the austerity of tabulated legalism', suitable to give individuals the full measure of the fundamental rights and freedoms referred to.

Similarly, the Strasbourg Court construes the Convention in a purposive way. It chooses the interpretation which best reflects the democratic purpose of the Convention. As the Strasbourg Court put it in *Soering v UK*:

> ... any interpretation of the rights and freedoms guaranteed has to be consistent with the general spirit of the Convention, an instrument designed to maintain and promote the ideals and values of a democratic society.[8]

The Strasbourg Court also adopts the principle known as the principle of dynamic or evolutive interpretation. The Convention uses concepts linked to societal values and these change from time to time. The object of interpretation is to seek the current, not the historic, meaning. As one judge put it: 'The Convention is written in the present tense.' Thus, while birching was considered acceptable in the 1950s, matters had changed when the Strasbourg Court came to consider the matter in 1978. Similarly, the Strasbourg Court's attitude to illegitimate children and transsexual people has changed over the course of time. In relation to transsexual people, the Strasbourg Court at one time held that no violation was involved in a failure to change the birth certificate of a transsexual person because there was no generalized approach in the member states of the Council of Europe to the treatment of transsexual people in certain circumstances. However, in the recent case of *Goodwin v United Kingdom*,[9] the Strasbourg Court held that there was no justification for barring a transsexual person from enjoying the right to marry under any circumstances, and that the treatment of transsexual people for legal purposes was no longer within the United Kingdom's margin of appreciation. In reaching this

---

[7] [1980] AC 319, 323.   [8] [1989] 11 EHRR 439, 467 para 87.
[9] [2002] 35 EHRR 447.

conclusion, the Strasbourg Court took into account the evidence of a continuing international trend in favour of the increased social acceptance and legal recognition for transsexual people.

Because the interpretation of Convention rights is dynamic and changes from time to time, special problems may arise for the statute law of member states. A statute may be passed which may fully respect all Convention rights as they are then understood. However, ten years later, Convention jurisprudence may have moved on, so that conclusion is no longer correct. Section 3 of the 1998 Act will require the court to construe the Act not against the context of Convention rights as they stood when the legislation was enacted but against the context of Convention rights as they stand at the time of the judgment. Accordingly, the meaning of a statute may change as the Convention rights which it touches change with the course of time.

An analysis of s 3 of the Human Rights Act 1998

I now turn to look at the exact words used in s 3 of the 1998 Act, starting with the phrase 'so far as it is possible to do so'. I have already expressed the view that this states in more modern language what Lord Diplock had stated in the *Garland* case. This particular formula gives the courts the maximum room for manoeuvre. Indeed, Lord Diplock in the *Garland* case specifically left open the question whether anything short of an express statement in an Act of Parliament that a particular provision was intended to be made in breach of an obligation under European Community law would justify an English court in construing that provision in a manner inconsistent with a Community treaty obligation of the United Kingdom. However, the courts do not go that far under s 3 of the Human Rights Act 1998.[10]

The words 'so far as it is possible to do so' clearly confer maximum flexibility when attempting to find a compatible interpretation. The wording also gives the courts maximum flexibility to develop new principles or canons of convention to enable them to carry out their new interpretative duty in a principled way. Nonetheless, Parliament clearly envisaged that there would be cases where statutes could not be construed in a manner compatible with Convention rights. In that situation, the courts might instead make a declaration of incompatibility under s 4.

The next phrase to examine in s 3 is 'read and take effect'. The view has been expressed judicially and by academic writers that it is open to the court, even if it has construed a statute in a manner incompatible with a Convention right, to hold that a statute should not 'take effect' in that way in the instant case, for example, by withholding a remedy. I question whether Parliament intended that interpretation. It would, in effect, be giving the courts a dispensing power whenever legislation violated a Convention right. Moreover, it is clear that the word 'and' is used

---

[10] See *Re S (Minors) (Care Order: Implementation of Care Plan)* [2002] UKHL 10, [2002] 2 AC 291, 313 at [40].

conjunctively in s 3(1). I venture to think that the drafter might have considered that it was necessary to say both 'read' and 'take effect' in case a court should be sufficiently perverse to conclude that the statute should be interpreted to give effect to Convention rights but that this was not its natural interpretation and that it should give effect to the statute in accordance with its natural interpretation. This would deprive s 3(1) of any effect or alternatively give the courts an option to decide when to follow it or not. Section 3 is, of course, also arguably a mandatory direction to persons other than courts who have to apply the relevant statutory provisions.

The next word to focus on is 'compatible'. It is sufficient if the statute passes the test of compatibility with no room to spare. The interpretative obligation does not require the courts to give the fullest expression to Convention rights or to find a meaning which would promote them to the fullest extent.

Next, it is to be observed that s 3(1) of the 1998 Act applies to enactments whenever enacted.[11] Accordingly, courts must construe statutes in accordance with s 3(1) even if it is obvious that, at the time the statute was passed, no-one had ever heard of the Convention. This is another example of the courts being required to impose on a statute a regime which was not intended to be employed by the legislature at the time of enactment.

The House of Lords' interpretation of s 3(1)

The next task is to look at some of the cases where s 3(1) of the Human Rights Act 1998 has been in point. All the cases which I shall consider have been decided by the House of Lords, rather than in the lower courts. It will be seen that there has been a steep learning curve for the courts in relation to s 3(1).

The first case is *R v A (No 2)*.[12] In this case, the appeal was by a defendant to a criminal charge of rape and concerned the question of whether certain evidence concerning the sexual behaviour of the complainant would be admissible at trial. The defendant wanted to adduce evidence of the complainant's sexual behaviour in the three weeks prior to the alleged rape. However, s 41 of the Youth Justice and Criminal Evidence Act 1999 prohibits the admission of evidence as to the complainant's sexual behaviour unless certain conditions are fulfilled. The conditions permit the admission of evidence of sexual behaviour on the issue of consent if the prior sexual behaviour was so similar to sexual behaviour of the complainant that the similarity cannot be explained as a coincidence. But further conditions are attached to this exception, including a condition that the behaviour should have taken place as part of the event or at or about the same time as the alleged rape.[13] The House of Lords held that an accused's Convention right to a fair trial might be violated if relevant evidence of the kind sought to be addressed by the appellant was excluded. The question then arose whether s 41 could be construed so as to prevent

---

[11] As to the separate question whether s 3 affects vested rights, see *Wilson v First County Trust (No 2)* [2003] UKHL 40, [2004] 1 AC 816.
[12] [2001] UKHL 25, [2002] 1 AC 45.   [13] Section 41(3)(c).

any violation of the defendant's rights. On this, their Lordships expressed different views. First, Lord Steyn made some general observations about s 3:

[44]   On the other hand, the interpretative obligation of section 3 of the 1998 Act is a strong one. It applies even if there is no ambiguity in the language in the sense of the language being capable of two different meanings. It is an emphatic adjuration by the legislature: *R v. Director of Public Prosecutions, ex parte Kebilene* [2000] 2 AC 326, per Lord Cooke of Thorndon, at p. 373F; and my judgement at 366B . . . In accordance with the will of Parliament as reflected in section 3 it will sometimes be necessary to adopt an interpretation which linguistically may appear strained. The techniques to be used will not only involve the reading down of expressed language in a statute but also the implication of provisions. A declaration of incompatibility is a measure of last resort. It must be avoided unless it is plainly impossible to do so. If a *clear* limitation on Convention rights is stated in terms, such an impossibility will arise: *Secretary of State for the Home Department, ex parte Simms* [2000] 2 AC 115, 132A-B per Lord Hoffmann. There is, however, no limitation of such a nature in the present case.

[45]   In my view, section 3 requires the court to subordinate the niceties of the language of section 41(3)(c) and in particular the touchstone of coincidence, to broader considerations of relevance judged by logical and common sense criteria of time and circumstances. After all, it is realistic to proceed on the basis that the legislature would not, if alerted to the problem, have wished to deny the right to an accused to put forward a full and complete defence by advancing truly probative material. It is therefore possible under section 3 to read section 41, and in particular section 41(3)(c) as subject to the implied provision that evidence or questioning which is required to ensure a fair trial under article 6 of the Convention should not be treated as inadmissible. The result of such reading would be that sometimes logically relevant sexual experiences between a complainant and an accused may be admitted under section 41(3)(c) . . .

Lord Hope of Craighead took a different view. He considered that the question whether s 41 was incompatible with the Convention could not be finally determined at the pre-trial stage. Accordingly, he considered it was neither necessary nor appropriate to resort to the interpretative obligation in s 3 of the Human Rights Act 1998. Lord Hope added:

[108]   I should like to add, however, that I would find it very difficult to accept that it was permissible under section 3 of the Human Rights Act 1998 to read into section 41(3)(c) a provision to the effect that evidence or questioning which was required to ensure a fair trial under article 6 of the Convention should not be treated as inadmissible. The rule of construction which section 3 lays down is quite unlike any previous rule of statutory interpretation. There is no need to identify any ambiguity or absurdity. Compatibility with Convention rights is the sole guiding principle. This is the paramount object which the rule seeks to achieve. But the rule is only a rule of interpretation. It does not entitle the judges to act as legislators . . .

[109]   In the present case it seems to me that the entire structure of section 41 contradicts the idea that it is possible to read into it a new provision which would enable the court to give leave whenever it was of the opinion that this was required to ensure a fair trial. The whole point of this section, as was made clear during the debates in Parliament, was to address the mischief which was thought to have arisen due to the width of the discretion which had previously been given to the trial judge. A deliberate decision was taken not to

follow the examples which were to be found elsewhere, such as in section 275 of the Criminal Procedure (Scotland) Act 1995, of provisions which give an overriding discretion to the trial judge to allow the evidence or questioning where it would be contrary to the interests of justice to exclude it. Section 41(2) forbids the exercise of such discretion unless the court is satisfied as to the matters which that section identifies. It seems to me that it would not be possible, without contradicting the plain intention of Parliament, to read in a provision which would enable the court to exercise a wider discretion than that permitted by section 41(2).

[110]   I would not have the same difficulty with a solution which read down the provisions of sections (3) or (5), as the case may be, in order to render them compatible with the Convention right but if that were to be done it would be necessary to identify precisely (a) the words used by the legislature which would otherwise be incompatible with the Convention right and (b) how those words were to be construed, according to the rule which section 3 lays down to make them compatible. That, it seems to me, is what the rule of construction requires. The court's task is to read and give effect to the legislation which it is asked to construe...

The other members of the House in substance agreed with Lord Steyn's approach. Lord Slynn held:

It seems to me that your Lordships cannot say that it is not possible to read section 41(3)(c) together with article 6 of the Convention rights in a way which will result in a fair hearing. In my view, section 41(3)(c) is to be read as permitting the admission of evidence or questioning which relates to a relevant issue in the case and which the trial judge considers is necessary to make the trial a fair one.[14]

Lord Clyde held:

If a case occurred where the evidence of the complainant's sexual behaviour was relevant and important for the defence to make good a case of consent, then it seems to me that the language would have to be strained to avoid the injustice to the accused of excluding them from a full and proper presentation of the defence.[15]

Lord Hutton held:

... pursuant to the obligation imposed by section 3(1) that section 41 must be read and given effect in a way which is compatible with article 6, I consider that section 41(3)(c) should be read as including evidence of such previous behaviour by the complainant because the defendant claims that her sexual behaviour on previous occasions was similar, and the similarity was not a coincidence because there was a causal connection which was her affection for, and feelings of attraction towards, the defendant.[16]

The next case is *R v Lambert*.[17] There were a number of issues in this case including an issue as to retrospectivity of the Human Rights Act 1998. I propose to refer to the case only in so far as it is relevant to s 3 of the Human Rights Act 1998. As to the facts, the appellant was found in possession of a package which contained controlled drugs and he was charged with an offence of possessing controlled drugs

---

[14] *R v A (No 2)* at [13].   [15] *R v A (No 2)* at [136].   [16] *R v A (No 2)* at [163].
[17] [2001] UKHL 37, [2002] 2 AC 545.

contrary to s 5(3) of the Misuse of Drugs Act 1971. He was convicted. His defence was that he did not know or suspect that the package contained controlled drugs. Section 28(2) of the 1971 Act provides that subject to section 28(3):

... it shall be a defence for the accused to prove that he neither knew of, nor suspected, nor had reason to suspect the existence of some fact alleged by the prosecution which it is necessary for the prosecution to prove if he is to be convicted of the offence charged.

Section 28(3) provides that the accused is not to be acquitted simply because he does not know that the substance was not the particular controlled drug but that he should be acquitted 'if he proves that he neither believed nor suspected nor had reason to suspect that the substance or product in question was a controlled drug'. At trial, the appellant failed to make out his defence under s 28 and was convicted. One of the grounds of his appeal against his conviction was that s 28 was in violation of Art 6 of the Convention since by reversing the onus of proof it violated the presumption of innocence. All the members of the House of Lords, excluding Lord Hutton who did not find it necessary to deal with the point, but including Lord Steyn who dissented in the result, held that, in accordance with s 3(1) of the 1998 Act, s 28 could be read as merely imposing an evidential burden. As the judge had given the correct direction, the conviction stood. Lord Clyde indeed considered that it required no straining of the language of s 28 to construe the references to proof as intending an evidential burden and not a persuasive one. Accordingly, in his judgment, the construction was well within the word 'possible' for the purposes of s 3.[18]

The application of s 3 was dealt with in most detail by Lord Hope. First, he repeated the point that he had made in *R v A (No 2)* that s 3 did not enable the courts to legislate but merely to interpret legislation. Secondly, he held that it was necessary to identify the word or phrase which, if given its ordinary meaning, was incompatible with Convention rights and to say how the word or phrase was to be construed if it was to be made compatible. He held that the justification for this approach was to be found in the nature of s 3:

[80] ... Its primary characteristic, for present purposes, is its ability to achieve certainty by the use of clear and precise language. It provides a set of rules by which, according to the ordinary meaning of the words used, the conduct of affairs may be regulated. So far as possible judges should seek to achieve the same attention to detail in their use of language to express the effect of applying section 3(1) as the Parliamentary drafter would have done if he had been amending the statute. It ought to be possible for any words that need to be substituted to be fitted into the statute as if they had been inserted there by amendment. If this cannot be done without doing such violence to the statute as to make it unintelligible or unworkable the use of this technique will not be possible. It will then be necessary to leave it to Parliament to amend the statute and to resort instead to the making of a declaration of incompatibility.

Lord Hope then discussed the techniques that could be used under s 3:

---

[18] *R v Lambert* at [157].

[81]   As to the techniques that may be used, it is clear that the courts are not bound by previous authority as to what the statute means. It has been suggested that a strained or non-literal construction may be adopted, that words may be read in by way of addition to those used by the legislator and that the words may be 'read down' to give them a narrower construction than their ordinary meaning would bear: Clayton & Tomlinson, *The Law of Human Rights* (2000), vol. 1, p. 168, para. 4.28. It may be enough simply to say what the effect of the provision is without altering the ordinary meaning of the words used: see *Brown v. Stott* 2000 JC 328, 355B-C, per Lord Justice General Rodger. In other cases, as in *Vasquez v. The Queen* [1994] 1 WLR 1304, the words used will require to be expressed in different language in order to explain how they are to be read in a way that is compatible. The exercise in these cases is one of translation into compatible language from language that is incompatible. In other cases, as in *R v. A (No. 2)* [2002] 1 AC 45, it may be necessary for words to be read in to explain the meaning that must be given to the provision if it is to be compatible. But the interpretation of a statute by reading words in to give effect to the presumed intention must always be distinguished carefully from amendment. Amendment is a legislative act. It is an exercise which must be reserved to Parliament.

Lord Hope went on to hold that the words 'to prove' in s 28(2) should be read as 'to give sufficient evidence' and that the same meaning should be given to the words 'if he proves' in s 28(3).[19]

R v A (No 2) and *R v Lambert* represent the high water mark of the application of the interpretative obligation. There have been at least three other cases in which use of the interpretative obligation in s 3 has been rejected and declarations of incompatibility have been made. In the first, *Re S (Minors) (Care Order: Implementation of Care Plan)*,[20] the issue was whether the court could, by using s 3 of the Human Rights Act 1998, interpret the Children Act 1989 as enabling the judge to establish milestones in a care plan and impose obligations on the local authority to act if those milestones were not met. This was called a 'starring' system.

The House of Lords held, in essence, that it was a cardinal principle of the Children Act 1989 that the courts were not empowered to intervene in the way local authorities discharged their parental responsibilities under final care orders and that the starring system introduced by the Court of Appeal was inconsistent with that cardinal principle and went beyond the boundary of interpretation. The principal speech was given by Lord Nicholls, with whom all the other members of the House agreed. This speech contains some important observations on the effect of s 3 of the 1998 Act. Lord Nicholls starts by making the point that s 3 is 'forthright, uncompromising language', but he continues:

[38]   But the reach of this tool is not unlimited. Section 3 is concerned with interpretation. This is apparent from the opening words of section 3(1): 'so far as it is possible to do so'

. . .

[39]   In applying section 3 courts must be ever mindful of this outer limit. The Human Rights Act reserves the amendment of primary legislation to Parliament. By this means the Act seeks to preserve Parliamentary sovereignty. The Act maintains the constitutional

---

[19] *R v Lambert* at [94].   [20] [2002] UKHL 10, [2002] 2 AC 291.

boundary. Interpretation of statutes is a matter for the courts; the enactment of statutes, and the amendment of statutes, are matters for Parliament.

Lord Nicholls continued by saying that the area of real difficulty was in identifying the limits of interpretation in a particular case. He observed that the problem was more acute today than in the past because courts are more liberal in their interpretation of all manner of documents. Lord Nicholls continued:

> For present purposes it is sufficient to say that a meaning which departs substantially from a fundamental feature of an Act of Parliament is likely to have crossed the boundary between interpretation and amendment. This is especially so where the departure has important practical repercussions which the court is not equipped to evaluate. In such a case the overall contextual setting may leave no scope for rendering the statutory provision Convention compliant by the legitimate use of the process of interpretation. The boundary line may be crossed even though a limitation on Convention rights is not stated in express terms. Lord Steyn's observations in *R v. A (No. 2)* [2002] 1 AC 45, 68D-E, para. 44 are not to be read as meaning that a clear limitation on Convention rights in terms is the only circumstance in which an interpretation incompatible with Convention rights may arise.[21]

Lord Nicholls went on to say, effectively in agreement with Lord Hope, that when applying s 3:

> ...it is important the court should identify clearly the particular statutory provision or provisions whose interpretation leads to that result. Apart from all else, this should assist in ensuring the court does not inadvertently stray outside its interpretation jurisdiction.[22]

It is not, therefore, surprising that in two further cases the House of Lords has also made declarations of compatibility. The first was *R (Anderson) v Secretary of State for the Home Department*[23] where the issue was whether the statutory provision which enabled the Secretary of State to fix the tariff period to be served by mandatory life sentence prisoners was inconsistent with Art 6 of the Convention. The House of Lords held that it was, and went on to make a declaration of incompatibility. The House rejected the submission that the statutory provision could be interpreted in such a way as to be compatible with the Convention under s 3(1) of the 1998 Act. Memorably, Lord Bingham held:

> To read section 29 as precluding participation by the Home Secretary, if it were possible to do so, would not be judicial interpretation but judicial vandalism: It would give the section an effect quite different from that which Parliament intended and would go well beyond any interpretative process sanctioned by section 3 of the 1998 Act. (*In Re S (Minors) (Care Order: Implementation of Care Plan)* [2002] 2 AC 291, 313–314, para. 41).[24]

Lord Steyn added:

> It would not be interpretation but interpolation inconsistent with the plain legislative intent to entrust the decision to the Home Secretary, who was intended to be free to follow or reject judicial advice. Section 3(1) is not available where the suggested interpretation is

---

[21] *Re S* at [40].   [22] *Re S* at [41].
[23] [2002] UKHL 46, [2003] 1 AC 837.   [24] *Anderson* at [30].

contrary to expressed statutory words or is by implication necessarily contradicted by the statute: *In Re S (Minors) (Care Order: Implementation of Care Plan)* [2002] 2 AC 291, 313-314, para. 41, per Lord Nicholls of Birkenhead.[25]

The third case was *Bellinger v Bellinger*.[26] In this case, the petitioner, who was registered as male at birth, had undergone gender reassignment and subsequently went through a ceremony of marriage with a man. She sought a declaration that her marriage was valid. Section 11(c) of the Matrimonial Causes Act 1973 provides that 'a marriage . . . shall be void on the following grounds only, that is to say . . . that the parties are not respectively male and female . . .'. The House of Lords held that this provision referred to a person's biological gender at birth and thus that the appellant was not entitled to a declaration that her marriage to a male was valid and subsisting. The House of Lords further held that, since there was no provision for the recognition of gender reassignment for the purposes of marriage, s 11(c) was a continuing obstacle to the petitioner entering into a valid marriage with a man and that s 11(c) of the 1973 Act was therefore incompatible with her right to respect for her private and family life and her right to marry pursuant to Arts 8 and 12 respectively of the Convention. Accordingly, the House of Lords made a declaration of incompatibility. Only Lord Hope and Lord Hobhouse specifically referred to s 3. Lord Hope contented himself by saying that he did not consider that the House of Lords could solve the problem judicially by means of the interpretative obligation in s 3(1) of the 1998 Act.[27] Lord Hobhouse came to the same conclusion. He said:

This would, in my view, not be an exercise in interpretation however robust. It would be a legislative exercise of amendment making a legislative choice as to what precise amendment was appropriate.[28]

Conclusions

I will now endeavour to draw the threads together.

First, as the recent decisions of the House of Lords make it clear, s 3(1) only creates an interpretative duty, and does not impose a duty on the courts to rewrite the law. Section 3(1) requires the courts to read and give effect to legislation. It does not provide that 'nothing in any enactment can violate a Convention right and that it should be given effect accordingly'. The duty is only one of interpretation, and there may come a stage where interpretation in a manner compatible with Convention rights is impossible, as the last three cases to which I have referred show.

Second, it has never been open to doubt that s 3(1) is not a judicial override. Usually bills of rights enable courts to strike down legislation, as happens in the United States. But that is not the position in the United Kingdom. The reason is the reason that I gave at the outset, namely that the Human Rights Act 1998 also

---

[25] *Anderson* at [59].   [26] [2003] UKHL 21, [2003] 2 AC 467.
[27] *Bellinger* at [69].   [28] *Bellinger* at [78].

preserves Parliamentary sovereignty. Another way of putting this point is that the United Kingdom does not have a proper bill of rights. But that is what Parliament has decided should happen.

Third, although the task is one of interpretation, it is not the traditional task of interpretation. New rules and canons of interpretation apply to it. In particular, the doctrine of precedent does not apply in the same way. If a statute was interpreted before the commencement of the Human Rights Act 1998, that interpretation will not be binding on a court after the commencement of the Act if it is shown to result in violation of a Convention right. Where the position is that the courts have construed legislation on a previous occasion in accordance with the Convention but Convention jurisprudence has since then itself moved on in accordance with the evolutive approach adopted by the Strasbourg Court, it is an open question whether the doctrine of precedent applies so that only a higher court may depart from a previously Convention-compliant interpretation.

Fourth, *Re S (Minors) (Care Order: Implementation of Care Plan)* makes it clear that Lord Hope's view has prevailed that, when a court is applying s 3, the court must identify the word or phrase which given its ordinary meaning is incompatible with the Convention and say how the word or phrase is to be construed if it is to be made compatible. To this extent, the process of statutory interpretation is the same as in any other case.

Fifth, there are, however, features of interpretation under s 3 which are inconsistent with statutory interpretation in other circumstances. As Lord Hope's discussion on various techniques shows, it may be necessary to write in words or give them a different meaning in order to ensure compatibility. Further, there is no need to identify any ambiguity or absurdity before applying s 3. The only touchstone is incompatibility. Moreover, s 3 applies even if the statute was passed before the Human Rights Act 1998. The courts are not, therefore, seeking the intention of Parliament when it enacted the statute in question. They are seeking to apply the will of Parliament as subsequently expressed.

There are all sorts of consequences of this new approach. One of the reasons given for requiring the identification of the precise wording of the enactment to be construed is that this is likely to achieve greater certainty. However, there is still a very large area of uncertainty. If a statute is incompatible with human rights, there may be a number of ways in which it could be construed in order to make it compatible. For example, in *R v A (No 2)* the majority applied s 3(1) by reading s 41 as subject to an implied provision that evidence or questioning required to ensure a fair trial under Art 6 of the Convention should not be treated as inadmissible. This is a very open-ended type of construction since it does not resolve the problem of what evidence or questioning would violate Art 6. Moreover, there is bound in any case to be a number of ways in which the court can resolve a question of incompatibility. For instance, in *R v Lambert*, the court could have held that s 28 required the prosecution to prove the negative in all circumstances.

The fact that there is a spectrum of ways of construing a provision which is incompatible in order to make it compatible introduces considerable uncertainty into the statute book. This is obviously undesirable because it means that more and more questions of construction have to be litigated in the courts.

The interpretative duty may also shatter long-held beliefs about statutory interpretation. One of the sacred cows of statutory interpretation is that a word must have the same meaning every time it is used. This is a great anchor for drafter and judge alike. But if an expression in a particular section has to be given a special meaning for Convention reasons, it does not necessarily follow that it should have the same meaning in the rest of the Act.

Before the decisions in *Re S (Minors) (Care Order: Implementation of Care Plan)*, *Anderson* and *Bellinger*, it seemed to me that the proper approach to s 3(1) was very unclear. The House of Lords has now provided considerable guidance. However, it is still true to say that the courts are feeling their way towards a set of rules and canons of construction that will apply where s 3(1) is in point. It is perhaps not surprising that those rules and canons of construction have not been developed already. They are bound to take many years to develop. Nevertheless, the process is still one of interpretation and the courts' traditional role in that respect has not been radically altered.

8

The Changing Judicial Role: Human Rights, Community Law, and the Intention of Parliament

This chapter is based on a paper delivered as the Annual Lecture of the Constitutional and Administrative Law Bar Association in November 2007 and subsequently published in the Cambridge Law Journal.*

Introduction

A member of the Bar who appeared before us recently said that he was an engineer by training, and that what he did when he was looking at a problem was to turn it by 90 degrees and examine it on a different plane. The aim of this paper is to discuss statute law and statutory interpretation and to use those subjects as a platform from which to draw some conclusions about the judicial role. I hope to do so from a new angle. My principal premise is that statutory interpretation is now capable of being analysed into two distinct models, which I call the 'Agency Model' and the 'Dynamic Model'. I will start with the Agency Model, and in the course of describing this model I will make a short detour into the rule of law. In principle, legislation should comply with the rule of law. Then I will turn to the Dynamic Model. This has only been developed over the last 35 years but it is distinct from the Agency Model. In the course of looking at the Dynamic Model, I will look at the extremely liberal approach to interpreting legislation under s 3 of the Human Rights Act 1998.[1] I will contrast this with the courts' more restricted approach to the question whether, having taken account of Strasbourg jurisprudence, they should ever go beyond it. I will call that the 'take account' point after s 2 of the Human Rights Act 1998 which provides that when determining any question in connection with a Convention right the court 'must take account of' Strasbourg

---

* The lecture was subsequently published in the Cambridge Law Journal, 2013 © Cambridge Law Journal. It is reproduced here with the kind permission of the Publisher.

[1] The Convention rights incorporated by the Human Rights Act 1998 and the principal provisions of that Act are set out in the Appendix.

jurisprudence. The development of the Dynamic Model is one of the factors which has led to a debate about whether judges now have too much power. When I come to my conclusions, I will draw attention to this debate and make three points in response. They will be about checks and balances, the 'take account' point and the sources which judges use when determining questions derived from a statute.

I should say at the outset that this paper represents my thinking at the present time. My thinking is not fixed and I might well take a different view if the matter was argued out in front of me. I would also make the general point that when I refer to 'the Convention' or 'Convention rights', I am of course referring to the European Convention on Human Rights and the rights guaranteed by that Convention.

The Agency Model

The general approach to statutory interpretation

Statutes are the means by which the legislature imposes its will on the citizen. Statutory interpretation therefore has constitutional implications. When the court decides a question of statutory interpretation, it is deciding how far the state can go in controlling some aspect of an individual's activities. Statute law is increasingly important in the United Kingdom because of the sheer volume of statute law enacted each year by Parliament and also by the devolved Parliaments of the United Kingdom, that is the Scottish Parliament, the Northern Ireland Assembly, and the Welsh Assembly. Some legislation is enacted to fulfil international obligations, such as the obligation to implement Community instruments, that is, legislative measures of various kinds adopted by the European Community and requiring implementation in the member states. Statutory interpretation is the prerogative of the courts, including tribunals, and the courts alone. We do not, for instance, have a principle such as exists in the United States of America whereby, in a case involving a challenge to executive action carried out on the basis of the executive's view as to the meaning of an ambiguous statute, the court does not ask whether the interpretation is correct, but simply whether the administrative agency's interpretation is a permissible one.[2] The principles of statutory interpretation are not codified. They are governed by the common law and are therefore capable of endogenous development by the courts to meet new technical problems or social needs. Since the principles of interpretation are governed by the common law, it might be thought that statutes mean what judges say they mean, rather than what Parliament may have intended. But that is not so: in general, the court's function is to ascertain the intention of Parliament and that is done from the language that Parliament has used. Thus we can say that the basic model for statutory interpretation is an 'Agency Model'. The essential feature of this model is that the judge sets out to interpret what is written in front of him, rather than to think about constitutional issues. In doing this he is fulfilling, as faithfully as he can, the will of the

---

[2] *Chevron v Natural Resources Defense Council* (1984) 467 US 837.

democratically elected Parliament. I should make it clear that the expression 'the intention of Parliament' is a term of art which refers to the intention of Parliament to be found (almost exclusively) in the legislative provision under consideration.

It follows naturally from the court's function in interpretation that judges cannot rewrite statutes. Moreover, they must always act within judicial constraints. But, in practice, there are situations where it is not clear what Parliament would have intended if it had thought about the situation that has emerged and presents itself in the case before the court. Parliament may have intended one thing, but the language which it has used may not bear that meaning. The court has to find the meaning of the statute from the language used and the indications given in the statute read as a whole. This means that it is possible that its interpretation will turn out not to have been what Parliament in fact intended. Since the role of the courts is to interpret legislation, and not to rewrite it, the courts cannot cure a gap in a legislative scheme. However, by careful interpretation they may be able to prevent the gap from arising in the first place.

In principle, the same method applies to all kinds of legislation, whatever the subject matter. In determining the intention of Parliament from the language used, the main rules that the court applies are that the statute must be read as a whole and that all the words must be given a meaning. There are other rules such as the limited class, or *eiusdem generis*, rule. Under this rule, where there are a number of specific terms followed by a general word, the general word is to be interpreted as limited to the same class of thing as the earlier specific terms. Some of the rules appear to contradict others, such as the rule that every word must be given a meaning, as opposed to the rule that permits the court to reject words in certain circumstances as surplusage. It could be said that the rules are simply a form of language—like a diplomatic language that the court is using to systematize the complex process of reasoning it is actually undertaking.

After a statute is passed, changes often occur, for example, changes in social conditions or technological developments. Exceptionally, a statute is limited to a state of affairs existing at a particular point in time, but more generally it is silent about its effect in changed circumstances. As already explained, the courts cannot fill gaps in legislation, and so they have to determine whether the existing statute applies to the changed state of affairs. The legislation may express a clear purpose that can only be fulfilled if it is applied to the new state of affairs. The House of Lords held that this was the case where the statute provided for a process of statutory licensing for in vitro fertilization of human embryos and a new method of creating embryos outside the human body was discovered.[3] In other cases, it may be that the legislation refers to a concept, which is sufficiently wide to embrace changes in circumstances. This is the case, for instance, in companies legislation, which requires company accounts to show 'a true and fair view'. The content of the concept of a true and fair view may change over the course of time but the concept itself is unaltered.

---

[3] *R (Quintavalle) v Health Secretary* [2003] UKHL 13, [2003] 2 AC 687.

In some jurisdictions, the courts, when interpreting a statute, can take into account what was said in Parliament when the Bill was considered. In England and Wales, the use of legislative history as an aid to the interpretation of the statute was not permitted prior to 1993. It can now be used as an aid to interpretation only if the statute is ambiguous and if a government minister, or other promoter of the Bill, made a statement in Parliament dealing clearly with the point of dispute.[4] This is a very limited exception to the general rule excluding legislative history. The court cannot, for example, use legislative history to show that a particular change in the law was considered and rejected in the course of pre-legislative scrutiny.

I want to make one last important point about statutory interpretation. Very few judges have ever written about statutory interpretation. Of course, there are books written by scholars in statute law, constitutional law, and legal philosophy but what the books do not tell you is this: that, in practice, when the court is interpreting a statutory provision, whether it is an important general provision or a highly technical piece of secondary legislation, it will often approach the matter by peeling away the layers of meaning and by analysing the policy choices that have been made to arrive at the form of words that has been used. In other words, statutory interpretation is an intensive exercise that involves *drilling down* into the substratum of meaning of the statutory provision. This is a point to which I wish to return later. It applies whether the judge is in agency mode or in the dynamic mode, which I have yet to describe.

I now want to make one or two points about statute law itself. Statutes are enacted on the basis that principles of the general law apply to supplement the statute unless Parliament has excluded them expressly or by implication. The principles in question may be principles of public law or of private law. For example, where a statute creates a public body and gives it powers, it will be presumed by the courts when they interpret the statute that the public body will, in the exercise of its powers, be subject to the supervisory jurisdiction of the courts on the principles of administrative law developed by the courts. These general principles of law do not need to be set out in the statute and in general it is better not to set them out. To set them out may throw doubt on their application in statutes where they are not set out, and developments in the case law may not apply. If the principles set out in the statute go beyond the principles permitted by the courts, a citizen may unintentionally obtain additional remedies over and above those to which the citizen would be entitled in similar situations under public law. Of course, where a statute extends not just to our own jurisdiction but to jurisdictions of other parts of the United Kingdom, the principle that statutes are enacted on the basis that the principles of the general law apply means that the statute may have a different effect in another part of the United Kingdom.

---

[4] *Pepper v Hart* [1993] AC 593.

The rule of law

The most important of the general principles of law is undoubtedly the rule of law itself. I am going to take this opportunity to say a little about the rule of law and what that concept means. The rule of law is absolutely fundamental, and in principle all statute law should comply with the rule of law. When the Constitutional Reform Act 2005 reformed the office of Lord Chancellor, it was thought desirable to state that the reforms to his office did not affect his function to uphold the rule of law. Accordingly, s 1 of that Act provides:

This Act does not adversely affect—
(a) the existing constitutional principle of the rule of law, or
(b) the Lord Chancellor's existing constitutional role in relation to that principle.

The rule of law has never been comprehensively defined. It is like a tree that is perpetually developing and has many branches. The fundamental principle of the rule of law is that there is a state of affairs in which law rules and in which people are equally subjected to the law. The branches of the rule of law include access to justice, the principle of limited government, the principle of separation of powers, the principle that the law must achieve a certain quality, and the principle that the law must guarantee certain basic rights. The Senior Law Lord of the United Kingdom, Lord Bingham of Cornhill, has set out a number of the features of the rule of law in a paper now published in the *Cambridge Law Journal*,[5] and it is well worth reading in full. He said that the core of the existing principle of the rule of law is that all persons and authorities within the state, whether public or private, should be bound by, and entitled to the benefit of, laws publicly and prospectively promulgated and publicly administered in the courts. He said that it was important to understand the implications of the rule of law, and he conveniently broke these down into eight sub-rules, which he stated he did not intend to be exclusive. Those sub-rules were that:

(1) the law must be accessible, and so far as possible intelligible, clear and practicable;

(2) questions of legal right and liability should ordinarily be resolved by the application of the law, not by the exercise of discretion;

(3) the laws of the land should apply equally to all save to the extent that objective differences justified differentiation;

(4) the law must afford adequate protection of fundamental human rights;

(5) means must be provided for resolving without prohibitive cost or inordinate delay bona fide disputes which the courts themselves are able to resolve;

(6) ministers and public officers at all levels must exercise the powers conferred on them reasonably, in good faith, for the purposes for which the powers were conferred and without exceeding the limits of such powers;

---

[5] [2007] CLJ 67.

(7) adjudicative procedures provided by the state should be fair; and

(8) the existing principle of the rule of law requires compliance by the state with its obligations in international law.

Very many scholars have also written about the rule of law. One of the most relevant for the purposes of this paper is Professor Lon Fuller from Harvard. In his book, *The Morality of Law*,[6] Professor Fuller created a character called King Rex, who attempted to legislate for his kingdom. Professor Fuller concluded that an attempt to create a legal system might miscarry in at least one of eight ways. Indeed, he went on to conclude (although this conclusion is not necessary to my argument) that a total failure in any one of eight ways that he identified would result in something that could not properly be called a legal system at all 'except perhaps in the Pickwickian sense in which a void contract can still be said to be one kind of contract'. The eight elements of law, which according to Professor Fuller are necessary for a society aspiring to institute the rule of law, are as follows:

(1) Laws must exist and be obeyed by all, including government officials.

(2) Laws must be published.

(3) Laws must be prospective in nature, so that the effect of the law may only take place after the law has been passed. For example, the court cannot convict a person of a crime committed before a criminal statute prohibiting the conduct was passed.

(4) Laws should be written with reasonable clarity to avoid unfair enforcement.

(5) Laws must avoid contradictions.

(6) Laws must not command the impossible.

(7) Law must stay constant throughout time to allow the formalization of the rules.

(8) Official action should be consistent with the declared rule.

Elements (4), (5), and (6) can be applied directly to statute law. For instance, statute law should generally be prospective in nature, avoid contradictions, and not command the impossible. Professor Fuller's rules may occasionally have practical implications for the work of the courts. I would like to give the example of a case in which I sat called *FP (Iran) v SSHD*.[7] This case concerned the power of the Lord Chancellor to make rules for asylum appeals. The statutory power provided that, in making these rules, the Lord Chancellor should 'aim to secure . . . that the rules are designed to ensure the proceedings before the tribunal are handled as fairly, quickly and efficiently as possible . . . '. The power also enabled the Lord Chancellor to make a rule requiring a tribunal to hear an appeal in the absence of the parties.

Under this power, the Lord Chancellor made a rule requiring the tribunal to hear an appeal in the absence of a party or his representative if it was satisfied that the

---

[6] Lon L Fuller, *The Morality of the Law* (Yale University Press, 1964).
[7] [2007] EWCA Civ 13.

party or his representative had been given notice of the date, time, and place of the hearing and had given no satisfactory explanation for his absence. This rule was in contrast to the rule which applies in normal civil proceedings,[8] which enables the court to proceed to a trial in the absence of a party, but provides that that party may apply for the judgment to be set aside. The court may grant that application if the applicant acted promptly, has a good reason for not attending the trial, and has a real prospect of success at trial. There was no equivalent in the asylum rules. If the appellant did not receive notice of the appeal hearing, he would be unable to give any explanation for his absence and thus could never satisfy the requirement that he should provide a satisfactory explanation for his absence, even though the rule had purported to give them that opportunity. The tribunal would have to hear and determine his appeal in his absence even if he was able subsequently to produce a good explanation for his absence. An appellant might be able to prove that he had a satisfactory explanation for his absence because, for example, he had had an accident and been in hospital when the notice was sent and had not seen it until it was too late. In the cases before us, the parties had failed to appear because they did not receive any notice of the appeal hearing. They had changed their addresses and asked their solicitors to give notice of change of address to the tribunal, which those solicitors had failed to do.

The Secretary of State argued that the appellants' remedy was to apply for judicial review of the tribunal's decision. However, judicial review is not available where there is a mistake of fact which is the responsibility of the party applying for judicial review or his legal representatives, or if the mistake involves disputed questions of fact.

In the circumstances, the relevant rule removed the right of a party to provide a satisfactory explanation for his absence by providing that the tribunal must proceed in his absence, even if he did not know he had to put forward such an explanation. I held that the situation in which a party was given a right and it was then taken away before he had a chance to exercise it did not fulfil the basic requirements of the rule of law as identified by Professor Fuller. The rule was accordingly held to be *ultra vires* the Lord Chancellor's rule-making power. The Lord Chancellor accepted the court's decision and altered the rules.

But the important point to note about *FP (Iran)* is the scope of the rule-making power. The rule had to be fair. There is no such general rule applying to Acts of Parliament. It would be wrong to suppose that a statute has never been passed which offends the rule of law as described by Lord Bingham or Professor Fuller. For example s 33 of the Taxes Management Act 1970 provides that a person's right to recover a payment of tax made under a mistake due to an error in a return is to a payment at the discretion of the Inland Revenue in certain limited circumstances. This may offend the second sub-rule enunciated by Lord Bingham but no-one has ever suggested that it is not on that account a valid and binding law.

---

[8] Civil Procedure Rule 39.3.

The Dynamic Model

Introduction

I now turn to the Dynamic Model, and I start by referring to the relationship between statutes and obligations in international law. International treaties are not enforceable in our domestic law unless they are approved by Parliament. But, where an international treaty is adopted into English law, an important statutory presumption arises, which is the springboard for a more dynamic approach to statutory interpretation than the Agency Model, which I have hitherto discussed. It is presumed by the courts that, where Parliament has made an international treaty part of our domestic law, then, when it enacts subsequent legislation, it intends that legislation to comply with its international obligations. This is now of crucial importance in relation to Community law and human rights. I am going to start by considering the interpretation of legislation when human rights are said to be involved.

The Dynamic Model in relation to legislation when human rights are said to be involved

The legislative framework for the court's interpretative duty in the context of human rights is contained in s 3 of the Human Rights Act 1998. This imposes a specific mandatory obligation on the courts to interpret legislation 'so far as it is possible to do so' in conformity with the Convention rights. This approach is built on the presumption that domestic law must be interpreted in accordance with international treaty obligations adopted by Parliament. Accordingly, s 3(1) of the Human Rights Act 1998 provides:

So far as it is possible to do so, primary legislation and subordinate legislation must be read and given effect in a way which is compatible with Convention rights.

The courts have been given powers to make declarations of incompatibility in respect of legislation which cannot be interpreted so as to be compatible with Convention rights. But any such declaration does not affect the result in the particular proceedings or constitute any precedent on which other parties can rely. It simply acts as a signal to Parliament and also to the government that it should consider introducing some measure to amend the enactment in question. The scheme of the Human Rights Act 1998 was intended to preserve Parliamentary sovereignty in that regard.

What does the interpretative duty mean in practice? Significantly, in relation to the interpretation of legislation under the Human Rights Act 1998, we move from an Agency Model to the 'Dynamic Model'. The judge is not simply looking at the wording and trying to apply it. He is looking at the wording critically. He is considering whether it complies with the Convention. This approach works on the basis that what Parliament intended was that statutes should have the effect of operating in conformity with human rights unless the contrary conclusion could not be achieved as a matter of interpretation. But, in truth, it is no longer a matter of looking at Parliamentary intention. This is highlighted by the fact that the new approach applies to legislation whenever passed. At the highest level of generality, the court is acting as the guardian of human rights and constitutional rights. Its role is a dynamic one, and hence I call the model in this context the Dynamic Model.

Just how dynamic is this model? After a little trial and error on the part of the House of Lords, if I may respectfully say so, there was an important case called *Ghaidan v Godin-Mendoza*.[9] This case concerned the question whether statutory rights of succession in respect of a tenancy were transmitted to a person who lived with a deceased original tenant of the same sex. The relevant condition in the statute was that the person should have lived with the deceased original tenant 'as his or her wife or husband'. If the legislation did not benefit same sex couples, it would discriminate against them in violation of Art 14 of the Convention read with Art 8 of the Convention.[10] The House of Lords held that the statute in question applied to the survivor of a same-sex relationship as much as it did to a surviving spouse. The court gave important guidance as to the limits of s 3 of the Human Rights Act 1998. I will merely refer to the speech of Lord Nicholls.

Lord Nicholls held that the effect of s 3 was that the court might be required to depart from the unambiguous meaning of the statute. The difficult question was how far the court should go. He held that the answer to this question did not depend upon the actual wording used by Parliament. He continued:

32 From this the conclusion which seems inescapable is that the mere fact the language under consideration is inconsistent with a Convention-compliant meaning does not of itself make a Convention-compliant interpretation under section 3 impossible. Section 3 enables the language to be interpreted restrictively or expansively, but section 3 goes further than this. It is also apt to require a court to read in words which change the meaning of the enacted legislation, so as to make it Convention-compliant. In other words, the intention of Parliament in enacting section 3 was that, to an extent bounded only by what is 'possible', a court can modify the meaning, and hence the effect, of primary and secondary legislation.

33 Parliament, however, cannot have intended that in the discharge of this extended interpretative function the court should adopt a meaning inconsistent with a fundamental feature of legislation. That would be to cross the constitutional boundary that s 3 seeks to demarcate and preserve. Parliament has retained the right to enact legislation in terms which are not Convention-compliant. The meaning imported by application of s 3 must be compatible with the underlying thrust of the legislation being construed. Words implied must, in the phrase of my noble and learned friend, Lord Rodger of Earlsferry, 'go with the grain of the legislation'. Nor can Parliament have intended that s 3 should require courts to make decisions for which they are not equipped. There may be several ways of making a

---

[9] [2004] UKHL 30, [2004] 2 AC 557.   [10] See the Appendix to this Volume.

provision Convention-compliant, and the choice may involve issues calling for legislative deliberation.[11]

Ghaidan is a powerful statement of the courts' preparedness to interpret legislation so that it is compatible with human rights. It is very far from being aimed at the interpretation of legislation as a reflection of what Parliament must have intended. Francis Bennion says that the Human Rights Act 1998 has revolutionized our constitution. He is right in that. It also revolutionized statutory interpretation where there is a challenge on human rights grounds. Human rights challenges are significant, and so the exception made by the Human Rights Act is a significant one.

Where a question arises as to compatibility with the Convention, therefore, the courts do not have to seek the intention of Parliament in the particular text. The courts must adopt what is sometimes called a 'strained construction' in order to achieve compatibility with the Convention. I do not consider that future generations will necessarily regard this sort of interpretation as 'strained'. Rather, they will see it as an illustration of a more dynamic approach or the Dynamic Model. The court in this context is no longer an agent simply for the purpose of ascertaining Parliamentary intention. The court has at the highest level of abstraction an independent role as guardian of the rule of law and human rights. The interpretative obligation is a very extensive one and the test of 'going with the grain of the legislation' takes little account of the fact that in reaching its Convention-compliant interpretation of the legislation the court may have in effect to make a selection from a number of possible ways in which the legislation could have been drafted on a Convention-compliant basis.

When there is an issue as to compatibility with the Convention, the question may arise whether the legislative act is necessary in a democratic society or serves a legitimate aim. Article 8 of the Convention, for instance, provides that there can be interference by public authorities with the private or family life of an individual if that is necessary in a democratic society, proportionate, and in accordance with the law.

In respect of these questions, the judiciary is required to decide some novel and profound questions of moral and political significance. The decisions of the higher courts may have substantial societal and political implications. What is there to assist them? In the United States, there are two schools of thought. Some believe that judges should apply the view of the constitution which would have been adopted by those who ratified the constitution in the eighteenth century. But why are the views of the original founders of the Constitution superior? Their view of, say, equality may be quite different from the view that might be generally accepted in the twenty-first century. The opposing point of view is that the judges should reach their own decision as of the date of their decision on what the Constitution requires. Questions of interpretation can only be decided in the context and culture in which they arise. However, this approach is open to the objection that it can

---

[11] [2004] UKHL 30, [2004] 2 AC 557, [32]–[33].

confer too much power on the judges. People who favour this approach sometimes go further and say that, because Parliament is so busy and unable to deal with matters of detailed law reform, it should be for the judges to update laws when they need to be updated. But this runs even deeper into the objection that it would confer much too much power on judges.

The American debate does not apply as such in our jurisdiction. But we still have to ask ourselves where we should seek to find the answers to the difficult questions posed by the qualified Convention rights. Is public opinion relevant? It may be divided or not fully informed. It can be said that even recognition of relative institutional competence—that is, a decision that the executive or Parliament is better able to form a view on a particular matter—constitutes a form of moral or political judgment by judges and so in that situation the courts should exercise restraint. The question has to be asked: what is there to assist the judges, when travelling into apparently uncharted territory in cases involving the application of qualified rights, apart from (to the extent available) analogical reasoning from the common law and sound moral and political reasoning? I shall attempt a partial answer to that question when I come to my conclusions.

Before leaving the Convention, I want to talk about the 'take account' point. It is now established in English law that, save in special cases, the duty of national courts is 'to keep pace with Strasbourg jurisprudence as it evolves over time: no more but certainly no less' (per Lord Bingham in *R (Ullah) v Special Adjudicator*).[12] This is in one sense consistent with the function of the Strasbourg Court as the organ for authoritative interpretation of the Convention. But it does not acknowledge that the Strasbourg Court is only laying down minimum guarantees. Moreover, Art 53 of the Convention itself recognizes that citizens of the contracting states may have more far-reaching rights. Again, *Ullah*, on the face of it, sits uneasily with the duty which s 2 of our Human Rights Act 1998 imposes on courts: when 'determining a question which has arisen in connection with a Convention right', to 'take account' of Strasbourg jurisprudence, rather than to follow it. From that it might appear that it was intended that the courts should be free in an appropriate case to go further than Strasbourg case law or even (though this would have to be an exceptional case) not as far as Strasbourg case law.

The result of the 'take account' point is that the courts take a restrictive approach to the question of when to depart from Strasbourg jurisprudence. We can contrast this approach with the expansive view taken of s 3 of the Human Rights Act 1998. It is true to say that the question of what the Convention requires could well be a more difficult question than how to interpret a domestic statute, but it does not follow from this that the decision whether or not to use s 3 does not also involve substantial policy questions of the kind normally reserved to the legislature. It is therefore arguably paradoxical that the courts have not taken a more restrictive approach to s 3 as well.

---

[12] [2004] UKHL 26, [2004] 2 AC 323, 350.

The Dynamic Model and the interpretation of directive-based legislation

I now want to turn to Community law. At the time of the passing of the European Communities Act 1972, there was a fork in the road. The judges could have gone down the route marked 'Diceyan Parliamentary Sovereignty' and held that, if Parliament failed to legislate in accordance with Community law, Parliament must have intended to derogate to that extent from the Treaty of Rome. But that did not happen. The courts took the other route marked 'Community Law—Compliant Interpretation', and interpreted legislation, so far as they could, so that it was compatible with Community law. The traditional doctrine of Parliamentary sovereignty took on a new meaning. Parliament must have approved of the courts' approach because, as we have seen, it copied it when it enacted the Human Rights Act 1998. But the two forms of compatible interpretation are not identical. In the context of Community law, there is a fixed reference point, namely the law as laid down by the European Court of Justice (the 'Luxembourg Court'), whereas the Strasbourg Court only lays down minimum guarantees.

European Union legislation is much less exact than our own domestic law. Bismarck said: 'Laws are like sausages, it is better not to see them being made.' I sometimes think that he must have had Community legislation in mind. Community legislation frequently represents a compromise between the different member states, and leaves matters to be resolved by the courts. It is also drafted with less precision than we are accustomed to in the United Kingdom. The interpretation of Community legislation presents particular difficulties for any national judge, because it involves balancing more interests than are generally required to be balanced in a domestic situation.

When the court has to find the meaning of legislation designed to implement Community legislation, it has to consider the problem at two levels: first, the meaning of the underlying Community legislation, and, second, the meaning of the domestic legislation.

As to the interpretation of domestic legislation, the principle in England and Wales is that the court must interpret the domestic legislation so far as possible in conformity with Community law. The leading authority is *Litster v Forth Dry Dock & Engineering Co Ltd*[13] The *Litster* case involved the Acquired Rights Directive.[14] This directive is designed to safeguard the rights of employees when their employer's undertaking is transferred to another company. The persons protected by the United Kingdom implementing legislation were persons who were 'employed immediately before the transfer'. The employer in question became insolvent and had entered receivership. The issue was whether this wording quoted above covered employees who were dismissed by receivers one hour before the transfer.

---

[13] [1990] 1 AC 546.
[14] Council Directive 77/187/EEC of 14 February 1977 on the approximation of the laws of the member states relating to the safeguarding of employees' rights in the event of transfers of undertakings, businesses or parts of businesses.

The House of Lords held that, to give effect to the underlying directive as interpreted by the Court of Justice, there had to be read into the words 'a person so employed immediately before the transfer' the words 'or who would have been so employed if he had not been unfairly dismissed in the circumstances described in regulation 8(1)'. In other words, the House of Lords made a significant change to the wording of the legislation by adding words that were not there. This is not possible in statutory interpretation under purely domestic law. If the courts took the same approach to a purely domestic statute, it would probably be regarded as impermissible judicial legislation.

As regards the interpretation of the underlying Community legislation, the Court of Justice held in *Pfeiffer v Deutsches Rotes Kreuz*:[15]

118. In this instance, the principle of interpretation in conformity with Community law thus requires the referring court to do whatever lies within its jurisdiction, having regard to the whole body of rules of national law, to ensure that Directive 93/104 is fully effective, in order to prevent the maximum weekly working time laid down in Article 6(2) of the directive from being exceeded (see, to that effect, *Marleasing*, paragraphs 7 and 13).

In *Revenue and Customs Commissioners v IDT Card Services Ireland Ltd*,[16] it was contended that the distributors of phone cards in the United Kingdom were not liable to VAT on phone cards issued by an Irish company and redeemed by an associated Irish company. The supply of telecommunications services is liable to VAT under Community law but it was sought to take advantage of a difference in the rules between the United Kingdom and Ireland. The United Kingdom imposed VAT on the supply of telecommunications services to the end user and exempted distributors of phone cards unless the supplier who was liable to pay VAT failed to do so, whereas Ireland imposed VAT on the supply of the phone card to the end user. In these circumstances, the exemption, on the face of it, applied because the Irish company supplying telecommunications services could not be said to have failed to pay VAT which it was not liable to pay.

The Court of Appeal held that there was a general principle in the Sixth VAT Directive against the avoidance of non-taxation and that the United Kingdom exemption did not apply where the principle of the avoidance of non-taxation would be violated. The Court of Appeal held that the relevant test was that in *Ghaidan v Godin-Mendoza*, namely, whether the interpretation that would be required to make the statute in question compliant with Community law would involve a departure from a fundamental feature of the legislation or go against the grain of the legislation. The court recognized that that decision concerned interpretation under s 3 of the Human Rights Act 1998 but held that the differences were immaterial and applied the same principle to the interpretation of directive-based legislation.

---

[15] Cases C-397/01 to C-403/01 [2004] ECR I-8835.
[16] [2006] EWCA Civ 29, [2006] STC 1252. Permission to appeal to the House of Lords was refused.

The taxpayer contended that the interpretation in accordance with *Ghaidan* would offend the Community law principle of legal certainty. The Court accepted that the person affected by legislation must be able to foresee the manner in which it is to be applied and that that must particularly be so where the legislation has financial consequences for him such as flow from the imposition of the requirement to account for VAT. Moreover, a taxpayer was entitled to structure his business so as to limit his liability to tax and to take advantage of any loopholes that he could find. However, the Court of Appeal held that it was well-known that the provisions of the implementing legislation had to be interpreted in conformity with the Sixth Directive and that the supply of telecommunications services constituted a taxable supply for the purposes of the Sixth Directive. Therefore the principle of legal certainty was not infringed. Nor was it an objection to the application of the *Marleasing* principle that it might result in the imposition of a civil liability where such a liability would not otherwise have been imposed under domestic law. The court referred to *Centrosteel Srl v Adipol GmbH*[17] where the effect of interpreting Italian law in accordance with the directive on commercial agents was that a contract made by an agent who was not registered in accordance with the purely domestic provisions of Italian law was enforceable and not void.

Is the approach to statutory interpretation different in relation to devolution questions?

In the last decade there has been a transfer of legislative power by the Westminster government to the Scottish Parliament, the Northern Ireland Assembly, and the Welsh Assembly. The devolved powers are different in the case of Wales but that difference is not material for the purposes of this paper. The devolution dimension is a whole new area of statute law, calling for appropriate statutory interpretation.

The devolution arrangements in the United Kingdom do not constitute a fully federal system. As I explained in *R (Horvath) v Secretary of State*:[18]

The United Kingdom devolution arrangements lack some of the characteristics of a federal system. The Westminster Parliament has not given up its sovereignty over the devolved administrations and that means that in theory, subject to constitutional conventions, it could restrict or revoke the powers that it has given to the devolved administrations. Furthermore, there is no provision for judicial review of legislation passed by the Westminster Parliament on the grounds that it deals with devolved matters. The only qualification to that principle is if the court decides that the legislation of the Westminster Parliament violates Community law. If any such question arises, the courts of any part of the United Kingdom can refer a question to the Court of Justice for a preliminary ruling. In addition, there is no separate legislative body for England as opposed to Wales, Scotland or Northern Ireland. The judicial systems for England and Wales are not separate. There is no dual system of courts in any part of the United Kingdom. Moreover, the United Kingdom ministers have, as I have described, a reserve power with respect to the implementation of Community law.

---

[17] C-456/98 [2000] ECR 1-6007.   [18] [2007] EWCA Civ 620.

So the devolved assemblies are not independent sovereign parliaments, and they must act within powers conferred. The United Kingdom has no assembly of representatives of the devolved bodies. Relations with the Community are not devolved matters but in some cases the devolved assemblies can implement Community directives. In the *Horvath* case, a directive had been implemented by the devolved jurisdictions in different ways. There was a challenge to the English regulations on the grounds that the differential implementation of a Community measure for different parts of the United Kingdom violated the principle of non-discrimination in the EC Treaty. The Court of Appeal refused to set aside a reference to the Court of Justice for a preliminary ruling on this question. The EC Treaty binds the member state. The Strasbourg Court has applied the same principle and held that the Convention binds the contracting states to the Convention and they are responsible for actions of autonomous regions within the contracting state.[19] Accordingly, it has to be seen if the European Court of Justice will distinguish the situation where a unitary member state violates its obligations under the EC Treaty by implementing a directive in a way which discriminates unjustifiably between those affected, from the situation in *Horvath*, where the differentiation resulted from the internal constitutional arrangements of the United Kingdom.

The legislation enacting the devolution arrangements specifies the powers reserved to the Westminster Parliament. Hitherto, there has been no real dispute about those powers or the dispute had been resolved by some practical solution, such as legislative competence motions within the devolved Parliaments. But, with the recent changes in the political composition of the devolved Parliaments, disputes may start to occur which require the intervention of the courts.

The function of the courts deciding those issues may then be similar to that of the European Court of Justice when it considers whether a directive prevents a member state from enacting its own legislation on a particular subject. In those cases, the Court of Justice appears to have proceeded on the basis of looking not simply at the directive in question, but also at the wider objectives of the European Union. Indeed, it could be said that its approach has often been centralizing, with a nod in the direction of subsidiarity. Its function would seem to involve a special balancing of the interests of the member states and those of the Community and its institutions. This area could lead to further developments in the field of statutory interpretation. There is comparative material in the United States, Canada, India, South Africa, and Germany to draw on.

Conclusions

Recapitulation of the Agency and Dynamic Models

The principal approach used by the courts in England and Wales is one where the judge seeks to find the intention of Parliament as expressed in the language

---

[19] *Assanidze v Georgia* (Application No 71503/01), 8 April 2004.

Parliament has used. I have called this the Agency Model. Here the judge applies important presumptions, including the presumption that Parliament intended to fulfil its international obligations adopted into English domestic law. But this model is not the complete picture. The Agency Model imposes a different discipline from that imposed by the direction in the Human Rights Act 1998 that judges should interpret legislation, whenever passed, so far as possible in conformity with Convention rights. I have suggested that future generations will not regard this type of interpretation, that is, Convention-compliant interpretation, as a 'strained interpretation', as it is sometimes described. They will recognize that the basis in this context is that the judge is no longer an agent of ascertaining Parliamentary intention and that his function is as guardian of constitutional norms, including human rights. This model I have therefore called the Dynamic Model. The Dynamic Model is also applicable to the interpretation of domestic statutes, which have to be given a dynamic interpretation in order to make them compatible with Community law.

Drawing the threads together

The Dynamic Model leads naturally to arguments about changes in the judicial role and about whether judges now have too much power. This was the theme of the Justice 2007 Tom Sargant lecture given by Professor Conor Gearty. The provocative title of the lecture was 'Are judges now out of their depth?' He skilfully conjured up the graphic picture of judges, stripped down to their swimwear, in the deep end of a swimming pool, physically challenged and perhaps overwhelmed. He advanced three propositions. His first proposition was that, although judges are not yet out of their depth, they must be on constant guard against becoming so. Indeed, he thought that the guard of some had been dropping of late. His second proposition was that, if judges do find themselves out of their depth, they must on no account swim. They should move back to the shallow end, where they belong. Professor Gearty's third proposition was that it was essential for the integrity of the judicial function to clarify the judicial role along these lines. While he did not favour judges being too cautious, the 'deep end', as he colourfully called it, was for elected representatives and not the judges. With respect to Professor Gearty, it is difficult to avoid circularity here, because 'the deep end' is often defined as that which is outside the competence of the judiciary.

Interestingly, a similar debate has been taking place in Germany. The traditional view of the relationship between the legislature and the judiciary was that of master and servant. The then President of the Federal Supreme Court of Germany, Professor Dr Hirsch, in a journal article,[20] in which he referred (among other things) to the Europeanization of German domestic law, questioned whether this analogy was correct today. The judges breathe life into the dead letter of the written law. They help legislation to become what it should be. The President expressed a preference for the analogy of the pianist and composer rather than that of servant

---

[20] 'Auf dem Weg zum Richterstaat?' (2007) 62 *Juristen Zeitung* 854–8.

and master. The legislator is the composer. The judge is the pianist interpreting the binding requirements of the legislator. The judge has discretion in doing so but he must not falsify the piece. What more could a European or national legislator want than to have his laws interpreted by a judge with the same skill as that with which Horowitz or Rubinstein interpreted Chopin? But this article led to a protest. One critic said: 'In a country in which one judge might be Horowitz and another Rubinstein, judges pose a threat to freedom.' One must not carry this analogy with German law too far, because German judges have more discretion in statutory interpretation than English judges in some respects, and the analogy of the pianist could be read as suggesting that there is some latitude for the proclivity of the individual. The law is far greater than any individual judge. The law is not the fiefdom of any individual judge to develop as he wants. Even so, the debate in Germany is not without interest. It echoes the distinction I have drawn between the Agency Model and the Dynamic Model.

This debate about the proper role of the judiciary in a modern democracy raises deep political and philosophical questions. The answers to these questions cannot be summed up in a few words. But there are three points that I would make by way of a conclusion to this paper. First, co-incident with what is seen as a shift in power to the judiciary, there has been a spontaneous growth of checks and balances. The public has become more involved in various ways in the work of the courts. There has been an exponential growth in institutions involving the community in the organization of the justice system. For example, there are numerous user committees and justice councils, such as the Civil Justice Council, the Family Justice Council, and the Criminal Justice Council. There is also the Sentencing Guidelines Council. In these ways the public has much greater involvement in the administration of justice than they have had in the past. This is bound inevitably to have an effect on judges. There is bound over time to be a greater sense of connectedness between the courts and judges and the communities that they serve. The law used to be administered on the basis of a top-down process. Now it is more of a bottom-up process. Added to that, there have been changes in the way judges act. They have reduced the use of legal Latin, which many people find off-putting, and the judges are about to abandon their wigs in civil cases. There is a new system of judicial appointments, with substantial lay membership, and a new system of judicial complaints and discipline. Both new systems have a statutory basis. So, there has, to some extent, been a spontaneous growth of checks and balances.

My second point relates to the 'take account' point. The self-denying ordinance in *Ullah* is that, save in special cases, the courts should go as far as Strasbourg jurisprudence but no further. There are technical grounds for criticizing that holding. The reason given by the House of Lords in the *Ullah* case was that the Strasbourg Court was empowered to give authoritative pronouncements on the Convention. But this gives little weight to the point that the Strasbourg Court is merely laying down minimum guarantees. Moreover, the Convention specifically authorizes contracting states to give further rights if they wish. Also, it seems paradoxical to have the self-denying ordinance when the courts have taken such extensive powers under s 3 of the Human Rights Act 1998. In its favour, it can be said that the self-denying ordinance has the advantage of relieving courts of the need to look, save on rare occasions, at the way constitutional courts in other parts of the world have developed constitutional rights. Those courts are deciding constitutional rights for their own societies and therefore it may not be appropriate to transplant them to our own jurisdiction. Moreover, it is often said that the implementation of the Human Rights Act 1998 has not led to a constitutional crisis. This must be due in part to the restrained approach which the judges have taken to developing human rights jurisprudence.

But the 'take account' point illustrates another point, which I want to make. It reflects, and speaks volumes about, the relationship between the judiciary and Parliament. There is an unwritten principle of judicial restraint. There is respect for the will of Parliament, and an exercise of judgment by the judges as to when to concretize that respect by leaving a particular decision to another organ of the constitution. The 'take account' point may mean that, if the United Kingdom wants to go further than Strasbourg, Parliament will have to enact a domestic Bill of Rights. That will be a matter for politicians. It could, of course, give additional rights, for instance in the area of freedom of speech or housing. A domestic Bill of Rights would require a great deal of thought by judges and it might lead to yet further developments in statutory interpretation.

The third and final point I want to make is this. Statutory interpretation is an important area because every exercise in statutory interpretation involves, to a greater or lesser degree, a working out of the constitutional relationship between the legislature and the individual. Community law and human rights have caused the judges to develop new techniques of statutory interpretation over the last thirty-five years. Many issues which formerly did not come before the courts are now doing so, for example (to take a recent example of my own) the question of whether it would be a violation of the Convention right to freedom of thought, conscience, and religion to hold that a minister of religion was an employee of a church if such a relationship were contrary to the religious beliefs of the church in question. Not infrequently, though, I accept, not always, issues of human rights and Community law involve questions of statute law. Sometimes it is a question of statutory interpretation; sometimes it is a question of working out the proper scope of a statutory discretion. When the court is dealing with any question of interpretation, it digs deep into the statutory language, peeling away the different layers of thinking and working out the various policy choices that Parliament must have made to make the provision that it did in fact make. Even if the court comes to the conclusion that the Dynamic Model requires it to adopt its own conforming interpretation, that is, an interpretation which is not the natural interpretation but which is required to make the provision compatible with Convention rights or Community law, it may well find in the deeper layers of the legislation a seam of material to assist it. Indeed, it may discover that there is a range of policy choices and that it should be cautious about using the interpretative obligation in s 3 of the Human Rights Act 1998. Intensive statutory interpretation of this kind does not always provide the answer to a problem, but it may provide significant guidance in some cases. That is something that we should all remember.

9

Statutory Interpretation and Human Rights

This chapter is based on a paper presented to the Commonwealth Association of Legislative Counsel, London in September 2005.*

In this paper, I will concentrate my remarks on the statutory interpretation of human or constitutional rights. I do not simply mean the interpretation of statutes which legislate for human rights. I also mean those situations where it is said that a statute dealing with some other subject matter violates a constitutional or human right.

For a judge to address this subject might be said to be like looking down the wrong end of a microscope and seeing the clinician or microbiologist or whoever is using the telescope. But that metaphor must not be taken too far. Specimens seen under a microscope are usually put on a slide and extracted from all other matter. In statutory interpretation words have to be examined in their context. To find the meaning of even such simple words as 'the cat sat on the mat' requires some basic common understanding of the laws of gravity.

The determination of a question of statutory interpretation is in general an exercise in attributing a meaning where it is not obvious and has become a source of dispute between two or more parties. (I should explain that in the United Kingdom we do not have any system whereby the courts can give purely advisory opinions.) Speaking entirely for myself, I would be very cautious about describing the task for the judge as one of ascertaining the intention of Parliament, since I am not clear whose intention I would then be seeking or where I would find it if not in the words used. The evidence that is available to the judge is not in general that of the intention of Parliament but that of the government or the promoters of the Bill or of law reform agencies, and it does not follow that the intention of Parliament was their intention at all.

What then is the role of judges? Is their task the purely mechanical task of reading the words legislative counsel have drafted and Parliament has passed? The answer to that question is no, for many reasons. I could, of course, devote all my time to discussing that question. However, there is so much else that I want to cover so it is sufficient to quote what is said about the role of judges in the

* *Statutory interpretation and human rights* published in part by 'THE LOOPHOLE', the Journal of the Commonwealth Association of Legislative Counsel.

Commonwealth Principles on the Accountability of and the Relationship between the Three Branches of Government.

These Principles were agreed by the Law Ministers of the Commonwealth and endorsed by the Commonwealth Heads of Government Meeting in Abuja, Nigeria, in December 2003. These Principles state:

Independence of the Judiciary

An honest, impartial and competent judiciary is integral to upholding the rule of law, engendering public confidence and dispensing justice. The function of the judiciary is to interpret and apply national constitutions and legislation, consistent with international human rights conventions and international law, to the extent permitted by the domestic law of each Commonwealth country...

(c) *Judicial Review*

Best democratic principles require that the actions of government are open to scrutiny by the courts, to ensure that decisions taken comply with the Constitution, with relevant statutes and other law, including the law relating to the principles of natural justice.[1]

So the time when judges come into contact with human rights and statute law together is when they are being asked to interpret a constitutional provision or human right or when they are being asked to decide whether some other statute actually violates those rights.

Diversity of constitutional and human rights

The wide variety of constitutional systems and the wide variety of human or constitutional rights should be kept in mind. I am not familiar with by any means all of the Commonwealth systems but it is sufficient to give some examples.

Our human rights in the United Kingdom are those set out in the European Convention on Human Rights (the 'Convention').[2] These include: the right to life, the right to liberty and security, the right to a fair trial, the right to respect for home and private life, the right to freedom of thought, the right to freedom of expression, and so on. By and large, the Convention contains no socio-economic rights. There is moreover no self-standing right to equality in the Convention. There is, however, a right to freedom from discrimination on any ground in the enjoyment of Convention rights.

By contrast, in South Africa, the constitution confers socio-economic rights, such as the right of access to healthcare facilities or to adequate housing. These are sometimes expressed in a qualified form so to impose only an obligation to take reasonable legislative or other measures within available resources to achieve the

---

[1] *Commonwealth Principles on the Accountability of and the Relationship between the Three Branches of Government*, known as 'the 'Latimer House principles', published by the Commonwealth Secretariat and other Commonwealth organizations.

[2] Save for Arts 1 and 13 of the Convention. The Convention rights incorporated by the Human Rights Act 1998 and the principal provisions of that Act are set out in the Appendix, together with Arts 1 and 13.

progressive realization of the right of access to housing. Rights in this form leave open the argument that they are susceptible only to a low level of judicial review. These two examples show that constitutional and human rights can have very different content and they can be drafted according to very different models.

Diversity of constitutional systems

There are also different models when it comes to making decisions about who should decide what violates human rights. Somebody has to have that power. In some countries, this power is vested in the courts: the best known example is the US Supreme Court which has the power to strike down legislation which is unconstitutional. In the European Union, there are two levels of problems: first, is the legislation in accordance with EU law? Second, is the EU law in question consistent with constitutional rights conferred in the individual member states? The European Court of Justice ('ECJ') sitting in Luxembourg has the power to decide whether a law of a member state infringes European law or if a law of the EU is outside the competence of the EU. However, the German courts have a very interesting position on this. They take the view that, while the ECJ has the final say on EU matters, if there is also a question of whether an EU law contravenes the German constitution, that is a matter for the German Federal Constitutional Court although that Court would no doubt reach the same view as the ECJ in most cases. This problem reared its head when the German Federal Constitutional Court decided that the EU arrest warrant, which would enable one member state to ask for a person present in another member state to be arrested in connection with an offence under the requesting member state's laws, infringed the rights conferred by the German constitution to have questions of extradition considered by a German court. In Hong Kong the position is different again: the Court of Final Appeal in Hong Kong is empowered to strike down laws which offend the Basic Law, but on certain reserved matters the decision of the Court of Final Appeal can be re-interpreted by the Standing Committee of the Chinese National People's Congress. This Committee may find that the Court's interpretation is not in accordance with the intention of the People's Congress when the legislation was passed.

The system in Hong Kong is just another way of doing things. It could not be followed in the United Kingdom because the Convention provides that an independent and impartial tribunal established by law must determine all disputes as to rights and obligations. I will return to the UK solution later. But the point I am making is that there should be no necessary assumption that the judicial arm of government can only strike down legislation which is in violation of human rights. The courts do not have that power in the United Kingdom so far as primary legislation is concerned. But our law does provide that it is the role of the judges to interpret statute law in conformity with rights protected by the Human Rights Act 1998 (the '1998 Act'). Only if statute law cannot be interpreted so as to conform to the Convention can the courts make a declaration of incompatibility. As I shall explain later, if such a declaration is made, only Parliament can change the law or declare it inapplicable.

Diversity of approach by the courts

Another point on which we should reflect is the diversity of approaches to statutory interpretation. Not every court approaches questions of interpretation in the same way. Some courts approach questions of statutory interpretation with a close attention to the wording. Some adopt a more purposive approach. Each approach has its advantages and disadvantages. Where the courts give close attention to the wording this is likely to help people predict the results more easily and plan transactions so as to take advantage of the law. If, however, the courts give more weight to the purpose behind legislation, then it is arguably more likely that the rights, which the legislature intended to confer on citizens, will be recognized by the courts and enforced. Much depends on the constitutional framework in which the courts in question operate and the understanding as to their role in the society in which they operate. There is no 'one size fits all' here.

Relative importance of statute law

Then again, in some systems statute law is more important than it is in others. In the United Kingdom it is becoming increasingly important. There are very few areas of common law which have not been affected by statute law of one kind or another. Of course, where statute law applies, it will, unless it otherwise provides, displace the common law. The study of statute law is inter-disciplinary. It is relevant to all areas of law, for example company law, contract law, environmental law, damages, and so on. Many lawyers are not particularly interested in statute law. I think they are wrong not to think it deserves separate and careful study. Statute law may be adjectival law but to me it is very important. It raises technical and constitutional issues.

Diversity of subject matter

Yet again, not every question of interpretation is amenable to the same approach. This may be because of the nature of the subject. Courts across the world tend not to get involved with purely political issues: for example, in the *Belmarsh* case[3] concerning the detention of terrorist suspects, where the House of Lords accepted the view of the executive that there was a state of emergency threatening the life of the nation. It may be that the approach to statutory interpretation in one case is different from that in another case because of the objectives of interpretation. In the case of human (or constitutional) rights, courts have to give effect to a living instrument. Unless as a matter of law the constitution is to be interpreted exactly

---

[3] *A v Secretary of State for the Home Department* [2004] UKHL 56, [2005] 2 AC 68.

in the light of social circumstances as existing at the date of the constitution, then constitutional rights have to be updated as social conditions change. The European Court of Human Rights (the 'Strasbourg Court') adopts an approach of dynamic or evolutive interpretation: it interprets the Convention according to its current rather than its historic meaning. As one judge put it, 'the Convention is written in the present tense'.

The dynamic approach to the interpretation of Convention rights can be seen, for example, in the progressive recognition by the Strasbourg Court of the rights of illegitimate children and transsexual people. Since the principle of evolutive inter-pretation is embedded in the jurisprudence of the Strasbourg Court it will be easy for the English courts to adopt it in relation to Convention rights. Indeed, it has been held on the highest authority that, even though the 1998 Act does not oblige the English courts to follow the jurisprudence of the Strasbourg Court, in the absence of special circumstances the English courts should do so. In the interpret-ation of constitutional rights, dynamic interpretation is a common feature: as Justice Kirby of the High Court of Australia said extra-judicially in his Hamlyn lectures:

Construing a constitution with a catch cry about 'legalism', with nothing more than judicial casebooks and a dictionary to help, and with no concept of the way it is intended to operate in the nation whose people accept it as their basic law, is a contemptible idea. As one sage put it: if you construe a constitution like a last will and testament, that is what it will become.[4]

The principle of evolutive interpretation is not confined to human rights. It may apply, for example, where Parliament has used words which involve a value judgment, as in the statutory requirement that company accounts show a 'true and fair view'. What is true and fair is liable to change as the expectations of users of such documents change. There are statutes in many different fields which contain terms which require to be given a modern meaning even though they were enacted in the past. Such statutes have been described as 'always speaking'.

The Commonwealth

One of the remarkable things about the Commonwealth is that the members of it display such diversity in their systems. Some Commonwealth systems are pure common law, like the English system, but others are based in whole or part on the civil law, for example the law of Quebec or Mauritius. Others again are in whole or part based on Roman-Dutch law, such as South Africa and Sri Lanka. I am sure many other examples could be given. What is unique about an association such as this is that it offers a forum where so many jurisdictions come together to discuss

---

[4] The Hamlyn Lectures, 'Judicial Activism', By The Hon Justice Michael Kirby AC CMG, Justice of the High Court of Australia (2004), 40.

their approaches and broaden their own horizons. If we can pool ideas about how to solve problems and confront each other's ideas we will in my view reach better solutions to our own problems in our jurisdictions when we return to our normal tasks again.

Human rights in the United Kingdom

In the United Kingdom, we have no written constitution. In 1950, the United Kingdom instead became a party to the Convention, which is an international convention. For many years the United Kingdom did not incorporate the Convention into UK domestic law and so the domestic courts could not give effect to Convention rights. However, under the Convention individuals are given the right to petition the Strasbourg Court to determine whether there has been a violation. Prior to 1998, the only recourse open to a citizen of this country who asserted that his rights had been infringed was to petition the Strasbourg Court. In 1998 Parliament passed the Human Rights Act in order to give better protection to Convention rights in domestic law. I now turn to the relevant provisions of the 1998 Act.

Human Rights Act 1998

For my purposes the relevant provisions of the 1998 Act are ss 2, 3, and 4.[5] Sections 3 and 4 deal with the interpretation of statutes and the making of declarations of incompatibility. These two sections demonstrate that, when Parliament incorporated the Convention into UK domestic law, it did so in a way that preserved Parliamentary sovereignty. In other words, it was a term of the constitutional settlement then reached that the courts should not be able to strike down primary legislation passed by Parliament. They could, however, make a declaration of incompatibility. A declaration of incompatibility has no effect on the validity, continuing operation, or enforcement of the provision in question and is not binding on the parties to the proceedings in which it is made. Thus, the statutory provisions in issue remain unaffected unless and until Parliament changes them. The courts are also bound by the interpretative obligation in s 3 to interpret legislation, so far as possible, in conformity with the rights conferred by the Convention.

The general expectation, when the 1998 Act was passed, was that, when there was a final order of a court making a declaration of incompatibility, Parliament would respect the court's decision and change the law. It was recognized that Parliament should choose the way in which the law should be amended. But there is no provision in the 1998 Act compelling Parliament to change the law and it is doubtful whether there is any constitutional convention to that effect. Thus it is a

---

[5] Set out in the Appendix.

consequence of the constitutional settlement in the 1998 Act, which I described earlier, that, following a decision by the courts that primary legislation is incompatible with the Convention, Parliament could, at least in theory, decide that it did not wish to change the law to make it conform to the Convention or indeed that it wished to amend or repeal the 1998 Act.

This constitutional settlement has been tested. After 9/11,[6] Parliament passed the Anti-terrorism, Crime and Security Act 2001 which among other provisions conferred the right on the Home Secretary to detain terrorist suspects. In the *Belmarsh* case, to which I have already referred, the House of Lords found that those detention provisions violated the Convention rights to liberty and to freedom from discrimination because the provisions discriminated as against aliens and were disproportionate. They did not apply to terrorist suspects who were British subjects. The House of Lords could not strike the provisions down. All the House of Lords could do was make a declaration of incompatibility. But that did not lead to the release of the detainees. They had to apply for bail on the grounds that, if they were not released voluntarily by the Home Secretary, they would apply to the Strasbourg Court for their release and those applications were likely to be successful because of the decision of the House of Lords.

When the decision in the *Belmarsh* case was handed down, the Government did not take any immediate step to release the detainees, or to change the law. However, in due course it did introduce a Bill which became the Prevention of Terrorism Act 2005 (the '2005 Act'). The 2005 Act provides for the courts, or in some circumstances the Home Secretary, to make 'control orders' under which conditions are attached to a person's liberty, for example, conditions as to a curfew or a prohibition on using the internet or mobile phones, and so on. The detainees are no longer detained in a prison. In the main, they are now subject to control orders limiting their freedom of movement under this Act.

As we have seen, however, in the 1998 Act Parliament gave the courts an enhanced power to interpret legislation. Lord Nicholls has said that this is not interpretation in the usual sense of the term.[7] The courts are indeed empowered to adopt a strained meaning if this is required to make legislation compatible with human rights. Moreover, the courts are enjoined to apply this interpretation to statutes whenever passed, not just statutes passed after the 1998 Act itself became law. So the courts may no longer be concerned with the meaning of the words used by Parliament at the time it passed the legislation. However, there must be some limits to what may properly be called interpretation because Parliament has devised the alternative route of a declaration of incompatibility as already explained. I give two examples below of cases in which s 3 of the 1998 Act has been applied. They are both decisions of the House of Lords.

[6] '9/11' is the name often given to the terrorist attacks on the United States on 11 September 2001.
[7] Lord Nicholls, 'My Kingdom for a Horse: the Meaning of Words' (2005) 121 LQR 577, 590.

Human rights and the use of legislative history

It should be noted that, while on questions of statutory interpretation the English courts do not in general admit legislative history, they may be able to do so more freely where the question is whether the legislation is compatible with the Convention, or whether its provisions are proportionate to the legitimate ends to which the legislation is directed.

Human rights and the quality of legislation

The *Belmarsh* case also raises concerns about the quality of legislation. In the UK, statute law tends to be relatively prescriptive, and judges pay close attention to the actual words of the statute. Accordingly it is important that the legislative drafting should be of the highest quality. This is not always possible where the Parliamentary process is accelerated. The Anti-terrorism, Crime and Security Act 2001 went through its Parliamentary stages at speed. The position with the 2005 Act was even more striking: it was considered and passed by Parliament over only 18 days. When this happens, Parliament may require the legislation to be reviewed annually or impose a 'sunset' clause.[8] In addition, when a Bill is introduced into Parliament, the Minister responsible for it must make a statement to the effect that the provisions of the Bill are compatible with Convention rights.[9] These measures are some acceptance of the problem but not a total solution. The existing statute may still need to be interpreted by the courts. Where legislation has been passed at speed, it may be that Parliament did not give adequate consideration to human rights, and the courts may look at the statute with that possibility in mind.

Jurisprudence on s 3 of the Human Rights Act 1998

I now turn to give two examples of the way in which the House of Lords has interpreted legislation in reliance on s 3 of the 1998 Act. The first case is *R v A (No 2)*.[10] In this case, the appeal was by a defendant to a criminal charge of rape and concerned the question of whether certain evidence concerning the sexual behaviour of the complainant would be admissible at trial. The defendant wanted to adduce evidence of the complainant's sexual behaviour in the three weeks prior to the alleged rape. However, s 41 of the Youth Justice and Criminal Evidence Act 1999 prohibits the admission of evidence as to the complainant's sexual behaviour unless certain conditions are fulfilled. The conditions permit the admission of evidence of sexual behaviour on the issue of consent if the prior sexual behaviour

---

[8] A provision in a statute stipulating that the statute is to cease to be in force on a particular date or after a particular event or period.
[9] Human Rights Act 1998, s 19(1).   [10] [2001] UKHL 25, [2002] 1 AC 45.

was so similar to the sexual behaviour of the complainant that the similarity cannot be explained as a coincidence. But further conditions are attached to this exception, including a condition that the behaviour should have taken place as part of the event or at or about the same time as the alleged rape.[11] The House of Lords held that an accused's Convention right to a fair trial might be violated if relevant evidence of the kind sought to be addressed by the appellant was excluded. The question then arose whether s 41 could be construed so as to prevent any violation of the defendant's rights. On this, their Lordships expressed different views.

First, Lord Steyn made some general observations about s 3:

[44]   On the other hand, the interpretative obligation of section 3 of the 1998 Act is a strong one. It applies even if there is no ambiguity in the language in the sense of the language being capable of two different meanings. It is an emphatic adjuration by the legislature: *R v Director of Public Prosecutions, ex p Kebilene* [2000] 2 AC 326, per Lord Cooke of Thorndon, at p.373F; and my judgment at 366B . . . In accordance with the will of Parliament as reflected in section 3 it will sometimes be necessary to adopt an interpretation which linguistically may appear strained. The techniques to be used will not only involve the reading down of expressed language in a statute but also the implication of provisions. A declaration of incompatibility is a measure of last resort. It must be avoided unless it is plainly impossible to do so. If a *clear* limitation on Convention rights is stated in terms, such an impossibility will arise: *Secretary of State for the Home Department, ex parte Simms* [2000] 2 AC 115, 132A-B per Lord Hoffmann. There is, however, no limitation of such a nature in the present case.

[45]   In my view, section 3 requires the court to subordinate the niceties of the language of section 41(3)(c) and in particular the touchstone of coincidence, to broader considerations of relevance judged by logical and common sense criteria of time and circumstances. After all, it is realistic to proceed on the basis that the legislature would not, if alerted to the problem, have wished to deny the right to an accused to put forward a full and complete defence by advancing truly probative material. It is therefore possible under section 3 to read section 41, and in particular section 41(3)(c), as subject to the implied provision that evidence or questioning which is required to ensure a fair trial under article 6 of the Convention should not be treated as inadmissible. The result of such reading would be that sometimes logically relevant sexual experiences between a complainant and an accused may be admitted under section 41(3)(c) . . .

Lord Hope of Craighead took a different view. He considered that the question whether s 41 was incompatible with the Convention could not be finally determined at the pre-trial stage. Accordingly, he considered it was neither necessary nor appropriate to resort to the interpretative obligation in s 3 of the 1998 Act. Lord Hope added:

[108]   I should like to add, however, that I would find it very difficult to accept that it was permissible under section 3 of the Human Rights Act 1998 to read into section 41(3)(c) a provision to the effect that evidence or questioning which was required to ensure a fair trial under article 6 of the Convention should not be treated as inadmissible. The rule of construction which section 3 lays down is quite unlike any previous rule of statutory

---

[11] Section 41(3)(c).

interpretation. There is no need to identify any ambiguity or absurdity. Compatibility with Convention rights is the sole guiding principle. This is the paramount object which the rule seeks to achieve. But the rule is only a rule of interpretation. It does not entitle the judges to act as legislators . . .

[109]   In the present case it seems to me that the entire structure of section 41 contradicts the idea that it is possible to read into it a new provision which would entitle the court to give leave whenever it was of the opinion that this was required to ensure a fair trial. The whole point of the section, as was made clear during the debates in Parliament, was to address the mischief which was thought to have arisen due to the width of the discretion which had previously been given to the trial judge. A deliberate decision was taken not to follow the examples which were to be found elsewhere, such as in section 275 of the Criminal Procedure (Scotland) Act 1995, of provisions which give an overriding discretion to the trial judge to allow the evidence or questioning where it would be contrary to the interests of justice to exclude it. Section 41(2) *forbids* the exercise of such discretion *unless* the court is satisfied as to the matters which that subsection identifies. It seems to me that it would not be possible, without contradicting the plain intention of Parliament, to read in a provision which would enable the court to exercise a wider discretion than that permitted by section 41(2).

[110]   I would not have the same difficulty with a solution which read down the provisions of sections (3) or (5), as the case may be, in order to render them compatible with the Convention right but if that were to be done it would be necessary to identify precisely (a) the words used by the legislature which would otherwise be incompatible with the Convention right and (b) how those words were to be construed, according to the rule which section 3 lays down to make them compatible. That, it seems to me, is what the rule of construction requires. The court's task is to read and give effect to the legislation which it is asked to construe . . .

The other members of the House in substance agreed with Lord Steyn's approach. Lord Slynn held:

It seems to me that your Lordships cannot say that it is not possible to read section 41(3)(c) together with article 6 of the Convention rights in a way which will result in a fair hearing. In my view, section 41(3)(c) is to be read as permitting the admission of evidence or questioning which relates to a relevant issue in the case and which the trial judge considers is necessary to make the trial a fair one.[12]

Lord Clyde held:

If a case occurred where the evidence of the complainant's sexual behaviour was relevant and important for the defence to make good a case of consent, then it seems to me that the language would have to be strained to avoid the injustice to the accused of excluding them from a full and proper presentation of the defence.[13]

Lord Hutton held:

. . . pursuant to the obligation imposed by section 3(1) that section 41 must be read and given effect in a way which is compatible with article 6, I consider that section 41(3)(c) should be read as including evidence of such previous behaviour by the complainant because

---

[12]   *R v A (No 2)* at [13].   [13]   *R v A (No 2)* at [136].

the defendant claims that her sexual behaviour on previous occasions was similar, and the similarity was not coincidence because there was a causal connection which was her affection for, and feelings of attraction towards, the defendant.[14]

R v A (No 2) was one of the first cases where s 3 of the 1998 Act was considered. The House of Lords' approach has been developed in a number of other cases involving s 3, of which the most important is *Ghaidan v Godin-Mendoza*.[15] In that case the statute in question confers rights of succession in respect of a tenancy on a person who had lived with the deceased original tenant 'as his or her wife or husband'. The issue was whether this provision applied to same sex couples. If it did not do so, then it discriminated against them in violation of Art 14 of the Convention read with Art 8.

The House of Lords held that the statute in question had to apply to the survivor of a same sex relationship as much as it did to a surviving spouse. In the course of reaching that conclusion the courts gave authoritative guidance as to the limits of s 3.

The leading speech is that of Lord Nicholls. He held that the effect of s 3 was that the court might be required to depart from the unambiguous meaning of a statute. The question of difficulty was how far the courts should go. He held that the answer to this question did not depend on the actual wording used by Parliament. He continued:

[32]   From this the conclusion which seems inescapable is that the mere fact the language under consideration is inconsistent with a Convention-compliant meaning does not of itself make a Convention-compliant interpretation under section 3 impossible. Section 3 enables language to be interpreted restrictively or expansively. But section 3 goes further than this. It is also apt to require a court to read in words which change the meaning of the enacted legislation so as to make it Convention-compliant. In other words, the intention of Parliament in enacting section 3 was that, to an extent bounded only by what is 'possible', a court can modify the meaning, and hence the effect, of primary and secondary legislation.

[33]   Parliament, however, cannot have intended that in the discharge of this extended interpretative function the courts should adopt a meaning inconsistent with a fundamental feature of legislation. That would be to cross the constitutional boundary section 3 seeks to demarcate and preserve. Parliament has retained the right to enact legislation in terms which are not Convention-compliant. The meaning imported by application of section 3 must be compatible with the underlying thrust of the legislation being construed. Words implied must, in the phrase of my noble and learned friend, Lord Rodger of Earlsferry, 'go with the grain of the legislation'. Nor can Parliament have intended that section 3 should require courts to make decisions for which they are not equipped. There may be several ways of making a provision Convention-compliant, and the choice may involve issues calling for legislative deliberation.

Lord Rodger also considered the boundaries of s 3 and gave further helpful guidance. He held that in deciding how to interpret the legislation the courts should not produce a meaning which departed substantially from a fundamental

---

[14] *R v A (No 2)* at [163].   [15] [2004] UKHL 30; [2004] 2 AC 557.

feature or cardinal principle of the legislation. Likewise the courts should be less ready to interpret legislation so as to be compatible with Convention rights where there would be important practical repercussions which the courts are not quipped to evaluate.

The decision in the *Ghaidan* case is a powerful statement of the court's preparedness to interpret legislation so that it is compatible with human rights. The speeches, all of which repay careful study, contain extremely valuable guidelines. The House of Lords has recognized the force of the mandatory obligation in s 3. However, the words 'in a way which is compatible with the Convention rights' make it clear that the courts have the choice as to how to interpret the legislation to achieve the objective in s 3, namely that, where possible, the legislation should be compatible with human rights.

The courts are not bound to give effect to Convention rights in exactly the same way as the Strasbourg Court. As Lord Irvine LC put it in Parliament during the passage of the Bill, they can use the jurisprudence of the Strasbourg Court as a floor rather than a ceiling. Moreover, the House of Lords has made it clear that the courts do not have slavishly to follow a textual approach to achieve a compatible interpretation.

Where s 3 can be applied to part only of a statute, it is possible that words may mean one thing in the section subject to interpretation under s 3, and another in some other section of the statute which is interpreted in the ordinary way.

In his most illuminating speech Lord Rodger counsels against using jurisprudence of the Judicial Committee of the Privy Council since it is usually concerned with overriding constitutional provisions, rather than provisions such as s 3 which preserve Parliamentary sovereignty. These are of course wise words. Nonetheless, it is still a point worth making that, with the exception of such experience as judges have obtained in the Judicial Committee of the Privy Council, the English courts have comparatively little experience in constitutional interpretation. The United Kingdom has no single statute containing a constitution, although it now has a number of statutes which deal with some of the matters that would be dealt within a normal written constitution. Those statutes include the Parliament Acts 1911 and 1949 and the various statutes dealing with devolution and discrimination. It must be borne in mind that s 3 of the 1998 Act does not apply to all statutes of a constitutional nature. It applies only to those which have to be interpreted so as to conform to the Convention. So, even after the 1998 Act, it is still true to say that the United Kingdom has no special doctrine of interpretation applying to constitutional statutes in general.

The position that English law has reached on s 3, while clearly right, may only be the beginning of the road. It still leaves some unanswered questions. For example, on the basis that the Convention is a floor and not a ceiling, there must inevitably be a space between the floor and the ceiling which leaves the judges considerable room for the exercise of judgment. Is there any principle of interpretation which applies here? Likewise, is there any principle of interpretation which applies when the Court has to sort out conflicts between different rights, such as the right to freedom of expression as against someone else's right to respect for his private life? We may have a long way yet to go in this field.

We are likely to need different sorts of guidelines for different sorts of cases. For example, it may be that Kirby J's quotation from the sage who said that constitutions must not be interpreted like wills should not be taken too far. Even in the field of constitutional rights, there may be occasions when a relatively technical approach will be needed, for instance in constitutional provisions setting out money-raising powers, or setting out the description of a group who are to enjoy particular privileges or protection under a constitution. In addition there will be some occasions when a historical approach is relevant.

Conclusions

The United Kingdom is a relative newcomer in the field of statutory interpretation and human rights. But it is clear, even from domestic law developments thus far, that human rights require a fresh approach to some of the established ideas and concepts of statutory interpretation. Moreover, there is plenty of scope for the courts to develop further the approach to the interpretation of legislation where human rights are involved.

SECTION B

BALANCING DIFFERENT INTERESTS

Balancing the rights and interests of two or more groups is a feature of the Convention jurisprudence. This Section looks at two issues where such a balance is crucial: terrorism and privacy. In the context of terrorism, the law must strike a balance between the interest of the community in being protected against acts of terrorism and the rights of suspected terrorists. In the context of privacy, the courts may have to strike a balance between the right of a person to respect for his or her private life and the right of the media to publish material about that person. The chapters in this Section demonstrate the considerable impact which Strasbourg jurisprudence has had in both these contexts.

Preface by Bernard Stirn and Matthias Gyomar, members of the French Conseil d'Etat

It is a great honour for two French judges, members of the French Conseil d'Etat (Council of State), to have been invited to write a preface for a book by The Rt Hon Lady Justice Arden, who continues to contribute successfully, with insight and nuance, to judicial dialogue in Europe. The different papers collected in this book will be welcomed by all those concerned with issues of state power and human rights. Her excellent study of 'hard cases' in the United Kingdom is especially timely.

This Section examines the topic of balancing of different interests, which is central to the very existence of a meaningful democracy. Mary Arden focuses on issues that are of enduring significance, such as balancing human rights and national security, and balancing public and private interests in relation to privacy. Terrorism laws and privacy have been much affected by human rights developments. In this field, Mary Arden provides a remarkable comparative study, describing some English decisions but also dealing with different cases in leading courts throughout the world. Her speeches and articles show to what extent proportionality is a key principle that must guide judges in this balancing of different interests.

Mary Arden underlines the influence of European law, especially the European Convention of Human Rights, on national jurisdictions. France implemented the Convention by ratifying the protocol on individual applications in 1981. This has had considerable impact on the French legal order, comparable with the effect of the Human Rights Act 1998 in the United Kingdom.

This book will be of interest to those dealing with such matters within legal systems other than the United Kingdom, especially those in political, judicial and academic circles. In France, comparative law has become, for judges and in particular for administrative judges, a way of thinking and a part of legal reasoning. Indeed, developing the use of comparative law has become a policy of the Council of State, which is more and more open to foreign influence. Since 2009, the Centre for Legal Research and Documentation (Centre de Recherche et de Documentation Juridique), a service of the Judicial Chamber of the Council of State, has included a small team of comparative lawyers led by a scholar from Cornell University. There is absolutely no doubt that this book will be very useful for French judges, not only to help them find the 'right answer' in balancing different interests, but also to enable them to understand themselves better.

Bernard Stirn, président de la section du contentieux
(judicial chamber) du Conseil d'Etat
Mattias Guyomar, conseiller d'Etat

PART IV

BALANCING HUMAN RIGHTS AND NATIONAL SECURITY

After 9/11,[1] the UK adopted a number of laws which could be used to restrict an individual's rights where the authorities suspected that that person might be connected with terrorism. Individuals could be detained. They could be searched for items which might be used in connection with terrorism. Associations could be proscribed and could then no longer raise money for their activities. On the other hand, the Human Rights Act 1998 enabled individuals to challenge actions which were in breach of human rights. Thus, the courts were faced with completely novel challenges.

Each of the chapters in this Part is ultimately searching for a principled answer to the question of how courts should balance national security and human rights. The first case in the House of Lords to give guidance on this was *A v Secretary of State for the Home Department*,[2] known as the '*A* case' or the '*Belmarsh* case'. The paper on which Chapter 10 is based, *Human Rights in the Age of Terrorism*, was delivered in 2005, shortly after this decision was handed down. It examines the *Belmarsh* decision, which concerned the question whether the Home Secretary could detain indefinitely suspected terrorists who had no right to reside here but who could not be deported because they would be at a risk of torture in their own country. The right to freedom from torture guaranteed by the European Convention on Human Rights prohibits the return of a person in those circumstances. The detainees were held in the Belmarsh prison. The House of Lords famously held (by a majority) that it was a violation of the Convention for the Home Secretary to detain them.

Two things particularly struck me about this momentous decision. First the majority clearly saw that what was at stake was liberty of the person. Second, the majority dealt with each of the main issues—national security and proportionality—in different ways. They considered that national security was, in the particular circumstances, a matter for the executive. But they importantly rejected the idea that there were 'no go' areas into which (having regard to their nature) the courts would not venture: whether they would do so depended on the particular

---

[1] '9/11' is the name often given to the terrorist attacks on the United States on 11 September 2001.
[2] [2004] UKHL 56, [2005] 2 AC 68.

circumstances. Proportionality, on the other hand, was a matter for the court. The government lost on that issue because only aliens could be detained on these grounds and there was no logical reason for distinguishing between aliens and persons entitled to reside in the United Kingdom, who might pose an equal risk of terrorist activity. The speech of Lord Bingham put the issue of freedom of the person in its historical context, and this gave his judgment a magisterial tone.

I contrasted the *Belmarsh* decision with the way in which the US courts dealt with the detainees in Guantanamo Bay. It took a long time for cases to wind their way to the Supreme Court of the United States. The courts did not give persons who were not American citizens the same rights as American citizens. Thus, aliens have been subjected to continued detention at the will of the executive and have been tried under military law. The general response of American law to terrorism was a blot on a legal system that in my time at Harvard I had come greatly to admire.

In my final remarks in *Human Rights in the Age of Terrorism* I suggest the need for a higher degree of scrutiny by the courts of the reasons put forward by the state to justify restrictions on individual rights. I also propose that suspected terrorists should, if possible, be charged and tried under the ordinary criminal law. This is preferable to their being detained without trial. Overall, I conclude that anti-terrorism laws should not interfere with an individual's rights unless it is necessary and proportionate that they should do so.

The extract from my speech *Balancing Human Rights and National Security*, which follows in Chapter 11, is included because it pursues the question of what factors would be relevant to deciding whether it was proportionate for a law to interfere with individual liberty. Those considerations would include the value of the democratic way of life, and the likelihood that the anti-terrorist law would not, in the event, ensure that innocent civilians were safe from terrorist outrages. These would have to be weighed in the balance as factors which militate against having anti-terrorist measures which intrude on people's rights.

I gave this speech to the Constitutional Court of South Africa in Johannesburg. This was another leading court with which I have been privileged to spend some time. I am full of admiration for the way in which that court acted as guardian of the new constitutional settlement in South Africa when apartheid was abandoned.

Chapter 12, *Meeting the Challenge of Terrorism: The Experience of English and Other Courts*, is a study of pairs of cases on terrorism in leading courts throughout the world where the courts were seeking to devise solutions to similar problems, for example, detention, the use of torture, and the need for special trial procedures where defendants cannot be given access to certain sensitive information. As the lecture on which this chapter is based was given in Sydney, I used an analogy based on the Sydney Harbour Bridge. That bridge has an expansion joint to allow for appropriate movement. So, too, the law has had to find solutions to new legal issues resulting from terrorism, but the solutions must be principled, not expedient.

Courts are sometimes asked to approve some substantial and expedient interference with individual rights in order to increase the chances of bringing a suspected terrorist to justice. But courts need to be sceptical about this. I point out that in making decisions about measures intended to protect society against the risk of terrorism, both courts and legislators have to balance the need for security against individual freedom. The problem of terrorism is not likely to be resolved for some time to come, and the question of how the balance is to be struck between human rights and national security will have to be addressed with care in many new situations.

10

Human Rights in the Age of Terrorism

This chapter is based on the Third University of Essex and Clifford Chance Lecture which was given on 27 January 2005.*

Introduction

Terrorism is the defining issue of the present time. It raises political, legal, ethical, and other issues of great difficulty. Most relevantly for the purpose of this paper, anti-terrorist laws present a great challenge to human rights. Indeed, one anti-terrorist law in particular, the Anti-terrorism, Crime and Security Act 2001 (the '2001 Act'), posed the first great challenge to the operation of the Human Rights Act 1998.[1]

Terrorism is not new. Terrorism of the modern kind has been manifesting itself since the 1960s and the 1970s. Accordingly the bombing of the World Trade Centre in New York in 2001 (which I will refer to as '9/11') was not a one-off event. However, the methods that terrorists use have changed. They have become more desperate. They now use suicide bombers, women, and children. Their weapons are changing—the terrorists have used planes as missiles, and chemical and biological weapons. The intelligence material quoted in the Butler report[2] states that Al Qaeda had been trying to obtain fissile material to make nuclear weapons. The terrorist threat has been building up for some years. We must take it seriously, and we must assume that it will not be eradicated for many years. There is a great need for effective national security, and we need counter-terrorism laws.

In these circumstances, as I see it, we also need to develop a principled approach to resolving the principal issue arising from counter-terrorism laws, that is, the conflict that arises between the need for national security and human rights. My object in this paper is to endeavour to put forward such an approach and hopefully to start a debate. The principled approach will, of course, be derived from human rights jurisprudence.

---

* First published in (2006) 121 LQR 604. It is reproduced with the kind permission of the Publisher.

[1] The Convention rights are incorporated by the Human Rights Act 1998, and the principal provisions of that Act are set out in the Appendix.

[2] *Review of Intelligence on Weapons of Mass Destruction*, 14 July 2004, HC 898.

To achieve my objective, I will use the decision of the House of Lords in *A v Secretary of State for the Home Department*[3] as a launch pad. My paper has three sections:

(1) *A v Secretary of State for the Home Department.* This will contain a summary of the decision and some preliminary observations.

(2) A comparison with the decisions of the US Supreme Court on the Guantanamo Bay detainees.

(3) The wider picture and the principled approach to balancing human rights and national security.

I should give two explanations. First, there is a vast amount of material on this subject, and much of the material for this paper has had to be ruthlessly cut and allowed to fall on the cutting room floor. That means that I have had to condense many points. Second, I want to make clear some of the issues which I am *not* going to cover in this paper. They include:

- the causes of terrorism;
- the political response to terrorism;
- the possible courses of action open to the Government, on the one hand, and the detainees, on the other hand, in the light of the decision of the House of Lords;
- the Home Secretary's ministerial statement of 26 January 2005;
- the legal and ethical issues arising from torture.

The difficult subject of torture was brilliantly captured in Lord Hope of Craighead's University of Essex and Clifford Chance lecture in 2004.[4] In the same way, Lord Bingham of Cornhill gave an illuminating account of the treatment of slavery in English law in the first University of Essex and Clifford Chance lecture in 2003.[5]

Nothing I say in this paper is intended to make light of the dangers posed by terrorism, or of the responsibility imposed on the government to keep the public safe, or of the difficult and dangerous task performed by the security and intelligence services. There are in the world today groups who seek to obtain publicity for their political cause by brutally causing death and injury to innocent civilians.

A v Secretary of State for the Home Department

The result in this case was remarkable. The House of Lords, in exercise of the powers conferred by the Human Rights Act 1998, quashed the Human Rights (Designated Derogation) Order 2001, and made a declaration that s 23 of the 2001

---

[3] [2004] UKHL 56, [2005] 2 AC 60.
[4] David Hope, 'Torture' (2004) 53 ICLQ 807.
[5] Tom Bingham, 'The Law Favours Liberty: Slavery and the English Common Law' (First University of Essex and Clifford Chance lecture, 2003).

Act was incompatible with Arts 5 and 14 of the European Convention on Human Rights (the 'Convention'). In so doing, the House of Lords restored the order of the Special Immigration Appeals Commission ('SIAC'), which had been set aside by the Court of Appeal. The *A* case may well be the first time that a court of the United Kingdom has dealt such a body blow to legislation conferring powers on the executive to meet a threat to national security.

The decision is a lengthy one. It extends to 240 paragraphs. The leading judgment is that of Lord Bingham, but each of the other members of the House, apart from Lord Carswell, also provides reasons for their decision. It is impossible to do justice to all the reasoning and learning in these judgments here. On the other hand, I suspect that not everyone will have had time to read the judgments in full or to draw them together, so I propose to start with a summary of what the case decides and then make some observations about it.

The relevant events start with the conferral of preventive detention powers conferred on the Home Secretary by s 23 of the 2001 Act in the wake of 9/11. By 'preventive detention' I mean detention which is imposed by the executive and which is for an indefinite period of time determined by the executive.

Part 4 of the 2001 Act enables the Home Secretary to issue a certificate if he or she reasonably believes that a specified person's presence in the United Kingdom is a risk to national security and suspects that that person is a terrorist. The Home Secretary can then make a deportation order against that person. Where, however, a person faces the prospect of torture or inhuman treatment in the country to which he would otherwise be deported, then, under Convention jurisprudence, he cannot be deported.[6] To meet that situation, s 23 of the 2001 Act then provides that that person may be detained even if he cannot be removed from the United Kingdom.[7] The person detained cannot apply for habeas corpus. He has to challenge the order for his detention by using the procedure for appeals set out in the 2001 Act. He can appeal against his detention to SIAC. SIAC is given exclusive jurisdiction to determine whether the United Kingdom was entitled to derogate from the Convention. A party who has been unsuccessful before SIAC can appeal, on a point of law only, to the Court of Appeal. The appellants in the *A* case were detainees who had unsuccessfully appealed to SIAC against their detention under certificates issued by the Home Secretary under Part 4 of the 2001 Act.

It was accepted by the government when the 2001 Act was passed that the detention provisions were incompatible with Art 5 of the Convention. The government

    [6] *Chahal v United Kingdom* (1996) 23 EHRR 413.

    [7] As at the date of writing in 2005, in all sixteen people have been detailed under Part 4 and twelve remain subject to Part 4. One has had his certificate quashed by SIAC, whose ruling was upheld in the Court of Appeal: *Secretary of State for the Home Department v M* [2004] EWCA Civ 324, [2004] 2 All ER 863; another had his certificate discharged by the Home Secretary, and two others left the jurisdiction. In addition, one detainee has been transferred to Broadmoor and one has been released on bail (on very strict conditions) because of his mental condition. These figures are taken from the speech of Baroness Hale of Richmond (at [223]) though it has been widely reported that seventeen persons have in fact been detained. According to the press, they are all North African Muslims. According to *The Times*, 18 December 2004, the detainees have now applied to SIAC for release on bail.

therefore elected to derogate from the Convention in this respect, pursuant to Art 15(1) of the Convention, which provides:

In time of war or other public emergency threatening the life of the nation any High Contracting Party may take measures derogating from its obligations under this Convention to the extent strictly required by the exigencies of the situation, provided that the measures are not inconsistent with its other obligations under international law.

The derogation issue

The threshold question in the *A* case was whether a state of emergency had arisen entitling the United Kingdom to derogate from Art 5. No party to the Convention other than the United Kingdom has derogated from Art 5 in the wake of 9/11. The House of Lords (by a majority of 8:1,[8] but Lord Scott of Foscote *dubitante*[9]) rejected the appellants' arguments on this point. The question had been one for SIAC; SIAC had heard evidence that had not been disclosed to the House of Lords; there was no misdirection by SIAC. In one of its earliest decisions on this issue, the European Court of Human Rights (the 'Strasbourg Court') had accepted that Ireland could derogate from the Convention even though it was not shown that there was widespread loss of life or an attack on the territorial integrity of the state was involved. In addition, the House was prepared to attach great weight to the judgment of the Home Secretary and Parliament on the issue whether there was a public emergency threatening the life of the nation. In the words of Lord Bingham:

... the more purely political (in a broad or narrow sense) a question is, the more appropriate it will be for political resolution and the less likely it is to be an appropriate matter for judicial decision ... Conversely, the greater the legal content of any issue, the greater the potential role of the court ...[10]

The question whether the circumstances amounted to a public emergency threatening the life of the nation was at the political, rather than the legal, end of the spectrum and, therefore, a matter in which the views of the other organs of government were entitled to great weight. Lord Nicholls of Birkenhead agreed. He was emphatic that it was for the executive to decide how to respond to terrorism. He held that:

All courts are acutely conscious that the government alone is able to evaluate and decide what counter-terrorism steps are needed and what steps will suffice. Courts are not equipped to make such decisions, nor are they charged with that responsibility.[11]

Both Lord Scott and Lord Hoffmann made reference to the shortcomings of intelligence in relation to Iraq and weapons of mass destruction. Even though courts are not able to second-guess intelligence, they can be sceptical about it.

---

[8] The dissenting judgment was that of Lord Walker, who usefully summarizes his views at [209].
[9] At [154].   [10] At [36].   [11] At [79].

On the derogation issue, the lone dissenting voice was that of Lord Hoffmann. He held that, although he was prepared to accept that there was credible evidence that terrorist outrages were planned against the United Kingdom, there was no emergency threatening the life of the nation for the purposes of Art 15. 'Terrorist violence, serious as it is, does not threaten our institutions of government or our existence as a civil community.'[12] None of the other members of the House in terms addresses this point.

The proportionality issue

The second issue in the *A* case was whether the provisions of the 2001 Act relating to detention violated the detainees' rights under Art 5 to an extent greater than that strictly required by the exigencies of the situation, and so exceeded the limits within which derogation was permitted under Art 15. The House considered that proportionality was a question of law.[13] On proportionality, the argument focused on the fact that the powers of detention related only to foreign nationals who could not be deported. It could not be said that foreign nationals were the only threat; if they were a threat, they could under the 2001 Act go abroad and carry on their activities from abroad. Furthermore, foreign nationals could in theory be detained even if the threat which they presented was not as members of Al Qaeda but of some other organization altogether which had not been responsible for the state of emergency justifying the derogation. The House of Lords (by a majority of 7:1, Lord Hoffmann not expressing a view on this or the next issue) accepted these arguments: in a word, s 23 was irrational. The fact that the detention could be reviewed by SIAC did not overcome these points. According to Lord Scott, the Home Secretary 'should at least . . . have to show that monitoring arrangements or movement restrictions less severe than incarceration in prison would not suffice'.[14]

The discrimination issue

The House of Lords also held that the powers of preventive detention under the 2001 Act violated Art 14 of the Convention by discriminating unjustifiably between non-UK nationals and UK nationals, who could not be detained on suspicion. The appropriate comparators were UK nationals who were suspected terrorists, and not, as the government contended, non-UK nationals who were suspected terrorists but who could be deported to third countries. To accept the government's comparator would be to accept the correctness of the government's choice of immigration control to address the terrorist threat when it was that means of addressing the threat that was in issue.

---

[12] At [96].   [13] At [44] per Lord Bingham.
[14] At [155]. These criticisms of Part 4 may make it difficult for the government to seek to meet human rights considerations simply by extending Part 4 to United Kingdom nationals.

Lord Hoffmann did not express a view on this point. He did not wish to give the impression that all that was necessary was for the government to extend the powers to foreigners; any preventive detention was unconstitutional. Lord Hoffmann added:

The real threat to the life of the nation, in the sense of a people living in accordance with its traditional laws and political values, comes not from terrorism but from laws such as these. That is the true measure of what terrorism may achieve.[15]

Consequences of the decision

The government is not bound to release the detainees as a result of this decision,[16] and it has not done so.

On 26 January 2005, the Home Secretary made a ministerial statement in Parliament, which I will now summarize. The Home Secretary stated that Part 4 of the 2001 Act had played an essential part in containing the threat posed by the detainees, and had deterred other suspected terrorists from entering or remaining in the United Kingdom. The Home Secretary stated that he accepted the declaration of incompatibility made by the House of Lords in the *A* case. He also accepted that new legislative measures had to apply to United Kingdom nationals as well as non-nationals. There continued to be a public emergency threatening the life of the nation. The government proposed to adopt a twin-track approach, that is, deportation with assurances for foreign nationals who could be deported, and a new mechanism, namely control orders, for those who could not be prosecuted or deported. The government did not intend to change the law so as to make intercept evidence admissible. Legislation would therefore be introduced to enable the Home Secretary to impose control orders. These could be made irrespective of the suspected terrorist's nationality. They would only be imposed in serious cases, and they would be subject to appeal to SIAC. Control orders could be used to impose a range of controls restricting movement, and association and communication with named individuals; control orders could also be used to impose curfews and tagging, and restrictions on access to telecommunications and the internet. A person against whom a control order was made could be required to remain in his home. The Home Secretary also stated that the government would seek to renew the powers in Part 4 of the 2001 Act until the new legislation could be put in place and either the persons presently in detention could be deported, or were prosecuted, or became subject to control orders, or the Home Secretary was satisfied that he could revoke his certificate under Part 4 in relation to them. The Home

[15] At [97].
[16] Immediately following the decision, the Home Secretary, The Rt Hon Charles Clarke, made a written statement in the House of Commons in which he stated that he would not be revoking any of the certificates or releasing the detainees, whom he believed to be a 'significant threat to [our] security'. Instead the provisions would remain in force until Parliament decided how the law should be amended: *Weekly Hansard*, Issue No 2017 (Pt II), 16 December 2004, col 152 WS.

Secretary stated that he believed that these changes were justified in the interests of national security.[17]

There has been considerable criticism in the media of these proposals contained in the Home Secretary's ministerial statement.

According to the press, the detainees have applied to SIAC for bail and propose to apply to the Strasbourg Court, if they are not released. The Strasbourg Court may be able to make an order for their release.

I will comment on the wider issues of the *A* case in the third section of this paper. In this section, however, I want to make some preliminary observations on it.

Characterization of the issue

It is fundamental to an understanding of the decision to note that the House of Lords saw the issue as one of the right to liberty, not as one about the executive's power to control persons with no right to remain here.[18] If the issue had been one of immigration control, the law could have legitimately discriminated between nationals and aliens. Discrimination could not be justified by treating the issue as if it were one of immigration. As it was, the issue was whether aliens posed a sufficiently different risk to national security from that posed by UK nationals to justify the different restrictions imposed on them. The answer was no.

The House of Lords' approach to the discretionary area of judgment

There is one issue which permeates, in greater or lesser measure, all three issues in the *A* case. It is the extent to which the courts should give weight to the views of the executive or the legislature on matters, such as national security, relied on as justifying a restriction on a person's human rights. To what extent does the executive or the legislature have (as it is often put) 'a discretionary area of judgment' into which the courts will not intrude? Put another way, with what level of intensity will the court scrutinize the acts of the executive or the acts of the legislature? Does it depend on the circumstances and, if so, which circumstances?

Lord Walker of Gestingthorpe (who dissented in the result) accepted that the question of the level of intensity of judicial review presented a real dilemma. He expressed the view that the question was fully discussed in the speeches of the other members of the House.[19] With respect, I do not think that this is so.

The state of the law is complicated by a number of decisions of the House of Lords, notably *Secretary of State for the Home Department v Rehman*.[20] The detailed facts of this case do not matter, save that the issue again was whether SIAC had adopted the right approach to the views of the Secretary of State when making a

---

[17] *Weekly Hansard*, Issue No 2020, 26 January 2005, col 305. See the postscript below for a summary of the legislation on control orders, which led to the release of the detainees. The legislation on control orders was itself superseded in 2011 by legislation introducing Terrorist Prevention and Investigation Measures ('TPIMs').
[18] See per Lord Bingham (at [68]), Lord Hope (at [105]), Lord Rodger (at [171])).
[19] At [196].   [20] [2001] UKHL 47, [2003] 1 AC 153.

deportation order on the grounds that the person to be deported constituted a threat to national security. In the *Rehman* case, Lord Hoffmann, with whom Lord Clyde and Lord Hutton agreed, appeared to say at one stage in his speech that the executive was entitled to an exclusive say in matters of national security.[21] The courts would be bound to accept their assessment. However, Lord Hoffmann also said that the courts would nonetheless retain certain functions, including the function of scrutinizing the evidence supporting the Minister's opinion that a particular course of action was in the interests of national security, and the function of determining whether the Minister's opinion was perverse. Lord Hoffmann also held that, when SIAC was considering, on appeal to it, whether the circumstances justified a derogation from the Convention, it should not ordinarily interfere if it considered that the view was one which the Home Secretary could reasonably entertain.

There has been criticism of Lord Hoffmann's apparent view in the *Rehman* case that the executive has an exclusive say in matters of national security. In a lecture given shortly before the speeches in the *A* case were handed down, Lord Steyn pointed out that it would be wrong to use the doctrine of separation of powers as a reason for not exercising the court's jurisdiction.[22] He quoted with approval a passage from the judgment of Madam Justice Beverley McLachlin, now the Chief Justice of Canada, in which she said among other things that the courts have a role in determining, 'objectively and impartially, whether Parliament's choice falls within the limiting framework of the Constitution'.[23] Lord Steyn expressed the view that 'it cannot be right to say that there are issues which constitutional principle withdraws from decision by the courts'. Lord Steyn supported his argument by reference to the decisions of the Strasbourg Court in *Tinnelly v UK*,[24] *Smith and Grady v UK*,[25] *Brannigan and McBride v UK*[26] and other cases. Lord Steyn pointed out that the mindset in troubled times that 'after all we are all on the same side as the government' is a slippery slope which tends to sap the will of the judiciary to stand up to a government guilty of an abuse of power. One must not forget that the principles which the courts develop in times of an emergency will probably outlast the emergency and have to be applied in normal conditions as well.

The passages in the *Rehman* case which Lord Steyn criticized are not referred to in the *A* case. In the circumstances, my view is that Lord Hoffmann's speech should be interpreted consistently with the speeches in the *A* case. There is no question of its having been expressly overruled in the *A* case. It may be that it was unnecessary for the House to refer to the relevant passages in the *Rehman* case because SIAC had principally applied *R (on the application of Daly) v Home Secretary*,[27] rather than the

---

[21] At [50]. See also [53].
[22] 'Deference: A Tangled Story': lecture given by The Rt Hon Lord Steyn, Lord of Appeal in Ordinary (2004), Judicial Studies Board Lecture, Belfast, 25 November 2004, published in [2005] PL 346.
[23] *RJR-MacDonald v Att-Gen of Canada* [1995] 3 SCR 199, paras 133–7. This case is referred to in *A v Secretary of State for the Home Department*.
[24] (1998) 27 EHRR 249.   [25] (1999) 29 EHRR 493.   [26] (1993) 17 EHRR 539.
[27] [2001] UKHL 26, [2001] 2 AC 532.

Rehman case. The House of Lords was satisfied that SIAC had not misdirected itself on the derogation issue.

On the question of the discretionary area of judgment, I have already summarized the nuanced, spectrum approach of Lord Bingham, and his view that the question whether there existed a public emergency threatening the life of the nation was at the political end of the spectrum. Lord Bingham did not examine any evidence on the threat to the life of the nation, or express a view on it. He simply held that it had not been shown that there was any error of law by SIAC.

I next turn to Lord Hope of Craighead's speech. While Lord Hope was also prepared 'to accept that the questions whether there is an emergency and whether it threatens the life of the nation are pre-eminently for the executive and Parliament',[28] he considered that there had to be a two-stage enquiry: first, the nature of the emergency had to be examined; second, the court had to determine if the measures were strictly required by the emergency. He held that notwithstanding the weight to be given to the views of the executive on the question whether there was an emergency:

> ... it is nevertheless open to the judiciary to examine the nature of the situation that has been identified by government as constituting the emergency, and to scrutinise the submission by the Attorney-General that for the appellants to be deprived of their fundamental right to liberty does not exceed what is 'strictly required' by the situation which it has identified.[29]

Thus, Lord Hope took the view that the House could not decide whether measures were strictly required by the situation without understanding what was said to be the nature of the emergency. In consequence, Lord Hope proceeded to examine the evidence as to the emergency (the first stage). Informed by that exercise, he then considered whether the detention provisions were strictly required (the second stage). He held that that test was not met because the threat from UK nationals who were also suspected of terrorism was dealt with without detention of the suspects. This two-stage approach seems to me to leave some scope for the court to form a view about the scale of the threat. But another consequence that flows from Lord Hope's approach is that it is not enough for the executive to state that there is a threat, and to support it with meagre evidence. On his approach, the weight of the evidence may be used to assess the proportionality of the measure.

Lord Rodger of Earlsferry came to a similar conclusion. He pointed to the right of appeal to SIAC on derogation matters.[30] He held that '[i]f the right is to be meaningful, the judges must be intended to do more than simply rubber-stamp the decisions taken by ministers and Parliament'.[31]

Later, Lord Rodger held:

> [176]   If the provisions of section 30 of the 2001 Act are to have any real meaning, deference to the view of the Government and Parliament on the derogation cannot be taken too far. Due deference does not mean abasement before those views, even in matters relating

---

[28] At [116].   [29] At [116].   [30] Section 30 of the 2001 Act.   [31] At [164].

to national security. Even in such matters what Simon Brown LJ said in *International Transport Roth GmbH v Secretary of State for the Home Department* [2003] Q.B. 728, 754, holds true: 'There are limits to the legitimacy of executive or legislative decision-making, just as there are to decision-making by the courts.' Indeed the considerable deference which the European Court of Human Rights shows to the view of the national authorities in such matters really presupposes that the national courts will police those limits. Moreover, by enacting section 30, Parliament, including the democratically elected House of Commons, gave SIAC and the appellate courts a specific mandate to perform that function—a function which the executive and the legislature cannot perform for themselves—in relation to this derogation. The legitimacy of the courts' scrutiny role cannot be in doubt.

[177]   On a broader view, too, scrutiny by the courts is appropriate. There is always a danger that, by its very nature, a concern for national security may bring forth measures that are not objectively justified. Sometimes, of course, as with the Reichstag fire, national security can be used as a pretext for repressive measures that are really taken for other reasons. There is no question of that in this case: it is accepted that the measures were adopted in good faith. But good faith does not eliminate the risk that, because of an understandable concern for national security, a measure may be taken which, on examination, can be seen to go too far. For example, even though it was a bona fide response to the crisis facing the nation in the summer of 1940, the mass detention of German and Italian enemy aliens, including many refugees, is sometimes thought—rightly or wrongly—to be a case in point. So, in these proceedings, even though detention of foreign suspects was introduced in good faith on grounds of national security, SIAC and the appellate courts have a limited, but nonetheless important, duty to check whether, as article 15(1) stipulates, the measure was strictly required by the exigencies of the situation.

So Lord Rodger too would be prepared to examine the nature of the emergency in order to determine whether the measures were strictly required for the purpose of dealing with the emergency.

My conclusions thus far on the discretionary area of judgment are as follows:

(i) The House of Lords did not accept the extreme view of deference derived from the *Rehman* case. It did not take the view that there were 'no go' areas into which the courts could not enter. It did not treat the question of the discretionary area of judgment in relation to matters of national security as a question of jurisdiction. It applied a flexible approach to the question of the discretionary area of judgment.

(ii) Like many other issues, the issue of national security is multifaceted. There are elements in it which are not reviewable save at the level of reasonableness, but likewise there are other elements which can be reviewed more intensely. Thus, when it came to the effect of the measures on the right to liberty of the detainees, the House of Lords in fact applied a level of scrutiny of higher intensity. It did so because there was a substantial legal content in the issue. I would add that another reason (as it seems to me) why the House could apply a high level of intensity was that the majority's reasoning on the proportionality issue required little in the way of evidence. Indeed, one could say that it was the lack of evidence from the Home Secretary that enabled the House to reach the conclusion that it did. However that may be, it is important to point out that the courts do not intervene to substitute their own view on a policy matter: the courts' intervention is limited to intervening in order to determine the legality of a measure or action. The choice of options belongs to the executive or legislature. As the President of the Supreme Court of Israel put it: 'The court's role is to ensure the constitutionality and legality of the fight against terrorism. It must ensure that the war against terrorism is conducted within the framework of the law.'[32]

(iii) The House of Lords did not formulate a detailed approach to the discretionary area of judgment. The House gave valuable guidance, but much has been left to be worked out in the future development of the case law.

I shall have to return to the discretionary area of judgment in the third section of my paper. Before I leave the subject (temporarily), I would add one comment. The concept of a discretionary area of judgment should be to executive discretion what the verdict of non-proven is to a criminal lawyer. The courts should not, simply because a matter is within the discretionary area of judgment, make the assumption with respect to that matter that the government must have taken the best decision that could have been taken on the information then available. In my view, it is a necessary consequence of judicial independence that, if the courts cannot review a matter on its merits, they should not make any assumption about those merits. The doctrine of the discretionary area of judgment must not be turned into a presumption that executive action within that area was necessarily correct.

Lord Hoffmann's view of the derogation issue

A different approach was taken by Lord Hoffmann. Lord Hoffmann's approach appeals to those who take the view that the risk of terrorist activity is greatly overstated. He took a minimalist approach to the circumstances in which a derogation may be made, and his approach greatly restricts the circumstances in which the other branches of government can use a derogation. This has the advantage of protecting the public against abuse by the government of the power to derogate. Abuse could occur if a government not acting in good faith could make an unfounded claim that there was a significant terrorist risk, and then seek to control the public or to secure votes, by appearing to control the terrorist risk by measures such as preventive detention. Abuse could also occur even if the government is in perfect good faith but, arguing from an exaggerated view of the risk to security, promotes measures that are oppressive or objectionable on human rights grounds. It is worth remembering that one of the first reactions of the Home Office after 9/11 was to seek to make the punishment for bomb hoaxers more severe and indeed to make the increase in penalty retrospective. Lord Hoffmann's approach is the best protection against abuse of both kinds. The difficulty, however, that I have

---

[32] President Aharon Barak, 'Foreword: A Judge on the Role of the Supreme Court in a Democracy' (2002) 116 Harvard L Rev 19 at 160.

with his interpretation is that it treats that which threatens 'the life of the nation' as something that threatens its death, but perhaps this is playing with words.

I now turn to Lord Hoffmann's now famous dictum: 'The real threat to the life of the nation, in the sense of a people living in accordance with its traditional laws and political values, comes not from terrorism but from laws such as these.' My colleagues may disagree with me, but I have had some doubts whether, with great respect to Lord Hoffmann, this is truly an expression of a legal judgment. It seems to me to be more a matter of political science. Indeed, political scientists would also probably express different views on how civil society is best protected. I also think that I myself would have wanted to see the closed material which SIAC saw, but which the House of Lords did not see, before coming to a view on such an issue.

Use of Parliamentary materials and opinions and resolutions of international institutions

The judgments in the *A* case are remarkable for the use which they make of other Parliamentary materials, and the opinions and resolutions of international institutions, such as the Council of Europe and the UN Human Rights Committee. The Parliamentary materials include reports of the Parliamentary Joint Committee on Human Rights, and this shows the importance of those reports and the influence which they are having on the development of human rights jurisprudence. The speeches also refer to the important report (referred to below as the Newton Report[33]) of the review committee chaired by Lord Newton. This report was prepared under s 122 of the 2001 Act, which provides for a committee of not less than nine Privy Counsellors to carry out a review of the operation of the 2001 Act within two years of its passing. I will refer to the Newton Report again in section three of this paper.

The contrast with *Liversidge v Anderson*

There is a startling difference of approach to preventive detention between the *A* case and *Liversidge v Anderson*,[34] in which the House of Lords effectively held that the detention of persons in wartime under reg 18B of the Defence (General) Regulations 1939 could only be successfully challenged if the Home Secretary could be shown not to have acted in good faith. As Professor Simpson has pointed out,[35] although habeas corpus was not suspended in World War II, that fact made little difference to the detainees under reg 18B. As he put it, the judges were prepared to behave as mice provided that they were treated as lions. Moreover, reg 18B applied to British nationals, not to enemy aliens, who could be detained under other legislation. The approach in the *Liversidge* case meant that the balancing of

---

[33] *Anti-Terrorism, Crime and Security Act Review: Report*, 18 December 2003.
[34] [1942] AC 206.
[35] See AW Brian Simpson, *In the Highest Degree Odious, Detention Without Trial in Wartime Britain* (Oxford University Press, 1995).

the interests of national security against those of the individual was the sole prerogative of the Home Secretary. In the *A* case, the House of Lords held that that balancing of those interests by the Secretary of State could be reviewed by the courts to ensure that appropriate regard was paid to the human rights considerations.

I would add as a footnote that indirect references by some of their Lordships to reg 18B reveal some misunderstandings about that regulation.[36] First, reg 18B was not, as stated, in general used to detain enemy aliens, but rather to detain nationals of this country or its colonies. Secondly, habeas corpus was not in fact suspended though the courts did not encourage such applications because of the width with which they—ultimately with the blessing of the House of Lords in the *Liversidge* case—construed the regulation. The history of reg 18B was therefore even more shocking than their Lordships who referred to it thought. However, any historical inaccuracy is minor and beside the point. In my view, the House of Lords in the *A* case are to be congratulated for not having had historical amnesia over the experience of preventive detention in the two World Wars.

Other objections to the statutory scheme?

Because the House of Lords were satisfied that s 23 was incompatible with the Convention, they did not have to consider whether the detail of the statutory scheme for preventive detention was consistent with the Convention. Lord Scott, however, noted that the Secretary of State does not have to tell a detainee of the grounds on which he is being detained.[37]

Indefinite imprisonment in consequence of a denunciation on grounds that are not disclosed and made by a person whose identity cannot be disclosed is the stuff of nightmares, associated whether accurately or inaccurately with France before and during the Revolution, with Soviet Russia in the Stalinist era...[38]

Baroness Hale of Richmond noted that it was part of the Attorney General's case that the safeguards were greater than under any other internment powers.[39] So the question is undecided: if there are circumstances in which preventive detention is justifiable, what safeguards must there be? Clearly there must be a system of appeals and the means of applying for bail. But what arrangements have to be made for legal representation? Where are the detainees to be held? What particulars must they be given of the grounds for their detention? What arrangements must be made to inform their families of where they are being held, and so on?

Explanation of Convention values—conspicuous by its absence?

The reaction of the general public to the decision in the *A* case has not been uniformly favourable. Some members of the public have expressed the view that the

---

[36] See generally, Simpson, *In the Highest Degree Odious*; and see Lord Bingham's 2002 Romanes Lecture, 'Personal Freedom and the Dilemma of Democracies' (2003) 52 ICLQ 841.
    [37] At [155].   [38] At [155].   [39] At [223].

judges had taken over the government's role in deciding how to react to a terrorist threat. The answer, of course, is that the House of Lords were applying the Convention. However, there is no explanation in the speeches of why the power to derogate from the Convention is so restrictive, even when national security is threatened. I think it would have been helpful if there had been some discussion on those lines. The absence of any such discussion may be due to the fact that the appellants were prepared to accept that terrorism poses a threat to western democracies. But that concession does not explain why the Convention, and, in the absence of the Convention, the English courts, approach any departure from civil liberties so restrictively.

An explanation can be found in the judgment of the Supreme Court of Israel in the 'ticking bomb' case. I will come to the passage below, but the gist of it is that 'sometimes, a democracy must fight with one hand behind its back'. An explanation of the way democracies subjected to terrorist threat should approach civil liberties can also be found, for instance, in the decision of the Supreme Court of India in *People's Union of Civil Liberties v Union of India*. The Supreme Court of India said:

> Terrorist acts are meant to destabilise the nation by challenging its sovereignty and integrity ... The protection and promotion of human rights under the rule of law is essential in the prevention of terrorism ... Here comes the role of law and the Court's responsibility. If human rights are violated in the process of combating terrorism, it will be self-defeating. Terrorism itself should also be understood as an assault on basic rights. In all cases, the fight against terrorism must be respectful to human rights. Our Constitution laid down clear limitations on the State actions within the context of the fight against terrorism. To maintain this delicate balance by protecting 'core' Human Rights is the responsibility of courts in a matter like this. [The] Constitutional soundness of [the Prevention of Terrorism Act 2002] needs to be judged by keeping these aspects in mind.[40]

At the end of the day, however, my comment is only a presentational point.

A comparison between the *A* case and the decisions of the Supreme Court of the United States on the Guantanamo Bay detainees

Because the media have drawn parallels between the detainees in the *A* case and those in Guantanamo Bay, it is important to distinguish clearly the legal issues which arise in that case from those which arose in *A*. There is a major difference between the ways in which the United Kingdom and the United States have approached the problem of terrorism at a legal level. The American approach to the problem of detention has a very different starting point. The US government takes the view that it is fighting a war, which it calls the war on terror.

If this is, legally speaking, a war, then the President of the United States has, under United States constitutional law, very considerable executive powers.

---

[40] Writ petition (civil) 389 of 2002, 16 December 2003.

The position is quite different in the United Kingdom, where the government remains responsible to Parliament even if there is a war. President Bush has the authority of Congress to use 'all necessary and appropriate force against those organisations or persons he determines planned, authorised, committed or aided the [9/11 attacks] . . . or harboured such organisations or persons'. In those circumstances his acts within that authority have, under the law of the United States, a very considerable degree of legitimacy. Accordingly, in the exercise of wartime powers, the President has considerable discretion to do things which under English law would require explicit sanction. The resolutions which I have just quoted are relied on to justify invading Iraq and holding the Guantanamo Bay detainees.

The circumstances which led to the detainees being taken to Guantanamo Bay are well known. Following 9/11, the United States and its allies took military action against Al Qaeda installations and the Taliban regime in Afghanistan. In the course of this exercise, the US took prisoner a number of Al Qaeda and Taliban suspects, some of whom were transferred to Camp X-Ray, a detention centre at a US naval base in Guantanamo Bay in Cuba. Many of those prisoners remain there. The US government at first claimed that all the prisoners were unlawful combatants who were not entitled to the protection of the Geneva Conventions. It has, I believe, since accepted that the Taliban prisoners are prisoners of war and thus entitled to the benefit of the Geneva Conventions. The US proposes to detain the prisoners until the war on terror is over, and to try them, where appropriate in military tribunals. Guantanamo Bay is not part of the sovereign territory of the United States, but is leased to it by Cuba.

Relatives of the Guantanamo Bay detainees have sought to establish in the US courts that the detainees are entitled to be tried in civilian courts in the United Kingdom.

On 28 June 2004 the Supreme Court handed down its historic decisions in a number of cases concerning detainees held following American military operations in Afghanistan. One of these, *Rasul v Bush*,[41] concerned the right of the Guantanamo Bay detainees to challenge their detention. The Supreme Court (by a majority of 6:3) reversed the lower court's decision to deny habeas corpus to the detainees. The majority (Stevens, O'Connor, Souter, Ginsburg, Breyer, and Kennedy JJ) held that the detainee did not have to be present in a federal district of the United States: it was sufficient that the United States had complete jurisdiction and control over the Guantanamo Bay base.

But the decision left unresolved a number of further important issues, such as the basis on which the detainees could challenge their detention. To some extent, these issues were considered in the further decision of *Hamdi v Rumsfeld*,[42] which was also handed down by the Supreme Court on 28 June 2004. Mr Hamdi is both an American national and within the territory of the United States. He had been captured in Afghanistan and taken to Guantanamo Bay. On its being discovered that he was an American citizen he was returned to the United States, where he

---

[41] 124 S Ct 2686 (2004).   [42] 124 S Ct 2633 (2004).

remains in detention. The Supreme Court held, by a majority of 8:1, that Mr Hamdi had the right to challenge his status in the US courts. The court divided on its reasons for so concluding, but it is not possible for me to go into that here.

The next question is: how could Mr Hamdi show that he was not a terrorist? He was faced with the difficulty in effect of proving a negative. On the other hand, courts traditionally do not involve themselves in issues of national security. These are matters for the executive. The judgment of the four justices who considered that the resolutions were wide enough to authorize Mr Hamdi's detention dealt with this point. They rejected the standard proposed by the government, namely that it should be sufficient for the government to meet the habeas corpus claim to show that there was some evidence that Mr Hamdi was an enemy combatant. It struck a middle ground between the contentions of both parties and held that, provided that the government showed that there was some credible evidence that Mr Hamdi was an enemy combatant, the onus would shift to him to rebut the evidence with more persuasive evidence that he was not in that category. Moreover the four justices referred to the possibility that military tribunals could be set up to give alleged enemy combatants an appropriate opportunity to challenge their status. Souter and Ginsberg JJ also rejected the government's approach but did not agree with the approach of the four justices on these issues (or propose their own).

Recently, the Federal Court for the District Court of Columbia made an order stopping the trial of a Guantanamo Bay detainee (said to have been Osama Bin Laden's driver) by military commission until the US government complied with the Geneva Conventions.[43] The US Supreme Court refused permission for a 'leapfrog' appeal to be taken to the Supreme Court. The case has now returned to the Federal Court of Appeals, whence it might in due course find its way back to the Supreme Court.[44]

It is immediately apparent that there is a sharp difference in the legal response to terrorism in our respective countries. Most importantly, in the United Kingdom, there is detailed legislation dealing with terrorism and containing (among other matters) a number of specified safeguards for suspects and other members of the public. By contrast, the United States has no equivalent of the 2001 Act. There are therefore no democratically decided upon conditions for the detention of suspected terrorists.

Before I leave this subject, I must explain that, for reasons of space, I cannot go further here into the position of the Guantanamo Bay detainees. Their position raises legal and humanitarian issues, many of which were addressed by Lord Steyn in his FA Mann lecture, 'Guantanamo Bay: the Legal Black Hole'.[45] It is a matter of regret that Guantanamo Bay constitutes one of the most enduring images of President Bush's war on terror.

---

[43] *Hamdan v Rumsfeld* 344 F Supp 2d 152 (DCC) (8 November 2004).
[44] (cert denied) 124 S Ct 2633 (2004). On 15 July 2005 the Federal Court of Appeals for the District of Columbia Circuit reversed the decision of the District Court.
[45] (2004) 52 ICLQ 1.

The wider picture and the principled approach to the legal issue of balancing human rights and national security arising from counter-terrorism laws

I now turn to the third section of my paper, in which I will examine the wider picture.

Over the last few years, writers in the field of human rights and terrorism[46] have struggled with the question of how to balance civil liberties and national security. For example, I myself, writing in March 2003, said that the balance could only be struck with difficulty. The question—how precisely does the court strike that balance?—struck me at that time as virtually unanswerable. However, in my view, the *A* case (and other case law) now provide considerable guidance in answering that question.

First, however, I must try to answer a different question: what is the significance of the decision of the House of Lords in the *A* case? Some measure of the importance of the issues can be gleaned from the fact that it is a decision of nine members of the Appellate Committee, which normally sits in constitutions of five. In my view, the significance of the decision may be expressed in these terms: the decision in the *A* case is a landmark decision that will be used as a point of reference by courts all over the world[47] for decades to come, even when the age of terrorism has passed. It is a powerful statement by the highest court in the land of what it means to live in a society where the executive is subject to the rule of law. Even the government, and even in times when there is a threat to national security, must act strictly in accordance with the law.

The decision is also a statement of what it means to live in a democratic society. Lord Bingham powerfully addressed this issue in the following passage:

I do not accept the distinction which [the Attorney-General] drew between democratic institutions and the courts. It is of course true that the judges in this country are not elected and are not answerable to Parliament. It is also of course true, . . . that Parliament, the executive and the courts have different functions. But the function of independent judges charged to interpret and apply the law is universally recognised as a cardinal feature of the modern democratic state, a cornerstone of the rule of law itself. The Attorney-General is fully entitled to insist on the proper limits of judicial authority, but he is wrong to stigmatise judicial decision-making as in some way undemocratic. It is particularly inappropriate in a case such as the present in which Parliament has expressly legislated in s.6 of the 1998 Act to render unlawful any act of a public authority, including a court, incompatible with a Convention right, has required courts (in s.2) to take account of relevant Strasbourg jurisprudence, has (in s.3) required courts, so far as possible to give effect to Convention rights and has conferred a right of appeal on derogation issues . . . The 1998 Act gives the courts a very specific, wholly democratic mandate . . . [48]

---

[46] For example, President Barak, 'Foreword' at 148–56.

[47] The speech of Lord Woolf in the Court of Appeal in *A v Secretary of State* was, for instance, referred to by the Supreme Court of India in December 2003: *People's Union of Civil Liberties v Union of India*, writ petition (civil) 389 of 2002, 16 December 2003.

[48] At [42].

I entirely of course agree with all of this but I think I would go further. The authority of the courts is not in some way inferior to that of the government or of Parliament because the judges are not elected. What happens when the democratically elected members of the legislature enact a law is that the courts must enforce it. This is the effect of the rule of law. In a democracy, the courts have a separate function of upholding the rule of law. The rule of law is the reason for the legitimacy of the decisions of the courts on legal issues. In short, the fact that judges are not elected by popular vote does not mean that what they say lacks legitimacy.

The priority which I have placed on the rule of law is somewhat different from the emphasis of the President of the Supreme Court of Israel. As we all know, Israel has faced the threat of terrorism for many years. The Israeli Supreme Court has developed a unique jurisprudence on the judicial approach to counter-terrorism laws. President Barak has given many judgments on this issue, notably the decision in the 'ticking bomb' case. The influence of President Barak can, I think, be perceived in the passage from the speech of Lord Bingham which I have just quoted.

President Barak's approach is illustrated by one of the oft-quoted passages in the 'ticking bomb' case, in which he said:

We conclude this judgment by revisiting the harsh reality in which Israel finds itself . . .

We are aware that this decision does not make it easier to deal with that reality. This is the fate of democracy, as not all means are acceptable to it, and not all methods employed by its enemies are always open before it. Sometimes, democracy must fight with one hand tied behind its back. Nonetheless, it has the upper hand. Preserving the rule of law and recognition of individual liberties constitute an important component of its understanding of security. At the end of the day, they strengthen its spirit and this strength allows it to overcome its difficulties.[49]

In this passage, President Barak tests the acceptability of executive or legislative acts against terrorism by what is acceptable in a democracy. On his approach judges have the role of protecting democratic principles, and thus of reviewing legislation for compliance with those principles. He has said extra-curially: 'Only a strong, safe and stable democracy may afford and protect human rights, and only a democracy built upon the foundation of human rights can have security.'[50] The rule of law is, of course, one of the principles of a democracy, but President Barak's emphasis is on democratic principles in general.

However, I would suggest that, as the democratically elected legislative body in this country has enacted the Human Rights Act 1998, the real basis of the English court's intervention is the rule of law rather than democratic principles in general. I repeat: in my view, the decision in the *A* case is a powerful statement by the highest court in the land of what it means to live in a society where the executive is subject to the rule of law. The importance of that message amply justifies the

---

[49] *Public Committee Against Torture v Israel*, 26 May 1999, HC 5100/94.53(4) PD 817, 845.
[50] President Barak, 'Foreword' at 155.

unusual approach which Baroness Hale took of providing in her judgment a simple summary of the principles underlying the decision and the reasons for the decision. President Barak noted that judges meet their supreme test in times of war and terrorism,[51] and the House of Lords surely rose to the challenge.

The decision in the *A* case should not be misinterpreted as a transfer of power from the executive to the judiciary. The position is that the judiciary now has the important task of reviewing executive action against the benchmark of human rights. Thus, the transfer of power is not to the judiciary but to the individual. The rights, which the courts are enjoined to protect, are those of the individual. The decision accordingly marks the transition to a rights-based democracy. In passing, I would observe that this new role for the judiciary increases the urgency for the reforms in the Constitutional Reform Bill now before Parliament.[52] The Bill contains a guarantee of judicial independence and a provision about the rule of law. It also provides for the establishment of a new independent judicial appointments commission which will make recommendations to the Lord Chancellor about the persons whom it considers should be appointed judges. Unless the judges are truly independent, they will not command the respect and confidence of those whose rights they are charged to determine.

I now go back to that question: how exactly should courts balance national security and human rights? We need a general principle because the question arises in so many contexts. I have spent much of this paper examining the *A* case, but laws for the detention of suspected terrorists are not the only laws restricting civil liberties designed to meet the terrorist threat. Other civil liberties most obviously liable to be restricted in times of emergency are: the right to a fair trial (Art 6), freedom of expression (Art 10), and freedom of assembly and association (Art 11). Counter-terrorism legislation has a corrosive, and sometimes imperceptible, threat on these human rights. Take, for example, the facts of *R (Gillan) v Commissioner of Police for the Metropolis*.[53] The appellants were two individuals who were stopped and searched on their way to the Docklands Arms Fair in September 2003. They were stopped under s 44 of the Terrorism Act 2000. This enables the police to be authorized for periods of up to 28 days at a time to stop and search members of the public. The senior officer giving the 28-day authorization must consider it expedient to give it for the prevention of acts of terrorism and the Home Secretary must confirm the authorization.

One of the appellants was on his way to join a peaceful demonstration. The other was a journalist who was going to film the protesters. There was no basis for suspecting them of any offence. They were searched. The journalist was searched even though she produced her press cards. She was told to stop filming.

The fact that the power in the Terrorism Act 2000 could only be given for a maximum of 28 days would suggest to anyone reading the statute that an authority under s 44 was intended to be temporary. In fact, unknown to the general public, the power had been exercised on a rolling basis every 28 days for a period of

---

[51] President Barak, 'Foreword' at 149.   [52] Now the Constitutional Reform Act 2005.
[53] [2004] EWCA Civ 1067, [2005] QB 388 (Lord Woolf CJ, Buxton and Arden LJJ).

two-and-a-half years. Not surprisingly, part of the appellants' argument was that authorizations under s 44 had become a regular part of policing.

Thus the tentacles of counter-terrorism legislation can stretch into all sorts of places. Other examples could be given. Moreover, as I explained at the outset, terrorism is not likely to be a transient phenomenon. Thus, if society makes expedient compromises over its civil liberties to deal with the terrorist threat, it is likely that the restrictions on liberties will become part of ordinary life. To reduce that risk, we need a principled approach to balancing human rights and security.

Exactly how should courts balance human rights against the needs of national security? Even though the *A* case deals only with the paradigm situation of the preventive detention of suspected terrorists, it does, I think, represent a beacon of light, a beacon of light that not only illuminates itself, but also shows us the direction in which we should travel. I say that for three reasons:

(1) The defence of liberty in the face of counter-terrorism legislation depends on the court's ability to review the actions of the executive in the sphere of national security. The approach of the House of Lords in the *A* case represents a positive, flexible step forward to such review. The approach of Lord Hope and Lord Rodger in particular may lead to further developments. Their approach may lead to a more proactive approach by the court to examining the evidence on which national security decisions are based. I do not suggest that the court needs to intervene more readily. However, it is likely to avoid abuse and the unnecessary curtailment of civil rights if the executive is required to satisfy the court on a fuller, and more frequent, basis that its national security decisions have been reached after proper enquiry, that they have a sufficient factual basis, that they are within an acceptable margin of reasonableness and that the decisions that were made were actually made on the basis of that material. Greater interrogation by the courts of the executive would, as I see it, be likely to improve standards of governance in these troubled times.

(2) The decision in the *A* case builds upon the Newton Report. I have referred to this above. Among other matters, that report took the principled stand that legislation against terrorism should approximate as closely as possible to ordinary criminal law and procedure. I would broaden that into a general principle: in counter-terrorism legislation, any departure from the principles of our ordinary law—whether common law or statute—should have to be justified. We should start from the footing that the ordinary law of the land, for instance the ordinary law as to search and seizure, should suffice. That, for any new legislation or rule, is the principled starting place.

(3) In very broad terms, and at the risk of over-simplification, the detention provisions in the *A* case were incompatible with the right to liberty because the provisions were not shown to be necessary and proportionate. I would seek to broaden that into a principle too. I would suggest that, whenever, in future, we have to balance national security against human rights, we should apply that simple test: is the curtailment of the right necessary and proportionate? The test is a very simple one, but I suggest that it will be found to provide a principled solution in most cases. If it does, then the decision of the House of Lords in the *A* case will have

done far more than provide a remedy for the seventeen Belmarsh detainees, important though that is. It will also have unlocked the door which will enable us in future confidently to answer the challenge posed by counter-terrorism laws to human rights and enable us to adopt a principled approach to that conundrum, the balancing of human rights and national security.

The *A* case is a very high profile case and it will rightly command great attention here and abroad. But the principled approach had, I think, already been worked out in the *Gillan* case even though the detention in that case had lasted only somewhere between five and thirty minutes. In the *Gillan* case, Lord Woolf CJ, giving the judgment of the court, examined the general approach that the court should adopt when reviewing the exercise of a power provided by Parliament for the prevention of terrorism. He spoke of the difficulties for the executive and the unlikelihood that the court would interfere with the executive's assessment of the risk and the steps necessary to counter that risk. He continued:

[34] This does not mean the courts do not have an important role in supervising the decisions and actions of the authorities. 'Although terrorism necessarily changes the context in which the rule of law must operate, it does not call for the abdication of law' (*In re an Application under section 83.28 of the Criminal Code* 2004 SCC 42, para.6 (*per* McLachlin C.J. and Iacobucci, Major and Arbour JJ., with whom Bastarache and Deschamps JJ. agreed)). Courts can ensure the authorities do not stray beyond the four corners of the power they have been given. They can ensure that the power is used only in furtherance of the purpose for which the power was provided and they can ensure its use is necessary and proportionate.

Lord Woolf then examined proportionality, referring to the approach of Lord Steyn in *R (Daly) v Secretary of State for the Home Department*.[54] I have not set out the whole passage but it is worthy of study and repetition. However, it is Lord Woolf's concluding words 'necessary and proportionate' that I would repeat and emphasize. Necessity and proportionality are, I suggest, the answer to that seemingly intractable question, how exactly do courts balance human rights and national security? Human rights are only to be curtailed if the restriction is necessary in the interests of national security and proportionate to the end to be achieved. The monumental case of *A v Secretary of State for the Home Department* has shown us that that indeed is the principled approach.

Postscript

Successive legislation has reduced the restrictions which can be imposed on persons who are suspected of terrorism and who have not been convicted of any offence. The two principal changes came about in 2005 and 2011.

---

[54] [2001] UKHL 532, [2001] 2 AC 532 at [27].

On 11 March 2005, after intense debate, Parliament passed the Prevention of Terrorism Act 2005 (the '2005 Act'), which repealed ss 21–32 of the Anti-terrorism, Crime and Security Act 2001. In place of those sections, the 2005 Act provided for 'control orders' to be made in respect of individuals suspected of being involved in terrorism-related offences. If the order involved no derogation from the right to liberty in Art 5 of the European Convention on Human Rights, the Secretary of State could make the order with the permission of the court, and the function of the court was to consider whether the decision of the Secretary of State that there were grounds to make the order was obviously flawed. A non-derogating order lasted for 12 months but could be renewed. If, however, a control order was of a kind which violated Art 5, there had to be a derogation order in force under the Human Rights Act 1998 and the control order could only be made by the court, which could also make interim orders. The court could only confirm an interim order at a full hearing if, among other things, it was satisfied on a balance of probabilities that the defendant was or had been involved in terrorism-related activity. Such an order lasted for six months but was subject to renewal. Control orders could contain a variety of restrictions, including restrictions on movement and communication. Provision was made for appeals against control orders and for the modification or revocation of control orders.[55] On the day that the 2005 Act was passed, the persons in detention under Part 4 of the 2001 Act were released. Strict conditions were imposed on them, including conditions as to electronic tagging, living at their home addresses and a curfew from 7pm to 7am.

Control orders were in turn abolished by the Terrorist Prevention and Investigation Measures Act 2011. This Act introduced TPIMs.[56] TPIMs are similar in some respects to control orders but a higher evidential burden must be satisfied before they can be imposed. Many of the same restrictions as can be applied by a control order can be applied by a TPIM, but not the most serious. Moreover, a TPIM cannot last more than two years. TPIMs are controversial. One major criticism is that they restrict the liberty of individuals who have not been convicted of any offence.

These changes have not materially affected the need to search for a principled approach.

The *Gillan* case (footnote 53 above) went to the House of Lords (see further pages 182–5 below), and to the Strasbourg Court. The Strasbourg Court held that Art 8 of the Convention was violated because the stop and search powers were wide and lacked sufficient safeguards against abuse. The Strasbourg Court did not express a view on whether Art 5 was violated: *Gillan v UK* (App. No. 4158/05) [2010] ECHR 4158/05.

---

[55] Control orders are discussed further at pages 191–4 below.
[56] As at 1 September 2014, this legislation was still in force.

11

Balancing Human Rights and National Security

This chapter is an extract from a speech given to the Constitutional Court of South Africa in Johannesburg, 2005.*

How is national security to be balanced with human rights? Is it ever possible to do so? As South Africa knows, if we make expedient compromises it is all too likely that restrictions on liberty will become part of everyday life and that the character of a democratic society will be altered and possibly lost. Until his retirement last October, Lord Steyn was one of the three members of the Appellate Committee of the House of Lords from South Africa. He pointed out that the mindset in troubled times that 'after all we are on the same side as the government' is a slippery slope which tends to sap the will of the judiciary to stand up to a government guilty of an abuse of power. One must not forget that the principles which the courts develop in times of emergency may be applied in normal conditions as well.

So the courts have to be vigilant. At the same time they have to have a consistent and principled approach. I would now like to suggest to you the way in which a principled approach might be developed.

I said elsewhere that in my view the key to dealing with the question of how human rights and national security are to be balanced is through the doctrine of proportionality. This was the approach put forward by the Court of Appeal in the *Gillan* case.[1] The Court said:

Courts can ensure that the authorities do not stray beyond the four corners of the power that they have been given. They can ensure that the power is used only in furtherance of the purpose for which the power is given and they can ensure that its use is necessary and proportionate.[2]

* Subsequently published as 'Balancing Human Rights and National Security', South African Law Journal, vol.124:1, 2007. It is reproduced here with the kind permission of the Publisher.

[1] *R (Gillan) v Commissioner of Police of the Metropolis and another* [2004] EWCA Civ 1067, [2005] QB 388 (Lord Woolf CJ, Buxton and Arden LJJ).

[2] *Gillan* at [34].

But what the Court of Appeal did not have to do in that case was expand on how to apply the test of proportionality. I would like now to consider how the doctrine might be developed.

Proportionality means that you have to balance two interests: here, the interest of the state in security and the interest of the individual in the preservation of his human rights. The right of liberty is not inviolable. As the *Gillan* case shows, it is possible that it can properly be restricted. But the result of balancing in any given case must depend on the relevant circumstances. The fact that liberty can be restricted on one occasion does not mean that it should be restricted on other occasions.

But in order to know how to balance the interest of national security and the interest of the individual the courts need to have some idea of what is to be balanced against the infringement of the individual's right. We would all accept that terrorism must never be allowed to destroy the democratic way of life in society or to endanger the safety of its citizens. But in weighing up the interest of national security, the court has, I think, to look below the surface as Lord Hope indicated in the *Belmarsh* case.[3] Thus the courts may well have to be satisfied that the measure will have a material effect in preventing terrorism or on the safety of the public, and that there is no downside in other respects such as damage to community relations. The onus of proving all this must logically lie on the state, which has the resources at its disposal to state the likelihood of this being the case.

One of the lessons of 7/7 (the attack on London transport in July 2005 in which fifty-two people died) is that counter-terrorist measures do not ensure the safety of individual members of the public. Even with control orders the public was still at risk. So the question that society has to ask itself is whether the incomplete security which counter-terrorist measures provide for the protection of its members justifies their effect on the liberty of the individual members. We have to see terrorism as a long-term problem and avoid the temptation to deal with it by short-term solutions. We must also try to keep the problem in perspective. More people are killed in natural disasters than terrorist incidents. Some intrusion of personal liberty is of course acceptable, such as searches at airports and the entrance to buildings. But major intrusions into the right to liberty may well be a different matter. But the truth is that some risk from terrorism is bound to remain however intrusive the counter-terrorist measures are. No measures will make us absolutely secure from terrorism. It would seem pointless so to restrict individual liberties in the hope of making people more secure if the result is to destroy the essential characteristics of a free and democratic society. To preserve those characteristics, therefore, we may have to accept some risks will remain.

As I see it, understanding these issues is essential to solving the problem implicit in the title to this paper. I would be interested to know whether the jurisprudence of South Africa has another approach to offer. I am a strong supporter of a dialogue between judges of different jurisdictions particularly for the purpose of discussing

---

[3] *A v Secretary of State for the Home Department* [2004] UKHL 56, [2005] 2 AC 68 at [116].

problems which they have in common. One of the benefits of a comparative discussion is that participants can see what solutions are suggested by another system with a view to unlocking their potential for solving the problem for their own system. But this is not just a matter of dialogue between judges. Judges today have a role of educating society about the meaning of constitutional rights. It follows that it may very well be that what judges have to do in the future is to explain to society why the law cannot always put national security first, so that people understand the decisions like that in the *Belmarsh* case.

I conclude with a reference to a play written by Robert Bolt called *A Man for all Seasons*.[4] I think it describes the issue of balancing national security and individual rights graphically and memorably. Sir Thomas More was a Lord Chancellor who was eventually executed by Henry VIII for his failure to support the disestablishment of the Church. In this passage, Robert Bolt describes an imaginary conversation between the Lord Chancellor, Sir Thomas More, who was about to be betrayed, and his son-in-law, William Roper. Roper suspects that someone is about to betray More. He is an impetuous young man and he demands that More has the man arrested. But More refuses: the man has done nothing illegal, and until he does, he, and even the devil himself, is entitled to the protection of the law. The conversation was on the following lines:

ROPER So now you'd give the Devil benefit of law!

MORE Yes. What would you do? Cut a great road through the law to get after the Devil?

ROPER I'd cut down every law in England to do that!

MORE Oh? And when the last law was down, and the Devil turned round on you, where would you hide, Roper, the laws all being flat? This country's planted thick with laws from coast to coast—man's laws, not God's—and if you cut them down—and you're just the man to do it—do you really think you could stand upright in the winds that would blow them? Yes, I'd give the Devil benefit of laws, for my own safety's sake.

This passage reminds us that, if the rights of suspected terrorists are diminished, so potentially is the protection for other members of society, who may be entirely innocent of any crime or wish to harm society. In that way, the values of a democratic society are put in danger. Any balancing of national security with human rights has to remember that kind of risk.

---

[4] R Bolt, *A Man for all Seasons*, Heineman, 1960.

12

Meeting the Challenge of Terrorism: The Experience of English and Other Courts

This chapter is an edited version of the John Lehane Memorial Lecture given in Sydney in 2006.*

Introduction

I first came to Australia in April 2003 and during my visit I gave a lecture on terrorism and human rights. The circumstances were very different. The terrorist attack which has become known as '9/11' has been followed by stringent counter-terrorist legislation across the world, including Australia. In October 2001, the United States and its allies had entered Afghanistan to prevent the Taliban regime from supporting terrorists. The appalling bombing incident in Bali, in which 202 people lost their lives, had by then occurred. The UK legislation for the executive detention of suspected terrorists had just begun its way up the English courts and the US courts were starting to engage with the problems of Guantanamo Bay. The invasion of Iraq had started (on 23 March 2003). But things have moved on. In March 2004, some 173 people were killed in terrorist bomb attacks in Madrid. In September 2004, nine people were killed when a bomb exploded outside the Australian Embassy in Jakarta. In July 2005, fifty-two people were killed by suicide bombs on the London Underground, followed two weeks later by the Stockwell killing in which a person was fatally wounded by the police on the Tube because it was mistakenly thought that he was a suicide bomber. In July 2006, 207 people were killed by bombs left on trains in Mumbai. There have been many other incidents and in all these incidents many people have suffered serious injury.

In addition, the British and the Australian Parliaments have both been busy enacting new anti-terrorist laws. There are political and other developments day in and day out. There are many ways of tackling the problem of terrorism. For example, one way of tackling it, and I suggest the best way there is at the moment, is by improving our intelligence capability so that the authorities can stop terrorist plots before they are executed. Another way is to control terrorist funding by

---

* This lecture was first published in (2006) AJLR 818. It is reproduced here with the kind permission of the Publisher.

imposing strict controls on the movement of large sums of money. A further way is to impose strict immigration control so that suspected terrorists with no right of entry are denied entry. People can, of course, seek to hide their identity at ports of entry but the techniques to prevent this are improving through use of biometric information and information as to the vital measurements of a person's face. But it will also be necessary to use other more obvious measures such as imposing restraints on the use of information, creating new offences for activities associated with terrorism, and detaining or deporting persons suspected of connections with terrorism and bringing them to trial. I will call these 'law and order measures' to distinguish them from intelligence and hi-tech measures such as the interception of communications.

It is inevitable that governments will wish to control terrorism through law and order measures of this kind. It is the duty of governments to take reasonable steps to keep persons within their control secure from threats to life. The European Court of Human Rights, (the 'Strasbourg Court'), has indeed held that the right to life means that for a government not to take such action could result in a violation of the right to life conferred by the European Convention on Human Rights[1] (the 'Convention').

My basic thesis is that the courts cannot respond to the situation posed by terrorism in a totally inflexible way. They are the guardians of individual rights, but at the same time they have to take account of the seriousness of the terrorist threat. I will seek to draw an analogy with an expansion joint. Consider the expansion joint in the Sydney Harbour Bridge. There has to be an expansion capability so that the structure can endure changes of temperature. The bridge has to be able to expand and contract in line with those changes. So it is with the law and threats such as the threat of terrorism. As I will endeavour to show you, there are ways in which the law must adapt to the new challenges that it now faces. I will return to the analogy of the Sydney Harbour Bridge in due course.

The legal issues raised by law and order measures are extensive. When I started to prepare this paper, I had a choice as to whether to present my material chronologically, or by topic, or by country or region. In the end my choice was not to confine myself to any particular topic or type of terrorist measure, but to choose pairs or groups of cases that would serve two purposes. The first purpose is to convey information about some of the major developments in the jurisprudence in this field. The second purpose is to use the material to draw conclusions about lessons for the future. So, once I have outlined the cases in question, I will seek to draw some conclusions and to conclude with some ideas for further consideration and discussion.

The cases I have chosen concern a number of different legal topics within terrorism. They are not confined to any single legal system. The comparison of cases from different jurisdictions needs to be done with caution. Different legal systems are likely to have different rules and benchmarks for the validity or

---

[1] *Osman v United Kingdom* [1999] Crim LR 82.

constitutionality of rules. Additionally, each legal system lives within a particular social and political context and thus the driving factors behind the jurisprudence of the courts will vary. But I am concerned not with the first tier question that arises in any case of establishing precisely what is the rule the court has to apply, but with the second tier questions that arise in any legal system simply because rules are rarely perfectly clear or complete in themselves. For example, under certain rights guaranteed by the Convention, an English court may have to assess the compatibility of a measure by reference to what is 'necessary in a democratic society'.[2] Those words 'necessary in a democratic society' have a dynamic content that requires them to be constantly updated. Thus the court that has to apply those terms at any particular point in time is likely to have to make a value judgment as to what they should entail. It is those value judgments that I seek to compare and contrast. What this comparison shows is that here is considerable common ground in the common law world. This in itself is a potential source of strength for decision-making in this sphere.

The Convention and the Human Rights Act 1998

It may be helpful at this point to summarize the position in English law regarding the Convention and the UK Human Rights Act 1998.[3] It is well known that the United Kingdom has neither a codified constitution nor its own indigenous Bill of Rights. The domestic courts of the United Kingdom are, however, empowered to give protection to the rights guaranteed by the Convention. This was drafted after the experiences of the Second World War and British lawyers played an important role in its drafting.

The Convention is an international treaty to which the states who are members of the Council of Europe are parties. Theses states stretch from Ireland in the West to Russia in the East. The principal rights under the Convention are the rights to life, freedom from torture, liberty, fair trial, freedom to manifest one's religion, and freedom of expression.[4] There is a provision that enables a member state to derogate from the right to liberty and certain other rights if there is a 'war or other public emergency threatening the life of the nation'.[5]

The UK courts could not enforce the rights guaranteed by the Convention without domestic legislation implementing the Convention. In the case of England and Wales, this was the Human Rights Act 1998, which was commenced on 2 October 2000. By s 2, the courts 'must take into account' Strasbourg jurisprudence when deciding questions in connection with Convention rights. Section 3 is then directed to the interpretation of legislation. It requires an English court so far as

---

[2] See eg European Convention on Human Rights, Arts 8 (right to respect for private and family life) and 10 (freedom of expression).
[3] The Convention rights and the principal provisions of that Act are set out in the Appendix.
[4] European Convention on Human Rights, Arts 2, 3, 5, 6, 9, and 10.
[5] European Convention on Human Rights, Art 15.

possible to interpret legislation (whenever enacted) so that it is in conformity with Convention rights. But this does not empower the court to rewrite legislation or interpret it in a manner which is inconsistent with a fundamental feature of the legislation.[6] Nor does it empower the court to strike down primary legislation, ie legislation enacted by Parliament as opposed to secondary legislation made under powers conferred by Parliament. If the court cannot interpret primary legislation so that it conforms to the Convention, it can (if it is one of the higher courts) make a declaration of incompatibility (s 4). There are two consequences of this. First, in the case before it, the court must apply the legislation as it stands (and it will not be able to give effect to the Convention). Second, the government may use a streamlined procedure to introduce an amendment to make the legislation conform to the Convention (s 10). In this way, Parliamentary sovereignty is preserved.

Section 6 of the Human Rights Act 1998 provides that it is unlawful for public authorities to act in a manner that is incompatible with Convention rights. So, if a department of state wishes to exercise a discretionary power, it must do so in conformity with the Convention. The Act does not define 'public authority'. However s 6 states that the court is a public authority. It, too, has a duty not to act incompatibly with the Convention. However, Parliamentary sovereignty is preserved, because the new duty does not apply to an act if the public authority could not have acted differently because of primary legislation (s 6(2)(a)).

Section 19 is also important because it provides that, when a government bill is introduced into Parliament, the relevant government minister must make a statement as to whether the bill complies with the Convention. This makes it difficult in practice for the government to introduce legislation that does not comply with the Convention.

The Convention provides in Art 6 for the establishment of the Strasbourg Court to ensure the observance of the Convention. It thus has the power to give authoritative rulings on the interpretation of the Convention.

With that digression, I now return to the main theme of this paper. The roadmap that I will be taking through those cases is from deportation to detention, then to torture, control orders[7] and special trial procedures.

Deportation: *Chahal* and *Mohamed*

I will deal with these first two cases briefly. They are important because they establish a principle that has influenced the development of the law in this field. The first is the decision of the Strasbourg Court in *Chahal v United Kingdom*[8] (the '*Chahal* case'). In this case the British government wished to deport Mr Chahal to India on the grounds that his continued presence in the United Kingdom was not

---

[6] *Ghaidan v Godin-Mendoza* [2004] UKHL 30, [2004] 2 AC 557.

[7] Control orders are discussed below. They constitute orders which restrict the movements of a terrorist suspect but do not involve full-time detention.

[8] (Application No 22414/93) (1997) 23 EHRR 413.

conducive to the public good, including the fight against terrorism. Mr Chahal was a well known Sikh separatist. He, however, claimed that on his return he would suffer inhuman and degrading treatment, contrary to Art 3 of the European Convention on Human Rights, at the hands of the Indian police. The British government contended that, although generally a deportation which resulted in a violation of the deportee's rights under Art 3 on his return would normally violate the Convention, this did not apply where the activities of the deportee were considered to be damaging to national security or, alternatively, this damage was certainly a matter the court could take into account in deciding what course to take. The Strasbourg Court rejected these arguments and stressed the importance of Art 3. It held that the activities of the individual in question could not excuse a violation of Art 3. The effect of this decision is that, in the absence of satisfactory assurances from the receiving state, even a dangerous terrorist could not be deported. This principle is often referred to as the *Soering* principle.[9]

The Constitutional Court of South Africa came to a similar conclusion in *Mohamed v President of South Africa*[10] (the '*Mohamed* case'). I would like to summarize this case because it helps to demonstrate the near universality[11] of the philosophical position taken in the *Chahal* case. The *Mohamed* case also concerned an alleged terrorist, in this case a Tanzanian who was alleged to have conspired to bring about the bombing of the United States embassies in Dar-es-Salaam and Nairobi in 1998. These were particularly serious acts of terrorism. Over 220 people were killed in these incidents and over 4,500 persons were injured. Mr Mohamed moved to South Africa and applied for asylum under an assumed name. In the meantime a grand jury in New York had concluded that the attacks were the work of Al-Qaeda. Mr Mohamed was spirited out of South Africa and put on trial in New York for an offence which, upon conviction, could lead to the death penalty. It was held that this was a violation of Mr Mohamed's constitutional rights. The South African Constitution protects the right to life. The Court referred to a number of cases, including *Chahal*, and held that it was a breach of Mr Mohamed's constitutional rights for the South African authorities to hand him over to the American authorities without obtaining an assurance that the death penalty would not be exacted.

It is the *Soering* principle which led the British government to introduce legislation for the executive detention of foreign terrorist suspects. In the next section I will examine a major decision on that legislation.

---

[9] After the decision in *Soering v United Kingdom* [1989] 11 EHRR 439, where this principle was first applied. In the *Soering* case, however, it was not alleged that the deportee was a terrorist.
[10] 2001 (3) SA 837.
[11] The Supreme Court of Canada has, however, left open the question whether in exceptional circumstances an individual might be deported to a receiving state where he might be tortured or subject to inhuman or degrading treatment: *Suresh v Canada* [2002] 1 SCR 3.

Detention: the *A* case, the *Gillan* case and Guantanamo Bay

After 9/11, Parliament passed the Anti-terrorism, Crime and Security Act 2001 (the '2001 Act'). This was a substantial piece of legislation. The most controversial part of the 2001 Act, however, was Part 4 under which the Home Secretary was given authority to issue against an alien a certificate of the Home Secretary's reasonable belief that the individual's presence in the United Kingdom constitutes a threat to national security and that the person was accordingly a suspected terrorist. Such a person might then be detained and deported. However, if the *Soering* principle applied, so that the alien could not be deported without risk of torture or death in the country to which he was to be returned, the 2001 Act enabled the Secretary of State to detain him indefinitely. Significantly, the alien did not have to be brought to trial in that period. This made it necessary for the UK government to enter a derogation under Art 15 of the Convention. The United Kingdom was the only signatory to the Convention to do this. The derogation was from Art 5(1)(f), which permits detention with a view to deportation but not indefinite detention if deportation is not possible.

The 2001 Act conferred rights of appeal in lieu of the right to apply for habeas corpus. The Secretary of State's certificate was subject to an appeal to the Special Immigration Appeals Commission ('SIAC'). This tribunal has three members, at least one of whom must be a judge who holds or has held high judicial office and at least one of whom must be an immigration judge. It sits without a jury.

SIAC had power to cancel the certificate if it considered that it should not have been issued. The issue then for SIAC was whether there were reasonable grounds for the Home Secretary's belief or suspicion, and SIAC had to reach an objective judgment on this question against all the circumstances in which the judgment was to be made. SIAC also had jurisdiction to determine whether the derogation satisfied the conditions of Art 15 of the Convention. There was an 'open' element in the proceedings before SIAC, which considered the information that the Home Secretary is prepared to disclose to the detainee. There was also a 'closed' element to these proceedings, in which SIAC examined material that the Home Secretary was not prepared to make public. In this part of the process a special advocate represented the detainee. Once a special advocate has received the closed material he may no longer communicate with the detainee or his legal representatives. The detainee could further appeal, but on a point of law only, to the Court of Appeal. If he was unsuccessful in the Court of Appeal he could appeal again, with permission, to the House of Lords.

SIAC had to review the certificate at regular intervals. SIAC could grant bail, where appropriate, subject to conditions. If a detainee agreed to leave the United Kingdom, his detention came to an end. The 2001 Act provides for a derogation from Convention rights under Art 15 of the Convention to be challenged before SIAC.

I have now set the scene for the decision of the House of Lords in the *A v Secretary of State for the Home Department*[12] (the '*A* case'; sometimes called the '*Belmarsh* case' after the prison where the detainees were held). This is a landmark decision for many reasons. It is also an unusual decision in that it is a decision of nine members of the House, which normally sits in constitutions of five.[13] By its decision, the House of Lords, in exercise of its powers conferred by the Human Rights Act 1998, quashed the Human Rights (Designated Derogation) Order 2001, and made a declaration that s 23 of the Anti-terrorism Crime and Security Act 2001 (providing for detention without trial) was incompatible with Arts 5 and 14[14] of the Convention. In so doing, the House of Lords restored the order of SIAC, which had been set aside by the Court of Appeal. It must be one of the first times that the courts of the United Kingdom have dealt such a body blow to legislation enacted by Parliament to confer powers on the Executive to meet a threat to national security. The decision shows the measure of the change made by the Human Rights Act 1998.

The decision is a lengthy one. It extends to some 100 pages. The lead judgment is that of Lord Bingham, but each of the other members of the House, other than Lord Carswell, also provides reasons for their decision. It is impossible to do justice to all the reasoning and learning in any summary of them. I have given a lecture devoted to this case, now published in the *Law Quarterly Review*,[15] in which more detailed comments can be found.

It was of course accepted by the government that provisions of Part 4 of the 2001 Act were incompatible with Art 5 of the Convention as the government had entered a derogation pursuant to Art 15 of the Convention. The relevant part of that article reads:

15(1)   In time of war or other public emergency threatening the life of the nation any High Contracting Party may take measures derogating from its obligations under this Convention to the extent strictly required by the exigencies of the situation, provided that the measures are not inconsistent with its other obligations under international law.

The threshold question in the *A* case was whether a state of emergency had arisen entitling the United Kingdom to derogate from the articles specified above. The House of Lords (by a majority of 8:1,[16] but Lord Scott of Foscote *dubitante*[17]) rejected the appellants' arguments on this point. In essence, the question had been one for SIAC. SIAC had heard evidence that had not been disclosed to the House of Lords and there was no misdirection by SIAC and therefore no error of law. In one of its earliest decisions on this issue, the Strasbourg Court had accepted that

---

[12] [2004] UKHL 56, [2005] 2 AC 68.

[13] According to *The Economist* (18 December 2004), this is only the second time that it has sat with a constitution of nine since the Second World War.

[14] This prohibits discrimination, on any ground, in the enjoyment of Convention rights.

[15] M Arden, 'Human Rights in the Age of Terrorism' (2005) 121 LQR 604. (Reproduced at Chapter 10.)

[16] The dissenting judgment was that of Lord Walker, who usefully summarizes his views in *A v Secretary of State for the Home Department* at [209].

[17] *A v Secretary of State for the Home Department* at [154].

Ireland could derogate from the Convention even though it was not shown that a widespread loss of life or an attack on the territorial integrity of the state was involved.

Moreover, the House was prepared to attach great weight to the judgment of the Secretary of State and Parliament to the issue whether there was a public emergency threatening the life of the nation. In the words of Lord Bingham (at [29]):

It is perhaps preferable to approach [the question of the deference owed by the courts to the political authorities] as one of demarcation of functions or what Liberty in its written case called 'relative institutional competence'. The more purely political (in a broad or narrow sense) a question is, the more appropriate it will be for political resolution and the less likely it is to be an appropriate matter for judicial decision. The smaller, therefore, will be the potential role of the court. It is the function of political and not judicial bodies to resolve political questions. Conversely, the greater the legal content of any issue, the greater the potential role of the court, because under our constitution and subject to the sovereign power of Parliament it is the function of the courts and not of political bodies to resolve legal questions. The present question seems to me to be very much at the political end of the spectrum.

Lord Nicholls was more emphatic than Lord Bingham in his rejection of the appellants' arguments on the validity of the derogation. He held that (at [79]):

All courts are acutely conscious that the government alone is able to evaluate and decide what counter-terrorism steps are needed and what steps will suffice. Courts are not equipped to make such decisions, nor are they charged with that responsibility.

Both Lord Scott and Lord Hoffmann made reference to the shortcomings of intelligence in relation to Iraq and weapons of mass destruction. They took the view that, even though courts are not able to second-guess intelligence, they are able to have a substantial amount of scepticism about it.

On the derogation issue, the lone dissenting voice was that of Lord Hoffmann. He held that, although he was prepared to accept that there was credible evidence that terrorist outrages were planned against the United Kingdom, there was no emergency threatening the life of the nation for the purposes of Art 15. He wrote (at [96]):

Terrorist violence, serious as it is, does not threaten our institutions of government or our existence as a civil community.

He further held (at [97]):

The real threat to the life of the nation, in the sense of a people living in accordance with its traditional laws and political values, comes not from terrorism but from laws such as these. That is the true measure of what terrorism may achieve.

There has been considerable protest from politicians over this passage. In my article in the Law Quarterly Review, I respectfully expressed doubts as to whether this was an expression of a legal judgment as opposed to one of political science.[18]

---

[18] M Arden, 'Human Rights in the Age of Terrorism' (2006) 121 LQR 604 (reproduced at Chapter 10).

A journalist in *The Observer* newspaper wrote that 'The slyness of the sentiment infuriated [many politicians and civil servants]' and that Lord Hoffmann had 'allowed no room for argument about the balance between liberty and security'.[19] I am not convinced that this is a fair criticism since there was no balancing exercise of that kind to be performed in the *A* case.

In South Africa, at the time of the apartheid, the regime used anti-terrorist legislation as a means of stifling opposition. That is, however, a very different situation from that in which the United Kingdom finds itself.

The second issue in the *A* case was whether the provisions of the 2001 Act relating to detention violated Convention rights only 'to the extent strictly required by the exigencies of the situation' for the purposes of Art 15. Here the argument focused on the fact that the powers of detention related only to foreign nationals who could not be deported. It could not be said that foreign nationals were the only threat; if they were a threat, they could under the 2001 Act go abroad and carry on their activities from abroad. They could be detained even if the threat which they presented was not as members of Al-Qaeda but of some other organization altogether which had not been responsible for the state of emergency justifying the derogation. The House of Lords (by a majority of 7:1, Lord Hoffmann not expressing a view on this or the next issue) accepted these arguments: in a word, s 23 was irrational. The fact that the detention could be reviewed by SIAC did not overcome these points. As Lord Scott put it, the Secretary of State:

should at least . . . have to show that monitoring arrangements or movement restrictions less severe than incarceration in prison would not suffice.[20]

Lord Scott's reference to movement restrictions was taken up by the government after its defeat in the *A* case when the government introduced a bill to enable control orders to be imposed on suspected terrorists. I will explain what the courts have said about that later in this paper.

In the *A* case, the House of Lords also held (and this was the third issue) that the powers of preventive detention discriminated unjustifiably between non-UK nationals and UK nationals, who could not be detained on suspicion.

What is the significance of the decision of the House of Lords in the *A* case? It is a landmark decision in a favour of liberty and freedom of the individual. It will be cited in the English courts for many years to come. It is also likely to be cited in courts in other countries. The analysis of the legal issues is also very important. On the question whether there was a 'public emergency threatening the life of the nation' for the purposes of Art 15 of the Convention, the view of the majority was deferential to that of Parliament largely because the question of the scale of the terrorist threat was one of political judgment in which the courts had a more limited role to play. It should be noted that the appeal was limited to the question

[19] N Cohen, 'Save us from the Crackpots who see Zionist Conspiracies in Everything', *The Observer* (13 August 2006).
[20] These criticisms of Part 4 would make it difficult for the government to seek to meet human rights considerations simply by extending Part 4 to UK nationals.

of whether SIAC had made an error of law; there was no rehearing of the evidence. The question was not whether the individuals who were being detained[21] presented a threat of the seriousness required by Art 15; their position fell to be examined on the second question before the House. As noted earlier, Lord Hoffmann dissented. The passages from his speech already quoted have been much criticized. It is, however, possible to point to regimes where legislation about terrorism has been used to maintain a particular regime in power. Lord Hoffmann's observations would have been very relevant if there had been a finding that the government intended to use the powers of detaining individuals for ulterior purposes or if the House had concluded that the government's assessment of the situation was wholly unreasonable. But that was not so in this case.

The view of the majority on the first question contrasts sharply with its view on the question whether the provisions for detention were 'strictly required by the exigencies of the situation' as required by Art 15 of the Convention. Here the House rejected the government's argument. The House was on firmer and more familiar ground on this aspect of the case and the question of proportionality. It could conclude that the power of detention did not prevent any person who was content to return to his own country from doing so and carrying on terrorist activities from there. (To prevent a person acting in this way, it would have been necessary to bring criminal proceedings against him and obtain a conviction and a sentence of imprisonment.) Nor did the power of detention prevent UK nationals from carrying on terrorist activities because they could not be detained under this power.

My view is that the importance of the decision is its bottom line. The House rejected the idea of detention of alien terrorists without trial, notwithstanding the pressure of arguments as to national security. The deprivation of liberty by indefinite detention without trial is such an extreme measure that very special circumstances are needed to justify it. The decision is a powerful statement of the value to be placed on the Convention right to liberty.

I now turn to another case decided in 2006 by the House of Lords, namely *R (Gillan) v Commissioner of Police for the Metropolis*[22] (the '*Gillan* case'). This decision also arises out of powers conferred by anti-terrorist legislation. The contrast which it provides with the *A* case is what makes it interesting in the context of the present discussion. It shows that the deprivation of freedom does not simply mean placing an individual under lock and key or under a control order. There is a range of different ways in which liberty can be affected by anti-terrorist legislation. The facts of the case also show that the liberty in question may be that of an ordinary citizen and not that of a suspected terrorist. I was a party to the decision of the Court of Appeal in this case.

The facts were simple. The appellants were stopped and searched on their way to watch a peaceful demonstration outside an arms fair under powers contained in the Terrorism Act 2000. That Act provides that a chief police constable or an assistant

---

[21] There were sixteen individuals in all who were detained.
[22] [2006] UKHL 12, [2006] 2 WLR 537. See postscript pp 168–9 above.

police officer can, if he is satisfied that it is expedient to do so for the prevention of acts of terrorism, issue an authorization to police officers to stop and search persons without having to have any suspicion of their having committed any offence. The authorization has to be confirmed by the Home Secretary, but it is not made public. The power of search may only be used for the purpose of searching for articles of a kind that could be used in connection with terrorism. The principal issue before the Court of Appeal was whether the detention involved in a search of this kind was a restriction on liberty that violated the right to liberty in Art 5 of the Convention. If it was it did not fall within the exceptions to Art 5. The Court of Appeal held that there had been no violation of Art 5 in these circumstances. The House of Lords upheld this decision. The *Gillan* case thus recognizes the need to have some restrictions on liberty in order to ensure effective policing. By contrast with the *A* case, the invasions of liberty were minor. This shows that the more serious the invasion of a person's right to liberty, the stricter will be the scrutiny by the courts.

Another question raised by the *Gillan* case is the difficult question of racial profiling for security purposes. Would it be unlawful discrimination to select a person for search by reference to a profile which included his race or ethnic origin, for example on the basis that, or which included the fact that, he was an Asian or a Muslim? Certainly many Muslims have expressed the view that the police when exercising anti-terrorist legislation unfairly target them. Discrimination on the grounds of race, colour, ethnic origin, or nationality is made unlawful by the Race Discrimination Act 1976 (the '1976 Act').

In the *Gillan* case, it was argued that the statutory power of search was unlawful in that there were insufficient safeguards to prevent it from being abused or exercised arbitrarily. The appellants submitted that the power would fail this test because, although there was a code of practice for the police that advised the police that the powers should not be used in a way that discriminated against minority groups, there was nothing to prevent persons being selected for search on the ground of their ethnic or racial origin. Therefore, on the appellants' submission, the police could only lawfully stop everyone, or (say) every fifth person because there would be no discrimination in that event. Neither Lord Bingham nor Lord Walker dealt with the point, which did not arise on the facts.

The other members of the House—Lord Hope, Lord Scott, and Lord Brown— dealt with the point *obiter* and rejected it. In short, they indicated that in principle racial profiling for security purposes did not constitute unlawful race discrimination provided that race was only one ingredient in the objectively justifiable selection of a person for searching.

In particular, Lord Brown observed that that result would make random searches impractical or futile. He noted that there was value in an intuitive stop. He also held that it was not unlawful discrimination to take a person's ethnic background into account in deciding whether to exercise these powers, provided that the reason for stopping the person was a reason connected with the perceived terrorist threat and not on grounds of racial discrimination and that the power was used sensitively. On the contrary it would not be lawful to use the power against persons who were perceived to present no terrorist threat. Lord Brown distinguished an earlier case (the '*Roma Rights* case')[23] in which the House held that it was unlawful to treat asylum applications by a particular ethnic group, the Roma, routinely with more suspicion. In that case, the Roma applicants had been treated stereotypically rather than as individuals. In the case of the search of an Asian or Muslim individual, those characteristics were, so long as Al-Qaeda were perceived as a terrorist threat, part of a profile of a person who might have connections with a terrorist organization.

The speech of Lord Hope is also of great interest. Lord Hope considered the issue in two stages. First, he posed the question: how in practice is discriminatory use to be prevented given the nature of terrorist threats it is designed for? Second, he asked: how did the fact that it is likely to be difficult to detect whether the use of the power was discriminatory square with the principle of legal certainty? As to the first question, the nature of the terrorist threat was bound to pay a large part in the selection process. Discrimination on racial grounds is unlawful even if the assumptions on which it is based turn out to be justified.[24] Therefore, the police could not rely on a person's Asian origin alone. There had to be something more than this. This was likely to be the case. As to the second question, Lord Hope said that in view of the fact that the legal framework and code of practice were published there was sufficient compliance with the requirement for accessibility even if the authorizations themselves were not published. Lord Scott agreed with Lord Brown.[25]

As the question of racial profiling only arose *obiter*, the House did not consider in detail what the limits of legitimate lawful discrimination would be or whether any safeguards were required to meet possible abuse or racial profiling for other purposes. Lord Hope's speech suggests that some caution is necessary[26] though passages in Lord Brown's speech[27] can be read as suggesting that ethnic origin could be a dominant reason for deciding to search a particular individual. No defence of justification would be available because that defence only arises under the 1976 Act if the discrimination is indirect, rather than (as here) direct.

Racial profiling by the police as a basis for exercising their counter-terrorist powers is clearly capable of leading to the inappropriate exercise of those powers, such as the exercise of those powers on the sole or predominant basis of stereotypical assumptions about a person's race and ethnic origins. The assumption that a terrorist would be a Muslim from an Arab country would be such an assumption, as it is now well known that terrorist incidents connected with Al-Qaeda have involved persons of different nationality or racial origin. Furthermore, not all terrorists are Muslims. The identification of persons on the basis of assumptions of this kind is also open to operational objection for the same reason: it will not be

---

[23] *R (European Roma Rights Centre) v Immigration Officer at Prague Airport (United Nations High Commissioner for Refugees Intervening)* [2004] UKHL 55, [2005] 2 AC 1.
[24] *Gillan* at [44].
[25] Lord Scott also added that even if the search required some degree of stereotyping this was validated by ss 41–2 of the Race Relations Act 1976, as amended.
[26] *Gillan* at [47].   [27] *Gillan* at [92].

adequate to catch all persons who are in fact terrorists. Moreover, the profile of terrorists has changed over time.[28]

In all the circumstances, it would seem more prudent to concentrate on other approaches to fighting terrorism generally, such as better intelligence, more effective security measures, and investigation, or, in relation to the exercise of the powers of search, on the behaviour of persons against whom the powers should be exercised, rather than their racial or ethnic origin.

Over the years there have been worrying allegations of improper racial profiling by the police in other fields such as drugs and traffic offences. In the particular context of terrorism, racial profiling is productive of mistrust by Muslims in the fairness of the police and thus may lead to a lack of co-operation from that part of the community with respect to the provision of information about potential terrorists. In those circumstances, there must be a case for more detailed guidance for the police than at present,[29] and also a case for having a legislative framework. This would enable a central record to be kept of the exercise of counter-terrorist powers on grounds that include racial profiling, and for monitoring their use. Inappropriate racial profiling is likely[30] to involve unlawful racial discrimination. In addition, it can lead to damage to the individual concerned and to harm to community. For all these reasons, it must be taken most seriously.

Guantanamo Bay

No discussion of detention in the context of terrorism would be complete without some reference to the position of the detainees held at Guantanamo Bay. The history of this matter is well known. Following 9/11, the United States and its allies took military action against Al-Qaeda installations and the Taliban regime in Afghanistan. In the course of this exercise, the United States took a number of suspected terrorists prisoner. Some of them were transferred to the United States naval base at Guantanamo Bay, Cuba. This is not part of the sovereign territory of the United States, but is leased to it by Cuba. Relatives of the Guantanamo Bay detainees have sought to establish in the American courts that the detainees are entitled to be tried in American courts. According to the media, there are some 480 prisoners in Guantanamo Bay who have been held there without trial for more than four years.

On 28 June 2004, the United States Supreme Court handed down its historic decisions in a number of cases concerning detainees held at Guantanamo Bay. In one of these, *Rasul v Bush*,[31] the Supreme Court held by a majority that in order to challenge his detention the detainee, who was not an American citizen, did not have to be present in a federal district of the United States. It was sufficient that the United States had complete jurisdiction and control over the Guantanamo Bay

---

[28] For instance, it now includes women and teenagers.
[29] The current guidance is set out in *Gillan*.
[30] Subject to the views of Lord Scott above.   [31] 124 S Ct 2686 (2004).

base. The detainees were not therefore in a 'legal black hole' as it has been described.[32] A detainee who was an American citizen was entitled to have his status determined by an American court wherever he was apprehended.[33]

It is of course very welcome that the United States Supreme Court has held that the detainees in Guantanamo Bay have the right to have their status judicially determined. A decision to the contrary would certainly have been at variance with the principles of habeas corpus as established in England.[34] The jurisdiction to grant habeas corpus is not territorial only and thus it would not be an answer to an application for relief by way of habeas corpus that the UK authorities holding a person in custody did not have sovereignty over the place where he was held. Furthermore, as a matter of principle, there must be a right for a detainee to assert in an appropriate tribunal or court of law that 'You have got the wrong person', and to have a court determine whether the detention is lawful. Even in wartime, or in times when national security is threatened, the Executive can make mistakes.

The United States Supreme Court did not, however, decide in *Rasul v Bush* whether a military tribunal was an appropriate tribunal to determine the status of a detainee at Guantanamo Bay, or what a detainee must show in order to obtain his release. The Supreme Court handed down a further decision in the case of *Hamdan v Rumsfeld*.[35] In this case Hamdan, who was detained at Guantanamo Bay, challenged the United States government's decision to try him for criminal conspiracy before a specially convened military commission. The Supreme Court there held (by a majority) that the President of the United States had no power to cause a detainee to be tried by a military tribunal other than under the laws of war. Moreover if the detainee was detained during a conflict, he was entitled to the protection of the Geneva Conventions whether or not he was supported by a state signatory to the Convention. The majority further held that the Geneva Conventions required Hamdan to be tried before ordinary military courts, not, as was proposed, by military commissions that had different rules of procedure and evidence for which no special need had been shown.

The *Hamdan* decision is a welcome decision. As a result of this decision, the US administration has accepted that it should apply the Geneva Conventions to all the Guantanamo Bay detainees. This is a step forward as the US administration has not previously accepted that all the detainees there were entitled to be treated as prisoners of war. Furthermore, it has had to introduce new legislation about the military commissions used to try detainees at Guantanamo Bay. Under this new legislation,[36] the principles of law and rules of evidence used in courts martial will in general apply, and the detainees will be legally represented if they so wish. Moreover, the new legislation prohibits the use before military commissions of evidence obtained by torture. An enemy combatant has a right of appeal to a further

---

[32] See Lord Steyn, 'Guantanamo Bay: The Legal Black Hole' (2004) 52 ICLQ 1; see *R (Abbasi) v Secretary of State for Foreign and Commonwealth Affairs* [2002] EWCA Civ 1598, (2003) UKHRR 76.

[33] *Hamdi v Rumsfeld* 542 US 507 (2004).　　　　[34] See *Ex parte Mwenya* [1960] 1 QB 241.

[35] 126 S Ct 2749 (2006).

[36] Military Commissions Act 2006 (US), s 3930. This Act was passed in September 2006, after this lecture was given in Sydney, and the written text of the paper has been amended to reflect this fact.

military tribunal and from there he can appeal on a point of law to the federal courts. However, the new legislation appears to provide for the removal of the right of any alien enemy combatant to apply for habeas corpus in the ordinary courts. In addition, the new legislation provides that enemy combatants may not rely on the Geneva Conventions in any civil proceedings brought in the US courts against the United States or its agents. Moreover, the new legislation states that in some circumstances the President of the United States has authority to interpret the meaning of the Geneva Conventions and their application to the United States. Some of the provisions of this legislation may well be challenged before the United States Supreme Court in due course. Opponents of this legislation have pointed out that any departure from international law in relation to the treatment of detainees at Guantanamo Bay undermines the moral case for military action against terrorists and may put at risk the lives of American soldiers and those of its allies.

The European Union and others continue to press for the closure of Guantanamo Bay. It appears that the US administration does not consider that this can be done until the detainees can be brought to justice either in the United States or in their home countries. The British government refused to give any assurances to the United States government that it would bring criminal charges against the British subjects held at Guantanamo Bay before their release.[37] In all the circumstances there would appear to be no likelihood that Guantanamo Bay will be closed in the near future and so the legal battles over Guantanamo Bay may continue.

The history of detention at Guantanamo Bay is remarkable for many things. It is remarkable that Guantanamo Bay was ever established just outside the territorial jurisdiction of the US courts. It is also remarkable how long the issues relating to detainees have taken to reach the United States Supreme Court. English courts treat matters concerning the liberty of a person as urgent and often give them priority over other cases. It is also remarkable that the detainees were not treated as prisoners of war for the purposes of the Geneva Conventions.

The fate of the detainees at Guantanamo Bay is a cause of considerable concern across the world for the message it sends about the justice in the United States. The Attorney General for England and Wales, Lord Goldsmith, has referred to the position as 'unacceptable' and as 'a symbol to many—right or wrong—of injustice'.[38] If the detainees are indeed terrorists who have committed crimes, it should be possible for the American authorities to adduce sufficient evidence to determine their status and to bring criminal charges against them. If they are not persons whom the American authorities are entitled to detain, they should be released as soon as possible.

---

[37] It has been said that David Hicks, the Australian citizen held there, has also not committed any offence under Australian law.

[38] Lord Goldsmith, Attorney General for England and Wales, Speech to a conference on International Homeland Security & Resilience (Royal United Services Institute, London, 10 May 2006). In his Magna Carta lecture given in Sydney on 13 September 2006, the Lord Chancellor, Lord Falconer, referred to the action of the United States in seeking to put terrorist suspects beyond the reach of the law in Guantanamo Bay as a 'shocking affront to the principles of democracy'.

Torture: *Public Committee* and *A v Secretary of State for the Home Department (No 2)*

Under this heading I wish to compare two cases dealing with torture. The use of torture is the subject of an absolute ban under the Convention and international law. I want to explain why this is so. Evidence obtained by torture is often unreliable but in addition it is contrary to the laws of civilized nations to allow torture. Torture involves an attack on the integrity of an individual who is defenceless at that point in time and who at that moment poses no threat. It is liable to lead to yet more inhumanity of man to man. The common law of England has always prohibited it.

In a well known case, *Public Committee against Torture in Israel v State of Israel* (sometimes called the 'ticking bomb case'),[39] the Israeli Supreme Court of Israel held that it was not open to the General Security Service (GSS) of Israel (the Israeli secret services) to use torture, which in that case involved shaking a suspect or holding him in a painful position for a lengthy period, or depriving him of sleep. The Israeli Supreme Court said that torture was one of the methods that it was not open to a democracy to use in the fight against terrorism. That court left open the 'ticking bomb' paradigm where a person (who might be a child, or a person not responsible for creating the danger) has information about a bomb which is ticking and will kill many innocent people if it explodes. In such a situation, the Israeli Supreme Court ruled that the GSS might have a defence of necessity if it used unlawful coercive interrogation methods. However, the situation which the Israeli Supreme Court left open has never, so far as I am aware, had to be considered by a court. It is, I suggest, likely to be a very remote case and the use of force even in that situation would probably be illegal under international law. The Israeli Supreme Court further held that it was for the Knesset to decide whether special legislation was required with regard to interrogation methods of the GSS, subject to the provisions of the Basic Law: Human Dignity and Liberty.

In the course of his judgment, President Barak uttered the words that are often quoted:

We conclude this judgment by revisiting the harsh reality in which Israel finds itself... We are aware that this decision does not make it easier to deal with that reality. This is the fate of democracy, as not all means are acceptable to it, and not all methods employed by its enemies are always open to it. Sometimes democracy must fight with one hand tied behind its back. Nonetheless, it has the upper hand. Preserving the rule of law and recognition of individual liberties constitute an important component of its understanding of security. At the end of the day, they strengthen its spirit and this strength allows it to overcome its difficulties.

Under the Convention, torture is absolutely prohibited in any circumstance, as is inhuman or degrading treatment or punishment, so that the issue that arose in the

---

[39] *Public Committee against Torture in Israel v State of Israel*, Applications HC 5100/94, HC 4054/95, HC 6536/95, HC 5188/96, HC 7563/97, HC 7628/97, HC 1043/99.

Israeli case could not arise in the United Kingdom. However, some people (not, I think, in Europe) have put forward the idea that torture might be made lawful if it was conducted under a judicial warrant in times of emergency. One of the proponents of this idea is Professor Alan Derschowitz, a leading American lawyer. Such a system would require fine judgments to be made as to the seriousness of the emergency and the measure of force. More importantly, it would be the beginning of a slippery slope. Once torture is used it would become difficult to control. In fact the Detainee Treatment Act 2005 of the United States now provides that no individual in the custody, or under the control, of the United States government can be subjected to cruel, inhuman, or degrading treatment.[40] This prohibition can, however, under the Detainee Treatment Act 2005 be repealed by later legislation but the amending legislation must specifically refer to the Detainee Treatment Act 2005.

Not all states observe the ban on torture. There has been considerable concern throughout the world at the interrogation techniques authorized by the US government and reputed to be used by a number of other governments. The use of torture by other countries is important to the United Kingdom because many countries now share intelligence and there is accordingly a possibility that the Executive in the United Kingdom is making decisions, for example, as to whether a person should be subjected to a control order, on the basis of evidence obtained by a foreign state as a result of the use of coercion against other persons in its control. Thus the context in which torture has been the subject of litigation in England is entirely different from that in which it arose in Israel.

In the next case I wish to discuss, *A v Secretary of State for the Home Department (No 2)* (the '*A* case'), the question arose whether, when determining the legality of a certificate given by the Secretary of State that a person was a suspected terrorist and could therefore be detained, SIAC could rely on evidence which the appellant suspected had been obtained from overseas governments who had obtained it by torture of other persons.

The House held that, while the Executive would not act unlawfully if in its decision-making it took account of evidence provided by foreign states which was liable to have been obtained by them by the use of torture, evidence obtained by torture was inadmissible in a court of law. Lord Bingham pointed out that the common law had regarded torture and its fruits with abhorrence for over 500 years (at [51]). In addition, Art 15 of the United Nations Convention Against Torture and Other Cruel, Inhuman or Degrading Treatment or Punishment 1984 (the 'Torture Convention'), although not expressly implemented in English law, prohibited the use of evidence obtained by torture in legal proceedings. The House of Lords accepted that two strong reasons for the prohibition on the use of evidence obtained by torture to be found in Art 15 of the Torture Convention were that

---

[40] Cruel, inhuman, or degrading treatment is defined as such treatment as defined in certain amendments to the United States Constitution, as defined in the United States' reservations, declarations, and understandings in relation to the United Nations Convention Against Torture and Other Cruel, Inhuman or Degrading Treatment or Punishment.

evidence obtained by torture was likely to be unreliable and that such a prohibition served to discourage its use.[41] In addition, the House held that the admission of evidence obtained by torture was inconsistent with integrity of the proceedings.[42]

However, different views were expressed about what the suspect had to demonstrate before the evidence was rendered inadmissible. The majority held that the appropriate test of whether the evidence should be admitted and taken into account was for SIAC to ask itself whether it was established, by means of such diligent inquiries into the sources as it was practical to carry out, and on a balance of probabilities, that the information relied on by the Secretary of State had been obtained by torture. The majority held that that was the approach that Art 15 of the Torture Convention[43] took and that that approach was the best guide to what was practical. If it were established, by that appropriate test, that the information was obtained under torture, that information had to be left out of account in the overall assessment of the question whether the Home Secretary had reasonable grounds for a belief or suspicion of the kind necessary for the purposes of issuing a certificate which could lead to restrictions on the liberty of a suspected terrorist.

The minority took a different view. They considered that once the suspect adduced plausible grounds for believing that the evidence had been, or may have been, obtained by torture, the evidence had to be left out of account unless it was established that there was no real risk that it was obtained by torture. The minority took the view that it would, in practice, be very difficult to show that evidence met the test laid down by the majority.

Neither case discusses the level at which a coercive interrogation technique would constitute torture. Under the Convention, such questions are unlikely to arise since both torture and inhuman and degrading treatment are prohibited. Press reports would suggest that a narrower view has at least in the past been taken in the United States[44] of what constitutes torture from that under the Convention and

---

[41] *A v Secretary of State for the Home Department (No 2)* at [39] (Lord Bingham).

[42] *A v Secretary of State for the Home Department (No 2)* at [39] (Lord Bingham), [91] (Lord Hoffmann).

[43] United Nations Convention Against Torture and Other Cruel, Inhuman or Degrading Treatment or Punishment, Art 15 provides: 'Each State Party shall ensure that any statement which is established to have been made as a result of torture shall not be invoked as evidence in any proceedings, except against a person accused of torture as evidence that the statement was made.'

[44] See eg Editorial, 'The Vote on Mr Gonzales', *Washington Post* (16 January 2005): 'Mr Gonzales made a second bad judgment about the Geneva Conventions: that their restrictions on interrogations were "obsolete". Quite apart from the question of POW status for detainees, this determination invalidated the Army's doctrine for questioning enemy prisoners, which is based on the Geneva Conventions and had proved its worth over decades. Mr Gonzales ignored the many professional experts, ranging from the Army's own legal corps to Secretary of State Colin L Powell, who told him that existing interrogation practices were effective and that setting them aside would open the way to abuses and invite retaliation against Americans. Instead, during meetings in his office from which these professionals were excluded, he supported the use of such methods as "waterboarding", which causes an excruciating sensation of drowning. Though initially approved for use by the CIA against al Qaeda, illegal techniques such as these quickly were picked up by military interrogators at Guantanamo and later in Afghanistan and Iraq. Several official investigations have confirmed that in the absence of a clear doctrine—the standing one having been declared "obsolete"—US personnel across the world felt empowered to use methods that most lawyers, and almost all the democratic world, regard as torture. Mr Gonzales stated for the record at his hearing that he opposes torture. Yet he made no effort to

one day it may be necessary for some definition to be found. What is noticeable in the cases referred to here is the similarity of approach between the Supreme Court of Israel and the House of Lords in their outright rejection of torture.

Control Orders: *MB* and *JJ*

As I have explained, the UK government lost the *A* case on executive detention. It was far from clear what the government would do next. Under the Human Rights Act 1998, Parliament was not bound to amend the legislation. However, since the decision in the *A* case, Parliament has in fact repealed the legislation held to be incompatible with the Convention and enacted a new law providing for control orders to be made restricting the freedom of terrorist suspects.[45]

When the Prevention of Terrorism Act 2005 was being debated in Parliament, concern was expressed about judges becoming involved in what was really an executive activity: this could affect their independence and breach the principle of the separation of powers. For this and other reasons, control orders are very controversial. There is still no requirement in law to charge a person subject to a control order or to bring him to trial. In June 2005, Alvaro Gil-Robles, the Human Rights Commissioner for the Council of Europe, criticized the Prevention of Terrorism Act on the basis that control orders were intended to 'substitute the ordinary criminal justice system with a system run by the executive'. Moreover, he recommended that control orders should only be made for an aggregate period of 12 months, after which the suspect would be released unless charged with a criminal offence. So far as I am aware, the government did not accept these criticisms. Indeed the primary usefulness of such orders must surely be to place restrictions on an individual before he commits an offence with which he can be charged in order to prevent the commission of acts connected with terrorism.

The scheme relating to control orders in the Prevention of Terrorism Act may be summarized as follows:

(a) The function of a control order is to impose obligations on individuals suspected of being involved in terrorism-related activities. The obligations are designed to restrict or prevent further involvement by individuals in such activities. The intention is that each order is tailored to the particular risk posed by the individual concerned. Obligations that may be imposed include prohibitions on the possession or use of certain items, restrictions on

---

separate himself from legal judgments that narrowed torture's definition so much as to authorize such methods as waterboarding for use by the CIA abroad. Despite the revision of a Justice Department memo on torture, he and the administration he represents continue to regard those practices as legal and continue to condone slightly milder abuse, such as prolonged sensory deprivation and the use of dogs, for Guantanamo.' In 2006, however, the Pentagon issued a new army manual that would prohibit waterboarding.

[45] Prevention of Terrorism Act 2005.

movement to or within certain areas, restrictions on communications or associations and requirements of place of abode.

(b) If a control order does not derogate from the rights guaranteed by the Convention, particularly the right to liberty, it is called a 'non-derogating control order'. (As to the circumstances in which a control order derogates from the right to liberty in the Convention, there has been some case law in the Court of Appeal in England to which I will refer below.) The court's permission is required for the Secretary of State to make a non-derogating control order. However, if the matter is urgent, the Secretary of State can make an order without seeking permission of the court but he must apply to the court for confirmation immediately. Before making a non-derogating control order, the Secretary of State must have reasonable grounds for suspecting that the individual has been involved in a terrorism-related activity and he must consider that it is necessary for purposes connected with protecting members of the public from the risk of terrorism to make a control order imposing obligations on that individual. A non-derogating control order may last for twelve months but is renewable. A derogating control order may last for six months only but it is also renewable.

(c) When considering whether to grant permission for a non-derogating control order, or when considering whether to confirm a non-derogating control order made by the Secretary of State, the court may hold a hearing without notice to the person on whom the order is to be imposed, and it must consider whether the Secretary of State's decision was 'obviously flawed'. If it finds that it was obviously flawed, the order cannot be made or must be quashed. If it finds that it was not obviously flawed, the court must refer the control order for a full hearing on notice to the other party. At this hearing the court will apply the judicial review test to the control order in order to decide if it should continue in force.

(d) The 2005 Act also enables control orders to be made that derogate from the Convention. These can only be made by the court on the application of the Secretary of State. Again, there will be a preliminary hearing, which may be without notice, and if the court decides there is a prima facie case for the order to be imposed, the court will make the order and give directions for a full hearing on notice to the other party to be held.

(e) The court must confirm a derogating control order at that hearing if:

 (i) it decides on the balance of probabilities that the controlled person is or has been involved in terrorism-related activity;

 (ii) it considers the obligations imposed as part of the control order are necessary for purposes connected with protecting members of the public from the risk of terrorism;

 (iii) it appears to the court that the risk arises out of or is associated with a public emergency in respect of which there is a designated derogation from the whole or a part of Art 5 of the Convention;

(iv) the obligations imposed by the control order are in a list of derogating obligations set out in the derogation order.

(f) At the hearing of any proceedings for the making or confirmation of a control order, or permission to make a control order, the court may hear evidence in open and closed sessions. If the session is closed, the subject of the proposed control order and his legal representative are excluded but a special advocate who represents the interests of the individual concerned will be appointed. The special advocate cannot communicate with the subject of the proposed control order after that person has been served with the closed material.

There have been two recent decisions of the Court of Appeal, presided over by Lord Phillips, Lord Chief Justice of England and Wales, concerning control orders. The two cases provide an interesting contrast with each other and indeed with the *Gillan* case (the case considered above about the detention of the two observers who were stopped on their way to a peaceful demonstration). In the first case, *Secretary of State for the Home Department v MB*,[46] the subject was prevented by the order made by the Secretary State from a number of specified activities, including a restriction on leaving the United Kingdom. The object of the order was to prevent the subject from going to Iraq to fight against the coalition forces. The judge (Sullivan J) held that the procedure for judicial review made the non-derogating control order system incompatible with Art 6[47] of the Convention. The Court of Appeal disagreed. The court had to decide whether the decision of the Secretary of State was flawed on the basis of the material presented at the time of the court's adjudication, rather than just at the time of the Secretary of State's decision as the judge below had held, and this gave the court a more substantial role. Moreover, the court had to consider whether the suspect's Convention rights were violated. Furthermore, the standard of review open to the court in determining whether the decision of the Secretary of State was flawed did not (as the judge had held) fall short of the standard of review required to meet the requirements of Art 6 of the Convention.

However, the Court of Appeal accepted that the Secretary of State was better placed than the court to determine the measures necessary to protect the public from the activities of a terrorist suspect and that accordingly a degree of deference was required to be paid to the decision of the Secretary of State. But the court still had to give intense scrutiny to each of the restrictions to be imposed by the control order. The Court of Appeal likened this exercise to fixing the conditions for bail. Since Art 6 of the Convention was concerned only with fair procedure and not with the content of rights or obligations, the judge hearing the application did not, as the judge in the instant case had thought, have to be satisfied as to the facts on which the suspicion was based but only as to whether the Secretary of State had reasonable grounds for his suspicion.

---

[46] [2006] EWCA Civ 1140, [2007] QB 415.
[47] This provides for the rights of fair trial and access to an independent court or tribunal for the determination of civil rights and obligations.

The Court of Appeal (not without some misgivings) held that the court hearing the application could examine 'closed material', ie material that would not be shown to the subject of the order or made public in court, and decide whether it should be shown to the subject, without violating the subject's rights to a fair trial. For this purpose the special advocate procedure could be used. The Court of Appeal noted that in the *Chahal* case, the Strasbourg Court, drawing on the experience of the Canadian courts, had recognized that the use of confidential material may be unavoidable where national security is at stake.

In the second case, *Secretary of State for the Home Department v JJ*,[48] the Court of Appeal had to consider more extensive forms of control order. In this case, each of the subjects of the control orders had to remain in their own one-bedroom flat (not their own home) for 18 hours a day and in the remaining hours they could only visit specific areas. The flats were subject to spot searches. The Court of Appeal agreed with the judge (Sullivan J) that the restrictions imposed by the order were so extensive that they violated Art 5 of the Convention and, as there was no derogation order in place, the orders had to be quashed. This, therefore, is a case where the deprivation of liberty was not transient, as it had been in the *Gillan* case. It obviously raises the question at what precise point a control order amounts to a deprivation of liberty for the purposes of the Convention in any particular case, and that question may have to be worked out in later cases.

Special trial procedures

My last group of cases illustrate the way in which courts have sought to fashion procedures that address the special problems affecting the trial of suspected terrorists and yet preserve sufficient freedom to ensure that justice is still done. They illustrate the variety of different ways in which Parliament may seek to change the trial process and the judgments which the courts have to make as to whether the essential requirement of fairness to the defendant is met or whether the balance is swung too far in favour of those who prosecute or investigate terrorism.

In the first case, *Kartar Singh v State of Punjab*[49] (the '*Kartar Singh* case'), the Supreme Court of India had to consider a comprehensive constitutional challenge to the then anti-terrorist legislation in India. The court found that most of the legislation satisfied the Constitution of India. It reached this conclusion by reading in safeguards to protect against abuse. It read into the offence of abetting a terrorist act a requirement for mens rea. In relation to a provision in the legislation rendering suspect's confessions to a police officer admissible, the Supreme Court gave guidelines, including a guideline that the maker of the confession should be taken without delay before the Chief Judicial Magistrate who would record the statement and order a medical examination if there was any question of torture. The Supreme Court also laid down guidelines for the periodic review of cases

---

[48] [2006] EWCA Civ 1141, [2007] QB 446.   [49] (1994) 3 SCC 569.

registered under the legislation and also of the prevailing situation in the areas notified as the ones affected by terrorist activities. The Supreme Court also laid down guidelines on when a witness whose life was in danger could remain anonymous. Substitute safeguards were put in place to make up for the fact that the defendant would not be able to cross-examine the witness, such as the appointment of a special advocate to address the court on the weight to be attached to the evidence and the administration of written questions.

The detailed facts of *R v Lodhi*[50] are well known. It concerned a criminal trial in New South Wales of an alleged terrorist. A question was raised as to the constitutionality of a statutory provision requiring the Attorney General to be given the right to object if information was to be disclosed in a criminal trial that related to national security. The application would be dealt with in the absence of the defendant or his representatives. One of the questions considered was whether the legislation exceeded the powers of the Commonwealth Parliament on the ground that it authorized judicial power to be exercised in a manner inconsistent with the essential character of a court or with the nature of judicial power. The judge rejected this challenge, holding that the powers related to pre-trial disclosure rather than to the calling of evidence in the course of a trial. The judge would, moreover, have power to stay the proceedings if there was a substantial adverse impact on the fairness of the proceedings.[51] The court sought to strike the balance between the position of the state and the accused by making this reservation.

Finally, I would briefly refer to the decision of the Supreme Court of Canada in *Re Art 83.28 of the Canadian Criminal Code*.[52] This concerned an application by the Crown to examine under oath an unco-operative witness during the trial of two persons charged with the explosion on board an Air India jet in 1985. The Crown wanted to examine the witness in private in the absence of the accused. The examination would be under oath and in private, and the witness would not be entitled to decline to answer. A judge other than the trial judge made the order for the examination. Counsel for the accused only then became aware of what was afoot and he challenged the order on constitutional grounds. In the end, the order was varied so that counsel for the accused could attend but on terms that he would leave if information was elicited which did not relate to the trial. Moreover, no information acquired during the examination was to be given to the accused.[53] The case went to the Supreme Court of Canada. Applying a presumption of constitutionality and a purposive approach the majority held that it was implicit in the statutory power that counsel for the accused should be able to participate in the examination of the witness. The Supreme Court also held that the witness would be able to rely on the privilege against self-incrimination in extradition or deportation proceedings as well as criminal proceedings if it was sought to use his evidence against him.

[50] [2006] NSWSC 571.
[51] It is understood that there has been no appeal from this decision.
[52] [2004] 2 SCR 248, 2004 SCC 42.
[53] It does not appear that consideration was given to the use of a special advocate.

The defendants in the criminal trial sought to challenge the new powers on the grounds that they infringed judicial independence. The Supreme Court by a majority rejected this challenge and the further argument that the judge was co-opted into performing an executive function. The judge's role was the traditional role of ensuring that the investigation was conducted fairly. The purpose of the investigation was to investigate a terrorist offence. There was a presumption that such proceedings would be held in public but in the instant case the hearing would be in private and the information would not be published until after the criminal trials had concluded. Judicial independence was preserved because the judge would be empowered to ensure that the questioning was fair and relevant. This then was another case where the court's decision mitigated the apparent adverse impact of the legislation on the rights of the accused.

Drawing the threads together

I said in the introduction to this paper that I had two purposes. The first purpose was to provide information about some of the major developments in the jurisprudence in this field. I hope that I have fulfilled that purpose. My second purpose was to use those cases to draw some conclusions together about lessons for the future. It is to that second purpose that I now turn. I will do this under four headings: the terrorist threat, legislative and executive action, the role of the courts, and some closing thoughts.

The terrorist threat

The terrorist threat is undoubtedly serious and nothing I have said in this paper should be taken as underestimating the threat. Terrorism is a feature of modern society. Effective police action or military action within the law can reduce it but it is not likely to be completely eradicated unless terrorist groups themselves decide to abandon their armed struggle. Governments have a duty to protect the public and they will inevitably seek ways to qualify the normal rules of criminal procedure, immigration and other laws to protect the public.

Legislative and executive action

Since 9/11, there has been intense legislative activity in the United Kingdom. In addition to the Prevention of Terrorism Act 2005 to which I have already referred, Parliament has passed the Terrorism Act 2006. Section 1 of this Act makes it an offence intentionally or recklessly to publish a statement likely to be understood by those to whom it is directed as encouraging terrorism. Such statements include statements which glorify the commission or preparation of acts of terrorism and which constitute statements from which persons to whom they are addressed could reasonably be expected to infer that what is being glorified is being glorified as conduct which should be emulated by them in existing circumstances. Section 5 of this Act also makes it an offence for a person, with the intention of committing acts of terrorism or assisting another to commit such acts, to engage in conduct in preparation for giving effect to his intention. These provisions are cast in wide terms and were hotly debated in their passage through Parliament. I note that in its Review of Sedition Laws,[54] the Australian Law Reform Commission took the view that it was undesirable to introduce an offence of glorifying terrorism. It expressed the view that the offence would represent 'an unwarranted incursion into freedom of expression and the constitutionally protected freedom of political discourse'. It noted that the Convention would be a crucial safeguard against an overly broad interpretation of the offence but that that safeguard would of course be absent in Australia.[55] However, I note that the Criminal Code of Australia includes an offence of urging inter-group violence.

The 2006 Act also permits the detention of terrorist suspects for up to 28 days before they are charged. The original proposal by the government was for a three-month period of detention but this was rejected by Parliament. It has been reported in the press that as a result of the alleged plot by terrorists to blow up several transatlantic airliners which was made public in August 2006 the government would again ask Parliament to approve a pre-charge detention period of 90 days.

In addition, the Racial and Religious Hatred Act 2006 creates offences involving stirring up hatred against persons on religious grounds, and confers powers of arrest in relation to both racial and religious hatred. These offences can be committed by words or behaviour or the publication or distribution of written material. There is a provision that states that the offences are not to restrict discussion or criticism of religions or religious beliefs or practices.

So the British Parliament has been busy creating new powers for the Executive and new offences for the citizen. Powers to detain or make control orders are potentially particularly troubling. There is a risk that powers of detention or to make control orders that are based on a subjective assessment of intelligence may turn out to be wrong so that innocent people suffer. Judges must always bear in mind the possibility that innocent people have become caught up in the activities which give rise to suspicion. Likewise, if criminal offences are defined too broadly, innocent people may also be wrongly convicted of offences in circumstances for which those offences were not intended.

---

[54] Australian Law Reform Commission, *Fighting Words: A Review of Sedition Laws*, Report No 104 (2006). My attention has been drawn to the decision of the High Court of Australia in *Al-Kateb v Godwin* (2004) 219 CLR 562, [2004] HCA 37. In this case, the High Court of Australia by a majority upheld legislation for the mandatory (administrative) detention of an illegal immigrant pending his removal from the jurisdiction, even though he was a stateless person and no country had been found to accept him. His detention was therefore indefinite. There was no suggestion that he was a terrorist suspect. It may be that the decision would have been different if the illegal immigrant had been able to invoke a bill of rights or some unwritten constitutional norm. As to the latter, see generally, McLachlin CJ, *The Judicial Conscience* (Osgoode Hall Law School, 2006) (published in the conference proceedings of the Raoul Wallenberg International Human Rights Symposium 2006); see also the decision of the Court of First Instance of the European Communities in *The Yusuf and Al Barakaat International Foundation v Council and Commission* OJ C 44 (2002) (the '*Yusuf* case') (Case T 306/01).

[55] Australian Law Reform Commission, *Fighting Words* at 6.24.

We saw in the *Gillan* case that in the fight against terrorism Parliament had given the police new powers of search that were more extensive than would generally be thought acceptable. This is not untypical of anti-terrorist measures. Where legislation is passed giving the Executive new and extensive powers, it is important that the same legislation makes the government accountable for the exercise of those powers given to it. This will serve to prevent any temptation to act in an unconstitutional fashion as happened when the Watergate affair in the United States took place. There are healthy signs, however, that the British Parliament is developing legislative techniques to make the Executive more accountable for the way it uses new anti-terrorist statutory powers. Sometimes sunset clauses are included so that the government has to come back and ask for an extension of its anti-terrorist powers. In other cases, there may be a provision for independent reviews at regular intervals of the way in the new powers are being used. I would interpose that the reports of independent review bodies can be of great use to the courts. In the *A* case, the House of Lords placed great emphasis on a Privy Counsellor review of the relevant provisions of the 2001 Act. As an alternative, the use of the new powers could be made subject to more continuous review by a separate agency. That agency could monitor the use across different government departments of measures introduced for reasons of national security to meet the terrorist threat.

Where it is said that the ordinary liberties of the individual have to be restricted in some way, the legislation should contain as many safeguards as practicable for the individual. For example, it can be argued that a person should never be at risk of losing his liberty on the basis of evidence that he or she has not seen. But, if Parliament considers that the court or tribunal should have access to sensitive information that cannot be shown to the defendant, then safeguards must be provided. For instance, the court should be able to see that information and the court should be able to appoint a special advocate who can make submissions on this material for the assistance of the court. The decision of the Supreme Court of India in the *Kartar Singh* case goes one stage further: it is an example of the courts taking the initiative to ensure that these safeguards are provided.

The general approach should not, however, be to create new criminal offences or processes save where the existing criminal law cannot be used. The same standards and procedures should apply in terrorist cases as in other cases. That should be the starting point and there should only be a departure from it if a good reason to the contrary is made out. Using the ordinary criminal process is the best way of ensuring that rights and freedoms are not whittled away.

The above points about legislative techniques for ensuring accountability and the creation of new anti-terrorist offences are really points for policymakers and legislators. I turn below to the role of the courts but before I do, it is necessary to consider the relations between judges and politicians. I can of course only speak for the United Kingdom. Following the delivery of the decisions on control orders to which I have referred, the Prime Minister, Tony Blair, was reported as having said that the judges were frustrating the government's efforts to protect the United Kingdom from terrorist threats by repeatedly striking down anti-terrorist laws on the grounds that they infringed the suspects' human rights.[56] In the crisis over the invasion of Lebanon by Israel, Tony Blair also referred to an arc of extremism and to the need for a 'renaissance' in the way the United Kingdom deals with terrorists. Politicians have often expressed their anger at decisions in the courts which have in some way prevented executive action or which have resulted in laws that were passed by Parliament being declared incompatible with human rights. They point out that judges do not have any responsibility if, as a result of legal action, a terrorist plot cannot be stopped.

Much of the tension has arisen from the exercise of the powers conferred by the Human Rights Act 1998, and there have been suggestions by the government and by the leader of the opposition to amend the Human Rights Act 1998 in some not very clearly identified way. As yet, there has been no legislative measure brought forward for that purpose and it is difficult to see what Parliament could do because, even if the Human Rights Act 1998 were repealed, individuals would still have the right to go to the Strasbourg Court and obtain relief against the UK government there. If the Strasbourg Court ruled that particular legislation breached the Convention, the United Kingdom would be under a treaty obligation to remedy that violation for the future by taking steps to repeal the legislation. I therefore leave aside the possibility of any amendment of the Human Rights Act 1998, and return to the relationship between judges and politicians. Judges cannot become involved in a public debate with politicians about why they have decided certain cases in a certain way. Still less can they do so in private discussions with politicians. If ministers do not like the courts' decisions, they should not seek to undermine the administration of justice by criticizing the judiciary, still less by attacking their decisions on a personal level. The role of making decisions on legal issues is constitutionally that of the judges. Ministers should appeal a decision to a higher court or, so far as they can, bring about a change in the law.

The role of the courts

So I now turn to the role of the courts. Their duty is to decide cases. As Lord Bingham said in the *A* case in the passage which I quoted, when the issue is a legal issue it is the duty of the court to decide that issue. The traditional role of the courts is to be the guardians of individual rights and liberty. The terrorist threat has enhanced that role. With increasing emphasis in public life on transparency, there is today another role, and that is the role of explaining decisions clearly and educating people as to their rights and duties. The courts' willingness to do this will help improve the transparency of judicial decision-making. The most important place for the voice of the judges to be heard is in general in their judgments.

There are some other points worth noting here. The brief survey of cases across the common law world that I have undertaken in this lecture demonstrates as it seems to me the remarkable adaptability of the common law to deal with the

---

[56] G Jones, 'Judges "Frustrate Fight Against Terror"', *Daily Telegraph*, 4 August 2006.

challenges of terrorism and to find new solutions. I illustrated a point earlier in this paper by comparison to the expansion joint in the Sydney Harbour Bridge. If that room for expansion were not there, the bridge would have fallen down long ago. Of course a great deal of skill and scientific calculation went into creating that expansion joint. The amount of expansion needed to make the bridge stand up will depend on a number of variables. We have need of creative and bold judges who are able to apply the same level of skill to the law to make it meet modern circumstances. Yet, at the same time, it is important to be absolutely clear what the expansion joint is for. It is not for expedient short-term solutions. The bottom line for the courts in meeting the challenge of terrorism is the preservation of a plural society and democratic way of life, subject to the rule of law, and the essence of our individual freedoms. That involves the retention of the courts' vital role as the guardians of individual rights.

In fact, these values happen to be the values that underlie the Convention. The advantage of a statement of rights is that it enables people more easily to identify fundamental values. The years since 9/11 have also brought home in the United Kingdom the point that one of the other advantages of statement of rights is that it enables some control to be exercised over excessive intrusions by the other branches of government into individual rights and freedoms. It is quite possible that but for the Human Rights Act 1998 there would today be many people being held in detention in the United Kingdom as terrorist suspects. Yet, of course, those detentions would not have prevented the London bombing since the persons responsible for those events were not aliens who could be detained under the 2001 Act but Britons. Nor would 18-hour control orders necessarily have prevented them.

You will notice that in that statement of the bottom line I made no reference to the maxim that 'he who comes to equity should come with clean hands'. I know that New South Wales is a stronghold of equity, and long may it remain so. But this particular maxim cannot, I think, be deployed in the field of human rights. Politicians may want to say that those who break the rules of society should not be entitled to its benefits and that bills of rights are not suicide pacts. But those two propositions are not the same. Of course human and constitutional rights should not be pushed too far and that is why, for instance, we have seen the courts adopting the special advocate technique for dealing with the disclosure of evidence that cannot be shown to the suspect without risking national security. Where, however, national security and the fundamental values to which I have referred are not genuinely and seriously compromised, everyone should have equal rights in a court of law. That is the principled approach and the approach that will reduce so far as we can the risk that innocent people will suffer miscarriages of justice. Likewise, it was the view of the Strasbourg Court that everyone should have equal rights in the first case discussed above, namely the *Chahal* case.

This brief journey around the common law world also demonstrates something else, and that is the value of international discourse between judges. There is, at the end of the day, an extraordinary similarity of thought between the different jurisdictions involved in the various cases to which I have referred, even if they use different techniques. The international discourse between judges at the highest levels transcends national boundaries and is not subject to political control. Professor Anne-Marie Slaughter, author of *A New World Order*,[57] may be right that this international judicial discourse will one day lead the way to a new world order based on the rule of law. A body of global constitutional and human rights law is being created. There is an extraordinary congruence of thinking. Looking at the challenge of terrorism across the common law world is like watching the wind make ripples in a field of grass. Some stalks are more blown than others but at least they are all blown in the same direction.

Some concluding thoughts

Despite the scale of the threat from terrorism, we must keep the threat in perspective. More people are killed in natural disasters than terrorist incidents. Security measures intrude upon the ordinary liberties of citizens (see eg the *Gillan* case). The question that society has to ask itself is whether the incomplete security which counter-terrorist measures provide for the protection of its members justifies their effect on the liberty of the individual members. It would not be much fun living in a society in which the police could search our homes at any time of day and without showing any grounds for suspicion.

Some intrusion of personal liberty is of course acceptable, such as searches at airports and the entrance to buildings. But major intrusions into the right to liberty may well be a different matter. The truth is that some risk from terrorism is bound to remain, however intrusive the counter-terrorist measures are. No measures will make us absolutely secure from terrorism. It would seem pointless to restrict individual liberties in the hope of making people more secure if the result is to destroy the essential characteristics of a free or democratic society, or indeed to cause disharmony between the groups who feel that they are wrongly made the targets of the new powers. There is no point in being more secure if you are also less safe. So an appropriate balance has to be struck between liberty and national security. It is worth noting that, even if the House of Lords in the *A* case had accepted the validity of the detention provisions of the 2001 Act, it would not have prevented the London bombings, which were carried out not by aliens with no right to remain in the United Kingdom but by terrorists who were British citizens.

An analogy has recently been drawn between the war on terrorism and the Cold War. There are many differences of course between the Cold War and the war on terror. Nonetheless, it is worth remembering that during the Cold War there were many moments when things could have gone badly wrong, such as during the Korean War and the Cuban crisis. There were also those who thought that there should be a stronger military response against the communist threat. It all turned out the right way in the end. After a long wait, the Cold War came to an end partly

---

[57] A Slaughter, *A New World Order* (Princeton, 2004).

because the authoritarian regimes failed to deliver economic success and also social and political justice. In the end, it was democracy and freedom that triumphed. So we too should remain quietly confident. If we hold on to the fundamental values of a plural, democratic society, subject to the rule of law, and all that that involves, there is surely a good chance that terrorism too will be defeated and that freedom will survive. There is, moreover, no better way of ensuring that that happens.

PART V

PRIVACY: BALANCING PUBLIC AND PRIVATE INTERESTS

In the first chapter in this Part, Chapter 13, *The Future of the Law of Privacy*, I examine the state of the English law of privacy as it stood prior to the Human Rights Act 1998. It gave little protection to a person whose privacy was invaded by, say, the publication of photographs taken without permission on a private occasion. There was no right to privacy although there might be some remedy on some other ground, such as breach of confidence. This paper is historically important because it shows how inadequate our law was in this respect before the Human Rights Act 1998, which substantially changed the remedies for breach of confidence. At the time when I wrote this paper, I was considering how the law might be developed using European Convention on Human Rights ('Convention') rights to protect private information that it was not in the public interest to disclose. I contemplated that the courts might develop existing torts using Convention case law to protect individual rights of privacy, which indeed happened, as the following chapter shows.

In Chapter 14, *Human Rights and Civil Wrongs: Tort Law under the Spotlight*, I review the developments which the courts were able to make following the incorporation of human rights into domestic law. The courts developed the law of breach of confidence to provide a remedy for what in other systems would have been treated as invasions of privacy. To do this, the courts drew on the jurisprudence of the European Court of Human Rights (the 'Strasbourg Court') under Art 8 (right to respect for private and family life) and Art 10 (freedom of expression). They did this even in cases between private persons when the state was not involved—that is, cases which could not be pursued in Strasbourg. This cast a new light on the debate that had taken place before the Human Rights Act around whether human rights would only be enforceable 'vertically'—that is, against the state or some state body. In privacy cases, the defendant (often the media) had to show that there was a public interest in disclosure.

Chapter 15, *Media Intrusion and Human Rights: Striking the Balance* shows how the Strasbourg Court has built up a remarkable body of case law about responsible journalism. If the media wished to assert its Convention right of freedom of expression, the court would take into account the extent to which the media had followed these guidelines. Our domestic courts have been able to draw on this jurisprudence, since the Human Rights Act 1998 took effect, in deciding whether to prevent the disclosure of information by the media.

The case law on responsible journalism makes it clear that the media's right to exercise freedom of expression must be upheld in appropriate cases. Save in those cases, undoubtedly the effect of the Human Rights Act 1998 was substantially to strengthen the rights of individuals to obtain injunctions to prevent the disclosure of private information about them where there was no public interest in disclosure.

13

The Future of the Law of Privacy

This chapter is based on an article published in 1999.*

For many years people have argued whether there should be a legal remedy for infringement of privacy.[1] This question has now moved on. The new government has introduced a Human Rights Bill which will require the courts to enforce the individual's right to respect for his private and family life. There seems little doubt that that bill will become law. The question now is: assuming that the Human Rights Bill becomes law in its present form, when should an individual be able to claim that his right of privacy has been infringed? That is the question to which we should now be directing our attention, and on which the public debate should now focus.

If I had called this paper 'The Future of the Right of Free Speech', I suspect that you would have been very shocked. We are all very accustomed to believing that the right of free speech is so important that the law should always respect it and never interfere with it. That is of course the right place to start but the fact is that the right of free speech is not sacrosanct in law, nor is it absolute. There are many restrictions on it which we take for granted: the law against obscene publications,[2] defamation, official secrets,[3] contempt of court,[4] and shortly we shall have restrictions on the payments which the media can make to potential witnesses in criminal trials.[5] In my view, the right of free speech is of the greatest importance: without it a free press, a cornerstone in a democratic society, could not survive. But in the field of privacy, as in the field of contempt of court or payments by the media to witnesses, there have to be some necessary restrictions. The question is what those restrictions

---

* First published in [1998–9] 9 KCLJ 1. It is reproduced here with the kind permission of the Publisher.

[1] See for example Warren and Brandeis, 'The Right to Privacy' (1890) 4 Harv L Rev 193, Winfield, 'Privacy' (1931) 47 LQR 23, Markesinis, 'Our Patchy Law of Privacy—Time to do something about it' (1990) 53 MLR 802 and 'The Calcutt Report must not be Forgotten: A Reply to Peter Preston' (1992) 55 MLR 118; Eady, 'Opinion: A Statutory Right to Privacy' [1996] EHRR 243.

[2] See Obscene Publications Act 1959.

[3] See Official Secrets Act 1920 and 1989.

[4] See the Contempt of Court Act 1981.

[5] See *Payments of Witnesses*, consultation paper, Lord Chancellor's Department and others, October 1996, and the response of the Lord Chancellor to the Second Report of the National Heritage Committee, Session 1996–7, October 1997.

have to be and how they can be imposed with least damage to our democratic tradition.

One matter that I should make clear at the outset is that privacy is not a topic which the Law Commission currently has on its agenda and so the views I am expressing are my own and not those of the Commission. The Commission is often described as the government's law reform body, and that is correct in so far as it is intended to imply that our statutory powers only enable us to look at questions of law reform at the instance of the government.[6] The government has stated that it does not intend to legislate on the question of privacy but to rely on self-regulation of the press by the Press Complaints Commission.[7] I will proceed on the basis that that policy is maintained. In so far as the description of the Law Commission as 'the government's law reform body' suggests that we make recommendations at the behest of the government, I would reject that as wholly inaccurate. We are emphatically an independent body in the recommendations we make. That is the key characteristic and great strength of the Law Commission. It follows from the government's decision that, although other law commissions[8] have been asked to make recommendations as to the law of privacy or on related topics, we have not been asked to do so and I therefore assume that the law will develop by the traditional methods of the common law. We could no doubt debate whether that is the right way for the law to develop in this particular field but it would appear, at present at least, that for all practical purposes that question has been decided.

Accordingly, I would prefer to stimulate debate on the question: in what circumstances in the foreseeable future will there be a legal remedy for infringement of privacy? That is the only issue that I can address in the space available, but it must be noted that a right of privacy may be a relevant consideration in all sorts of other cases, such as cases on discovery, interrogatories, freedom of information, defamation, contempt of court, arbitration, *Anton Piller* orders, the admission of evidence in criminal trials, applications involving children or concerning medical treatment, rules for hearing cases in private, disclosure of bank accounts, and so on. The right of privacy could be a many-headed hydra which appears in all sorts of contexts in the future, but I am concerned with it here only in so far as it results in a cause of action.

So the question I want to discuss, is, in what circumstances will there be a legal remedy for infringement of privacy? Obviously I can only state my view about this; the actual outcome after discussion in many cases may well turn out to be different, but I will do the best I can to deal with the issues that I think will arise.

The courts do not decide this sort of question in isolation or even on the basis only of what earlier courts have said, unless there is earlier case law which is binding under the doctrine of precedent and cannot be distinguished. One of the things

---

[6] Law Commissions Act 1965, s 3(1)(c),(e).

[7] See for example Lord Irvine Lord Chancellor, *Hansard*, House of Lords, vol 582, 3 November 1997, col 1229.

[8] See for example Ontario Law Commission, *The Protection of Privacy in Ontario* (1968), Law Reform Commission of South Australia, *Report Regarding the Law of Privacy* (1973), Australian Law Reform Commission, *Unfair Publication: Defamation and Privacy* (1979) and *Privacy* (1983).

that will influence the development of the law of privacy is an informed debate as to what the right of privacy should be. That is why in writing this paper I hope to stimulate a public debate on these issues. There are of course other factors that will influence the way that the courts develop the law, and they include previous decisions in England, decisions from other jurisdictions, Law Commission reports[9] and other authoritative studies,[10] of which in this field there are many.

The question that I have posed has to be tackled in stages:

- First, we must ask: to what extent is infringement of privacy protected by the law, apart from the European Convention on Human Rights?

- Second, we need to ask: in what further respects will the right of privacy be protected by the Convention?

Having considered those two questions, we can then move to the third question: in what circumstances might a remedy be available in future which is not available today?

To what extent is infringement of privacy already protected by the law?

It is well known that English law does not recognize a tort of infringement of privacy. The best known authority for this is *Kaye v Robertson*.[11] Mr Kaye, a television actor, was lying critically ill in hospital as he recovered from brain surgery, when reporters from a tabloid newspaper entered his room despite signs on the door. They proceeded to photograph him and conduct an 'interview' of which he was barely aware and had little recollection later. Mr Kaye sought an injunction preventing publication. The Court of Appeal held that there was no right of privacy recognized by the common law and that the only relief to which the plaintiff was entitled was an interlocutory injunction in malicious falsehood preventing not the publication of the reporters' photographs and interview, but anything which would give the impression that he had co-operated with them. In the case of *R v Khan*[12] it was argued that evidence obtained by illegal electronic listening devices ought not to be admitted in evidence in a criminal trial because the means by which the evidence had been obtained had been in breach of the defendant's right of privacy.

---

[9] See for example Ontario Law Commission, *The Protection of Privacy in Ontario* (1968), Law Reform Commission of South Australia, *Report Regarding the Law of Privacy* (1973), Australian Law Reform Commission, *Unfair Publication: Defamation and Privacy* (1979) and *Privacy* (1983).

[10] See for example the Report of the Committee on Privacy (Chairman: The Rt Hon Kenneth Younger) (1972); the Report of the Committee on Privacy and Related Matters (Chairman: David Calcutt QC) (1990) (Cm 1102); Review of Press Self-Regulation by Sir David Calcutt QC (1993) (Cm 2135); *Privacy and Media Intrusion*, Fourth Report of the National Heritage Committee Session 1992–3 (1993); *Infringement of Privacy*, a consultation paper, the Lord Chancellor's Department and the Scottish Office (July 1993); *Privacy and Media Intrusion: the Government's Response*, Department of National Heritage (July 1995) (Cm 2918).

[11] [1991] FSR 62, CA.　　　[12] [1997] AC 558.

However the House of Lords held that they did not have to decide whether there was a right of privacy as a matter of English law because the evidence was admissible even if it had been unlawfully obtained and that on the facts fairness did not require it to be excluded.

There are, however, a number of separate remedies already available for intrusion into the private life of a person. I will now summarize the principal ones.

(1) Breach of confidence

The conditions for a claim for breach of confidence are encapsulated in the following passage from the judgment of Megarry V-C in *Malone v Comr of Police of the Metropolis (No 2)*:[13]

... three elements are normally required if a case of breach of confidence is to succeed: 'First, the information itself, in the words of Lord Greene M.R.... must "have the necessary quality of confidence about it". Secondly, that information must have been imparted in circumstances importing an obligation of confidence. Thirdly, there must be an unauthorised use of that information to the detriment of the party communicating it' ...

A claim for breach of confidence thus lies if information, which has been obtained in the course of a relationship giving rise to an obligation of confidence,[14] is subsequently published, and there is no public interest in that information being made public.[15] The circumstances in which an obligation of confidence can be imposed are now generously construed. Those circumstances are not limited to a situation where there is some formal relationship between the parties. Rather, as Lord Goff put it in *A-G v Guardian Newspapers Ltd (No 2)*:[16]

... the broad general principle (which I do not intend in any way to be definitive) [is] that a duty of confidence arises when confidential information comes to the knowledge of a person (the confidant) in circumstances where he has notice, or is held to have agreed, that the information is confidential, with the effect that it would be just in all the circumstances that he should be precluded from disclosing the information to others.

Such a claim is, however, conceptually quite different from a claim for infringement of privacy since it depends upon the imposition of an obligation of confidence. A claim for infringement of privacy on the other hand would focus on the nature of the information: it would be *because* the information in question is of a personal or domestic nature, which the person whom it concerned would normally expect not to be revealed to third parties, that the claim would arise. However there is certainly an overlap between confidence and privacy. Where information of a confidential

---

[13] [1979] 2 All ER 620 at 645, [1979] Ch 344 at 375.

[14] This would include the relationship of husband and wife in respect of domestic secrets and any other relationship in which confidential information is imparted: *Stephens v Avery* [1988] Ch 449.

[15] See for example *Seager v Copydex Ltd* [1967] 1 WLR 923. For cases where it was contended that the publication was in the public interest, see for example *Initial Services v Putterill* [1968] 1 QB 396 and *Lion Laboratories v Evans* [1985] QB 526.

[16] [1990] 1 AC 109 at 281B.

and personal nature is given or received in circumstances in which an obligation of confidence is imposed, the victim of the infringement of privacy can utilize the law of breach of confidence. Thus in *Stephens v Avery*[17] the plaintiff wanted to prevent further publication by the press of information given to a friend about her sexual conduct. She claimed that she had given the information under an obligation of confidence, that this had been agreed between the parties and that the newspaper knew that the information had been given in confidence. It was argued among other things that there was no claim in confidence because there was no pre-existing relationship or contract between the parties. Sir Nicholas Browne-Wilkinson V-C rejected that approach: it was not the relationship between the parties that determined whether there was a claim for breach of confidence but rather whether the conscience of the recipient of the information was affected. The Vice-Chancellor made it clear that he appreciated the sensitivity of the issues involved in developing a law of privacy:

To my mind this case undoubtedly does raise fundamental difficulties as to the relationship between on the one hand the privacy which every individual is entitled to expect, and on the other hand freedom of information. To many, the aggressive intrusion of sectors of the press into the private lives of individuals is unpalatable. On the other hand, the ability of the press to obtain and publish for the public benefit information of genuine public interest, as opposed to general public titillation, may be impaired if information obtained in confidence is too widely protected by the law. Moreover, is the press to be liable in damages for printing what is true? I express no view as to where or how the borderline should be drawn in such a case.[18]

On this basis, the law relating to breach of confidence would now, subject to any defence of public interest, cover the 'kiss and tell' type situation. In this type of case, A has a relationship of a sexual nature with B. B tells C in confidence that he or she has had a relationship with A. C sells the story to the newspaper. Information relating to B's sexual conduct would be protected by the law of confidence, unless the conduct was grossly immoral or it was in the public interest that the information should be disclosed: B would have a claim in breach of confidence against both C and the newspaper. What is not so clear is whether A would have any claim against B, C, or the newspaper. In *Stephens v Avery* there was an express obligation of confidence and the court distinguished an earlier case[19] in which there had been no express obligation of confidence and an injunction had been refused. The court in that earlier case also held that the mere existence of a homosexual relationship did not give rise to an obligation of confidence. However, in the *Stephens* case, the Vice-Chancellor left open the question whether that earlier case was correctly decided and the better view today must be that the court would recognize other relationships, apart from those resulting from marriage or a contract, as giving rise to an obligation of confidence. But if for some reason the court finds that there is no obligation of confidence the plaintiff will not be able to prevent the disclosure of personal

---

[17] [1988] Ch 449. [18] [1988] Ch 449 at 456–7.
[19] *M and N v Kelvin Mackenzie, and News Group* (unreported) 18 January 1988.

information, however embarrassing. This exposes the difference between a claim for breach of confidence and what a claim for infringement of privacy would cover.

There are other differences between privacy and confidence: for example breach of confidence would cover any kind of confidential information, including commercial information. A claim for infringement of privacy would in general[20] only cover information of a personal nature. Breach of confidence focuses on the need to uphold the obligation of confidence whereas in enforcing a claim for infringement of privacy the court would be concerned with damage to the plaintiff as a result of the unauthorized publication.

Breach of confidence is a dynamic tort and its scope is by no means settled. One of the issues surrounding the law of confidence is whether it covers the acquisition of confidential information by reprehensible means but not in the course of a confidential relationship. As a matter of policy, it would be odd if a person could steal confidential information belonging to another and not be liable if he published it without the true owner's authority, whereas if he had been given the same information in confidence he could have been sued for damages for breach of confidence. This anomaly is highlighted by Laws J (obiter) in the context of the unauthorized taking of photographs and it received from him a robust response:

If someone with a telephoto lens were to take from a distance and with no authority a picture of another engaged in some private act, his subsequent disclosure of the photograph would, in my judgment, as surely amount to a breach of confidence as if he had found or stolen a letter or diary in which the act was recounted and proceeded to publish it. In such a case, the law would protect what might reasonably be called a right of privacy, although the name accorded to the cause of action would be breach of confidence. It is, of course, elementary that, in all such cases, a defence based on the public interest would be available.[21]

This is a different view of the law from that expressed in cases such as *Malone v Metropolitan Police Commissioner*[22] in which Megarry V-C said that the Post Office did not by tapping a telephone line breach any obligation of confidentiality to the subscriber and accordingly the subscriber could not recover damages when the Post Office passed the information to the police. It presupposes that a claim for breach of confidence can exist where there is no relationship giving rise to an obligation of confidence. There is some support for this proposition in some of the most recent case law, although it would involve reconstructing the tort.

If a claim for breach of confidence can exist where there is no relationship giving rise to an obligation of confidence, then to take, by means of a photograph, a record of information concerning a person who is on private property, when the person taking the photograph knows from the nature of the information and the circumstances in which the photograph is taken that the subject of the photograph would not have consented to its disclosure, would give rise to a claim for breach of confidence. If the view expressed by Laws J prevails, the law of confidence will give victims of infringements of privacy considerable protection.

---

[20] But see below, with respect to Art 8 of the European Convention on Human Rights.
[21] *Hellewell v Chief Constable of Derbyshire* [1995] 1 WLR 804.   [22] [1979] Ch 344.

In 1981, the Law Commission recommended that a new tort of breach of confidence be created.[23] This report was accepted by the government, but it has not yet been implemented by legislation. The report was concerned with breach of confidence and not with the creation of a claim for infringement of privacy.

(2) Trespass and nuisance

I need say very little about these torts, other than to note their relevance to privacy and their limitations. A person invading another's privacy may commit trespass to his person or property, and he may be liable for damages for trespass accordingly. But of course a person who stands for example in the public highway in order to take photographs[24] does not commit trespass so it is possible for this sanction to be avoided.

Nuisance may be committed by a persistent intruder or harasser if this interferes with the enjoyment of land. However, only the person who has an interest in the land on which the nuisance occurs can bring the action,[25] and accordingly this tort is of little use in protecting victims of infringements of privacy.

(3) Tort of harassment

The Protection from Harassment Act 1996 creates a new civil remedy[26] which in appropriate circumstances will be capable of being used by the victim of harassment. The victim of harassment may apply to the court for an order to restrain the harassment. If the defendant is in breach of the restraining order, the plaintiff may apply for a warrant of arrest and is not required to proceed by way of an application for contempt of court. The court may award damages for the mental anxiety caused by the harassment and the financial loss resulting from the harassment. The Act was introduced to meet cases of stalking, but there is no reason why it should not be capable of being used on appropriate facts by victims of harassment against journalists or private detectives who invade their privacy. The Act also creates a criminal offence of harassment.[27] There are certain circumstances where neither the civil remedy nor the offence apply, such as where the course of conduct was pursued for the purpose of preventing or detecting crime.[28]

(4) Defamation

The tort of defamation is also well known and will be available to a victim of an infringement of privacy without regard to motive for the publication of the defamatory matter. In general, matter is defamatory which would tend to lower

[23] *Breach of Confidence*, Law Commission (1981) (Cmnd 8388) (Law Com No 110).
[24] Compare *Bernstein v Skyways* [1978] 1 QB 333.
[25] *Hunter v Canary Wharf Ltd* [1997] 2 WLR 684, overruling in part *Khorasandjian v Bush* [1993] QB 727.
[26] Section 3.   [27] Section 2.   [28] Section 1.

the plaintiff in the eyes of right-thinking members of society. Neither actual damage nor lack of good faith have to be shown. If the defendant intends to show at trial that the alleged defamatory matter is true, the court will not grant an injunction to restrain publication. The defendant may also rely on absolute privilege (as for example where the alleged defamation occurred in court) or qualified privilege (as for example where the person who is under a duty to make a statement makes the statement, without actual malice, to a person who has an interest in receiving it). Certain changes to the law of defamation were made by the Defamation Act 1996.

(5) Data protection

Much information about individuals is today held on computer. There are already controls on the way information is stored in the Data Protection Act 1984, but the government proposes to introduce new measures to strengthen these controls in line with the European Community's Data Protection Directive.[29] These measures will include giving the subject remedies if he is denied access to information held about him. This information could include information held by the media on an individual. This would greatly increase the ability of an individual to monitor what information the press has about him before it was published. It is not yet clear whether, and if so to what extent, there will be any exemptions for the media.

Conclusion

So far as the right of privacy is concerned, this analysis suggests that there is no underlying principle in the different torts available in this situation and that the protection which the law provides is both fragmented and incomplete. It is almost as if the forms of action are ruling us from their grave! The good news however is that we may shortly be reaching the time when the courts will be able to review, systematize and restate the various different common law torts in a unified and principled way. A start was made by Lord Keith in *A-G v Guardian Newspapers*[30] when he said that: '... breach of confidence involves no more than an invasion of privacy.'

Rationalization along these lines seems to me also to be foreshadowed by the following passage from the speech of Lord Nicholls in *R v Khan*:[31]

the appellant contended for a right of privacy in respect of private conversations in private houses. I prefer to express no view, either way, on the existence of such a right. This right, if

---

[29] Directive 95/46/EC of the European Parliament and of the Council of 24 October 1995 on the protection of individuals with regard to the processing of personal data and on the free movement of such data.
[30] [1990] 1 AC 109 at 205. See also *British Steel Corp v Granada Television Ltd* [1981] AC 1096 at 1129–30, per Denning MR.
[31] [1997] AC 558.

it exists, can only do so as part of a larger and wider right of privacy. The difficulties attendant on this controversial subject are well known. Equally well known is the continuing, widespread concern at the apparent failure of the law to give individuals a reasonable degree of protection from unwarranted intrusion in many situations. I prefer to leave open for another occasion the important question whether the present, piecemeal protection of privacy has now developed to the extent that a more comprehensive principle can be seen to exist. It is not necessary to pursue this question on this appeal. Even if the right for which the appellant contended does exist, this would not lead to the consequence that obtaining evidence for the purpose of detecting or preventing serious crime was an infringement of the right or, even if it were, that the evidence was inadmissible at the trial.

The House of Lords did not decide whether a right of privacy existed in that case, and Lord Browne-Wilkinson, as well as Lord Nicholls, expressly left the issue open in terms which acknowledged the difficulty and importance of the law in this area.

It may very well be therefore that the law will be revisited and restated before the incorporation of the European Convention on Human Rights. The Human Rights Bill for this purpose is currently before Parliament. It is due to become law next year. The relevant provisions will not take effect immediately, but on a date to be appointed, so there is window of opportunity for the House of Lords to clarify the common law before the Convention becomes part of English law. Indeed, an article in the *New Law Journal*[32] suggested that there was also a case before the European Commission of Human Rights which turns on whether English law provides a legal remedy for the victims of infringements of privacy.

In what further respects will privacy be protected by the Convention?

As is well known, the European Convention on Human Rights, which is proposed to be made a part of English law by the Human Rights Bill now before Parliament, protects both the right to privacy[33] and the right to freedom of expression.[34] The relevant articles are in the following terms:

The Human Rights Bill now before Parliament provides (so far as material):

(1) that it is unlawful for a public authority to act in a way which is incompatible with rights conferred by the Convention (clause 6). A 'public authority' is defined as including a court and 'a person certain of whose functions are of a public nature' (clause 6 (3));

(2) that a person who claims that a public authority has acted in breach of Convention rights may bring proceedings against the public authority and the court may make any order it thinks fit, including in certain circumstances an award of damages (clauses 7 and 8);

---

[32] Patrick Milmo QC, 'Human Rights, Privacy and the Press', *New Law Journal*, 7 November 1997, p 1631.
[33] Article 8.   [34] Article 10.

(3) that when the court determines a question under the Human Rights Act in connection with a Convention right it must take into account any decision of the European Commission on Human Rights, the European Court of Human Rights or the Council of Ministers (clause 2).

The Human Rights Bill will apply mostly directly to cases against public authorities, which would include such bodies as the Press Complaints Commission. My principal concern in this paper is with the person who needs to apply to the court for an order restraining some action by a body which is not a public authority. The court will have to decide which bodies are 'public authorities', but assuming as I do that this expression does not include newspapers, any action which a victim of an infringement of privacy wishes to bring against a journalist or newspaper will continue to have to be brought under one of the remedies provided by the general law which I have already summarized.

Unlike (on this assumption) newspapers, public authorities will have a direct obligation to refrain from acting in a manner incompatible with the Convention. Precisely what this means for the courts is not clear.[35]

In what circumstances might a remedy be available in future which is not available today?

On one view the court is bound to provide a remedy for infringement of privacy—even if this involves creating a new tort. The creation of wholly new remedies is not a task which normally falls to the court. Indeed, the creation of a new remedy by the courts could produce a number of odd results. For instance the Bill in effect provides that a person may bring a claim under the Act against a public authority only in respect of an act occurring after the relevant provision of the Act takes effect (clause 22(3)). If the court decides to develop a new remedy, it may not be able to impose the same limitation.

The other view is that the courts' responsibility is to declare what the law is, and if it provides insufficient protection to an individual in respect of Convention rights which he seeks to pursue against non-public authorities, that is a question for Parliament to address.

Either construction is liable to produce anomalies. A person who sues a public authority for an infringement of his right of privacy may find he has a right if the defendant is a public authority but not if the defendant is not a public authority. Likewise, if the courts develop the law so that a person has a claim under the general law if his right to privacy is infringed by a body which is not a public authority for the purposes of the Human Rights Act, the court will not be under the same obligation with respect to decisions of, for example, the European Court of Human Rights, and the plaintiff may be able to recover damages assessed on a different basis

---

[35] See, for example, Milmo, 'Human Rights, Privacy and the Press' at p 1631.

from those that are awarded in his favour against a non-public authority, and in different circumstances. Neither result seems altogether satisfactory. I would expect the court to reject the first approach if it feels that it can but then to use the Convention as a catalyst to develop the law so as to diminish the differences between the rights against a public authority and the rights against a defendant who is not such an authority. However any such decision lies in the future and accordingly for the purposes of the next part of this paper, I will assume that the court decides to give protection to an individual whose right to privacy is infringed against not just a public authority as defined in the Human Rights Bill but also against a party who is not such an authority. This may be because the court conceives itself as bound to ensure equivalent protection in this situation or because it develops the existing torts. For example, following the lead given in *R v Khan* and *Hellewell v Chief Constable of Derbyshire*, the court may say that a claim for breach of confidence lies whenever there is an unauthorized breach of the claimant's privacy right.

I will not be dealing with the possibility of an action for judicial review against a 'public authority' for breach of a right conferred by the Convention.

All I can do here is try to identify the issues that are likely to arise and to express a view on them. In *Kaye v Robertson*, Bingham LJ regarded the difficulties of defining and limiting the tort as 'formidable'. I assume that the court would not wish to develop a remedy for an infringement of privacy beyond that which is required to give effect to the Convention. The European Commission on Human Rights held in 1986[36] that the absence of an actionable right to privacy under English law did not show a lack of respect for the applicant's rights under Art 8, but this was on the facts of the particular case before it.

I would identify the following issues as requiring to be resolved by the courts:

(1) When is there an infringement of the right of privacy?
(2) Will proof of damage be necessary?
(3) What defences will there be?
(4) When will the court grant interlocutory relief?

(1) When is there an infringement of privacy?

Under Art 8, information with respect to a person's private and family life, his home and correspondence is protected. It would appear to be primarily directed towards that which is personal or domestic in nature. But the Article also covers 'correspondence'. This word has been widely construed to include telephone conversations,[37] and the same authority also assumes that the correspondence need not relate to personal or private life: it can relate to business dealings. This

---

[36] *Winer v UK* (Application No 10871/84) (1986) 48 DR 154, EComHR.
[37] *Malone v United Kingdom* [1984] 7 EHRR 14.

would be an innovation since previous English reform proposals would only have introduced a tort of invasion of privacy to protect personal information.[38]

A more difficult question will be to know when there has been interference with this right. What a person does in their own home is clearly in general protected. But does the position change if something is done in public? After all the word 'privacy' suggests something done in private. Should the location where the information is imparted determine whether there is interference with the right of privacy if such information is taken without authority by someone who intends to publish it?

A German case[39] concerning Princess Caroline of Monaco, a member of the Monagasque ruling family, suggests that privacy can cover the conduct of private life in public. In that case the press took photographs of the Princess and her children at various public places. The Princess was constantly followed by the press. They also took photographs of her at a garden restaurant in France where she sat with a male friend. It appears to have been a romantic occasion. This is not a case on the Convention but on the interpretation of a provision of the German constitution which states that 'The dignity of man shall be inviolable'. German law in fact provides that in general pictures of a person may be distributed only with that person's consent but if the person is a person of contemporary history his or her consent is not required 'unless legally protected interests of the person are infringed'.

The Federal Court of Justice of Germany referred to the competing public interest in information protected by freedom of the press and the plaintiff's right to her personality. The Court held:

The protection of a person's private sphere of life has especial importance when the two interests are weighed against each other. The right to respect for one's own private sphere of life is an emanation of the general right to one's own personality, which grants every person an autonomous area of personal life within which he can develop and experience his own individuality, free from the interferences of others. The right to be left alone and 'to belong to oneself' forms part of this area. As a result, since 1954, the German courts have, especially in the area of civil law, given particular weight to the right to respect one's own private sphere of life, i.e. treated it as a basic right, guaranteed by the constitution which includes the right to one's own image.

The Court rejected an argument accepted by the Appeal Court that privacy stopped 'at the doorstep' and that therefore the press were entitled to take photographs of the Princess who was dining in the corner of a private restaurant. The Federal Court of Justice of Germany held that it was enough that the Princess had:

retreated to a place of seclusion where [she wished] to be left alone, as [could] be ascertained by objective criteria, and in a specific situation, where [she], relying on the fact of seclusion, acts in a way that [she] would not have done so in public. An unjustified intrusion into this area occurs where pictures of that person are published if taken secretly or by stealth.

---

[38] See for example the Report of the Committee on Privacy and Related Matters (the Calcutt Committee) (1991), para 12.18 (b), *Infringement of Privacy,* Consultation Paper issued by the Lord Chancellor's Department and the Scottish Office, July 1993, para 5.22.
[39] BGH 19 Dec.1995, BGHZ 131 pp 332–46.

A place of seclusion could be in a place open to the public so long as the person in question shut himself or herself off from the public. Such a place could include a garden restaurant so long as the fact that the person had shut himself or herself off from the public was reasonably obvious to third persons.

The Court continued:

When weighing up the various interests involved, the information value of the events depicted plays a significant role. The greater the interest of the public in being informed, the more the protected interests of the person of contemporary history must recede in favour of the public's need for information. Conversely, the need to protect the depicted person's privacy gains in weight as the value of the information which the public obtains from the photographs decreases. In this case the photographs which show the plaintiff with Vincent Lindon in a garden restaurant contain little, if anything of value. Here according to the Appeal Court, mere prying sensationalism, and the public's wish to be entertained, which is to be satisfied by pictures of totally private events of the plaintiff's life, cannot be recognised as worthy of protection.

On the other hand, when the Princess was in public, for instance dining or shopping, there was a public interest in knowing how she behaved even if she was not performing a public function. In these situations she had not retreated to a place secluded from the general public.

On this basis, under German law, a person in the position of Princess Caroline is in general entitled to privacy in respect of things done in private, or in exceptional circumstances things done in public. Those exceptional circumstances are where the claimant has made it clear that she has retreated to a place of seclusion. In that situation she is not exposed to photographers in the same way as if she had appeared normally in public. The exceptional circumstances will only rarely arise. It is in my view doubtful whether the result would have been the same in English law. The distinction which it seeks to draw is difficult to apply. But the case is a useful starting point for discussion. It also gives strong support to the notion that the public are not entitled to know every detail of the life of a public figure in her position. A line has to be drawn somewhere between the public's right to know, and the public figure's right to privacy and this case shows where the Federal Court of Justice of Germany decided that it should lie. It goes beyond the doorstep, but only a little way. What is clear however is that photographs taken of the Princess on private property using a long range lens would have been in breach of her right to privacy.

Different public figures must necessarily receive different levels of protection. This is illustrated by the English case of *Woodward v Hutchins*.[40] In that case a pop group sued their former manager because he threatened to reveal matters about their private lives. But in that case the group had tried to put forward the image of good behaviour. The information to be revealed would give the lie to that and the Court of Appeal refused to restrain its publication. Lord Denning MR said:

---

[40] [1977] 1 WLR 760.

No doubt in some employments there is an obligation of confidence. In a proper case the court will be prepared to restrain a servant from disclosing confidential information which he has received in the course of his employment. But this case is quite out of the ordinary. There is no doubt whatever that this pop group sought publicity. They wanted to have themselves presented to the public in a favourable light so that audiences would come to hear them and support them. Mr Hutchins was engaged so as to produce, or help to produce, this favourable image, not only of their public lives but of their private lives also. If a group of this kind seek publicity which is to their advantage, it seems to me that they cannot complain if a servant or employee of theirs afterwards discloses the truth about them. If the image which they fostered was not a true image, it is in the public interest that it should be corrected. In these cases of confidential information it is a question of balancing the public interest in maintaining the confidence against the public interest in knowing the truth. That appears from *Initial Services Ltd v Putterill, Fraser v Evans* and *D v National Society for the Prevention of Cruelty to Children* ([1976] 2 All ER 993 at 999, [1976] 3 WLR 124 at 132). In this case the balance comes down in favour of the truth being told, even if it should involve some breach of confidential information. As there should be 'truth in advertising', so there should be truth in publicity. The public should not be misled. So it seems to me that the breach of confidential information is not a ground for granting an injunction.

Accordingly politicians who propound family values in public but act differently in private must beware. The case of *Woodward v Hutchins* suggests that the law will not enable those who are hypocritical to be protected by the new law of privacy. But by the same token it does not follow that every detail of politicians' lives is a matter of public interest which merits exposure by the press. The press can make its point without going into every prurient detail, and even in the case of the hypocritical politician there may be a point beyond which they cannot go without infringing the politician's right to privacy or the right to privacy of his family.

Lastly on this issue, it should not be thought that in the area of privacy the court is concerned only with public figures. There are many people who are not public figures but who become caught up with some tragic event, such as the death of a child. They too can find their private lives under investigation by the press, often very suddenly and at a time when they are traumatized and at their most vulnerable and in need of privacy. The law must give them proper protection, just as much as it must give that measure of protection (and no more) to public figures.

(2) Will proof of damage be necessary?

Loss does not have to be shown where the claim is for breach of confidence, harassment, defamation, nuisance, or trespass unless damages are sought. The law regards the encroachment on the right as sufficient damage. It seems to me that the same must be true of a right of privacy to which there is no defence and so the real question is what defences there should be.

(3) What defences will there be?

In the absence of a defined tort, to start with the court will have to develop the defences as it goes along reasoning by analogy from the existing causes of action. It seems to me that the following defences are likely:

(a) Consent

If the plaintiff has courted the publicity, it is unlikely that he will be able to succeed in a subsequent claim for infringement of privacy. People who buy houses next to airports are not generally in a position to complain about the noise. Bridge LJ applied this principle to the plaintiff in *Woodward v Hutchins*, the case about the pop group, when he said in his judgment:

It seems to me that those who seek and welcome publicity of every kind bearing on their private lives so long as it shows them in a favourable light are in no position to complain of an invasion of their privacy by publicity which shows them in an unfavourable light.[41]

(b) Public domain

The essence of an infringement of privacy is that it should keep that which a person is entitled to keep private in that state. Therefore it should be a defence that the information has come into the public domain. But this may need refining. The fact that the information has been revealed in one country where the effect of disclosure was comparatively insignificant should not necessarily mean that there is no right to privacy in another.

(c) The defences provided by Art 8 itself

These comprise disclosure authorized by law and necessary in a democratic society for four purposes:

   i. in the interests of national security, public safety or economic well-being;
   ii. for the prevention of disorder or crime;
   iii. for the protection of health or morals;
   iv. for the protection of the rights or freedoms of others.

These defences would clearly enable an infringement to be justified on the basis that it was an exercise of free speech and similarly they would allow other infringements which are necessary in the public interest for the reasons given above. The above grounds cover much of the ground presently covered by the defence of public interest which is available in breach of confidence proceedings.[42]

---

[41] [1977] 1 WLR 760 at 765.
[42] See for example the discussion in paras 6.41 to 6.55 of the Law Commission's consultation paper, *Legislating the Criminal Code: Misuse of Trade Secrets* (Law Com No 150) (1997), and see also Breach of Confidence (Cmnd 8388), Law Commission (Law Com No 110) (1981) paras 6.77 to 6.84.

(d) Innocent infringement

As I have already pointed out, a person can commit defamation without a reprehensible motive. An important question for any tort of infringement of privacy is whether the plaintiff has to show that the defendant intended to infringe his privacy or had some other mental state. In my view the plaintiff should not have to show what the defendant had in his mind. On the other hand, there will be times when in the heat of the moment a person infringes the privacy of another in circumstances where he made a genuine mistake as to the relevant facts. He may have thought for instance that he had the plaintiff's permission to take photographs or that the plaintiff was not on private property. It would be just if the law was tempered to meet the possible harshness of this case. On the other hand, the fact of the matter is that the plaintiff's rights have been infringed so that the defendant cannot be given a complete defence, notwithstanding that he acted in perfect good faith.

The Defamation Act 1996 contains provisions,[43] at the time of writing not yet in force, which enable a person to make an offer of amends in relation to a defamatory statement. He can offer to correct and apologize for the statement, publish the correction, and pay compensation. The plaintiff can accept or refuse. If he accepts, the court can determine any further matter, such as the amount of the compensation, on which the parties cannot agree. If the plaintiff does not accept the offer of amends, the defendant may rely on the offer of amends by way of defence unless he knew or had reason to believe that the matter was defamatory. The new offer of amends procedure provides a means of dealing with defamation cases on a speedy basis.

What I suggest is that there should be some similar approach to infringement of privacy where the defendant had no reason to believe that his action would involve a breach of privacy. Thus if the defendant was prepared to make an offer of amends and the plaintiff accepted his offer, the court could proceed to deal with any outstanding issue as to the amount of any compensation on the basis of the parties' agreement the breach had occurred, perhaps on an expedited basis. Obviously there would be no publication in this case of any apology. There would be savings to the defendant in legal costs. It may be that some such procedure as this could be achieved simply by practice direction or procedural rule.

(e) The presence of an alternative remedy

The courts would probably be faced at some stage with the suggestion that there are sufficient remedies for the infringement of privacy in the self-regulatory systems such as the Press Complaints Commission and that therefore the court need not grant any remedy in respect of the infringement of privacy. Whether such an argument would succeed would, in my view, depend on the court's view as to the

---

[43] Sections 2–4.

adequacy of these alternative remedies. Any self-regulatory system which helps protect the right of privacy and also provides a means of alternative dispute resolution (not involving litigation) is clearly to be welcomed and encouraged. If it is successful, it will reduce the cost and delay involved in bringing legal proceedings and reduce the number of cases before the courts.

(4) When will the courts grant interlocutory relief?

In libel cases the courts do not restrain the publication of material if the defendant states that he intends at trial to show that the words are true. In breach of confidence cases, however, where the defendant relies on the defence of public interest, he must not only state that he intends to rely on the defence of public interest but also show that there is a serious defence based on public interest.[44] For infringement of privacy cases, the latter test is to be preferred. The libel rule would be unfair to a plaintiff, who is prejudiced by the disclosure of the information, where the defence based on public interest has no substance. The courts might decide that the defence of public interest has to be shown to some higher level on an application for an injunction, but there is the danger that, if proof is required to too high a level, the well-to-do plaintiff who wishes to stifle press comment will simply issue proceedings for an injunction to restrain publication of material which would infringe his privacy. Those writs will then be used as 'gagging writs' against the media.

Conclusion

There is considerable uncertainty over the future of the law of privacy. There are many new situations which the courts may have to resolve. In my view, after so many years of rhetoric on this sensitive subject, the time has come for an informed debate as to the appropriate limits to legal remedies for breach of the right to privacy if the courts find that such a breach is indeed actionable as such. As a start, I have endeavoured to raise some of the issues that I consider will have to be resolved. As I see it the problems are capable of solution. The law that is developed will have to have many qualities: it will have to be measured, reflective and flexible, and it will have to strike a proper balance between the right to privacy and freedom of expression. I think that all this can be achieved through the courts. Now that I have laid out one way in which it can be done it is for those who disagree with this point of view to participate in debate.

---

[44] *Lion Laboratories Ltd v Evans* [1985] QB 526.

14

Human Rights and Civil Wrongs: Tort Law under the Spotlight

This chapter is based on the Hailsham Lecture given in 2009.*

Lectures are regularly given, and articles written, about the effect of the jurisprudence of the European Convention on Human Rights on public law or criminal law. However, very little attention is given to its effect on the law of tort. This seemed to me to be a more unusual and challenging topic, and I have therefore chosen it for this paper.

Background

The Hailsham lecture is given in honour of a previous Lord Chancellor. When one of his successors, Lord Irvine of Lairg, gave the Tom Sargent Memorial Lecture in 1997, he expressed the view that:

As we move away from the traditional Diceyan model of the common law to a rights based system, the effects will be felt throughout the common law and in the very process of our judicial decision making. This will be a healthy and dynamic development in our law.[1]

Likewise, soon after new legislation came into force, Lord Hope said:

It is now plain that the incorporation of the European Convention on Human Rights into our domestic law will subject the entire legal system to a fundamental process of review and, where necessary, reform by the judiciary.[2]

In this paper, we will be looking to see how far these very general statements have been borne out in the law of tort.

---

* This chapter was first given as the Hailsham Lecture 2009, organized by Hailsham Chambers. It was subsequently published in the *Cambridge Law Journal*, 2013 © *Cambridge Law Journal*. It is reproduced here with the kind permission of the Publisher.

[1] Lord Irvine of Lairg, 'The development of human rights in Britain under an incorporated Convention on Human Rights' [1998] PL 221, 229.
[2] *R v DPP ex parte Kebilene* [2000] 2 AC 326, HL at 375.

The scheme of the European Convention on Human Rights (the 'Convention') and the Human Rights Act 1998 (the 'HRA') are now very familiar.[3] There are four particular points to note about the HRA for the purposes of this paper. First, when the courts are determining a question arising in connection with a Convention right, they are required 'to take into account' the Strasbourg jurisprudence.[4] They are not bound by it but the House of Lords has on several occasions said that English courts should follow Strasbourg jurisprudence, 'no more, but certainly no less'.[5] Second, it is only unlawful for *public* authorities to act incompatibly with human rights. Individuals are not so bound. Third, the HRA creates a right of action for violation of Convention rights.[6] But any award of damages must take account of the principles applied by the Strasbourg Court,[7] which awards only small amounts of damages, generally less than those available for a tort in domestic law. In addition, the limitation period under the HRA is in general only one year, whereas in England the limitation period for torts is generally six years from the wrongful act.[8] Fourth, in general, the HRA does not have retrospective effect.[9] Each of these points plays a part in the discussion that follows.

Aims of this paper

There is no obvious connection between the Convention and torts under the domestic law of a contracting state. The Convention does not guarantee that there will be any particular rights or remedies in the private law of contracting states. A further limitation in the Convention system is that it only protects the individual against the acts of public authorities and not the acts of other citizens. If the Convention were to have any impact on wrongs as between ordinary citizens, a way would have to be found round this restriction. If the matter stopped there, we should probably conclude that the development of the law of tort in ordinary cases between private citizens would be unaffected by the Convention.

But the matter is not as simple as that. There are two conflicting signals in the HRA as opposed to the Convention. The first signal suggests that Convention rights are to have no impact on domestic law: that signal is the provision in the HRA for its own system of remedies for violation of Convention rights. From this, it is arguable that Parliament intended that violations of human rights should only be actionable using that procedure. But there is another signal emitting the opposite message. The HRA makes the court a public authority.[10] When the Human Rights Bill was introduced, this was perceived to be the stronger signal. Before the HRA was passed, many thought that the courts would use the Convention proactively to develop

---

[3] The Convention rights incorporated by the Human Rights Act 1998 and the principal provisions of that Act are set out in the Appendix.
[4] HRA, s 2(1).
[5] On the application of *R (Ullah) v Special Adjudicator* [2004] UKHL 26, [2004] 2 AC 323, 350. This is not the case if the court is satisfied that the Strasbourg Court misunderstood English law or procedure: *Doherty v Birmingham City Council* [2008] UKHL 57, [2009] 1 AC 367.
[6] HRA, s 7.   [7] HRA, s 8(3).   [8] HRA, s 7(5).
[9] HRA, s 22(4).   [10] HRA, s 6(3).

common law rights of action. This raised an issue which became known as 'horizontality'.

I am not going to spend much time on explaining the debate on horizontality because it has ceased to be important due to the way the law has actually developed. Three main views were put forward. The first school of thought was that judges could never act incompatibly with the Convention. This led Professor Wade to conclude that 'the citizen can legitimately expect that his human rights will be respected by his neighbour as well as by his government'.[11] The second school of thought is exemplified by Murray Hunt. He argued that while the HRA does not permit direct horizontal effect, there is an indirect horizontal effect flowing from the duty imposed by s 6. Thus:

Law which already exists and governs private relations must be interpreted, applied and if necessary developed so as to achieve compatibility with the Convention. But where no cause of action exists, and there is therefore no law to apply, the courts cannot invent new causes of action, as that would be to embrace full horizontality.[12]

The third school of thought is exemplified by Gavin Phillipson. He accepted that the HRA would have some form of horizontal effect. This could be seen from the interpretive duty under s 3 in relation to legislation. However, he considered that the attempt to deduce from the HRA a general duty to achieve conformity of the common law with Convention rights would not be accepted by the courts.[13]

The discussion about the first two schools of thought, at least, on horizontality assumed that there would be a uniform approach to using Convention values in tort law. But that has not turned out to be the case. The position is more nuanced. In this paper, I will identify four techniques:

(a) The Convention has in some cases inspired change in the law. Thus the Convention has been used to develop the law on breach of confidence so as to provide stronger remedies against the wrongful disclosure of confidential information.

(b) In other cases, the courts have not sought to extend existing remedies so as to encompass violations of Convention rights. In particular, there is no general tort of wrongful invasions of privacy, and, in the field of negligence, domestic rights of action and remedies have been developed separately from remedies for breach of a Convention right. Indeed, the court has categorized the remedy under the HRA as a parallel remedy that ought to be developed separately.

(c) The Strasbourg jurisprudence has been used as a launch pad for new ideas for the way in which eg claims for damages might be developed.

(d) The Strasbourg jurisprudence has been used as a cross-check for conclusions already reached.

---

[11] W Wade, 'Horizons of Horizontality' (2000) 116 LQR 217, 224.
[12] M Hunt, 'The Horizontal Effect of the Human Rights Act' [1998] PL 423, 442.
[13] G Phillipson, 'The Human Rights Act, "Horizontal Effect" on the Common Law. A Big Bang or a Whimper?' (1999) 62 MLR 824, 845.

I will illustrate these four techniques by examples from the law of breach of confidence and negligence.

That survey leads to some general questions: How should the court use a statement of human rights when deciding cases about common law torts between individual citizens? What should be the respective roles of the Strasbourg Court and domestic courts in this field and more generally? On this latter question, Lord Hoffmann has given a powerful lecture in which he was critical of the Strasbourg Court, and I shall consider some of the points which he made.

Privacy

Before 1998, no cause of action in English law for invasion of an individual's privacy

English law historically failed to provide a remedy for breach of a person's privacy. Thus, in *Kaye v Robertson*,[14] decided before the HRA, a famous actor was photographed and interviewed by journalists in a hospital room having recently undergone surgery for serious head and brain injuries. The journalists claimed to have obtained Mr Kaye's permission to conduct the interview; however the evidence indicated that he was in no fit state to provide any informed consent. Mr Kaye sought to prevent publication of the interview and images. His case was pleaded on the basis of libel, malicious falsehood, trespass to the person, and passing off. Despite the obvious gross violation of his privacy, Mr Kaye succeeded only in obtaining an injunction restraining the newspaper claiming, by way of malicious falsehood, that he had voluntarily given the interview.

In 1999, I gave a lecture entitled 'The Future of the Law of Privacy'.[15] In it, I asked the question in what circumstances might a remedy be available in future under the HRA for invasions of privacy which was not then available. I referred to the debate on horizontality. I pointed out that it would be anomalous if the remedies available to an individual citizen against a public authority for an infringement of privacy were different from those available if the defendant was not a public authority. I stated that I would expect the court 'to use the Convention as a catalyst to develop the law so as to diminish the differences between the rights against a public authority and the rights against a defendant who is not such an authority'. I added that:

This may be because the court conceives itself as bound to ensure equivalent protection in this situation or because it develops the existing torts. For example, following the lead given in *R v Khan*[16] and *Hellewell v Chief Constable of Derbyshire*,[17] the court may say that a claim for breach of confidence lies whenever there is an unauthorised breach of the claimant's privacy right.

---

[14] [1991] FSR 62 Ca (Civ Div).
[15] [1998–9] 9 KCLJ 1, 12. (Reproduced at Chapter 13.)
[16] [1997] AC 558.   [17] [1995] 1 WLR 804, QBD.

This has turned out to be an accurate prediction of the way that the tort of breach of confidence has developed since the HRA came into effect.

Just six-and-a-half weeks after the HRA came into force, a celebrity wedding between Michael Douglas and Catherine Zeta-Jones gave rise to a dispute which would precipitate the first significant analysis by the English courts of the new HRA provisions in the context of an alleged breach of privacy. The couple had recently married at a lavish ceremony in a New York hotel and *OK!* magazine had paid a substantial sum of money for the exclusive right to publish photographs of the ceremony. Despite a heavy security operation, *Hello!* magazine, the main rival to *OK!*, had managed to obtain unauthorized photographs taken at the wedding. *Hello!* intended to publish these photographs as a 'spoiler' of *OK!*'s exclusive feature. The claimants sought an injunction restraining *Hello!* from publishing the unauthorized photographs.[18] The claim was pleaded as a breach of confidence. However counsel for the claimants said in argument that the case actually had more to do with privacy than confidentiality.

The Court of Appeal reversed the decision of the Divisional Court to grant an interim injunction. Sedley LJ in his judgment asked whether there was a right of privacy in English law. He replied that:

We have reached a point at which it can be said with confidence that the law recognises and will appropriately protect a right of personal privacy.[19]

Sedley LJ explained his reasons for reaching this conclusion:

The reasons are twofold. First, equity and the common law are today in a position to respond to an increasingly invasive social environment by affirming that everybody has a right to some private space. Secondly, and in any event, the Human Rights Act 1998 requires the courts of this country to give appropriate effect to the right to respect for private and family life set out in article 8 of the [Convention] . . . the two sources of law now run in a single channel because, by virtue of section 2 and section 6 of the Act, the courts of this country must not only take into account jurisprudence of both the Commission and the European Court of Human Rights which points to a positive institutional obligation to respect privacy; they must themselves act compatibly with that and the other Convention rights. This, for reasons I now turn to, arguably gives the final impetus to the recognition of a right of privacy in English law.[20]

Wainwright—no freestanding cause of action for invasion of privacy

The subsequent House of Lords decision in *Wainwright v Home Office* saw an emphatic repudiation of any notion that English law now recognized a general right to privacy.[21] In *Wainwright* the claimants had been strip searched during a prison

---

[18] *Douglas v Hello! Ltd (No 1)* [2000] EWCA Civ 353, [2001] QB 967, CA (Civ Div).
[19] *Douglas* at 997.   [20] *Douglas* at 997.
[21] *Wainwright v Home Office* [2003] UKHL 53, [2004] 2 AC 406.

visit. A number of prison rules were breached during the search, including the fact that the searches were conducted in front of a window overlooking a public street. The claimants brought an action against the Home Office alleging, inter alia, a breach of their right to privacy.

Although the events in question took place before the commencement of the HRA, the House of Lords considered whether there would have been breaches of any Convention right. The House of Lords specifically rejected a submission that, following the commencement of the HRA, English law should recognize a general cause of action for an invasion of privacy. The House also rejected a submission that the failure of English law to provide a remedy in these circumstances would leave the United Kingdom open to an adverse judgment of the Strasbourg Court. Lord Hoffmann stated that Sedley LJ's remarks in *Douglas* were nothing more than a suggestion that, in relation to personal information obtained by intrusion, the common law breach of confidence has reached the point at which a confidential relationship has become unnecessary.[22]

Breach of confidence and intrusive media attention

In *A v B plc*,[23] a prominent footballer sought an injunction against the *Sunday People* newspaper to prevent it from publishing a story which had been sold to it by two women who had each had an affair with the footballer. The court was confronted by the question of what duty it had to respect Convention rights in circumstances in which no public authority was involved. Did the state's positive obligations under Art 8 to afford respect to private life require the courts to offer a remedy against intrusion into private life by a non-state actor? The claimant obtained an interim from a High Court judge who held that there was no distinction between brief extra-marital affairs and sexual relationships within marriage. The Court of Appeal disagreed. While it did not rule out the possibility that information about brief extra-marital relationships would be protected from disclosure in some situations, in this case they were not the sort of relationships that the court would be astute to protect when the other parties to the relationships did not want them to remain confidential.

As to the role of Convention rights, Lord Woolf CJ held:

Under s.6 of the [HRA], the court, as a public authority, is required not to act 'in a way which is incompatible with a Convention right'. The court is able to achieve this by absorbing the rights which articles 8 and 10 protect into the long-established action for breach of confidence. This involves giving a new strength and breadth to the action so that it accommodates the requirements of those articles.[24]

---

[22] The Strasbourg Court subsequently held that there had been no violation of Art 3 in this case, but that there had been a violation of Art 8. It awarded the sum of €3000 to each of the applicants, together with their costs and expenses: *Wainwright v United Kingdom* (Application No 12350/04) (2007) 44 EHRR 40, ECHR.

[23] *A v B plc* [2002] EWCA Civ 337, [2003] QB 195.   [24] *A v B plc* at 202.

Lord Woolf CJ went on to hold that Arts 8 and 10 are:

the new parameters within which the court will decide, in an action for breach of confidence, whether a person is entitled to have his privacy protected by the court or whether the restriction of freedom of expression which such protection involves cannot be justified.[25]

The House of Lords developed this approach in *Campbell v Mirror Group Newspapers*.[26] The claimant was Naomi Campbell, a famous fashion model. The defendant was *MGN Limited*, publishers of *The Mirror*, a British tabloid newspaper. In February 2001 The Mirror had published a series of articles detailing her treatment for addiction, accompanied by photographs showing her leaving a meeting of self-help group, Narcotics Anonymous. The articles were accompanied by a series of pictures of the claimant leaving one of those meetings. (Modern technology can enhance the intrusiveness of invasions of privacy.) The claimant sought damages for breach of confidence. She complained about the level of detail given about her, and the photographs. The claimant succeeded in the House of Lords by a majority of 3:2 (Lord Nicholls and Lord Hoffmann dissenting), but the differences largely related to the way in which the right to respect for private life and freedom of expression should be balanced rather than to the statements of principle about the cause of action for breach of confidence.

Prior to the HRA, it had been necessary to show that the information had been disclosed in circumstances importing an obligation of confidence. Lord Nicholls began by confirming what was made clear in *Wainwright*—that in England there is 'no over-arching, all-embracing cause of action for "invasion of privacy"'. However he also noted that 'protection of various aspects of privacy is a fast developing area of the law' and specifically drew attention to the fact that development of the law had been spurred by the enactment of the HRA. Lord Nicholls then went on to say that following the HRA the cause of action for breach of confidence had firmly shaken off the constraint of the need for an initial confidential relationship. In so doing it had 'changed its nature' and was therefore 'better encapsulated now as misuse of private information'.

In essence, the right of the claimant to privacy had to be balanced against the right of MGN to freedom of expression. As Lord Hope put it:

Article 8(1) protects the right to respect for private life, but recognition is given in article 8(2) to the protection of the rights and freedoms of others. Article 10(1) protects the right to freedom of expression, but article 10(2) recognises the need to protect the rights and freedoms of others. The effect of these provisions is that the right to privacy which lies at the heart of an action for breach of confidence has to be balanced against the right of the media to impart information to the public. And the right of the media to impart information to the public has to be balanced in its turn against the respect that must be given to private life.[27]

---

[25] *A v B plc* at 202.   [26] [2004] UKHL 22, [2004] 2 AC 457.
[27] *Campbell* at [105].

Several strands of reasoning are reflected across the judgments of the House of Lords on the issue of how the HRA has influenced the common law in this area. Lord Nicholls did not consider it necessary to decide whether the duty imposed by s 6 of the HRA extended to questions of substantive law. Lord Hoffmann, on the other hand, held that the HRA does not have horizontal effect as between private citizens and considered that the new approach was due to the fact that a different view was now taken as to the underlying value that the law protects. Lord Hope considered that the exercise in balancing the parties' competing rights was essentially the same as before the HRA but that the jurisprudence of the Strasbourg Court offered important guidance as to how they should be approached and analysed.

Baroness Hale went further than the other members of the House. She held:

The 1998 Act does not create any new cause of action between private persons. But if there is a relevant cause of action applicable, the court as a public authority must act compatibly with both parties' Convention rights. In a case such as this, the relevant vehicle will usually be the action for breach of confidence.[28]

Lord Hope also relied on the court's duty not to act incompatibly with Convention rights.[29] Lord Carswell agreed with Lord Hope and Baroness Hale.

Campbell has been followed in several cases, usually brought by celebrities and public figures as a result of intrusive press reporting of their private lives. Another example is the case of *Mosley*, where a former president of a body responsible for organizing motor-racing succeeded in obtaining damages against a newspaper which had published details of his involvement in sadomasochistic activities.[30]

Some conclusions in relation to privacy

Effect of the Convention

Convention rights have had a powerful influence and they have led to the development of a right of action for breach of confidence, but not for invasions of privacy generally. The right of action for breach of confidence has been developed along the lines of Convention rights, not because English judges were compelled to do this, but because it was generally felt that the law did not provide adequate remedies against intrusions by the paparazzi. The English courts chose to accept the Convention value of privacy as interpreted by the Strasbourg Court.

Social value of privacy

It would go outside the scope of this paper to try to reach any conclusion about the value of privacy, because, as I have said, the English courts have simply chosen to accept a Convention value. The essence of the reason for protecting privacy is that

---

[28] *Campbell* at [132].   [29] *Campbell* at [114].
[30] *Mosley v News Group Newspapers* [2008] EMLR 10, [2008] EMLR 20, QBD.

privacy is a way of protecting individual autonomy. The individual should have as much freedom as possible so that he can develop his own personality, and the state should only interfere where the individual would cause harm to another member of society. This is in essence the harm principle put forward by JS Mill.[31] I have written elsewhere[32] about the analogy to be drawn between Convention rights and the harm principle, and privacy can be seen as one instance of that.

But there is certainly room for legitimate differences of opinion. In response to the development of the tort of breach of confidence, the media have often complained that the HRA has put too much power into the hands of the judges, and that this development has had a chilling effect on the press. We have to be wary of rights of privacy that are too extensive. It certainly appears that the court in *A v B* took a different view of the desirability of publishing information about a person's private life from that in *Mosley*.

It is to be noted that the English courts have adopted the Strasbourg tests without qualification. Indeed this is one of the objections that Paul Dacre, editor of *The Daily Mail*, has to the way that the courts have developed the law of breach of confidence. In this context, the courts have not left the victims of violations of Convention rights to rely on s 7 of the HRA. The courts have ordinarily incorporated Convention values because they considered that that was the best thing to do.

Liability of public bodies for negligence

The experience in the field of negligence in respect of acts of public authorities has been entirely different from that in the field of breach of confidence. Here the courts have not extended the law of tort to provide remedies for violations of Convention rights involved in claims for negligence against public authorities but left such claims to be dealt with in proceedings under s 7 of the HRA.

A fundamental element of negligence liability is the establishment of a duty of care owed by the defendant towards the claimant. The English courts will only hold that a duty exists if they consider it 'fair, just and reasonable'[33] to do so. This approach enables the courts to take account of policy considerations. In particular, it has been used to prevent the imposition of duties of care on public authorities in respect of the exercise of their statutory functions where this is considered to be contrary to public policy, for example because it might lead to defensive policing and divert resources from the police's primary functions. In other words, the determination that there is or is not a duty of care is a control device used by the courts to limit liability for negligence.

---

[31] JS Mill, *On Liberty* (2nd edn, London: John W. Parker & Son, 1859). Available online: <http://www.bartleby.com/130>.

[32] M Andenas and D Fairgrieve (eds), *Tom Bingham and the Transformation of the Law: A Liber Amicorum* (Oxford, 2009). (Reproduced at Chapter 3.)

[33] *Caparo Industries v Dickman* [1990] 2 AC 605.

Under English law a claim for negligence does not lie against a public authority in respect of the exercise of its statutory functions because the public authority owes no duty of care. This is illustrated by the case of *Jain v Trent Health Authority*,[34] where the owners of a nursing home were held to have no cause of action against a registration authority which applied to the court under a statutory power for its immediate closure based on allegedly inaccurate information. Needless to say, the holding that there is no duty of care operates harshly against individuals who suffer harm.

An episode occurred which illustrates the difficulty that England and Wales sometimes has as one of the few common law jurisdictions in Europe. In some other jurisdictions in Europe, the courts do not draw a distinction between public authorities and other defendants when imposing liability for negligent acts.[35] On the contrary, it is part of the political and legal tradition of some civil law countries that if an individual citizen suffers loss at the hands of an organ of the state, the loss should be borne by the whole community. If necessary, the state has to find the resources to meet the liability. Accordingly, the individual citizen would have a remedy of some kind.

It is therefore perhaps not surprising that the Strasbourg Court initially took the view that the determination by English courts that a public authority owed no duty of care in the exercise of its statutory functions was in effect the grant of an immunity to the state and a denial of access to court in breach of Art 6 of the Convention. In *Osman v United Kingdom*, an application was made to the Strasbourg Court by the relatives of a murder victim who was killed despite warnings to the police that he was in danger of serious harm from an identified individual.[36] Under domestic law, the police owe no duty of care to individual members of the public in the discharge of their general duty of combating and investigating crime.[37] The Strasbourg Court held that Art 2 is violated where the authorities knew or ought to have known at the time of the existence of a real and immediate risk to the life of an identified individual from the criminal acts of a third party, and failed to take measures within the scope of their powers which, judged reasonably, might have been expected to avoid that risk.

To the consternation of many English lawyers, the Strasbourg Court in *Oman* also held that the denial of a cause of action in this situation amounted to the grant of a blanket immunity on the police in respect of negligence claims and a breach of Art 6.

Osman was revisited by the Strasbourg Court in *Z v United Kingdom*.[38] In *Z* the applicants were children who had suffered severe abuse at the hands of their parents. They brought a claim in the English courts against their local authority, alleging that it had failed to take adequate protective measures in respect of the

---

[34] *Jain v Trent SVA* [2009] UKHL 4, [2009] 1 AC 853.
[35] See, eg, C Dadomo and S Farran, *French Substantive Law* (Sweet & Maxwell, 1997), 179–80; JWF Allison, *A Continental Distinction in the Common Law* (Oxford, 2000), ch 8.
[36] *Osman v United Kingdom* (2000) 29 EHRR 245, ECHR.
[37] *Hill v Chief Constable of West Yorkshire* [1989] AC 53, HL.
[38] *Z v United Kingdom* (2002) 34 EHRR 3, ECHR.

severe neglect which they were known to be suffering. The House of Lords struck out their claim on the basis that the local authority owed no duty of care. The applicants took their case to the Strasbourg Court which held that its earlier reasoning in *Osman* had to be reviewed in the light of subsequent domestic case law. The Court said that it was now satisfied that the 'fair, just and reasonable criterion' was an intrinsic element of the duty of care. Therefore the domestic rule that the local authority did not owe the applicants a duty of care was not an 'exclusion' or an 'immunity' and so did not violate Art 6. In this respect, *Z* heralded a significant retreat from *Osman*. However, while Strasbourg jurisprudence changed, there was no change in English law.

In 2008 the House of Lords considered two further police cases. In *Van Colle v Chief Constable of Hertfordshire Police*[39] the claimants were the relatives of a murder victim who had been killed by a man against whom he was due to give evidence. That man had made threats against the deceased, which had been reported to the police. The claimants brought an action under the HRA, alleging a breach of Art 2. The House of Lords ruled that there was no breach of Art 2 as it could not be said that the police should have anticipated that there was a real and immediate threat to life.

In *Smith v Northamptonshire CC*,[40] threats of violence had been made against the claimant by his former partner. These threats were reported to the police, who took no action to prevent the partner from carrying out his threats. The claimant brought an action in common law negligence, claiming that the rule that there was no duty of care owed by the police in this situation should no longer apply following the enactment of the HRA. The Court of Appeal held in *Smith* that English law on this point should change where the facts also involved a violation of Art 2 of the Convention. By contrast, however, the House of Lords (by a majority) held that the policy considerations still applied.

In this type of situation, domestic law will not mirror the Convention but provide parallel remedies. Lord Hope[41] and Lord Brown[42] also considered that the remedy in tort and the remedy under s 7 of the HRA should develop side by side, rather than converge. Lord Brown expressed the view that the function of the various remedies was different. A claim under s 7 of the HRA enabled breaches of Convention rights to be vindicated whereas the primary function of a claim in tort was to compensate for loss. The case of *Ashley*, considered below, shows that it is also a function of tort law to allow private rights to be vindicated, and not simply to provide damages to compensate for loss. It is not therefore always the case that the two remedies have a different function.

Lord Bingham dissented. He formulated a principle under which liability could be imposed on the police in the situation where the *Osman* principle applied. In a

---

[39] *Van Colle v Chief Constable of Hertfordshire, Smith v Chief Constable of Sussex Police (conjoined appeals)* [2008] UKHL 50, [2009] 1 AC 225.
[40] *Van Colle v Chief Constable of Hertfordshire, Smith v Chief Constable of Sussex Police (conjoined appeals)* [2008] UKHL 50, [2009] 1 AC 225.
[41] *Van Colle, Smith* at [82].   [42] *Van Colle, Smith* at [138].

powerful passage he gave muted encouragement to the general development of common law remedies in accordance with the Convention:

> ...one would ordinarily be surprised if conduct which violated a fundamental right or freedom of the individual did not find a reflection in a body of law ordinarily as sensitive to human needs as the common law, and it is demonstrable that the common law in some areas has evolved in a direction signalled by the Convention. I agree with...Rimer LJ...that 'where a common law duty covers the same ground as a Convention right, it should, so far as practicable, develop in harmony with it.'[43]

Using the Convention as a cross-check or launch pad—*Ashley v Chief Constable of Sussex Police*

The case of *Ashley v Chief Constable of Sussex Police*[44] raises a number of points relevant to this discussion. The events occurred before the HRA came into force and so the case did not directly concern human rights.

The claim arose out of a fatal shooting by the police. The policeman involved had been charged with murder but the charge had been withdrawn from the jury because his case was that he thought at the time of shooting that the deceased had a gun. For the purposes of the criminal law, a person may rely on the defence of self-defence even if his belief that he was in imminent danger was not reasonable. One of the issues was whether the belief had to be reasonably held when relied on in civil proceedings, on which there was no clear authority.

In the civil proceedings brought by the deceased's family for negligence, battery, and other claims, the police admitted negligence and offered to pay all the damages in full but the family still wished to proceed with their claim that there had been a battery as they wanted to know the full circumstances of the deceased's death. If the death had occurred after the HRA had come into force, the state would have been bound to hold an inquiry under Art 2 of the Convention.

The House of Lords by a majority, affirming the decision of the Court of Appeal, held (1) that in civil proceedings there had to be a reasonable belief in a threat for the defence of self-defence to lie, and (2) that the action could proceed notwithstanding the offer of settlement that had been made.

On the first point, even though the events occurred before the HRA came into force, I used Strasbourg jurisprudence to support my conclusion as to English law.[45] In a famous case about the killing by the SAS of IRA suspects in Gibraltar,[46]

---

[43] *Van Colle, Smith* at [58].

[44] *Ashley v Chief Constable of Sussex* [2008] UKHL 25, [2008] 1 AC 962, [2008] 2 WLR 975.

[45] *Ashley* at [211] to [214]. However, it has been said that where, in proceedings based on a claim in tort, the claimant's reliance on a Convention right deprives the defendant of a defence that he would otherwise have had to the claimant's claim, the claim should fall under s 7 of the Human Rights Act 1998: *Somerville v Scottish Ministers* [2007] UKHL 44, [2007] 1 WLR 2734 at 2785–7 per Lord Mance.

[46] *McCann v United Kingdom* (1995) 21 EHRR 97, ECHR, known as the 'Death on the Rock' case.

the Strasbourg Court had made it clear that the acts of the individual soldiers did not violate Art 2 where they reasonably but mistakenly believed that the suspects held remote devices for detonating bombs. I held:

There is of course no reason why the common law of battery should be the same as the jurisprudence of the Strasbourg court under article 2. But the co-incidence of jurisprudence affords some assurance that the common law remains up to date and in accordance with the standards to be expected of a modern democratic society. It provides a useful benchmark against which our common law can be tested, and against which it can be asked whether the rights of the parties are appropriately balanced.

This illustrates another way in which Strasbourg jurisprudence can be used in the development of tort law.

On the second point, the House by a majority held that the claim could proceed even though no further damages could be recovered. The claim was still intact. The result did not turn on the fact that the defendants were the police though the decision has obvious relevance to the current debate here about the accountability of the police for their actions involving members of the public.

Lord Scott referred to Lord Hope's observation in *Chester v Afshar* that:[47] 'The function of the law is to enable rights to be vindicated and to provide remedies when duties have been breached.'

Lord Scott explored another interesting point. He held that, in addition to the principal aim of compensating the claimants for a loss of dependency, there was no reason why compensatory damages should not also fulfil a *vindicatory* purpose. One might add that in human rights cases, as the jurisprudence of the Strasbourg Court on just satisfaction recognizes, vindication is often the very thing that the applicant really wants. If the Chief Constable's submission were allowed to succeed then this would prevent 'the deceased's right not to be subjected to a violent and deadly attack' from being vindicated. It was immaterial whether if the family succeeded they would be entitled to a declaration or to vindicatory damages. In reaching this conclusion Lord Scott drew upon the case law of several other common law jurisdictions where vindicatory damages can be awarded in respect of infringements of particular 'constitutional rights'. Lord Scott described such vindicatory damages as 'rights-centred, awarded in order to demonstrate that the right in question should not have been infringed at all'. Lord Scott referred to the right to life under Art 2 of the Convention which he described as 'at least equivalent to [those] constitutional rights'. Only Lord Scott dealt with this point but his view is a further illustration of the influence of human rights on the law of tort. It is an example of a situation in which the court has used a Convention right as a launch pad for a possible development of the law in future. In this way, Convention rights may be said to *energize* the common law.

---

[47] *Chester v Afshar* [2004] UKHL 41, [2005] 1 AC 134 at [87].

Conclusions

Early expectations

Before the HRA came into force, there was much debate about the implications of the statutory duty imposed by s 6 on courts not to act incompatibly with Convention rights. Many people expressed the belief that s 6 would lead the courts to develop the law of tort to make it consistent with Convention rights. Our tort law is largely case law, and its development is often policy-driven. Convention jurisprudence reflects the values of the Convention, and thus could provide inspiration for decisions about developing tort law.

Since the commencement of the HRA

The courts have indeed in some cases proceeded to develop the common law by reference to Convention rights. Certainly the law of breach of confidence has been transformed by using Convention rights and values. Undoubtedly, the lack of a remedy at common law for invasions of privacy was widely regarded as a deficiency. In actions for disclosure of information in breach of confidence, English law now 'mirrors' the Strasbourg jurisprudence.

But the developments have been subtler than forecast, and it is clear that s 6 does not have the full effect mooted before the HRA came into force. The law of England and Wales that public bodies should not in general owe a duty of care in the performance of statutory powers has not been qualified so as to provide a remedy where Convention rights have been violated. Another example can be taken from the law of nuisance. Even when a person suffers substantial interference with his home as a result of building work carried out by a public authority, and can show a violation of his Convention right with respect to his home, he has no remedy in nuisance at common law if he is merely an occupier with no interest in the land.[48]

Is there a principle?

The position would seem to be that the English courts are not necessarily going to develop the common law in the field of tort by reference to Convention rights and values, but will do so only in specific cases where that is appropriate for domestic law reasons. It will not be appropriate where the Convention goes against the grain of some established principle of domestic law. The disappointed litigant will then be confined to his statutory remedy for violation of Convention rights. At the moment this is in general distinctly less generous than a tort law remedy in English law but if the Strasbourg jurisprudence on just satisfaction were to change there

---

[48] *Hunter v Canary Wharf* [1997] AC 655 HL.

might well be a reason to reconsider the position in tort in domestic law rather than persist in the system of parallel remedies.

Other approaches

The use of the Convention in private law cases contrasts with the position in South Africa where the courts have used constitutional rights to develop private law since the adoption of the new Constitution in 1996. The Constitution in fact contains a provision for horizontality. Constitutional rights have been used to develop the liability of the police. Thus in *Minister of Safety and Security v Van Duivenboden*[49] the Supreme Court of Appeal found the police liable for failure to confiscate a firearm from a particular individual, who subsequently shot the claimant. The court said that what was needed was an assessment, in accordance with the norms of society, of the circumstances in which it should be unlawful to culpably cause loss. The Constitution being the 'supreme law', no norms or values that are inconsistent with the Constitution could have legal validity. The Supreme Court of Appeal said that although the imposition of a duty of care on public authorities is often inhibited by the belief that it is important to allow them to carry out their functions without the chilling effect of the threat of litigation, this argument ought not to be exaggerated as the need to establish negligence and legal causation meant that liability could be kept within acceptable boundaries.

The general position

The result is that there is a great deal of discretion in the hands of the judges to decide whether or not the common law will be developed in accordance with Convention rights, or whether a violation of a Convention right will be actionable only by means of the statutory remedy under s 7 of the HRA. It must be debatable whether Parliament intended to give this amount of discretion to the courts. The HRA does not provide that Convention rights shall apply horizontally and there must be some cases where the Convention right that an individual has against the state cannot be exercised in precisely the same way against a non-state actor. However, the absence of a provision for horizontality does not necessarily mean that Parliament did not intend the common law to be developed in accordance with Convention rights. The court is after all made a public authority for the purposes of the HRA. Parliament provided the statutory remedy in s 7 of the HRA. While this could be taken as an indication that there should be parallel remedies rather than that the common law of tort should be develop in line with Convention rights, s 7 is only a modest provision. Its intended function may simply have been as a fail-safe remedy to prevent the United Kingdom from being in breach of its obligation to provide a domestic remedy for all Convention violations.

---

[49] *Minister of Safety and Security v Van Duivenboden* (2002) (6) SA 431 (SCA).

Modernization?

The introduction of Convention values offered a means of modernizing the common law when it became out of touch with the needs of contemporary society but this has not happened on a uniform basis. In consequence, there is no straightforward answer to the question when the domestic court will either use or should use a statement of human rights when deciding cases about private wrongs between individuals.

Relationship of our courts with the Strasbourg Court and the views of Lord Hoffmann

The approach of the English courts in this field naturally proceeds on the basis that it is the English courts and not the Strasbourg Court that should be responsible for developing the substantive law of tort. The question of the application of Convention rights in the area of private wrongs has on occasion brought English law into conflict with the jurisprudence of the Strasbourg Court, and the UK courts have yet to work out the relationship between themselves and the Strasbourg Court. In a recent lecture,[50] Lord Hoffmann expressed the view that, while at the level of abstraction, statements of universal application could be made about human rights, their application had to be dealt with on a national basis and within their particular social context and that the Strasbourg Court had failed sufficiently to recognize this. Lord Hoffmann said that: 'Because, for example, there is a human right to a fair trial, it does not follow that all the countries of the Council of Europe must have the same trial procedure.'[51] Lord Hoffmann proceeded to criticize four particular decisions of the Strasbourg Court. I shall try in the short space of time remaining to answer some of his points.

This is not the place to engage in a debate as to when human rights can be regarded as universal or as to the composition of the Strasbourg Court, the appointment of its judges and its workload, which are other issues raised by Lord Hoffmann. These are matters for another day.

The principal issue raised by Lord Hoffmann, as it respectfully seems to me, is whether the Strasbourg Court should exercise more restraint about ruling on individual cases that affect established legal principles or practices in the member states. However, the Strasbourg Court already affords contracting states some measure of discretion about enforcing the standards it sets through what is called the margin of appreciation. Thus (in the case of qualified rights, such as Art 8) the Strasbourg Court leaves the decision on an issue to contracting states where it considers that the authorities in the contracting state are better able to determine some matter. The Strasbourg Court also leaves the decision as to what the animating principle on some moral issue should be (again on a qualified right) to the contracting states where there is no consensus on that issue within the contracting states. Lord Hoffmann states that the Strasbourg Court has not recognized that human rights have to be national in their application and so has not developed this doctrine sufficiently.

No doubt the doctrine of the margin of appreciation could be developed so as to give the contracting states more freedom to decide cases without interference, but one can readily understand that, from the point of view of the Strasbourg Court, there have to be limits on the margin of appreciation. Otherwise it would be liable to lead to a lowering of human rights standards in some countries. The whole point of an international human rights court is that it is able to give rulings that bind contracting states, and those rulings are bound to interfere with the way those states run their internal affairs, and to differ from rulings of the courts of the contracting states. Friction with contracting states is inevitable and interference in the internal affairs of contracting states is to some extent inherent in the Convention system.

Put another way, unlike the Court of Justice in Luxembourg, the Strasbourg Court does not give its judgment in the form of a ruling on a preliminary reference submitted by the national court. That is a system designed to encourage co-operation in decision-making between the national and supranational court. The Strasbourg Court is in general expected to give some decision on the particular case before it.

As it happens, it does not always disagree with our courts. It has on several occasions adopted and applied the reasoning of the Court of Appeal and House of Lords. One of those cases was *O'Halloran and Francis v United Kingdom*,[52] one of the four cases specially mentioned by Lord Hoffmann. He uses the reasoning in one of the dissenting judgments as an example of the type of reasoning in Strasbourg of which he is critical, but I respectfully do not myself think that this is a particularly powerful example given that it is taken from a dissenting judgment.

Lord Hoffmann also criticizes the liberal way in which the Strasbourg Court interprets the Convention. This is what is known as evolutive or dynamic interpretation. The language of the Convention is open-textured, and the Strasbourg Court gives it a dynamic interpretation so as to keep the Convention in line with present-day conditions. This occurred in another of the cases singled out for criticism by Lord Hoffmann, namely *Hatton v United Kingdom*.[53] In that case, the Strasbourg Court held that an issue could arise under Art 8 where an individual was seriously affected by noise or other pollution. On the facts, it found that there was no violation—by applying the margin of appreciation. Given the open-textured nature of the Convention, and the nature of its subject matter, it is not in principle, in my view, illegitimate for the Strasbourg Court to interpret the Convention dynamically. We may not always like its decisions, but we cannot pick and choose.

---

[52] *O'Halloran v United Kingdom* (2008) 46 EHRR 21, ECHR.
[53] *Hatton v United Kingdom* (2003) 37 EHRR 28, ECHR.

Lord Hoffmann took two other cases where he contended that the Strasbourg Court had overstepped the mark. As to *Saunders v United Kingdom*[54] he criticized the Strasbourg Court for holding that Mr Saunders had had 'to tell [Companies Acts] inspectors about his actions' during Guinness' takeover of Distillers. But the violation of Art 6 of the Convention did not occur at that stage but by the subsequent extensive use at Mr Saunders' criminal trial of those transcripts, which had been read to the jury over a period of three days. Lord Hoffmann further states that the Strasbourg Court expressed its criticism in crude terms, thereby encouraging other cases, but the Strasbourg Court was addressing the question of whether a Convention right had been violated not the subtleties in the privilege against self-incrimination under English law.

The last example which Lord Hoffmann takes is *Al-Khawaja and Tahery v United Kingdom*,[55] where the Strasbourg Court held that there was a violation of Art 6 when a defendant was convicted largely on the basis of hearsay evidence given by a witness whom he had not been able to cross-examine. I do not propose to deal with this case in any detail. Lord Hoffmann finds it extraordinary that the Strasbourg Court should have reached this conclusion given that the matter was governed by legislation that had in turn been informed by the work of the Law Commission. Suffice it to say that, when the Law Commission made recommendations on this topic, it warned that there was a possibility of a violation of the Convention.[56]

One of the problems identified by Lord Hoffmann is the right of individual petition to the Strasbourg Court once national remedies have been exhausted. But abolition of this right would probably mean that the United Kingdom had to cease to be a contracting party to the Convention and that it might well have to cease to be a member of the European Union. Some may not view that as an objection, but membership of the European Union has been approved by Parliament. By ceasing to be a party to the Convention, the United Kingdom would lose the advantage of being party to an international system for the enforcement of human rights. An international system of human rights has in fact considerable advantages for the United Kingdom. It subjects the institutions of the state to outside scrutiny, and that is particularly important when, as in the United Kingdom, there is a strong doctrine of Parliamentary sovereignty and the doctrine of *Wednesbury* unreasonableness. Even under the HRA, our courts cannot strike down primary legislation that violates the Convention. The existence of supranational courts, establishing human rights principles, also empowers the domestic judiciary, and strengthens their independence as against the other institutions of their own state. Furthermore, the Convention system gives us a legitimate interest in how other countries in Europe treat their citizens, and this is a more powerful position than could be achieved at a political level alone. The Strasbourg Court can bring about remarkable change and the raising of standards throughout Europe. In my experience, its

---

[54] *Saunders v United Kingdom* (1996) 23 EHRR 313, ECHR.
[55] Application Nos 26766/05 and 22223/06. Note: on 15 December 2011 the Grand Chamber of the Strasbourg Court held that the circumstances in these cases did not violate Art 6.
[56] *Evidence in Criminal Proceedings and Related Topics* (1997) (Law Com 245) para 5.13.

influence stretches far beyond the shores of Europe. As things stand, we have the opportunity to influence and contribute to its jurisprudence. If we left the Convention, we would be little Englanders rather than potential world leaders in the field of human rights.

The relationship with the Strasbourg Court in the future

The real question, as I see it, is how the relationship between Strasbourg Court and our own can be improved so that conflicts are minimized in future. In principle, the function of the Strasbourg Court is to set standards of human rights guaranteed by the Convention. These standards are set in a way that allows the contracting state a choice as to how to implement them. The principles formulated by the Strasbourg Court have been applied, sometimes with difficulty but often without difficulty, by the English courts.

However, it should be possible for the courts of the contracting state to apply the standards set by Strasbourg without the Strasbourg Court having to intervene. The Strasbourg Court suffers from a vast overload of cases: at the last count it had a backlog of some 100,000 cases and is said to be in danger of sinking under the weight of its own success. The Strasbourg Court needs to find ways in which it can focus its activities on important questions of principle. I would like to suggest there is one positive step that could be taken and that is to encourage the Strasbourg Court to remit back to the English courts cases where the principle has been established and all that remains is for the domestic court to apply the doctrine of proportionality or, in the event of a violation having been found, to decide on the amount of any just satisfaction. (This might involve some small amendment to the HRA.) If the English courts fail to do this work properly, the aggrieved party could always apply back to the Strasbourg Court. It would be for that Court to determine whether any such application was admissible.

In addition to this formal division of responsibility, there has to be a lively dialogue, in and out of court, between our courts and the Strasbourg Court. Although our courts take the view that they should apply the Strasbourg jurisprudence 'no more, but certainly no less',[57] there is no reason why they should not express their own views if they consider that the Strasbourg jurisprudence has taken a wrong turn. It is clear from the respect given to judgments of the Court of Appeal and the House of Lords in judgments of the Strasbourg Court that the views expressed by English courts are taken seriously. Moreover, if, exceptionally, the English courts consider the Strasbourg Court has simply misunderstood our domestic law, they do not consider themselves bound to apply it. That gives the Strasbourg Court a further opportunity to consider its position if an application is made to it. That is another example of the dialogue to which I have referred. In out-of-court discussions, we can obviously have a more free-flowing debate, and I agree with Lord Hoffmann that we should make it known when we disagree with the developments in Strasbourg jurisprudence.

---

[57] *R (Ullah) v Special Adjudicator* [2004] UKHL 26, [2004] 2 AC 323, 350.

Summary of conclusions

So, in conclusion, I return to the main theme of this paper, namely the impact of the Convention on the law of tort. The Convention has informed developments in some areas of our tort law, but in other areas, not at all. The decision has been that of the judges. This has given enormous discretion to the judges. The result has been that in some cases the claimant has been left his remedy under the Convention if he has one, but that is a less generous remedy than he would have had if the common law had been developed. It is not, of course, in every case that there is an overlap between domestic tort law and the Convention but certainly as we have seen it occurs in some cases.

It is open to argument that Parliament intended a more radical modernization of the common law in line with Convention values. This may in time happen. It is still early days. A fundamental rethinking of the impact that Convention rights should have on civil wrongs could well be the sort of issue that the new Supreme Court might consider.

Finally, we have seen that there has on occasion been a conflict between Strasbourg jurisprudence and the common law of tort. This raises a general issue about the relationship between the Strasbourg Court and our own. That question goes well beyond tort law. I consider that the role of the Strasbourg Court is to lay down principles that can be applied throughout Europe. The role of the domestic court is to apply those principles.

I put forward the suggestion that cases could in fact be remitted to it by the Strasbourg Court to help relieve the Strasbourg Court of its overload of cases. I propose that a dialogue between the Strasbourg Court and the domestic courts should take place at several levels. In my judgment this is a better way forward than the abolition of the right of individual petition.

The jurisprudence of the Strasbourg Court has made an enormous contribution to several areas of our law, such as breach of confidence and proportionality.

We should, in turn, support its work.

15

Media Intrusion and Human Rights: Striking the Balance

This chapter was originally published in 2012 as part of a Liber Amicorum in honour of Nicholas Bratza.*

President Nicolas Bratza has been a leading figure in European human rights for almost his entire professional career. It will be a long time, if ever, before anyone is able to rival his experience as a judge of an international court, still less the distinction he has brought to the role. So it gives me great pleasure to dedicate this paper to him. In this paper, I aim to summarize some of the achievements of the European Court of Human Rights in the area of media intrusion, a topical subject in the United Kingdom for reasons I shall also explain. The question of the balance to be struck between the media and the individual is one which has occupied the European Court of Human Rights on many occasions.

Media intrusion: the general approach of the European Convention on Human Rights

Media intrusion into private life, by which I mean the publication by the media of previously unpublished confidential information about an individual, entails consideration of two particular Articles of the European Convention on Human Rights (the 'Convention'), namely Arts 8[1] and 10.[2] An individual must be given respect for his or her private and family life under Art 8 but, at the same time, others including the media, have a right to freedom of expression under Art 10. Thus the risks against which private and family life are to be protected include unwarranted disclosures by the press, but otherwise freedom of the press is guaranteed. The

---

* This chapter was first published in J Casadevall, E Myjer, M O'Boyle, and A Austin (editors), *Freedom of Expression: A* Liber Amicorum *in Honour of Nicholas Bratza*, Wolf Publishers, 2012 © Council of Europe. It is reproduced here with the kind permission of the Publisher and of the Council of Europe.

[1] Article 8 guarantees the right to respect for private and family life. The full text of Art 8 can be found in the Appendix.

[2] Article 10 guarantees the right to freedom of expression. The full text of Art 10 can be found in the Appendix.

Strasbourg Court[3] has emphasized that the concept of 'private life' is a broad one. While it is not susceptible of exhaustive definition, it extends to the protection of one's reputation[4]—as well as to more obvious aspects relating to personal identity, such as a person's name, photograph, or physical, and moral integrity.[5] Traditionally, the Strasbourg Court has characterized an individual's right under Art 8 as, ultimately, being about self-realization, whereas the Art 10 right exercised by the media is the right to contribute to debate on matters of public interest in a democratic society.

By way of introduction, there are six points to be made about the approach of the Convention to the subject of media intrusion.

First, under the Convention system, there is no hierarchy among the rights protected apart from non-derogable rights. They are all fundamental rights and, as such, it cannot be said that Art 8 has priority over Art 10, nor vice versa.

Second, Arts 8 and 10 are qualified rights. The Convention thus recognizes that these rights have boundaries in a democratic and plural society. The obligation of the state to respect private life, for instance, can be outweighed by the considerations in Art 8(2), particularly the public interest.

Third, Arts 8 and 10 are often in conflict where the media, purporting to exercise its Art 10 right to freedom of expression, is alleged to have intruded on a person's private life, protected by Art 8. In those cases, there is a need for a balancing exercise to find the proper weight to be accorded to each right in the circumstances.[6] Because the rights have equal standing and importance, however, the Strasbourg Court has stressed that:

the outcome of [an] application should not, in theory, vary according to whether it has been lodged with the Court under Article 8 of the Convention, by the person who was the subject of the article, or under Article 10 by the publisher.[7]

Fourth, the Strasbourg Court has regularly affirmed the importance of a free press and its 'vital role' as a public watchdog.[8]

History shows that restrictions on rights to free expression often accompany or precede attacks on democratic principles.

Fifth, the Art 10 right to freedom of expression is not limited to popularly accepted ideas. It is:

applicable not only to 'information' and 'ideas' that are favourably received or regarded as inoffensive or as a matter of indifference, but also to those that offend, shock or disturb. Such are the demands of pluralism, tolerance and broadmindedness without which there is no 'democratic society'.[9]

---

[3] I use this expression to refer to the European Court of Human Rights or, where appropriate, the European Commission on Human Rights.
[4] *Axel Springer AG v Germany* (Application No 39954/08), [2012] ECHR 39954/08 at para 83.
[5] *Von Hannover v Germany (No 2)* (Application Nos 40660/08 and 60641/08), [2012] ECHR 40660/08 at para 95.
[6] See, for example, *In re S (FC) (a child)* [2004] UKHL 47, per Lord Steyn at [17].
[7] *Von Hannover v Germany (No 2)* at para 106.
[8] See, for example, *The Sunday Times v UK* (1992) 14 EHRR 229 at 241.
[9] *Von Hannover v Germany (No 2)* at para 101.

Sixth, the Strasbourg Court has in addition protected journalists' sources from disclosure. Without that protection, journalists could not perform their vital role.

With that introduction, I turn to consider the achievements of the Strasbourg Court in the field of media intrusion.

Development by the Strasbourg Court of the concept of responsible journalism

In my view, the greatest contribution made by Strasbourg jurisprudence to resolving the problems of balancing the rights of the individual with those of the media has been in the development of the concept of responsible journalism. The Strasbourg Court has developed a set of norms which the media must follow to avoid infringing the privacy rights of an individual. Examples of those norms can be seen in the cases to which I now turn.

In its case law the Strasbourg Court has drawn a distinction between fact and opinion. Thus, when reporting matters of fact, journalists must normally take steps to check that the information is correct. When they express value judgments, they must have a sufficient substratum of fact to enable the value judgment to be made. *Pedersen v Denmark*[10] illustrates these points. Two television journalists made allegations that a named Chief Superintendent of Police had intentionally suppressed evidence in the context of a murder trial. The Strasbourg Court held that, whilst public servants, such as policemen, are subject to wider limits of acceptable criticism than private individuals, they are not to be considered as on a plane with politicians. The allegations in *Pedersen* exceeded criticism and amounted to an accusation of a serious crime. Moreover, given the nature and seriousness of the allegations made, it held that it was not open to the journalists to rely on the statement of only one witness to justify the conclusions they had drawn.[11] Where there is a risk of damage to a person's reputation caused by the inferences made and allegations published, the press are expected to be particularly careful in checking their facts.

The Strasbourg Court, however, has been careful not to impose unduly onerous obligations on the press which might prevent them from discharging their important role. Journalists may therefore use information contained in an official report without checking its accuracy. In *Bladet Tromsø v Norway*,[12] a newspaper had published a series of articles covering the seal hunting trade. These articles had included a number of statements to which certain seal hunters took exception because they suggested that seal hunting regulations were breached, that the hunters were guilty of animal cruelty—the paper reported 'Seals skinned alive'— and that the hunters had, in one instance, assaulted the hunting inspector.

[10] (2006) 42 EHRR 24.   [11] See *Pedersen* at paras 78–80 and 84–9.
[12] (2000) 22 EHRR 125.

These allegations did not, however, emanate from the newspaper but were taken directly from a report prepared in an official capacity by a government inspector appointed by the Norwegian Ministry of Fisheries to monitor a seal hunt. The court considered that 'the press should normally be entitled, when contributing to public debate on matters of legitimate concern, to rely on the contents of official reports without having to undertake independent research. Otherwise, the vital public-watchdog role of the press may be undermined.'[13]

Moreover, when it comes to expressions of opinion, journalists are not necessarily required to counterbalance the view which they put forward with a statement of the opposite point of view. In *Jersild v Denmark*,[14] a television journalist had prepared a short piece about a group of extremists in Denmark known as the Greenjackets, who promoted racism and ideas of racial superiority. The Strasbourg Court held that, although he had not presented any counterbalancing or opposing points of view, the journalist had clearly disassociated himself from the racist comments of the interviewees, He had also challenged some of the statements made and made it clear that the racist statements were part of an anti-social trend in Denmark. The Strasbourg Court considered it important to determine whether the piece had as its object the propagation of racist statements and ideas, or was merely aimed at reporting on those matters to contribute to a wider debate.[15]

It is clear that the Strasbourg Court's assessment in these respects, and hence the assessment to be carried out under the Convention by domestic courts, is process-driven: did the journalist make proper enquiries? Did he or she have a sufficient substratum of fact on which to base an opinion or allegation? These questions have nothing to do with the content of a story. The emphasis on process is no doubt deliberate: as soon as the law starts interfering with content, there is a risk of a 'chilling effect'[16] on the press. The effect of these process-driven requirements is to encourage high standards of journalism. Thus the Strasbourg Court has developed a set of principles that have a real and beneficial effect in protecting individuals against press intrusion but yet also promote, rather than endanger, a strong press to perform its vital role in a democracy.

I now turn to those cases where the Strasbourg Court has developed the concept of public interest. I start with cases that deal with the role of the press in relation to the publication of matters about the private lives of politicians. Exposure of matters about politicians is often beneficial to democracy. For this reason, according to the Strasbourg Court's well-established case law, the limits of acceptable criticism are wider as regards a politician than as regards a private individual. In *Lingens v Austria*[17] the applicant journalist had been convicted in the domestic courts of criminal defamation in relation to two articles he published accusing the Austrian Chancellor of protecting former Nazi SS members for political reasons and facilitating their involvement in Austrian politics. The Strasbourg Court held that the margin for acceptable criticism of politicians is significantly wider than for private

---

[13] (2000) 29 EHRR 125 at para 68.   [14] (1995) 19 EHRR 1.   [15] *Jersild* at paras 34–5.
[16] A 'chilling effect' is said to occur where freedom of expression is inhibited by fears of sanctions.
[17] (1986) 8 EHRR 407.

individuals, since it is media reports on politicians that inform the public and enable it to form views on politicians. The Strasbourg Court rejected the idea expressed by the Austrian courts that the function of the media was to impart information but leave the interpretation of such information to the public. A politician 'inevitably and knowingly lays himself open to close scrutiny of his every word and deed by both journalists and the public at large, and he must consequently display a greater degree of tolerance'. Article 8 extends to politicians, even when they are acting in their public capacity, but 'in such cases the requirements of such protection have to be weighed in relation to the interests of open discussion of political issues'.[18]

Another illustration of the Strasbourg Court affording a greater degree of latitude to journalists in their coverage of public figures is the *Editions Plon* case.[19] There the Strasbourg Court upheld the right of a French publisher to put out a book containing details of the cancer suffered by the former French President, François Mitterand, shortly after his death. The details of President Mitterand's illness had not been made public during his lifetime. (Indeed the late President had released regular health bulletins but had never mentioned his illness.) The Strasbourg Court considered, however, that the book's publication fell within a widespread debate of general interest relating to the right of citizens to be informed of any serious ailments from which the head of state was suffering and to the suitability for highest office of someone who knew that he was seriously ill. By contrast, the Strasbourg Court held that there was no violation of Art 10 where an Austrian daily newspaper was censured by the domestic courts for publishing rumours about the intention of the wife of the then Austrian president to bring divorce proceedings and about her extra-marital affairs. There is, held the Court:

a distinction between information concerning the health of a politician which may in certain circumstances be a[n] issue of public concern . . . and idle gossip about the state of his or her marriage or alleged extra-marital relationships . . . the latter does not contribute to any public debate in respect of which the press has to fulfil its role of 'public watchdog', but merely serves to satisfy the curiosity of a certain readership.[20]

I now turn to the public interest in cases involving private citizens. The requirement of public interest applies in this context also. It plays a major role in protecting individuals from media intrusion. It is often difficult to identify. Nonetheless, the Strasbourg Court attaches considerable importance to the question whether disclosure of the matter in question is in the public interest. If there is no public interest in the disclosure of confidential information about an individual, a violation of Art 8 will normally be found.

---

[18] *Lingens* at paras 41–3.
[19] *Editions Plon v France* (2006) 42 EHRR 36. It is to be noted that the Court did not find a breach of Art 10 in the granting of an interim injunction prohibiting publication of the book in the short term. It was the continuation of that ban that was held to violate Art 10.
[20] *Standard Verlags GmbH v Austria (No 2)* (Application No 21277/05) at para 52.

In *Princess Caroline von Hannover v Germany*[21] (which will be referred to as '*von Hannover (No 1)*' to distinguish it from the second *von Hannover* case ('*von Hannover (No 2)*') which I shall discuss also), the Strasbourg Court held that:

A fundamental distinction needs to be made between reporting facts capable of contributing to a debate in a democratic society, relating to politicians in the exercise of their official functions for example, and reporting details of the private life of an individual who does not exercise such functions.... While in the former case the press exercises its role of 'public watchdog' in a democracy by imparting information and ideas on matters of public interest, that role appears less important in the latter case.

The determination of whether a matter is in the public interest depends on a careful consideration of all the circumstances. To qualify as being in the public interest, the publication of information about a person's private life must contribute to the debate in a democratic society. The decision of the Grand Chamber[22] in *von Hannover (No 2)* shows the Strasbourg Court's approach to these questions. In this case, the issue was whether photographs taken of the Princess during a skiing holiday could be published without violating Art 8. The media claimed that there was an issue of public interest because the Princess had chosen to take this holiday while her father, the late Prince Rainier III of Monaco, was seriously ill. The photographs had not been taken surreptitiously or in embarrassing circumstances.

The three photographs in question were as follows. One photograph showed the princess and her husband, Prince Ernst August, walking through St Moritz whilst on a skiing holiday, and accompanied an article about that holiday. Notwithstanding that they were on a busy street at the time, the photograph and article contributed nothing to public opinion and debate, and were, in essence, published for pure entertainment's sake. Holidays, even for high-profile public figures, fall within the core of an individual's private sphere.

The next photograph accompanied an article about the annual 'Rose Ball' in Monaco. Whilst the Rose Ball itself might conceivably qualify as an event of contemporary society, the photograph depicted the Princess on a ski-lift and had no connection whatsoever to the article or the Rose Ball. Given the low information value of the photograph, the public's curiosity must give way to the protection of the private sphere.

The final photograph, however, was held to be different. Whilst it also showed the Princess and her husband walking along a street on holiday, it accompanied an article dealing with the ailing health of her father. Given that Prince Rainier was the then reigning monarch, the story itself dealt with an event of contemporary society. Whilst the photograph, in and of itself, had no information value and contributed nothing to public opinion, it had to be considered taking account of the article that it accompanied. The German Federal Court of Justice decided that a legitimate aspect of the story was the question of how Prince Rainier's family was conducting

---

[21] (2005) 40 EHRR 1.
[22] References in this article to the Grand Chamber are to the Grand Chamber of the Strasbourg Court.

itself during his illness. In that context, a photograph of the Princess on holiday both supported and illustrated the story. The quality and presentation of the article were not relevant to this consideration, since taking those matters into account (barring something like offensive language) would interfere unduly with the wide margin of appreciation to be accorded to editorial decision-making.

The Grand Chamber did not differ from the assessment of the German Federal Court of Justice that the final photograph could be published without violating the Princess's Convention rights. It held that 'the characterisation of Prince Rainier's illness as an event of contemporary society . . . having regard to the reasons advanced by the German courts . . . cannot be considered unreasonable'.[23] As such, the press was entitled to report on 'how the Prince's children reconciled their obligations of family solidarity with the legitimate needs of their private life, among which was the desire to go on holiday'.[24] The Grand Chamber reiterated that it was not only a question of the press having the right to impart information and ideas on all matters of public interest, but also of the public's right to receive them.

It is not immediately obvious why there was a public interest in this case in knowing about the attitude of the reigning monarch's family to his serious illness. This seems, therefore, to be a very borderline case. The attitude of the monarch's family was not a matter of constitutional significance. On the other hand, the Grand Chamber may have been influenced by the national court's assessment in this case. Where there is room for doubt as to whether a matter is in the public interest, it is wise for the Strasbourg Court to have regard to whether the national courts considered that the publication in question engaged the public interest. Freedom of expression obviously includes, in principle, the right to publish pictures and photographs. But pictures and photographs can be more intrusive than text. As the Strasbourg Court observed, again in *von Hannover (No 1)*:

> this is an area in which the protection of the rights and reputation of others takes on particular importance. The present case does not concern the dissemination of 'ideas', but of images containing very personal or even intimate 'information' about an individual. Furthermore, photos appearing in the tabloid press are often taken in a climate of continual harassment which induces in the person concerned a very strong sense of intrusion into their private life or even of persecution.[25]

Likewise, in *von Hannover (No 2)*, the Grand Chamber recalled that for a 'private individual, unknown to the public, the publication of a photo may amount to a more substantial interference than a written article'.[26] Indeed, the 'publication of a photograph must, in the Court's view, in general be considered a more substantial interference with the right to respect for private life than the mere communication of the person's name'.[27]

Moreover, the circumstances in which a photograph is taken are relevant. Where, as in *von Hannover (No 1)*, the photographs are taken secretly, with a

---

[23] *Von Hannover (No 2)* at para 118.   [24] *Von Hannover (No 2)* at para 117.
[25] *Von Hannover (No 2)* at para 59.   [26] *Von Hannover (No 2)* at para 113.
[27] *Eerikäinen and others v Finland* (Application No 3514/02) at para 70.

telephoto lens, at a time when the subject of the photograph was in a private club to which journalistic access was strictly regulated, the Strasbourg Court will take this into account as a factor against publication, albeit not a decisive one.[28]

These then are the main aspects of the concept of responsible journalism developed by the Strasbourg Court. This concept is deployed to determine when the media can publish material which intrudes into a person's private life. In another decision, namely *Axel Springer AG v Germany*,[29] the Strasbourg Court has helpfully sought to bring together its jurisprudence in this field. This is a significant development, but, before turning to it, I will deal with the facts of the case.

The *Axel Springer* case concerned the arrest of a well known German actor at a beer festival on drugs charges 'of medium seriousness'. The Grand Chamber observed that:

96.... the articles in question concern the arrest and conviction of the actor X, that is, public judicial facts that may be considered to present a degree of general interest. The public do, in principle, have an interest in being informed—and in being able to inform themselves—about criminal proceedings, whilst strictly observing the presumption of innocence... That interest will vary in degree, however, as it may evolve during the course of the proceedings—from the time of the arrest—according to a number of different factors, such as the degree to which the person concerned is known, the circumstances of the case and any further developments arising during the proceedings.

The Grand Chamber held that there was a violation of Art 10 as the national courts had wrongly restrained publication of the articles in question. It is sufficient to indicate the main factors that led the Grand Chamber to its conclusion. The newspaper had acted responsibly in publishing details of the arrest. The newspaper's reporter had witnessed the arrest. It was particularly significant that the press officer at the public prosecutor's office had confirmed the nature of the arrest.[30] The newspaper did not pass any comment on the information; it merely published it. The Strasbourg Court held that the fact that one article 'contained certain expressions which, to all intents and purposes, were designed to attract the public's attention cannot in itself raise an issue under the Court's case law'.[31] The actor had previously discussed his private life in interviews, though the Grand Chamber noted that this does not deprive a person of all protection.[32] The information was capable of contributing to the debate in a democratic society. As the actor was well known, he could be regarded as a public figure.[33]

I now turn to the Grand Chamber's important distillation and collation in this case of the relevant criteria in its case law. By 'relevant criteria', I mean the criteria which it is necessary for national courts to take into account when balancing the right of an individual under Art 8 and that of the press under Art 10. This distillation and collation occupies a lengthy passage in the Grand Chamber's

---

[28] See *von Hannover (No 1)* at para 68; see also *von Hannover (No 2)* at paras 113 and 122.
[29] *Axel Springer AG v Germany* (Application No 39954/08).
[30] *Axel Springer* at paras 102–7.   [31] *Axel Springer* at para 108.
[32] *Axel Springer* at para 101.   [33] *Axel Springer* at paras 97–100.

judgment. It is not possible to set out the passage in this paper but the detailed criteria may be summarized as follows:

(1) *Contribution to a debate on a matter of public interest.* This is an essential pre-condition to any interference with a person's right under Art 8(1).

(2) *How well known the person concerned is, and the subject matter of the report.* The Strasbourg Court considered that it would for instance be a relevant consideration whether the person concerned was a private person. In addition, the Strasbourg Court warned against the use of photographs purely to satisfy the reader's curiosity.

(3) *Prior conduct of the person concerned.* The fact that the person involved had, for instance, previously discussed his private life with the press will be a relevant factor.

(4) *Method of obtaining the information and its veracity.* As discussed above, journalists must act on an adequate factual basis. It may not therefore be enough, for example, simply to have read the story on *Twitter*.[34] It may also be a factor against publication that it is based on confidential material removed from someone's dustbin, or known to have been obtained from a public official who was induced to act improperly in disclosing it.

(5) *Content, form and consequences of publication.* Did it, for instance, appear in a local or national newspaper?

(6) *Severity of the sanction imposed*, where a sanction is imposed by a tribunal.

This is a very structured approach to determining whether an intrusive report about a person should be published in pursuance of the press's freedom of expression. It will clearly be a point of reference for many years to come. As I have explained, the Grand Chamber went on to find, particularly in the light of the original disclosure by the public prosecutor, that there had been violations of Art 10 despite the wide margin of appreciation extended to national courts. However, it emphasized that, if the national court went through all the relevant criteria, it would require a strong case for the Strasbourg Court to come to a different conclusion.[35] The approach of the Strasbourg Court in establishing clear case law on the important subject of responsible journalism is to be welcomed. Moreover, for the reasons given above, there is great wisdom in the process-driven requirements that it has imposed, for example, in relation to the checking of facts.

However, there is also a wider conclusion that can be drawn. By recognizing a wide margin of appreciation for national courts, the Strasbourg Court has also recognized that there are different cultural approaches to press freedom and privacy throughout contracting states. The German courts' focus, for instance, on privacy rights in *Axel Springer* might strike an observer from another contracting state as quite surprising. It is apparent that, while one state might say that there should be

---

[34] *Twitter* is a widely-used online networking service that enables users to send and read text-based messages of up to 140 characters, known as 'tweets'.

[35] *Axel Springer* at para 88.

no disclosure of the name of the defendant as it may jeopardize his or her rehabilitation on completion of their sentence. Another state might say that on the contrary the public are in general entitled to know who committed a criminal offence. The implicit recognition of a legitimate plurality of approach among states in this field is important.

The further message from Strasbourg—and it is a very welcome message—is that provided that the national courts address at least all the specified criteria when they balance Arts 8 and 10, all will be well in Strasbourg. There has been a quantum leap here in terms of recognizing subsidiarity.

Moreover, the Strasbourg Court has driven forward the critical test of what is in the public interest by analysing the nature of media freedom. Media freedom is above all about the freedom to contribute to the debate in a democratic society. Media freedom is not, therefore, limited to seeking the truth, nor is it always limited by the ability to do harm. Rather it is about the communication needs of the audience.

Finally, siren voices of the press have frequently expressed the view that those communication needs are to be determined by the public. This would mean that any invasion of a person's privacy could be justified if there was a story that the public wanted to read. The Strasbourg Court has firmly resisted this temptation. It is clearly not enough for the press to say that, if the matter appeals to the public, it is something that it is in the public interest to publish.

Positive obligation on the state to require the press to give prior notice to individuals of their intention to publish potentially damaging confidential material

The press enjoys a powerful position in some countries. The right to damages for injury to one's reputation may be of little solace. Misconduct by the press involving an invasion of privacy may cause considerable damage to reputation. There is also a huge problem of containing the damage. The material can be republished on the internet and *Twitter*, and it may thus not be possible to recall the material. This can lead to untold damage to an individual whose privacy is wrongly breached.

Does the Convention impose a positive obligation on the state to redress the balance in favour of the individual? In *Mosley v News Group Newspapers*,[36] Mr Mosley sued the newspaper for damages in the English court for what was ruled to be the publication of information about his private life in which there was no public interest. He recovered damages but obtained no injunction. It was a pyrrhic victory because the information was already in the public domain. He then took his case to the Strasbourg Court. He argued that it was a violation of Art 8 for the state to fail to impose a pre-notification requirement. This would require a newspaper which was about to disclose private information to notify the individual involved in

---

[36] [2008] EWHC 1777 (QB), [2008] EMLR 20.

advance. He would then have a chance of getting an injunction preventing disclosure. He said that this was the only way of giving him an effective remedy for breach of his Art 8 right.

However, in *Mosley v UK*[37] the Strasbourg Court concluded that Art 8 does not require any binding pre-notification requirement. It considered that the limited circumstances in which a state may restrict the freedom of the press had to be borne in mind in carrying out the balancing exercise between Arts 8 and 10. It also considered that the potential efficacy of any such pre-notification requirement was open to serious doubt. The requirement would clearly have to be subject to a public interest exception so that the press could publish a story, without pre-notifying, where it considered it could defend itself on a public interest basis. To avoid a 'chilling effect' on the freedom of the press, the exception could only require a reasonable belief that publication was in the public interest. Furthermore, the efficacy of a system of pre-notification could only be ensured by setting damages for breach at a punitively high level. That could only be justified in the criminal context, which would risk breaching Art 10. Taking those factors into account, as well as the wide margin of appreciation afforded to states, the Strasbourg Court held that a pre-notification requirement was not required to ensure compliance with Art 8.[38]

Conclusions

What we have seen in the cases discussed in this paper is that the Strasbourg Court has made an enormous contribution in the field of freedom of expression by the press. It has worked out detailed principles of responsible journalism which both protect the individual and strengthen the press. In working these principles out, the Strasbourg judges have no doubt brought to the jurisprudence their wide knowledge and their experience from many parts of Europe. As an international court, the Strasbourg Court has the perspective not only of a developed Western democracy but also of a new democracy which has seen the problems for society where the press is controlled by the government. The rulings of the Strasbourg Court in this area display great sensitivity and wisdom. The advantages of an international court can be seen.

Instances of press misconduct in the United Kingdom have given rise to considerable public concern about the way some journalists behave.[39] In August

---

[37] Application No 48009/08.   [38] At paras 122–32.

[39] One of the reasons for the present public debate over media intrusion in the United Kingdom is that there is widespread concern about the way certain members of the press behave. One of the cases giving rise to that concern was that of Chris Jefferies. He was the landlord of a young woman, Joanna Yates, who was murdered in Bristol in December 2010. Chris Jefferies briefly fell under suspicion. He was arrested, and detained for questioning for two days. He was then released. Another man, Vincent Tabak, was later arrested and charged. He ultimately confessed. During Mr Jefferies' detention, however, certain newspapers published stories heavily critical of him, linking him positively with the murder, as well as making comment on his chosen solitary lifestyle and linking him to previous crimes with which he had never even been charged, much less convicted of. In proceedings brought against the

2011 the United Kingdom government set up an Inquiry, led by Lord Justice Leveson, in response to the now well-known accusations of telephone hacking by journalists at the *News of the World* and subsequent, related revelations. Confidential information about individuals was improperly obtained by accessing messages left for them on their mobile telephones. The Inquiry's terms of reference are far-reaching.

The United Kingdom, however, is not the only jurisdiction that is concerned with the regulation of the press. The European Commission has established a high level group on media freedom and pluralism. This will be making recommendations for the protection of the media in the autumn of 2012.[40] In Australia, the Finkelstein Inquiry, published in March 2012, recommended the establishment of a government-funded News Media Council to set and enforce journalistic standards. This investigation was launched after News Corporation closed the *News of the World* over illegal phone hacking allegations. News Corporation owns seventy per cent of Australia's newspapers. Many people in Australia argued that News Corporation's newspaper holdings were too large and were biased against the ruling party. In addition, in New Zealand, the Law Commission has issued a consultation paper seeking views on the extension of media regulation and the reform of civil wrongs.

There is clearly in the present climate an option for legislators to introduce a new system of regulation for journalists. An independent regulator could build up a code of practice that could help remove some of the present uncertainty and difference of opinion about what journalists can or cannot properly do. Regulation of the press is, however, extremely difficult as it may result in a 'chilling' effect on the press. If there were a system of statutory regulation, it would have to be carefully crafted. The nature of the issues to which press activity gives rise requires considerable judgment. Moreover, there would have to be an independent regulator appointed by some totally independent process to administer such a system of regulation. However, whether or not a state decides to have a system for the statutory regulation of journalists, there will always be a very considerable role to be played by the courts. The situations where problems are likely to arise are bound to be fact-sensitive. In addition, the law has to be kept up to date to reflect developments in technology and changes in social attitudes. It is difficult for any system of regulation to be sufficiently flexible.

---

newspapers by the Attorney General for contempt of court, Lord Judge CJ, giving the judgment of the court, described the newspaper articles as having 'vilified' Mr Jefferies. This was capable of constituting contempt even though he was only a suspect under arrest and was never charged. The vilification of him might prevent witnesses coming forward with information that might clear him of suspicion: *Attorney General v MGN Ltd and News Group International Ltd* [2011] EWHC 2074 (Admin), [2012] 1 Cr App R 1. On 7 March 2012 the Supreme Court of the United Kingdom refused permission to appeal in this case, saying the case did not raise an arguable point of law of general public importance which ought to be considered by the Supreme Court at that time, bearing in mind that the case had already been the subject of judicial decision and reviewed on appeal, and that this was a very clear case of contempt of court.

40　Terms of Reference, September 2011.

It is, therefore, the national courts who in the future are likely, by deciding privacy cases on a case by case basis, to do much of the work of providing an up-to-date definition of proper journalistic standards. In performing this task, national courts will, as they have in the past, look to the Strasbourg Court. They will look to the Strasbourg Court to continue to develop its case law in this area wisely. It has done that with spectacular success during the long period in which President Bratza has been involved in the development of its jurisprudence.

SECTION C
BEYOND OUR OWN HORIZONS

This Section looks beyond the horizon in two ways. First, it considers the value of looking at other jurisdictions and gives two examples of what we can learn: freedom of expression and prospective overruling. Second, it examines the evolving relationship between national and supranational courts in Europe. For example, different forms of dialogue can now take place between senior judges. Section C includes some recommendations for better reflecting the interrelationship of these courts and thus improving decision-making.

Preface by Prof Dr Andreas Voßkuhle, President of the Federal Constitutional Court of Germany

The success of a constitutional order depends, in my view, on three parameters: the constitutional order must be stable; it must be open to future developments; and it must ensure diversity—meaning its ability to absorb and come to terms with the dynamics of social and political processes.[1] These requirements also apply to orders that—like Great Britain and the European Union—feature constitutional law in substance if not in form, as they recognize human rights protection and certain basic rules that govern the interaction of state authorities.

In nurturing these characteristics of a constitutional order (in the formal or substantive sense), the courts have an important role to play. They have to strike the right balance between continuity and flexibility in interpreting and applying human rights and fundamental constitutional principles. Mary Arden shows convincingly that in doing this, looking beyond our own horizons can be more than useful.

In the first place, this involves comparative law. In interpreting law and adapting its understanding to current challenges, the comparison with other legal orders can be a valuable contribution. Of course, other countries' solutions can hardly ever be copied one-to-one into our own legal order. Nonetheless, they are helpful in identifying errors and in sharpening our own analysis.[2] In the wake of globalization, transnationalization, and Europeanization, national judges are—in Mary Arden's words—more and more often confronted with 'concepts that are not indigenous principles of one's own law'. Here, especially, we can learn from others.

Secondly, the same applies to dealing with overlapping jurisdictions in Europe. The member states of the European Union and the European Convention on Human Rights are firmly embedded in a complex multilevel system. Based on this, the courts increasingly engage in 'multilevel judging', as Mary Arden aptly describes it: a European lawyer must be able to play the keys of the different levels of law. Working out the 'right relationship' between the national and the European

---

[1] See Voßkuhle, 'Stabilität, Zukunftsoffenheit und Vielfaltssicherung—Die Pflege des verfassungsrechtlichen "Quellcodes" durch das BverfG' (2009) *JuristenZeitung* 917 et seq.

[2] Hoffmann-Riem, 'Justice, Bundesverfassungsgericht (Constitutional Court) Germany' (2005) *International Journal of Constitutional Law* 556 at 559.

supranational courts could be viewed as the fundamental theme of Mary Arden's activities and speeches. Mary Arden favours a structural approach and provides a whole toolkit of suggestions: more dialogue, more subsidiarity, more temporal limitations, and clearer judgments. These requests come from someone who knows what she is talking about: Mary Arden was among the first to call expressly for such a general dialogue, and she has committed herself to creating a lively and fruitful exchange of ideas between the national and the European courts in a unique manner. Of this, the papers collected in Section C, 'Beyond Our Own Horizons', are a particularly valuable, authentic, and inspiring testimony.

Prof Dr Andreas Voßkuhle,
President of the Federal Constitutional
Court of Germany

PART VI

THE VALUE OF THE INTERNATIONAL PERSPECTIVE

Judges learn from jurisprudence abroad how to do a better job at home. By looking at other legal systems, we may learn what lines *not* to follow or, conversely, pick up some new ideas (for instance, about an approach to some new legal problem) that will enable us to see our own domestic law in a different light and which may lead us to develop our own law in some new way. It may even be desirable to work towards harmonizing some aspects of the common law with the law of other countries to help keep the common law up to date and in accordance with the needs of society.

Judges may consider how other legal systems approach a particular subject before they start to write their judgments. Often they will not refer to the fact that they have done so. It is not necessary to be an expert in the entire legal system of another country to understand and learn from how they approach similar issues.

In some fields, such as family law, commercial law and insolvency law, where events may have legal effects in more than one jurisdiction, there are often procedures for enabling the courts to cooperate with one another.

In this Volume, there are several articles that draw on comparative law, that is, the practice of comparing the law of other systems with our own. I have included two particular examples in this Part.

In Chapter 16, *Freedom of Expression and the Role of a Supreme Court: Some Issues from Around the World*, I trace the development of the concept of freedom of expression in jurisdictions such as the United States, Australia, India, and the United Kingdom. The paper shows how the concept is affected by the culture in which the problem arises. The cases which I discuss range from the highly charged issue of flag burning in the United States to the right of an individual to criticize a former Nazi in West Germany in the period after the Second World War.

In Chapter 17, *Prospective Overruling*, I look at the question, at the time when the paper was written controversial in English law, whether judges could decide a case on the basis that the result would not, as is usual, apply retrospectively to all previous cases. I compared the practice in many other jurisdictions. The inspiration for this paper was an inconclusive discussion that I had on this subject with leading judges from many parts of the world at a conference in Australia. In a subsequent case, the House of Lords Appellate Committee, after a hearing in which my paper was cited, decided that the courts could limit the retrospective effect of their decision, but that this power should be exercised only in exceptional cases. The courts have not yet worked out when this power can be exercised.[1]

In many areas our domestic law is now based on international measures, often from the European Union. Accordingly judges are increasingly involved with law created outside our own jurisdiction, and they must take more account of the international perspective in their work.

---

[1] See, in particular, *A v HM Treasury* [2010] UKSC 2, [2010] 2 AC 534 at 689–96.

16

Freedom of Expression and the Role of a Supreme Court: Some Issues from Around the World

This chapter is based on a paper presented at a judicial-academic conference on 'Legal Boundaries, Common Problems and the Role of the Supreme Court' in July 2009.*

The purpose of this paper is to look at the subject of freedom of expression refracted through the lens of the role of a Supreme Court. This is a chance to do a little thinking out of the box. The case law, as I see it, shows that in this field Supreme Courts have exercised a leadership role. This is a function that, so far as I am aware, has not previously been publicly debated, at least in this jurisdiction.

Before we consider freedom of expression, it is worth spending a moment reflecting upon what makes a court a Supreme Court. Most importantly, it will be a final court of appeal in some area of law or other, though not necessarily in all areas of law with which it deals. Generally a Supreme Court has power to interpret a written constitution. (The United Kingdom does not, of course, have a single statute setting out its constitution.) Often a Supreme Court also has power to determine federal questions. The new UK Supreme Court will have power to determine devolution questions, and there are some parallels between devolution questions and federal questions.[1] If, as I suggest, a Supreme Court also has a leadership role in setting out how the law should develop, it also has a responsibility to select those cases that will enable it to set the law in a new direction.

Justice Sandra Day O'Connor of the US Supreme Court in her autobiography writes: 'When Congress . . . lights a fire by passing significant new legislation or taking bold new action, we are inevitably summoned to attend to the blaze.'[2]

---

* This is a modified version of a paper presented at the opening session of a judicial-academic conference on 'Legal Boundaries, Common Problems and the Role of the Supreme Court' on 31 July 2009 at King's College London. It was subsequently published in [2010] 21 KCLJ 529. It is reproduced here with the kind permission of the Publisher.

[1] On this point see the decisions of the Court of Appeal and the European Court of Justice in *R (on the application of Horvath) v Secretary of State for the Environment, Food and Rural Affairs* [2007] EWCA Civ 620 and Case C-428/07 (ECJ decision of 16 July 2009).

[2] Sandra Day O'Connor, *The Majesty of the Law* (Random House, 2004), 14–15.

However, she also concedes that the US Supreme Court occasionally starts a fire of its own. In putting out the fire, or perhaps dampening it down or sending it in a new direction, a Supreme Court is also responsible for more mundane matters such as giving clear guidance and laying down the law in a way that avoids unnecessary litigation.

So what about 'free speech'? The virtues of free speech and expression are well known. Freedom of speech is said to involve two basic principles: first, that there should be a marketplace in ideas with a view to public discussion winnowing out the truth, especially in political affairs; and second, that people should be able to express themselves as part of their right to self-realization. That right is part of the right to private life conferred by Art 8 of the European Convention on Human Rights.[3] But while freedom of speech is an important card in the pack, as we shall see it is not always the ace of trumps. Some cases, with the obvious example of defamation, are all about limiting freedom of expression.

Let us look at some examples of how some Supreme Courts across the world have shown leadership when dealing with issues of freedom of expression. Given that freedom of expression is a vast subject, the cases I recite are only the tip of an iceberg. It is well known that expression is by words. However, it may also be by conduct. The decision of the Supreme Court of the United States in *Texas v Johnson*[4] concerned expressive conduct, namely flag burning. The US Supreme Court, by a majority of 5:4, declared unconstitutional a State law that criminalized the burning of the American flag. Johnson had burnt the flag in an act of protest at the Republican National Convention. The First Amendment to the US Constitution enshrines the right to freedom of expression. The State argued that the flag should be preserved as a symbol of nationhood and national unity. The majority held that the First Amendment established a 'bedrock principle', namely, that the government could not prohibit the expression of an idea simply because society found the idea offensive or disagreeable. No official could force citizens to confess by word or action their faith in a particular belief. Prohibiting flag burning would 'dilute the freedom that this cherished emblem represents'. In the words of the Court: 'It is the nation's resilience, not its rigidity, that Texas sees reflected in the flag—and it is that resilience that we reassert today.'[5] That decision has, of course, proved very controversial. Congress tried to reverse it but its attempt to do so was also declared unconstitutional. Possibly as a result of both decisions of the Supreme Court, the pressure for legislation criminalizing flag burning then went away.

Sometimes the courts have had to balance the right of free expression with a constitutional right to protection of reputation. For example, in 1958 in *Lüth*,[6] the German Federal Constitutional Court had to determine the constitutionality of an order restraining the defendant from making repeated public calls for the public to

---

[3] Mary Arden, 'On Liberty and the European Convention on Human Rights' in Mads Andenas and Duncan Fairgrieve (eds), *Tom Bingham and the Transformation of the Law* (Oxford University Press, 2009), 3. (Reproduced at Chapter 3.) Article 8 of the European Convention on Human Rights is reproduced in the Appendix.
[4] 491 US 397 (1989).   [5] 491 US 397 (1989) at 491.
[6] *Lüth-Urteil* BVerfGE 7, 198.

boycott a film that had been produced by the film director Veit Harlan. According to the defendant, Harlan had been the 'Nazi film director number one' during Hitler's Reich. He had produced an infamous anti-Semitic film and had only avoided a criminal conviction for his activities on technical grounds. In the defendant's view he was therefore an unworthy representative of the German film industry, and his return to public life in Germany would reopen recent wounds. There were public disturbances. Harlan successfully obtained an order from the Regional Court restraining the defendant from calling for a boycott. The defendant argued that the injunction infringed his fundamental right to free expression under Art 5 of the Basic Law. The Constitutional Court noted that fundamental rights are primarily intended to guarantee the individual's sphere of freedom against the state. However, fundamental rights also had to be taken into account in disputes between individuals. The Court gave particular weight to the fact that the defendant was using his right to free expression to contribute to the formation of public opinion. In the circumstances, the right to free expression meant that the defendant should not have been restrained from publicly urging a boycott of Harlan's films. Anyone who felt injured by a public statement of another could similarly reply in public.

In Europe, the European Convention on Human Rights guarantees the right to respect for private life and the right to freedom of expression through Arts 8 and 10[7] respectively. However, these are qualified rights. This means that they may be subjected to restrictions that are prescribed by law, proportionate, and necessary, in a democratic society. The United Kingdom does not have its own Bill of Rights, but we shall see from the case of *Campbell v MGN*[8] that the House of Lords has used Arts 8 and 10 to produce a similar result to that in *Lüth* by applying those Articles in a private dispute. The authoritative court on the European Convention on Human Rights is the European Court of Human Rights in Strasbourg (the 'Strasbourg Court'). The extent, however, to which the Strasbourg Court has been prepared to permit contracting states to restrict freedom of speech has depended on the context.

In the case of political speech, for example, few restrictions are permitted.

This is illustrated by a series of cases concerning disputes between the Moldovan Government and '*Flux*', a national newspaper. The newspaper, in one case, had published an article which asked whether there was a connection between changes to tax laws and a party given by a businessman for some members of Parliament at a luxury hotel. One of the politicians involved successfully sued the newspaper for libel in the Moldovan courts and obtained the maximum award of damages. The Strasbourg Court held that the decision of the national court violated Art 10.[9] The article contained both statements of fact and value judgments. A requirement to prove the truth of a value judgment infringed freedom of opinion. The truth of a value judgment was not susceptible of proof. Even though the defendant had been unable to establish the truth of some of the facts, the Strasbourg Court held that in all the circumstances there had been a violation of Art 10. The Strasbourg Court

---

[7] Article 10 is set out in the Appendix.   [8] [2004] UKHL 22, [2004] 2 AC 457.
[9] *Flux v Moldova* (Application No 28702/03).

reiterated that journalists play a pre-eminent role in a democratic society and that contracting states have only a narrow margin of appreciation in freedom of expression cases concerning politicians. In these circumstances there was an unjustified infringement of the newspaper's right to free expression. By contrast, in relation to limitations on free speech for matters such as the protection of national security, the Strasbourg Court allows a wide margin of appreciation and leaves it to the national institutions to determine what restrictions are appropriate.

In another case, *NM & Others v Smith*,[10] the Constitutional Court of South Africa was required to strike a balance between the right to freedom of expression and the protection of individuals' privacy interests. The applicants were three HIV positive individuals who had participated in clinical research concerning possible HIV treatments. The respondents published a book which discussed those clinical trials. A passage in the book referred to the applicants by their real names and disclosed their HIV status. The applicants argued that the disclosure of this information without their consent had violated their fundamental rights to privacy, dignity, and psychological integrity. The Constitutional Court held that there had been a violation of their fundamental rights. The right to free expression had to give way to the fundamental right of human dignity. Madala J noted:

The disclosure of an individual's HIV status, particularly within the South African context, deserves protection against indiscriminate disclosure due to the nature and negative social context the disease has as well as the potential intolerance and discrimination that result from its disclosure.[11]

O'Regan J considered freedom of expression to be an 'indispensable element' of a democratic society. It enables individuals to form and share opinions and thus enhances human dignity and autonomy.[12] There are therefore 'close links' between freedom of expression and other constitutional rights such as human dignity, privacy, and freedom. The disclosure of a person's HIV status without their consent was an affront to human dignity that was not justified by reference to the right of free expression.

The media in the United Kingdom have been responsible for bringing shocking details of expense claims by members of Parliament into the limelight. In addition, a blogger, operating under the extraordinary name of *Guido Fawkes*, is said to have uncovered a sleazy plan on the part of prime ministerial aides to tar opposition politicians with scandals. There is no doubt about the value in a democracy of a free press. But that does not mean that there cannot be too much freedom or, as I put it earlier, that freedom of expression is always a trump card. Here in the United Kingdom, the House of Lords has given decisions which have developed the law,

---

[10] *NM, SM & LH v Charlene Smith, Patricia De Lille & New Africa Books (PTY) Ltd, Freedom of Expression Institute (Amicus Curiae)* (Case CCT 69/05) [2007] ZACC 6.
[11] CCT 69/05, [2007] ZACC 6 at para 42.
[12] This was a dissenting judgment. Contrary to the decision of the majority, O'Regan J considered that it was necessary to show that the respondents had been negligent or intentional in disclosing the names of the appellants without their consent and that on the facts this had not been shown.

on occasion by limiting the right of an individual to sue for defamation and on occasion by placing restrictions on media freedom.

One example is *Reynolds v Times Newspapers*.[13] This was a defamation case brought by a former Prime Minister of Ireland (Taoiseach) against *The Times* newspaper. The challenged article concerned a political crisis that had precipitated the collapse of his coalition government. Mr Reynolds claimed that the article was defamatory, as it suggested that he had deliberately misled the Irish Parliament and his Cabinet colleagues. *The Times* argued that the defence of qualified privilege should be developed by the creation of a new head of privilege for political speech, modelled on the decision of the Supreme Court of the United States in *New York Times v Sullivan*.[14] The House of Lords rejected *The Times'* argument but recognized the role of investigative journalism and approved the development of the existing law of qualified privilege so as to protect responsible journalism, even if what was said could not be shown to be true. The consequence of this decision is that, if the conditions necessary for the defence of responsible journalism are fulfilled, the individual about whom the statements were made will have no right to vindicate his reputation or to obtain redress through an award of damages for defamation.

On the other hand, in *Campbell v MGN*[15] the House of Lords developed the law in the other direction so as to protect the rights of the individual at the expense of those of the press. The claimant, Naomi Campbell, the famous fashion model, claimed in public that she did not take drugs. *The Mirror*, a British tabloid newspaper, published a series of articles detailing her treatment for drug addiction, accompanied by photographs showing her in a public place leaving a meeting of a self-help group, Narcotics Anonymous. The claimant sought damages for breach of confidence against the publishers. She complained about the level of detail given about her, and about the photographs. She succeeded in the House of Lords by a majority of 3:2 (Lord Nicholls and Lord Hoffmann dissenting on the facts). No new action for invasion of privacy was created but the House of Lords developed the existing tort of breach of confidence, using the newly incorporated Arts 8 and 10 of the Convention. The majority considered that there was a legitimate public interest in running a story that demonstrated that the claimant had misled the public over her use of illegal drugs but that the publication of details of her treatment and the photographs was unjustified. There is an analogy here between this case and *Campbell* undoubtedly extended the law in a way that resulted in a restriction on the freedom of the press.

To conclude, the content of the right to freedom of expression can only be understood in the context of specific legal cases. The cases I have outlined show that the content of the right depends upon the context and the environment in which the question arises. In these cases we can see apex courts developing their evaluation

13 [1999] UKHL 45, [2001] 2 AC 127.   14 (1964) 376 US 254.
15 [2004] UKHL 22, [2004] 2 AC 457.

of freedom of expression. In particular, we can see the House of Lords moving the law on and moreover doing so in *Campbell* by imposing new restrictions on freedom of speech. This was so even though, to use the words of the Lord Chief Justice, Lord Judge, 'free speech is bred in the bone of the common law'.[16]

Yet, for the Supreme Court, there are also some broader questions of principle. At a general level, the constitutional issues of 'free speech' raise the question of the extent to which a Supreme Court should exercise a leadership role. If it should, then one must ask exactly what such a leadership role should involve for it. The questions may be addressed as follows: is it a function of Supreme Courts to lead the development or the reordering of the law in response to changing social conditions? Should they do so against the weight of public opinion? Should they look for vehicles in which to modernize the law in areas that appear to them to require it? Do their decisions in turn lead to a change in attitudes and behaviour in society? As regards the United Kingdom, it is often said that the British media have changed their working methods in response to decisions such as *Campbell* and *Reynolds*, and that press reporting is now less invasive of individual privacy than hitherto. A free press is, of course, vital in a democracy, and British newspapers have some of the widest readership in the world. Even tabloid newspapers help disseminate information and encourage participation in public debate. On the other hand, one might equally ask: should the courts leave matters in this sensitive area to the democratically elected legislature?

Whatever the answers, one thing is already clear. We have much to learn from the way Supreme Courts have discharged their role both in other times and in other places. We must remain mindful, however, that what has served us well in the past may no longer serve us well in the future. It would be useful to investigate by comparative law study the extent to which, in the modern world, Supreme Courts derive assistance from looking at what other Supreme Courts do. With that information we would be better placed to make an assessment as to whether or not there is a common thread between the approaches of the various Supreme Courts when they deal with common issues of concern, such as free speech and freedom of expression. Moreover, we would have a better understanding about how a modern Supreme Court performs its important role.

---

[16] *R v Criminal Central Court, ex parte Bright* [2000] EWHC 560 (QB), [2001] 1 WLR 662, at 679.

17

Prospective Overruling

This chapter was first published in the Law Quarterly Review in 2004.*

In *Murphy v Attorney General*,[1] the Supreme Court of Ireland held that it was unconstitutional for legislation to provide for the aggregation of the income of married persons with the result that they would be taxed at higher rates than unmarried cohabitants. The Supreme Court further held that the legislation was void from the date of its enactment. Notwithstanding this, the Supreme Court ruled that the benefit of its decision should be limited to those persons who had already commenced proceedings by the date of its judgment, and then only in respect of the assessments which they had challenged. The effect of the decision was therefore denied as respects all other past assessments on the grounds that if the decision had retrospective effect in the usual way the practical consequences would be highly disruptive of the tax system. Tax had been collected and spent without challenge in those cases and it would be inequitable if those taxes had to be repaid.

The technique which the Supreme Court of Ireland invoked in the *Murphy* case was one of the techniques compendiously known as 'prospective overruling'. I use this term to cover any technique by which a court places an explicit limit on the retrospective effect of its decision. Various writers have considered the advantages and disadvantages of prospective overruling.[2] On the one hand, it has the advantage that the effect of a change in the law can be limited so as not to disturb past transactions. On the other hand, prospective overruling has the disadvantage of going beyond what is necessary to determine the case before the court and indeed (dependent on the technique used), like a declaration of incompatibility under s 4 of the Human Rights Act 1998, it may not give the benefit of any change in the law to the claimant in the case before it. Prospective overruling might also encourage courts to be bolder to an undesirable degree in developing the law. It has to be emphasized that there are many different circumstances in which prospective

* First published in the *Law Quarterly Review* 2004, 120(Jan), 7–11. It is reproduced here with the kind permission of the Publisher.

[1] [1982] IR 241.
[2] See, for example, AGL Nicol, 'Prospective overruling a New Device for the English Courts?' (1976) 39 MLR 543; K Mason QC, 'Prospective overruling' (1989) 63 ALJ 526; Corss and Harris, *Precedent in English Law* (4th edn, Clarendon Press, 1991), 228–32; MDA Freeman, 'Standards of Adjudication, Judicial Law-Making and Prospective Overruling' (1973) CLP 166.

overruling can take place. The *Murphy* case represents a relatively extreme situation where a limit was placed on the effect of a declaration of constitutional rights. Not all cases of prospective overruling fall within this category.

A number of English judges have expressed views on the idea of prospective overruling. In *Jones v Secretary of State for Social Services*[3] (on appeal from *R v National Insurance Commissioner, ex parte Hudson*), both Lord Diplock (at 1015) and Lord Simon of Glaisdale (at 1026) expressed the view that the technique was worthy of consideration. Other eminent judges, however, have opposed its introduction. Lord Devlin considered that prospective overruling which had the effect that the case before the court was decided under the former law while the law was changed for the future crossed 'the Rubicon that divides the judicial and the legislative powers'.[4] Lord Reid also rejected the idea of declaring that 'the law was one thing yesterday but is to be something different tomorrow'.[5] Likewise, in *Kleinworth Benson v Lincoln City Council*,[6] Lord Goff of Chieveley held that the system of prospective overruling 'has no place in our legal system'. More recently, however, the House of Lords has left open the question whether a ruling could be made with prospective effect only.[7]

The reaction of other courts has also been mixed. In *Ha v New South Wales*,[8] the High Court of Australia rejected a submission that, because of the serious implications which its decision had for the revenues of the states and territories involved, it should declare that a licence fee was unconstitutional with effect twelve months after the date of the decision. The High Court declared that it had no power to overrule cases prospectively. In that case the form of prospective overruling sought would have altered existing rights and obligations. Thus the High Court of Australia in effect took the opposite position from that adopted by the Supreme Court of Ireland in the *Murphy* case. Prospective overruling has also been rejected in Canada.[9] However, the courts in Canada have a wide discretion as to the form of the remedy in Charter and human rights cases and have made orders with prospective effect in such cases.

In addition to Ireland, there are a number of other jurisdictions which employ the technique of prospective overruling. They include the European Court of Justice, the European Court of Human Rights, India, and Israel.[10] The technique is well known in the United States of America. Its precise scope there is controversial. It has been employed by both state courts (in respect of state law) and by the US Supreme Court. The doctrine is known as the *Sunburst* doctrine following

---

[3] [1972] AC 944.   [4] *The Judge* (1979) 12.
[5] *West Midland Baptist Association v Birmingham Corporation* [1970] AC 874 at 898–9.
[6] [1992] 2 AC 349 at 379.
[7] *R v Governor of Brockhill Prison, ex p Evans* [2001] 2 AC 19.
[8] (1997) 189 CLR 465.
[9] *Re Edward and Edward* (1987) 39 DLR (4th) 654.
[10] See for example, *Defrenne v SABENA* [1976] ECR 455, ECJ and see generally *Zamir and Woolf: The Declaratory Judgment* (3rd edn, Sweet & Maxwell, 2001) at paras 3.047–3.048; see also *Marckx v Belgium* (1979) 2 EHRR 330, 352–3 and *Somaiya Organics (India) Ltd v State of Uttart Pradesh* AIR 2001 SC 1723.

Great Northern Ry Co v Sunburst Oil & Refining Co.[11] It has been used in civil cases as well as constitutional cases.

As one would expect, the reports of English cases do not disclose any detailed consideration of the merits or otherwise of prospective overruling. They do not indicate the circumstances in which it might be appropriate to use this technique. As the Law Commission pointed out in its report *Restitution: Mistakes of Law and Ultra Vires Public Authority Receipts*,[12] examples of prospective overruling can be found in the context of takeovers and monopolies references, and in rating.[13] It may be that, outside the sphere of public law, the closest one gets is the decision of the House of Lords in *Royal Bank of Scotland plc v Etridge (No 2)*.[14] The members of the House all gave their own judgments, (which require careful study, and raise many issues outside the scope of this paper).[15] But on the essential issue with which this paper is concerned they were in agreement with Lord Nicholls of Birkenhead: see *per* Lord Bingham of Cornhill at 793–4, per Lord Clyde at 815, Lord Hobhouse of Woodborough at 828 and Lord Scott of Foscote at 850.

Etridge was the lead decision in a number of similar cases raising the question whether a bank had rebutted the inference of undue influence which arose when a wife gave a charge over her property to support the debts of her husband. Significantly, the House of Lords applied its previous case law, established in *Barclays Bank plc v O'Brien*[16] to the cases before it. Under *O'Brien*, banks were expected to bring the matter home to the wife and advise her to take independent advice. The House recognized, however, that it was not the practice of banks to have private meetings with the wife but simply to seek confirmation from a solicitor acting for the wife that he has explained the nature and effect of the transaction to her. The House decided that *O'Brien* did not decide that a private meeting was the only way in which a bank could take the requisite steps to bring home to the wife the risks she was running.[17] The House of Lords laid down new guidelines for future cases. In the words of Lord Nicholls:

> For the future a bank satisfies these requirements if it insists that the wife attend a private meeting with a representative of the bank at which she is told of the extent of her liability as surety, warned of the risk that she is running and urged to take independent advice.[18]

Lord Nicholls enumerated in detail the course that a bank should take in future if it sought to obtain protection by taking steps to see that the wife was independently advised. These steps include (for the first time) routinely sending to the wife's solicitor financial information about the husband's affairs. Lord Nicholls added:

---

[11] 287 US 358 at pp 364–6 (1932).   [12] (Law Com No 227, 1994), para 11.23, n 50.
[13] See *R v Panel on Takeovers and Mergers ex parte Datafin plc* [1987] QB 815, at 842; *R v Panel on Takeovers and Mergers ex p Guinness plc* [1990] 1 QB 146; *R v Monopolies and Mergers Commission ex-parte Argyll Group plc* [1986] 1 WLR 763; *R v Paddington Valuation Officer ex parte Peachey Property Co Ltd* [1966] 1 QB 360, at 402.
[14] [2001] UKHL 44, [2002] 2 AC 773.
[15] See Sullivan, 'Developing O'Brien' (2002) 113 LQR 337.
[16] [1994] 1 AC 180.   [17] *Etridge* at 805–6 per Lord Nicholls of Birkenhead.
[18] *Etridge* at 804.

These steps will be applicable to *future* transactions. In respect of past transactions, the bank will ordinarily be regarded as having discharged its obligations if a solicitor who was acting for the wife in the transaction gave the bank confirmation to the effect that he had brought home to the wife the risks she was running by standing as surety.[19]

What lessons can be learnt about prospective overruling from *Etridge*? The matter was dealt with in a very low key way which attracts little attention. Importantly the issue was not one of statutory construction but a case of the court enunciating the effect of a doctrine which is established entirely by case law, that is, the doctrine of undue influence. Nor was any prior case law expressly overruled. However, it is not impossible that some earlier cases are by implication no longer good law.[20] Nonetheless, although *Etridge* is a very limited form of prospective overruling, it is an example of it. The method is different from that used in *Murphy* because the law as declared in *Etridge* for the future was not applied to the cases before the court. No doubt this was because the decision raises the requirements with which banks are expected to comply. Because the relevant ruling was prospective only, it could not be said that it altered accrued rights and obligations. Since many of the commercial parties before the House of Lords were 'repeat players' they could assist the court in setting the new standards and would have an interest in doing so.

There are a number of other features worth noting about this aspect of the *Etridge* case. The House of Lords set out the law for future transactions in the exercise of its inherent jurisdiction, thus demonstrating that the power to make rulings prospective only in appropriate cases is a function of common law adjudication. Second, *Etridge* was not a case about constitutional or public law, thus demonstrating that the prospective overruling is not a preserve of constitutional courts. Third, *Etridge* shows that the House of Lords is prepared to take a more pragmatic approach to the idea of prospective overruling. It did not define the limits of the cases when it would be appropriate to apply this concept. If the question of prospective overruling arises in the future, the circumstances in which the technique can be used will have to be identified with care by degrees so that the concept develops in accordance with the common law method in an incremental way. As *Zamir and Woolf*[21] indicates with respect to declaratory relief, there would appear to be power to grant relief prospectively. There are probably cases where it can be said with certainty that the concept should not be used, as where the decision turns purely on the construction of a statute. The question whether there should be relief in respect of past breaches of an Act of Parliament must surely be a matter for Parliament itself. Likewise the concept cannot in general be invoked so as to prevent a person from claiming a violation of his human rights. Nor should it be used so as to facilitate a development in the law which would go beyond the proper area of judicial law making. Within these boundaries, however, there may be a certain amount of territory where prospective overruling might be

---

[19] *Etridge* at 812, emphasis added.
[20] See *First National Bank plc v Achampong* [2003] EWCA Civ 487.
[21] At para 4.17.

productive of justice and properly employed. For example, where the question whether a person's right is or would be violated depends on the balancing of the interests of the state and the individual, the fact that the decision will not have retrospective or immediate effect may be a factor to be taken into account in striking that balance. The possibilities are manifold. It will be interesting to see how long it is before the technique of prospective overruling is employed again.

PART VII

WORKING OUT THE RIGHT RELATIONSHIP WITH THE EUROPEAN SUPRANATIONAL COURTS

Membership of the European Union carries with it an obligation to give effect to the decisions on EU law taken by the Court of Justice of the European Union (the 'Luxembourg Court'). And the Human Rights Act 1998 requires the courts of England and Wales to take into account the case law of the European Court of Human Rights (the 'Strasbourg Court') when they are deciding questions about the scope of European Convention on Human Rights ('Convention') rights. Working out the relationship with these two supranational courts has proved complex.

The unifying theme of the chapters in this Part is the growing appreciation of the possibilities for transjudicial dialogue in working out that relationship. The basic form of dialogue occurs informally through working meetings or formally through pronouncements in judgments on specific issues. But it is not restricted to this. Dialogue can today be defined as any activity which facilitates communication between national institutions and a supranational court. Transjudicial dialogue is dialogue between the national courts and a supranational court.

Dialogue has been developed against the backcloth of intense criticism in the United Kingdom and elsewhere of supranational courts. A particular source of criticism is the Strasbourg Court's 'living instrument' theory of interpretation of the Convention and its protocols: it seeks to develop its case law on rights in the light of modern day conditions. It is then said that its decisions on rights extend to matters which national institutions, and not the Strasbourg Court, should determine: this is often described as the 'democratic deficit'. The Luxembourg Court is also heavily criticized for the variable quality of its judgments and its seeming desire to speed up integration in the European Union.

Chapter 18, *Peaceful or Problematic? The Relationship Between National Supreme Courts and Supranational Courts in Europe,* was a cutting edge piece when it appeared in November 2009, promoting judicial dialogue in its primary form: through meetings between national and supranational judiciaries and through judges engaging with each other's approach in their judgments. Meetings between judiciaries give opportunities for discussion and provide the checks and balances to which a supranational court should be subject. Surprisingly there were no meetings between the UK judiciary and the Strasbourg or Luxembourg judiciary until about 2006, when I suggested such a meeting, and these have been held at regular intervals since. I also recommended the development of the concept of the margin of appreciation,[1] and that remains one of the most important tasks for the Strasbourg Court. I believe that this paper had considerable effect. In January 2010, I presented the same arguments at a seminar of judges from all of the states that are parties to the Convention.

As for dialogue through judgments, I had experience of this when sitting as a UK ad hoc judge in the Strasbourg Court, particularly in *Z v UK Ltd*,[2] when the Strasbourg Court decided not to follow an earlier case because the English courts had clarified that the tort law on which it was based was not as it had understood it to be. Initially, as I explain in the paper, the Appellate Committee of the House of Lords (the predecessor of the Supreme Court of the United Kingdom) took the view that our domestic courts had in general to apply Strasbourg jurisprudence. However, the Supreme Court has now held that this is not required in every case. It would not be required where the Strasbourg Court has misunderstood some provision of domestic law.[3] The exceptions are in fact quite limited, though they may be further extended.

Another frequent criticism made of the two European supranational courts is that they lead to a loss of the cultural, social, and constitutional identity of the United Kingdom. In Chapter 19, *Jurisdiction of the New UK Supreme Court*, I floated the idea that, even though the United Kingdom does not have a written constitution, nonetheless the Supreme Court should have jurisdiction to determine whether EU measures conflict with any fundamental rights conferred by national law.[4] This would follow the practice in France, Germany, and other member states. It would be yet another form of dialogue between our courts and the Luxembourg Court. The Luxembourg Court would be bound to note if some further authority was needed from Parliament or if there was a need for a referendum.[5]

The proposal was not taken up when the paper was written but still represents an idea that could be built on to provide a bulwark of protection for the United Kingdom, much the same as already exists through the courts in other member states. I suggested that the power should be given to the Supreme Court but there is no reason why the jurisdiction should be confined to the Supreme Court. It is often

---

[1] The concept of 'margin of appreciation' is explored at greater length in Chapter 4, *Proportionality: The Way Ahead?*

[2] (Application No 28392/95) (2001) 34 EHRR 97.

[3] See *R v Horncastle* [2009] UKSC 14, [2010] 2 AC 373, decided in December 2009.

[4] The paper considers two questions, both of which, as explained in the paper, remain relevant today.

[5] See now the European Union Act 2011, which provides for a referendum before the United Kingdom can agree to an amendment to the EU Treaties which would transfer competence from the United Kingdom to the European Union.

better for a Supreme Court to have the benefit of judgments in lower courts before it forms a final view.

The above proposal is amplified in the third chapter in this Part, Chapter 20, *An English Judge in Europe*, which pursues the question of the checks and balances for supranational courts. I pointed out that, like any other court, the Strasbourg and Luxembourg Courts do not always get it right, and that the relationship between national courts and supranational courts need not be seen as hierarchical, as in the domestic system. I explained that other constitutional courts in Europe hold that there is a sphere in which the supranational courts cannot interfere. I proposed, among other ideas, that, when the Strasbourg Court was about to make a significant development in its case law, it should first issue a non-binding provisional judgment which would enable national courts to respond before the judgment became final. This mechanism would enable the Strasbourg Court at least to be better informed about the consequences of any dynamic interpretation that it is considering, and promote greater transparency in its decision-making.

The Luxembourg Court has had an increasing role in developing fundamental rights since the adoption by the Lisbon Treaty of the Charter of Fundamental Rights and Freedoms. The Lisbon Treaty also provides for the Luxembourg Court to become a party to the Convention even though it is an international organization and not a state. These changes have not yet occurred but are bound to have important effects in practice. Particularly relevant here is the need for complex forms of formal dialogue between the two supranational courts in future.

This Part demonstrates that transjudicial dialogue can take many forms, and that it is a developing science. It is important not simply as a means of allowing national and supranational judges to get a better understanding of each other's law but also as a means of addressing some of the concerns, so vigorously expressed in civil society in recent years, about the constitutional position of both the Strasbourg and the Luxembourg Courts.

The development of dialogue could lead to national courts becoming stronger partners in the development of EU law and human rights jurisprudence or it could conceivably lead to the reverse, namely national courts or some of them accepting that one or both of the supranational courts is supreme in its own spheres. That would lead the way to a more integrated legal space in Europe. Either way, national courts have to work out their own priorities and what their role is to be.

18

Peaceful or Problematic? The Relationship Between National Supreme Courts and Supranational Courts in Europe

This chapter is based on the Thomas More Lecture given at Lincoln's Inn in November 2009.*

In this paper I propose to consider the implications for our legal system of the exponential growth in European law and human rights jurisprudence. This jurisprudence is now increasingly populating our domestic law. Accordingly, now is a very good time to ask questions such as: why is it important to have a system of supranational courts in Europe? What can be done to improve the way they relate to national courts at the highest level? For reasons which I will explain, a successful working relationship with national supreme courts is, in my view, one of the most important benchmarks of success for the European supranational courts.

To save time, I will refer to the European Court of Justice[1] and its jurisprudence as the 'Luxembourg Court' and 'Luxembourg jurisprudence', and to the European Court of Human Rights and its jurisprudence as the 'Strasbourg Court' and 'Strasbourg jurisprudence' respectively.

I am not the first person to have noticed the incoming tide of Community (now EU) law. Lord Denning, a Bencher of Lincoln's Inn, who was often ahead of his time, famously said:

... the flowing tide of Community law is coming in fast. It has not stopped at the high water mark. It has broken the dykes and the banks. It has submerged the surrounding land. So much so that we have to learn to become amphibious if we wish to keep our heads above water.[2]

Nor am I the first person to speak about difficulties of implementing the European Convention on Human Rights (the 'Convention'). Lord Hoffmann was highly critical of some of the jurisprudence of the Strasbourg Court in his lecture, 'The

---

* This is a modified version of the Thomas More Lecture given at Lincoln's Inn in November 2009. It was subsequently published in (2010) 29 *Yearbook of European Law* 1. It is reproduced here with the kind permission of the Publisher.

[1] Now renamed as the Court of Justice of the European Union under the Lisbon Treaty.
[2] *Shields v E Coomes (Holdings) Ltd* [1978] 1 WLR 1408 at 1416.

Universality of Human Rights'.[3] The press and the politicians have their own views on what should happen about human rights, but I come at these questions from a purely legal and judicial perspective and not a political one. This paper is therefore not concerned with questions such as whether there should be a British Bill of Rights or a repeal of the Human Rights Act 1998[4] or whether there should be restrictions on the powers of our courts in relation to Strasbourg jurisprudence.[5]

Whether there should be a British Bill of Rights or any amendment to the Human Rights Act 1998 are matters for the Parliament. What I am concerned with is how we absorb Strasbourg and Luxembourg jurisprudence into our legal system, how we manage the case load to which it gives rise, how we maximize the potential for working together, how we contribute to the creation of their jurisprudence, and how we can have the most influence on their work.

My view is that we should, in principle, support the work of the Strasbourg Court. By and large, human rights have made an important contribution to civil society in this country. A major challenge since the commencement of the Human Rights Act 1998 has been the balancing of freedom and security in relation to terrorism issues. Human rights have played a crucial role in the resolution of these issues.[6]

Likewise we have greatly benefited from the jurisprudence of the Luxembourg Court. It has brought us many benefits, for example, the doctrine of proportionality and the principles of equal treatment, effective protection, and so on.

However, we tend to react to each case or line of authority on an ad hoc basis instead of thinking in a long-term way about the relationship as a whole. Indeed, this may be the first occasion when a judge has raised the question of how the judiciary should react to the case law on a collective basis.

There is a very good reason for thinking about these issues. However much we value the jurisprudence of the supranational courts, there is always a risk, now that their jurisprudence is becoming ever more pervasive, of European law introducing concepts which do not sit easily with our own domestic law. European law very often has to be superimposed on to a body of domestic law and occasionally it also makes changes to the fabric of English law.

An example of this can be taken from the field of arbitration. In *West Tankers*[7] the Luxembourg Court held that, notwithstanding that arbitration is outside the Brussels Regulation,[8] which regulates jurisdiction over civil matters as regards defendants domiciled within the European Union, the courts of the law of the seat of an arbitration cannot issue an injunction restraining the pursuit of

---

[3] Judicial Studies Board Annual Lecture, 19 March 2009.

[4] However, I would ask anyone who seeks to remove or dilute any Convention rights to explain why this is necessary.

[5] See Malcolm Rifkind, 'Governed by Law or by Lawyers? International Treaties and Human Rights', Denning Lecture, October 2009.

[6] See, for example, *A v Secretary of State for the Home Department* [2004] UKHL 56, [2005] 2 AC 68 (also known as the '*Belmarsh* case').

[7] *Allianz SpA (formerly Riunione Adriatica Di Sicurta SpA) and others v West Tankers Inc* (Case C-185/07) [2009] WLR (D) 44.

[8] Regulation 44/2001/EC, Art 1.2(d).

proceedings in another member state (an 'anti-suit injunction'). The law of England and Wales is very commonly the law of the seat of an arbitration. The Luxembourg Court held that the anti-suit injunction was contrary to the principle of trust between courts of the member states that underlies the Brussels Regulation. This decision is contrary to the previous practice of the Commercial Court of England and Wales. The effect is that the other party can apply for a stay of those proceedings in that other court, and the arbitration can continue. However, there will be a risk of inconsistent findings in the arbitration and in the court of that other member state and the decision undermines the role given by English arbitration law to the law of the court supervising the arbitration. It is self-evident that it is also likely to cause the parties to incur additional costs.

The coherence of our domestic law is liable to be affected whether the basic approach of some area of law is changed or whether some ill-fitting and largely unnecessary principles are superimposed on to it. Change is, of course, an inevitable consequence of membership of the European Union. However, if we are satisfactorily to meet the challenges which European law presents we in the domestic courts need to think carefully about how to make the best of the system. I would like to start a debate at the level of national courts about how to achieve the most suitable form of supranational adjudication in Europe. I have no doubt that international courts discuss among themselves how to operate effectively. The supranational courts are not slow to say what they expect of national courts. But I would argue that the question of how to achieve the most suitable form of supranational adjudication must also be considered from the perspective of national systems. It is time to turn the tables and ask what the national courts are entitled to expect of supranational courts. So far as national courts are concerned, it is only natural that, where practical, national supreme courts should be asking this question and taking the lead in making any structural changes in the relationship.

The two European systems

Let us reflect for a moment on the major milestones and the major rudiments of the two systems. Those rudiments will be the foundations on which we have to build. There are important differences between the two systems of supranational adjudication.

Joining the European Union in 1973 brought about enormous constitutional change for the United Kingdom.[9] Parliament in effect ceded some of its sovereignty to the European Union, or at least transferred some decision-making powers to the institutions of the European Union.

The Human Rights Act 1998 is another milestone.[10] The Act gives further protection to the Convention in domestic law and makes the Convention in effect a shadow constitution for the United Kingdom. The courts are required to take

---

[9] See generally Vernon Bogdanor, *The New British Constitution* (Hart Publishing, 2009), 27 et seq.
[10] See generally Bogdanor, *The New British Constitution*, ch 3.

account of the jurisprudence of the Strasbourg Court and they are required to interpret legislation compatibly with the Convention, so far as they are able to do so. The domestic courts are not, however, given power to strike down primary legislation. Nonetheless, in respect of at least the qualified Convention rights,[11] the courts have to apply the doctrine of proportionality and balance competing interests and values. Judges when performing this task are *de facto* constitutional judges.

By contrast, the courts have the power and duty to displace domestic legislation if that is necessary to comply with EU law because of the doctrine of primacy enunciated by the Luxembourg Court. EU law sometimes simply adds to domestic law. Sometimes EU law and domestic law sit side by side and the litigant can invoke either. This happened in a case on equal pay in which I compared domestic law to the foot of Cinderella, on to which the slipper (then Community law) had to be fitted. I explained that, unlike Cinderella's slipper, the slipper of Community law is not made of glass but of some altogether technologically more advanced material that can expand and improve, to accommodate developments in Community law. I added that neither the foot nor the slipper can, however, be shrunk in the process of applying the slipper and that, in the context of equal pay, there are times when Cinderella is capable of dancing on her own without any slipper, that is, without any need to invoke Community law.[12]

The Luxembourg Court was set up to give authoritative rulings on the EU Treaties. The Treaties contains provisions which mean that the relationship which our courts enjoy with the Luxembourg Court is different from that which they enjoy with the Strasbourg Court. To take our relationship with the Luxembourg Court first, most commonly cases from the United Kingdom which end up in Luxembourg are cases referred to the Luxembourg Court by our courts for a ruling on the interpretation of EU legislation. This is, in form at least, suggestive of a partnership between our courts and the Luxembourg Court. We can ask a question and suggest an answer and the Luxembourg Court will rule. The Luxembourg Court will provide an answer on the EU law issues raised and will send the case back for the national judge to decide any issues of domestic law which arise and to apply the answer given to the facts of the case (as found by the national court). Of course there are many cases being referred to Luxembourg from other member states as well. The decisions in all those cases form part of the corpus of law which must be enforced by UK courts. Moreover, domestic courts must provide effective remedies for violations of rights conferred by EU law, even where no such remedies are conferred by domestic law.

With the Strasbourg Court, there is no preliminary ruling procedure. There is, however, the right of individual petition once domestic remedies have been exhausted. The domestic court has no control over which cases become the subject of an application to the Strasbourg Court, or over which cases are held to be admissible by the Strasbourg Court. Thus it may not be able to conduct a dialogue

---

[11] Articles 8–11.
[12] *Wilson v Health & Safety Executive* [2009] EWCA Civ 1074, [2010] ICR 302.

with the Strasbourg Court through its judgments so as to indicate to that Court what the domestic court thinks the answer should be.

Unlike the Luxembourg Court on a reference, the Strasbourg Court is expected to apply the human rights law, as enunciated by it, to the facts of the case. It will also be able to order just satisfaction (or compensation) for a violation though it cannot change the domestic law even if it is found to be in violation of the Convention.[13] Not every human rights case has to go to Strasbourg: the Convention requires contracting states to provide effective remedies in their own courts. The Strasbourg Court recognizes that it is not a fourth level of appeal from the decision of a trial judge. On the contrary, the mechanism for enforcement through the Strasbourg Court is said to be subsidiary to that of the member state. The notion of subsidiarity is expressed in the doctrines of subsidiarity and the margin of appreciation, which I will need to discuss further.

There is a famous saying, probably apocryphal, attributed to President Jackson of the United States after the Supreme Court of the United States had given judgment on a case about Cherokee rights: 'Marshall has given his decision; now let him enforce it.' Neither the Luxembourg Court nor the Strasbourg Court has any machinery of its own for enforcing its judgments.

The decisions of the Luxembourg Court are enforced through our domestic courts pursuant to the European Communities Act 1972.

Since the commencement of the Human Rights Act 1998, effect has also been given to Strasbourg jurisprudence by our domestic courts.[14] I shall consider below the extent to which domestic courts should regard themselves as under an obligation to follow Strasbourg jurisprudence. Strictly the United Kingdom is only bound to give effect to those decisions which are given in relation to the United Kingdom. It has been suggested that those are the only decisions which should be taken into account by domestic courts.[15] My view is that that suggestion is, with respect, absurd. Since it is likely that the Strasbourg Court would apply those decisions to other cases, the courts of England and Wales at least do not draw any such distinction.

Decisions of the Strasbourg Court are also enforced through the remarkable inter-governmental mechanisms of the Council of Europe, namely through the Committee of Ministers of the Council of Europe.[16] Article 46 of the Convention provides for the Committee of Minsters 'to supervise' the execution of judgments of the Strasbourg Court. This has proved very effective as a means of enforcement: very few judgments of the Strasbourg Court have not been implemented, although there have been delays. Enforcement through the Committee of Ministers is not

---

[13] I leave aside the 'pilot judgment' procedure: see, for example, *Kudla v Poland* (2000) 35 EHRR 198.

[14] The Convention rights incorporated by the Human Rights Act 1998 and the principal provisions of that Act are set out in the Appendix.

[15] Dominic Raab, *The Assault on Liberty* (4th Estate, 2009), 227.

[16] It should be noted that the decisions of the Strasbourg Court are generally directed only to the case before it and are declaratory only. They cannot in general require any change to be made to domestic law.

limited to the payment of any amount ordered by the Strasbourg Court. The Committee of Ministers expects to be told how the domestic legal system has been altered to prevent recurrence of the violation if this is needed. It is of the essence of the Convention system that it allows a range of methods of implementation: it is not a case of 'one size fits all'.

The system of implementation through the Council of Ministers give contracting states some time to reflect how best to make changes in their law consequent on Strasbourg decisions. In the United Kingdom, this freedom of choice may be taken away from them if the courts have meanwhile applied the Strasbourg jurisprudence in domestic law and decided what domestic law requires.[17] Accordingly the suggestion has recently been made that it should be possible in an appropriate case for an order to be made declaring that a new decision of the Strasbourg Court shall have no effect in the United Kingdom for a specified period until Parliament had had the opportunity to decide how to change the law.[18] The 14th Protocol to the Convention is relevant here. Now that it has come into effect, the Committee of Ministers will have a new power to go back to the Strasbourg Court for clarification of a judgment where the difficulty of interpretation is hindering implementation.[19] The United Kingdom government or Parliament might want a period of non-implementation to enable that step to be taken rather than to have to take an overcautious approach to what the decision requires. At the margins therefore, and in the context of the implementation of Strasbourg jurisprudence, the protection of Convention rights achieved by the Human Rights Act 1998 may have resulted in a less than perfect solution.

The challenge for national courts

Sometimes it is difficult to understand what exactly has been decided by the supranational court. This can happen with decisions of either the Luxembourg Court or the Strasbourg Court. I can give two examples from my own experience.

In *Wilson v Health & Safety Executive*,[20] the parties were at odds as to whether the Luxembourg Court had departed from its ruling in an earlier case known for short as *Danfoss*.[21] This established that an employer did not have to provide special justification for recourse to a length of service criterion in fixing pay scales. In a later case, *Cadman v Health & Safety Executive*,[22] the Luxembourg Court, after citing *Danfoss*, went on to hold that an employer had to show justification where the worker provided evidence capable of giving rise to serious doubts as to whether recourse to the criterion of length of service was appropriate. The Court of Appeal held that the Luxembourg Court had departed from its earlier jurisprudence, even

---

[17] Compare the controversial decision of the House of Lords in *Re G (Adoption: Unmarried Couple)* [2008] UKHL 38, [2009] 1 AC 73.
[18] See Rifkind, 'Governed by Law or by Lawyers?'.   [19] Article 16.
[20] [2009] EWCA Civ 1074, [2010] ICR 302.
[21] *Danfoss* (Case 109/88) [1998] ECR 3199.   [22] Case C-17/05 [2006] ECR I-9583.

though in its judgment it appeared to be simply applying the *Danfoss* decision. Occasionally there has to be a second reference to the Luxembourg Court to ask it to elucidate its earlier answer to a reference.

A similar problem can arise with Strasbourg jurisprudence. For example, in *Faisovas*,[23] the Court of Appeal had to decide whether it was a violation of Art 3 of the Convention[24] for prison authorities to handcuff a terminally ill patient while he was receiving treatment at a hospital outside prison. The Court was faced with the difficulty of ambiguous developments in the jurisprudence. Early jurisprudence of the Strasbourg Court had held that there was a violation where the prisoner was infirm as a result of his illness. However, in a subsequent case,[25] the Strasbourg Court held that there was a violation of Art 3 when a prisoner, sentenced to 22 years for membership of a terrorist organization, was subjected to a gynaecological examination while handcuffed, with (male) security officers behind screens and out of earshot. There was no question of the prisoner in that case being infirm and no finding that she was actually distressed. The principle had clearly been modified but it was not clear from the reasoning in the judgment precisely what the new principle was. The later decision seemed to turn on its own facts. The new power in the 14th Protocol is confirmation of the fact that from time to time there are ambiguities in Strasbourg jurisprudence.

Many of the decisions of the Luxembourg Court can readily be absorbed into the domestic system, but some of them result in profound change to our domestic law. This is particularly so in relation to cases based on the principle in the treaty against discrimination on the grounds of nationality. The Luxembourg Court has interpreted the treaty in these cases in a direction which paves the way for integration. An example of this is in the decision of the Luxembourg Court in *Bidar*,[26] where the Court reversed its previous jurisprudence in the light of treaty changes and held, on the strength of the prohibition on discrimination, that a student who is a national of one member state but lawfully resident in another member state is entitled to a student grant on the same basis as nationals of that state. There have been similar decisions in the field of social security and direct tax. Thus, tax relief given to resident companies cannot be denied to taxpayers resident in other member states.[27] Member states have had to make major alterations to their law and practice in consequence. What appears to be happening is that the Luxembourg Court is paving the way for integration by producing rulings which require a member state to give the same benefits that it gives to its own nationals and residents to persons from other member states. As one writer said, the Luxembourg Court regards itself as the engine of integration.[28] In some of these cases it appears that the Luxembourg Court has departed from its earlier tradition of incrementalism. These decisions can affect the way in which the social security benefits of many

---

[23] *R (Faisovas) v Secretary of State for Justice* [2009] EWCA Civ 373.
[24] 'No one shall be subjected to torture or to inhuman or degrading treatment or punishment.'
[25] *Uyan v Turkey* (Application No 7496/03), 8 January 2009.
[26] *R (Bidar) v Ealing LBC* [2005] ECR I-2119, [2005] QB 812.
[27] See, for example, *ICI plc v Colmer* [1999] 1 WLR 2035.
[28] Mitchel Lasser, *Judicial Deliberations* (Oxford University Press, 2004).

kinds are allocated, and the way tax laws in a variety of areas are administered. It can be very burdensome for a member state to have to change its system, and the workload of the courts and tribunals is greatly increased by the need to provide remedies in a wide range of cases. In the United Kingdom, remedies may be claimed for payments made as long ago as 1973.

A different problem for national courts arises when the Strasbourg Court has sought to develop its jurisprudence in a manner which demonstrates a misunderstanding of the domestic law position. For instance, the effect of the decision of the Strasbourg Court in *Osman v United Kingdom*[29] was that it was a violation of Art 6 on access to court for the court to conclude that it was not fair, just or reasonable to impose a duty of care. Happily a different conclusion was later arrived at in *Z v United Kingdom.*[30] In reality, the Strasbourg Court has been very receptive to reasoned criticism. It follows that the higher courts should not be expected as a matter of domestic law to implement the decision of the Strasbourg Court in every situation. There is however, a small domestic problem here generated by s 2 of the Human Rights Act 1998. This has been interpreted at the highest level as generally requiring domestic courts to follow Strasbourg jurisprudence, no more and no less. I shall need to return to this problem.

We are not the only member state to have had this experience of decisions that cause great disruption in the domestic system. For example, in *Princess Caroline's Case*, the German Federal Constitutional Court ruled in favour of freedom of expression that the rights of the Princess to protection of her personality under the German constitution had not been violated by intrusive press photography.[31]

Princess Caroline was a public figure trying to lead a private life. The Federal Constitutional Court held that she was a figure of contemporary history and that she only enjoyed protection of her private life outside her home if she was in a secluded place out of the public eye. Princess Caroline took her case to Strasbourg where the Third Section of the Strasbourg Court reached a different conclusion on the balance to be drawn between press freedom and privacy, and held that the Princess's right to respect for her private life had been violated.[32] This decision caused enormous difficulty for the German Federal Constitutional Court. It found itself in the embarrassing position of having to revise its interpretation of the constitutional right.

In the case of the Luxembourg Court, even though there is the doctrine of primacy, some constitutional courts in some member states have held that the law of the European Union is subject to their own constitution and that it is part of their function to guarantee their national constitutional rights not only as against state bodies but also as against the European Union.[33] When the Constitutional Reform Bill was being debated, I floated the idea that the new Supreme Court of

---

[29] (1998) 5 BHRC 293.   [30] (2001) 10 EHRR 384.
[31] *Re C* (1999) 10 BHRC 131.
[32] *Von Hannover v Germany* (Application No 59320/00) (2004) 16 BHRC 645.
[33] See, for example, *Brunner v The European Union Treaty* [1994] 1 CMLR 57, Federal Constitutional Court of Germany.

the United Kingdom should be given some similar power.[34] However, the intention was that the Supreme Court should, apart from acquiring the powers of the Privy Council in devolution matters, have the same powers as the Appellate Committee of the House of Lords. My idea was not pursued. In any event, it would be difficult, though not impossible, to achieve this position in a country that does not have a wholly written constitution.

How many cases go from the United Kingdom to Luxembourg or Strasbourg? The number of references to the Luxembourg Court from England and Wales is comparatively small: the Court of Appeal sends the most references. The number of references has been going up recently. However, the good news is that the United Kingdom is now one of the jurisdictions from which the Strasbourg Court receives the fewest applications. But that does not mean we do not have any problems. There is a great deal of jurisprudence being generated by the Strasbourg Court and the Luxembourg Court from many other member states of the Council of Europe or European Union, as the case may be, and this jurisprudence inevitably has a 'ripple' effect on our domestic law.

Why do we value the European supranational legal system and what are the benchmarks for success?

The above discussion must inevitably lead to the question why we value the European supranational legal system, and what we would regard as a sign of success.

I start with the Luxembourg Court. The Luxembourg Court is an essential part of the European Union. That Union is based on the rule of law and the Luxembourg Court has the function of ensuring that the acts of the member states and the EU institutions are in conformity with the laws of the European Union.[35] We could not do without a European supranational court to regulate the affairs of the European Union.

So far as the Strasbourg Court is concerned, we need a court with ultimate authority to interpret the Convention. Moreover, as I explained in my *Hailsham* lecture,[36] an international system of human rights has considerable advantages for the United Kingdom. It subjects the institutions of the state to outside scrutiny, and that is particularly important when, as in the United Kingdom, there is a strong doctrine of Parliamentary sovereignty, and the doctrine of *Wednesbury* reasonableness. Even under the Human Rights Act 1998, the courts cannot strike down primary legislation that violates the Convention. The existence of supranational courts, establishing human rights principles, also empowers the domestic judiciary and strengthens their independence as against other institutions of their own state.

---

[34] Jurisdiction of the new United Kingdom Supreme Court (Public Law) (2004) p 699. (Reproduced in Chapter 19.)

[35] See, for example, *Kadi v Council of the European Union* (Joined Cases C-402/05 P and C-415/05 P) [2008] 3 CMLR 41 at [281].

[36] 'Human Rights and Civil Wrongs: Tort Law under the Spotlight' [2010] PL 140. (Reproduced at Chapter 14.)

Furthermore, the Convention system gives us a legitimate interest in how other countries in Europe treat their citizens, and this is a more powerful position than could be achieved at the political level alone. The Strasbourg Court can bring about remarkable change in the raising of standards throughout Europe. In addition, in my experience, its influence stretches far beyond the shores of Europe. As things stand, we have the opportunity to influence and contribute to its jurisprudence.

However, it is still sensible to try to identify what we regard as the benchmarks for success in these European courts. Now what are the benchmarks for success for a supranational court?[37] This is a major question. I am going to take the European supranational courts together. I am going to suggest that what domestic legal systems value most about these courts are the following qualities:

(1) *Their independence.* This goes without saying and I need say no more about it.

(2) *Their effectiveness in creating a principled body of law within their jurisdiction.* This too is self-evident. We need a court to take the lead in EU law and human rights. We needed to create substantive law meeting the highest standards.

(3) *Quality of reasoning and ability to communicate clearly with their constituents.* This is a matter that I need to enlarge on below.

(4) *Respect for the role of national courts.* By this, I mean an awareness of where the boundaries are between the roles of the supranational and of the national courts, a sensitivity to national traditions and national legal systems and an appreciation that there may be constitutional ramifications for the national institutions flowing from their decisions. This is really a call for judicial restraint by the supranational courts.

Once we have understood what makes a good or bad supranational adjudication, we are better able to think about what we could do to make the system work better. I next move to the various suggestions that I want to make. I call this my 'toolkit'.

My toolkit for making improvements in the European system of supranational adjudication

My toolkit of suggestions for improving the relationship between the European supranational courts and the national courts and the system of supranational adjudication contains four main tools: (1) more dialogue, meaning dialogue between national judges and judges of the European supranational courts and dialogue between the judges of the national courts among themselves; (2) more subsidiarity; (3) more temporal limitations; and (4) clearer judgments.

---

[37] See generally, LR Heller and AM Slaughter, 'Towards a Theory of Effective Supranational Adjudication' (1997) 107 Yale LJ 273.

(1) More dialogue

Dialogue can take several forms and achieve several objectives. I start with informal dialogue between judges of the national courts, on the one hand, and judges of the two European supranational courts, on the other hand. There is a great value in personal contact. A quiet conversation between judges can head off steps which might prove ill-advised. It can also be an enriching exchange of experiences. The informal discussion can also give the national judges an input into the process of developing jurisprudence at the supranational level. In addition, the national judges can explain where the shoe pinches most and how the new jurisprudence can best be absorbed into their own system.

Furthermore, I see judicial dialogue of this kind as of constitutional importance in the European legal order. Any supranational court needs to be subject to checks and balances. In the case of the European supranational courts, dialogue with the national courts is an important means of providing such checks and balances.

Another form of judicial dialogue takes place at plenary meetings of judges from different member states, either with or without the judges of the European supranational courts. I would like to see more meetings between judges of national courts with interests in common, such as the judges of the common law jurisdictions within the European Union. This would enable them to forge a common approach. We also need meetings between judges in Europe who do not, on the face of it, have interests in common. This enables us to increase our understanding of our European legal heritage.

Another very important means of dialogue is through judgments. It is obviously of great benefit to the United Kingdom in terms of influencing the direction of the jurisprudence in the Strasbourg Court that the UK courts are able to give judgments interpreting the Convention rights, rather than rights conferred by domestic law. The national court can in effect send a message to the Strasbourg Court by reflecting its views on the Strasbourg jurisprudence in its judgment either in the case before it goes to Strasbourg or some other case raising the same issue. The Strasbourg Court is not bound to accept what the national court says but it has gone a very long way towards recognizing the role of superior national courts in assisting it in its role:

Where...the superior national courts have analysed in a comprehensive and convincing manner the precise nature of the impugned restriction, on the basis of the relevant Convention case law and principles drawn therefrom, this Court would need strong reasons to differ from the conclusions reached by those courts by substituting its own views for those of the national courts on a question of interpretation of domestic law (see *Z and Others...*) and by finding, contrary to their view, that there was arguably a right recognised by domestic law.[38]

This authority, which refers to *Z v UK*, means that the Strasbourg Court would equally be willing in an appropriate case to reconsider an earlier decision in the light

---

[38] *Roche v United Kingdom* (Application No 32555/96) (2005) 20 BHRC 99 at [120].

of disagreement by the superior national court. In my view, that is a good reason why in an appropriate case the superior national court should not simply apply the Strasbourg jurisprudence with which it has a serious disagreement, but should state its disagreement and, if it reaches a different conclusion from the Strasbourg Court, leave the applicant to his remedy in Strasbourg, where the national government can argue the matter fully. If necessary, it can seek a reference to the Grand Chamber of the Strasbourg Court.

But, to some extent, our domestic courts are disabled from having an active dialogue. This point derives from the way in which s 2 of the Human Rights Act 1998 has been interpreted. Section 2 of the Human Rights Act 1998 provides that when the court determines a question which has arisen in connection with a Convention right, it must *take into account* any jurisprudence of the Strasbourg Court, whenever made or given, so far as in the opinion of the court it is relevant to the proceedings in which the question has arisen. The obligation in relation to Strasbourg jurisprudence is thus much weaker than the obligation of British courts to give effect to the law of the European Union.[39]

However, it is now established in English law that, save in special cases, the duty of national courts is 'to keep pace with Strasbourg jurisprudence as it evolves over time: no more but certainly no less' (per Lord Bingham in *R (Ullah) v Special Adjudicator*).[40] There are advantages in this approach. It recognizes the function of the Strasbourg Court as the organ for the authoritative interpretation of the Convention, and at the end of the day domestic courts have to respect its authoritative role. Moreover, from the perspective of minimizing the risk of a decision of the national court being the subject of an application to the Strasbourg Court, and a finding of violation against the member state in question, this approach makes good sense.

However, there are also disadvantages to this approach. It does not, for instance, acknowledge that the Strasbourg Court is only laying down minimum guarantees. Article 53 of the Convention itself recognizes that citizens of the contracting states may have more far-reaching rights. More fundamentally, it is difficult to have an effective dialogue if the courts start from a position of deference. That deference must colour the national court's approach.

Moreover, *Ullah* on the face of it sits uneasily with the wording of the duty in s 2 of the Human Rights Act 1998 which imposes an obligation to 'take into account' Strasbourg jurisprudence, rather than to follow it. From that it would appear that Parliament intended that the courts should be free in an appropriate case to go further than Strasbourg case law (though this would have to be an exceptional case), or not as far as Strasbourg case law. Our courts should not in any event be expected to apply jurisprudence from another source without having investigated its reasoning.

---

[39] See s 2 of the European Communities Act 1972.
[40] [2004] UKHL 26, [2004] 2 AC 323 at [20].

It is said that the majority of courts in the other contracting states do not take the view that they are effectively bound by Strasbourg jurisprudence.[41] However, in these jurisdictions there are usually written constitutions so that precedence can be given to the rights contained in the constitution. In Germany, for instance, the obligation is again to take account of Strasbourg case law, which means that the courts attach considerable importance to the Strasbourg jurisprudence and must justify not following it. However, they are not bound by it.[42] In Germany a party may raise an objection based on a violation of the Convention as part of his complaint in proceedings before the German Federal Constitutional Court.

The result of the 'take into account' point is that domestic courts take a restrictive approach to the question when to depart from Strasbourg jurisprudence. The approach on this issue is in sharp contrast to the expansive view taken of s 3 of the Human Rights Act 1998, containing the interpretative obligation, which also involves substantial policy considerations. It is, therefore, arguably paradoxical that the courts have not taken a more restrictive approach to s 3 as well.

What we need is a *right of rebuttal*. We need to be able to say to the Strasbourg Court that it has not made the principle clear, or that it has not applied the principle, consistently, or that it has misunderstood national law or the impact of its decisions on the United Kingdom's legal system. I do not suggest there should be a free for all, or that domestic courts should be free to reinvent the wheel on human rights jurisprudence. However, I would argue in favour of an approach which is more flexible than the *Ullah* approach. Such an approach was adopted (without disturbing the status of the *Ullah* ruling) in *Doherty v Birmingham City Council*[43] where the House of Lords declined to apply Strasbourg jurisprudence so long as it failed to provide principles on which the courts could rely for general application.

In addition, after the 14th Protocol comes into effect, domestic courts may wish to allow time for a case to be referred back to the Strasbourg Court for clarification by the Committee of Ministers before they rule on its effect in domestic law.

Before I leave this topic I should refer to the extension of Strasbourg jurisprudence. Some people are concerned by the development by the Strasbourg Court of its own jurisprudence. The Strasbourg adopts what is known as evolutive or dynamic interpretation. The language of the Convention is open-textured, and the Strasbourg Court gives it a dynamic interpretation so as to keep the Convention in line with present-day conditions. Strasbourg has, for example, to keep pace with changes in technology, such as the storage of DNA. Lord Hoffmann, for instance, criticizes the liberal way in which the Strasbourg Court interprets the Convention. However, if Parliament does not like some development of the jurisprudence by the

---

[41] See *The Relations between the Constitutional Courts and the other National Courts including Interference in this Area of the action of the European Courts*, General Reports to the XIIth Conference of European Constitutional Courts, May 2002 (2002) 23 HRLJ 304 at 327.

[42] Görgülü BVerfGE 111. See further Hans-Jürgen Papier, 'Execution and Effects of the Judgments of the European Court of Human Rights from the perspective of German National Courts' [2006] 27 HMLJ 1.

[43] [2008] UKHL 57, [2009] AC 367.

Strasbourg Court, it is always open to pass primary legislation preventing our domestic courts from giving effect to the development. It will then be for the government to justify the course in Strasbourg. In appropriate cases, the Strasbourg Court should be willing to reconsider its jurisprudence. That still leaves the Strasbourg Court in the driving seat, but that position is inevitable, short of an amendment to the Convention.

What about dialogue with the Luxembourg Court? My view is that this is also very important as a way of achieving the best means of supranational adjudication. The judges of the national courts ought to be able to contribute to a debate on the key developments, but it is difficult to do so unless the judgments are more expansive, a point to which I return below.

(2) More subsidiarity

Subsidiarity for this purpose is the principle that a central authority should have a subsidiary function, performing only those tasks that cannot be performed effectively at a more immediate or local level.[44] It inevitably follows from subsidiarity that it is recognized that there can be a diversity of solutions to a particular problem.

Subsidiarity is consistent with democracy, and with the right of the individual to self-realization reflected in Art 8 of the Convention. This means that, so far as practical, decisions should be taken by the appropriate authorities in the areas most affected by those decisions. Examining the degree to which the supranational courts implement the principle of subsidiarity is therefore one way of testing my fourth benchmark for the supranational courts: respect for the role of national courts. Strasbourg jurisprudence and Luxembourg jurisprudence both have a principle called subsidiarity but they approach the concept differently and in each there is, in my view, room for expansion.

Although the ultimate rationale for subsidiarity is the same in both Strasbourg jurisprudence and Luxembourg jurisprudence, it has been developed in different ways and therefore it has to be examined separately in relation to the Strasbourg Court and the Luxembourg Court.

In Strasbourg jurisprudence, the doctrine of subsidiarity is well established. The Strasbourg Court is not a 'fourth instance'. Its role is supervisory. In general domestic remedies must be exhausted before any application can be made.

An allied doctrine is the doctrine of the margin of appreciation. The expression 'margin of appreciation' is used to describe those cases where the Strasbourg Court recognizes that the domestic authorities are in the best position to decide on measures in a particular area. The Strasbourg Court has held that there is a margin of appreciation in cases where the contracting state has asserted a derogation in times of a public emergency, or where there is a question of, for example, morals or the length of statutes of limitation on which there is no consensus among the member states. The doctrine is often controversial. Some feel that having a doctrine

---

[44] Oxford English Dictionary.

of margin of appreciation effectively compromises the role of the Strasbourg Court as the guardian of human rights because it leaves it to the national authorities to provide remedies, and they may fail to do so. After all, the most serious cases about breaches of human rights arise because the rights of some unpopular minority have been infringed.

But the margin of appreciation is not solely about the protection of rights. It is also about the competence of national institutions. The margin of appreciation ought not to be just about cases where there is no consensus in the contracting states. It is also about comparative institutional competence.[45] This aspect of the doctrine of the margin of appreciation should be recognized and developed. It is again relevant to my fourth benchmark: respect for the role of national courts.

National courts have to use the headroom permitted by the margin of appreciation specifically on a national basis. The self-denying ordinance in *Ullah* has no application when the national court is dealing with a case which falls within its margin of appreciation. As Baroness Hale pointed out in *Re G*,[46] Strasbourg jurisprudence is no help in this situation and our courts have to form their own judgment. If a matter falls within the margin of appreciation, and there is no legislation in place the courts have to exercise a delicate judgment as to whether the matter should be determined by the courts or by Parliament. The courts do not have power to determine the content of rights in a particular situation simply because a matter falls within the margin of appreciation.

My view is that subsidiarity, including margin of appreciation, is a concept which the Strasbourg Court should develop in its jurisprudence. It should also build on the idea of subsidiarity in another direction. The Strasbourg Court has a daunting burden of work. In 2008, the Strasbourg Court issued 30,200 decisions but it received 50,000 applications, increasing its backlog of cases to 97,000.[47] Some of these cases may be capable of being dismissed summarily as manifestly ill-founded. However, that would still leave a large residue. The only solution, as I see it, is to share the load with the national courts: however distasteful it may be to a human rights court, the Strasbourg Court should, at least until matters improve, seek to focus on the more important cases and leave the cases which are less important to be dealt with by the national courts without further recourse to the Strasbourg Court even if the litigant is dissatisfied with the result. There would have to be a clear definition of which cases were less important to contracting states in general, and the Strasbourg Court would have to have a discretion, but the definition ought to exclude cases which raise issues in areas of law where there is already a clear and constant case law, and with which the national courts ought to be able to deal. The Strasbourg Court might be able to use its 'pilot judgment'

---

[45] See for example, the speech of Lord Hope in *R (Kebiline) v Director of Public Prosecutions* [1999] UKHL 43, [2000] 2 AC 326 at 380–1.

[46] [2008] UKHL 38, [2009] 1 AC 73 at [120] and [121].

[47] Speech by President Jean-Paul Costa printed in *Dialogue between Judges*, European Court of Human Rights, 2009 at p 84.

procedure for this purpose. Excluding these cases would enable the Strasbourg Court to focus on areas of its jurisprudence that most call for its special expertise.

For the Luxembourg Court, subsidiarity can be seen as a form of proportionality review but it should also be seen as a separate principle since it forms the basis of a specific principle inserted by the Maastricht Treaty, which provides that EU institutions will not take any action which goes beyond what is necessary to achieve the objectives of the European Treaties.[48] But the principle has hardly been explored as yet by the Luxembourg Court. The principle is important because it recognizes the competence of member states.[49] It helps to create a corridor between what member states do and what EU institutions do. In any given case, however, it may be difficult for the Luxembourg Court to decide whether something could be effectively achieved by measures taken at the level of the member states. Even where this is so, the Luxembourg Court should insist upon strict review of any measure where the European Union view on this is challenged by a member state. This would be a practical way of fulfilling its role as a supranational court in ensuring respect for national institutions.

(3) More temporal limitations

I have a particular interest in this subject as I wrote a note on it in the *Law Quarterly Review*,[50] which led to counsel arguing before the House of Lords in *Re Spectrum Plus Ltd (in liquidation)*[51] that English law permitted the courts in an appropriate case to impose temporal limitations, that is, to direct that the effect of the order of the court should not have retrospective effect, but only prospective effect. There are many variants on the form of order that can be made.

Constitutional courts in other parts of the world have developed the doctrine. In an appropriate case, they declare that a particular act is unconstitutional, but that, if Parliament enacts legislation within a certain period, the order of the court will not come into effect.

The Luxembourg Court frequently acts as a constitutional court although it does not always say so. The government affected sometimes asks for a limitation on the effect of the order so that it is not fully retrospective. However, temporal limitations are only rarely imposed. It is generally not enough to show that the decision will have harsh financial consequences, such as having to meet claims going back over a substantial period of time, sometimes back to 1973. Generally, the Luxembourg Court takes the view that the interpretation which it gives to a provision of EU law clarifies and defines the meaning and scope of that provision as it should have been understood and applied from the time of its entry into force. For there to be a

---

[48] Now Art 5(3) of the TEU. This provision has been strengthened by the provisions of the Lisbon Treaty. The Lisbon Treaty enables a percentage of national parliaments to object to the Commission taking new measures in a particular area.

[49] And, where appropriate, the competence of their devolved administrations: see *Horvath v Secretary of State for the Environment, Food and Rural Affairs* (Case C-428/07) [2009] ECR I-6355.

[50] 'Prospective Overruling' (2004) 120 LQR 7. (Reproduced at Chapter 17.)

[51] [2005] UKHL 41, [2005] 2 AC 680.

temporal limitation, it considers that two essential criteria must be fulfilled, namely that those concerned should have acted in good faith and that there should be a risk of serious difficulties. The former condition may be satisfied by showing that the Commission led the party liable to a wrong belief as to the effect of European law. It can be difficult to satisfy this condition.

Some of the rulings of the Luxembourg Court have a seismic impact on national systems. Temporal limitations should be imposed more frequently where the Luxembourg Court makes a substantial change in the law. If the national court wishes to do so, it can make the point that consideration should be given to temporal limitations in its order for reference, explaining its view.

The Strasbourg Court has from time to time imposed temporal limitations but in the normal course it will be much less easy for it to do so as it will simply be dealing with the instant case and not with its impact on the domestic legal system. Nonetheless, there may be cases where, consistently with justice and subsidiarity, a temporal limitation should be imposed.

(4) Clearer judgments

The Luxembourg Court is probably very tired of common law courts making this point but it is an important one. The Luxembourg Court only issues single judgments. Judgments of the Luxembourg Court are often brief and contain little reasoning. Because they are single judgments, they are impersonal: no room for analogies with Cinderella or her slipper here! The Luxembourg Court frequently says that something follows when it does not follow and there is in fact a large and unexplained development in the law. Cases are referred to which are clearly not being followed and it is not distinctly said that they are being overruled.[52] What often prevails is some rather general EU law principle, like effectiveness. There should be dissenting judgments. When the Luxembourg Court fails to issue a judgment that is clear, it is not being transparent, and it does not meet the benchmark, which I have identified above, about the quality of reasoning.

But the point I am making goes beyond form: it is also a point about the substance of Luxembourg judgments. We need to encourage the Luxembourg Court to have a better debate in their judgments on the key thematic issues in EU law. The Luxembourg Court rarely discusses the constitutional ramifications or policy considerations of its decisions. If it did this more often, national courts could engage with these issues and make a contribution to their solution. What is often not appreciated is that, in jurisdictions like our own where there is no form of constitutional review, when the Luxembourg Court makes decisions which are effectively constitutional decisions the impression is given that constitutional decisions are being imposed on our jurisdiction without any scope for national debate before our national courts. That is a factor which can lead to hostility towards the institutions of the European Union.

---

[52] See, for example, *Cadman v Health & Safety Executive* (Case C-17/05).

For the Strasbourg Court, clarity of judgments is also sometimes an issue. We should continue to press the Strasbourg Court to maintain high standards in its judgments. Acceptance of its jurisprudence by the contracting states depends on the clarity of its jurisprudence. However, there is a partial remedy in the 14th Protocol in that Committee of Ministers will be able to refer cases back to the Strasbourg Court for clarification.

Conclusions

What I have sought to do in this paper is to pose some questions about what makes for effective supranational adjudication by our European supranational courts. I have sought also to put forward some criteria for assessing their work on a principled basis. It is in our own self-interest to think more structurally about the relationship of the national supreme courts and the European supranational courts. We should not allow the European supranational courts to revolve in their own orbit as if they occupied a separate planetary system. We want some influence on them, as the destiny of our legal system is now tied up with them.

Building a successful European system of supranational courts will also provide a model for other parts of the world and will help maintain the rule of law internationally.[53]

So to conclude. We have obtained substantial benefits from the Luxembourg jurisprudence and Strasbourg jurisprudence. So have other countries within Europe. Accordingly, the relationship has been beneficial and peaceful. However, for the reasons given in this paper, the relationship is also problematic. I have identified a number of practical issues and suggested solutions for how to manage the relationship to achieve the most effective system.

Where do we go from here? How should these ideas be taken forward? We shall have to wait and see. As the title of this paper suggests, the strategy for a national court may well be one which should be spearheaded by its supreme court. I look forward to seeing whether the new Supreme Court of the United Kingdom rises to the challenge.

---

[53] See generally Sir Francis Jacobs, *The Sovereignty of Law* (Cambridge University Press, 2006). I would like to thank Sir Francis Jacobs for our discussion on an early draft of this paper.

19

Jurisdiction of the New UK Supreme Court

This chapter is based on a paper first published in 2004.*

One of the objects of the Constitutional Reform Bill, which, at the time of writing this paper, is before Parliament, is to set up a new UK Supreme Court.

The general policy of the Bill in this regard is to transfer to the new UK Supreme Court the existing jurisdiction of the Appellate Committee of the House of Lords and the devolution jurisdiction of the Privy Council. In its report,[1] the Select Committee of the House of Lords on the Constitutional Reform Bill made no recommendation to the House about replacing the Appellate Committee with a UK Supreme Court. Nonetheless, it went on to consider certain specific issues about the new Supreme Court, such as the question whether it should have jurisdiction generally over Scottish criminal appeals, and whether permission should be required for Scottish civil appeals.

There are anomalies in both these fields. Apart from these matters, there was no discussion of the new Supreme Court's jurisdiction. However, further questions do arise as to the jurisdiction of the new UK Supreme Court in relation to EC law. The purpose of this note is to explore one or two of those questions.

The first question is that of jurisdiction to determine the ambit of EC law. The European Court of Justice[2] has jurisdiction to determine the legality under the EC Treaties of measures adopted by Community institutions and to give rulings generally on the interpretation of the EC Treaties.[3] Moreover, EC law has primacy over domestic law.[4] The obligations of the United Kingdom in respect of the EC Treaties have been incorporated into our domestic law by or pursuant to the European Communities Act 1972. Section 2(1) of the 1972 Act[5] provides:

(1) All such rights, powers, liabilities, obligations and restrictions from time to time created or arising by or under the Treaties, and all such remedies and procedures from time to time provided for by or under the Treaties, as in accordance with the Treaties are without further

---

* First published in (2004) PL 699. It is reproduced here with the kind permission of the Publisher.
[1] First Report (2003–04 HL 125-I).
[2] Now the Court of Justice of the European Union ('CJEU').   [3] Article 234 EC.
[4] *R v Secretary of State for Transport Ex p Factortame Ltd* [1991] 1 AC 603, ECJ.
[5] As amended by the European Communities (Amendment) Act 1986, s 2(a).

enactment to be given legal effect or used in the United Kingdom shall be recognised and available in law, and be enforced, allowed and followed accordingly...

Section 2(4) provides that:

[A]ny enactment passed or to be passed... shall be construed and have effect subject to the foregoing provisions of this section.

Section 3(1) provides that:

(1) For the purposes of all legal proceedings any question as to the meaning or effect of any of the Treaties, or as to the validity, meaning or effect of any Community instrument, shall be treated as a question of law (and, if not referred to the European Court, be for determination as such in accordance with the principles laid down by and any relevant decision of the European Court or any court attached thereto).

Other member states of the European Union are in a different position from the United Kingdom. Some of them are 'monist' systems in which the executive has power to cause their state to accede to an EC Treaty which becomes part of domestic law without domestic legislation. In their case, accession may give rise to a potential conflict in the state's domestic law between the domestic written constitution and a treaty. This may not have been addressed by a constitutional amendment at the time of accession.

Thus, for example, notwithstanding any treaty obligation of Germany, German troops cannot be committed to a NATO or UN peacekeeping operation without the agreement of the Bundestag, because that is what the German Constitution requires.[6] Under the proposed new constitutional treaty for the European Union, commonly known as the 'European Constitution', provision is made for a common security and defence policy.[7] This will provide the Union:

... with an operational capacity drawing on assets civil and military. The Union may use them on missions outside the Union for peace-keeping, conflict prevention and strengthening international security in accordance with the principles of the United Nations charter.[8]

Thus, in theory at least, if the Union decided to send a detachment of troops, including German troops, outside the European Union, a question could arise whether the process was in conformity with the German Constitution.

At first sight, this would be a question of the interpretation of the German Constitution. But others might say that the relevant question was one of the validity of the acts of an institution of the European Union. There would then

---

[6] Second Senat July 12, 1994—2BvE 3/92, 2 BvE 5/93, 2 BvE 7/93 and BvE 8/93 Karlsruhe, July 12, 1994.

[7] The European Constitution was not in the event adopted but in 2007 the member states of the EU adopted the Lisbon Treaty, which amended the EC Treaty. The common security and security policy remains largely outside the jurisdiction of the CJEU: see Art 275 of the Treaty on the Functioning of the EU (TFEU).

[8] Art 1–40. All references to the European Constitution are to the provisional consolidated version of the draft Treaty establishing a Constitution for Europe (CIG 86/04, 25 June 2004).

be an issue of who decides the legality of the acts of the Union. Under German law, it would appear to be the position, under a doctrine known as *Kompetenz-Kompetenz*, that the German national courts would be the final arbiter if a conflict between the German constitution and EC law arose.[9] No doubt the German Constitutional Court would seek to avoid any such conflict. However, the possibility of such a conflict exists, and it exists even without the new European Constitution. The risk may, however, be increased by the adoption of the European Constitution, particularly in areas such as the common foreign and security policy where the jurisdiction of the European Court of Justice is excluded.[10]

In this regard, the United Kingdom may be in a different position because it has no written constitution and the European Communities Act 1972 provides so seamlessly for the primacy of EC law. But there is a question worth debating whether the United Kingdom should be in any different position.

Lord Bridge may have had this point in mind when in *Factortame (No 2)*[11] he referred to 'according supremacy to rules of Community law in those areas to which they apply'. The courts have in any event left open for future consideration by them whether:

[I]f some particular European measure is brought into being under the powers of the Treaty of Nice, there could be a question whether it is so offensive to our domestic constitutional law that the general words of section 2(2) of the European Communities Act 1972 are insufficient to incorporate it.[12]

A committee of the House of Lords has considered the question of the relationship between the UK courts and EC law. This question was considered by the European Union Committee of the House of Lords in its report on *The Future of the European Court of Justice*.[13] It concluded:

88. Recognition of the effects of the Community's legal order and rules of Community law depends fundamentally on their acceptance by national courts. National constitutional/supreme courts are unlikely to relinquish their fundamental role as judicial guardian of their constitutions. That position is little different in the case of the United Kingdom, even though we do not have a written constitution, at least in the sense that that term is generally understood, or a constitutional court as such.

89. It is clear from the terms of the European Communities Act, and the judgments of our courts, that our courts should follow all rulings of the Court on matters which have been delegated through the Treaties. The scope of that delegation is in the first instance for the Court to construe. But the jurisdiction of our domestic courts is not necessarily excluded. We do not dismiss the possibility of the argument being advanced that Parliament, when

---

[9] German Constitutional Court, Maastricht judgment, 12 October 1993, BVerfGE 89 p 155, *Brunner v The European Union Treaty* (1994) 69(2) CMLR 57.

[10] Art 1–40 and Art III-282. The common security and defence policy is a part of the common foreign and security policy. See also n 7.

[11] *R v Secretary of State for Transport Ex p Factortame Ltd (No 2)* [1991] 1 AC 603.

[12] *R (McWhirter) v Secretary of State for Foreign and Commonwealth Affairs* [2003] EWCA Civ 384 (Laws LJ). Laws LJ added: 'That would be a question for the future. I decide nothing about it today.'

[13] Sixth Report (2003–04 HL 47).

referring, in section 2(1) of the ECA, to rights, powers etc. 'created or arising under the Treaties' under which the Community only has such powers as have been conferred upon Member States did not, notwithstanding Section 3(1), intend the final definition of those powers to be determined by the Court, a body itself dependent on the Treaties for its existence and powers. In short, Parliament did not hand over a blank cheque, legally or politically. The Government should set out their view on the *Kompetenz-Kompetenz* question clearly to Parliament and to citizens in the UK. This could go a long way in assuring the public that the Union is not some Frankenstein creation over which there may be little or no control . . .

91. The scope for the new Supreme Court to adjudicate on the reach of Union law may need to be considered further and possibly defined in the legislation establishing the new court.

For its part, the recent report of the Select Committee of the House of Lords on the Constitutional Reform Bill, which (as explained) will when enacted establish the new UK Supreme Court, did not consider 'the scope for the new Supreme Court to adjudicate on the reach of' EC law. Moreover, it is to be noted from the passages quoted above that the European Union Committee considered that the new Supreme Court might indeed already have this scope under the European Communities Act 1972. However, the issue remains for public debate and resolution.

The converse of the question considered above (and the second of the two questions raised by this paper) is whether, under the European Constitution, the jurisdiction of the UK courts, and the Supreme Court in particular, would need to be extended to cover questions of EC law over which the European Court of Justice has no jurisdiction. The European Committee considered this point too, taking again the example of the common security and defence policy. If the European Court of Justice has no jurisdiction on a particular issue, national courts would have to determine questions arising with respect to that issue, provided that they in turn have jurisdiction. Suppose a person is detained by a military force used by the Union outside the territory of the Union. He (like the Guantanamo Bay detainees) may seek a determination as to the legality of his detention. The European Court of Justice would have no jurisdiction.[14] In some circumstances, the European Court of Human Rights in Strasbourg may have jurisdiction.[15] National courts may or may not have jurisdiction under their own domestic law.

The European Committee warned that:

Recent events, including the detention of individuals at Guantanamo Bay, show that the rights of the individual may be seriously affected in the execution of foreign policy. The Union is becoming increasingly involved in peace-keeping operations and the possibility cannot be ruled out that challenges may be brought on human rights grounds in relation to the particular conduct of those acting in the name of the Union.

The European Committee invited the Government:

---

[14] See n 8 above.
[15] See eg *Bankovic v Belgium* (2001) 11 BHRC 435.

... to reflect on the problems to which maintenance of this position [the exclusion of the jurisdiction of the European Court of Justice in relation to the common foreign and security policy] could give rise, bearing in mind the need to safeguard the fundamental rights of the individual.

Whether there is a real problem here for detainees held by an EU force which includes British troops may depend on the detailed arrangements made for the command of those troops. If the United Kingdom retains control over the troops, habeas corpus may well be available.[16] But it would be unfortunate if it were discovered that there was a problem here only after the situation had arisen. Consideration should be given to this problem now.

For these reasons, the relationship between a new UK Supreme Court and EC law needs further thought and discussion. It would be a pity if, after a hard fought battle, the Supreme Court is established but future generations come to regret that these issues were not thought out and resolved.

---

[16] *Ex p Mwenya* [1960] 1 QB 241.

20
An English Judge in Europe

This chapter is based on the Neill Lecture given in Oxford at the invitation of All Souls College, Oxford, on 28 February 2014 in celebration of the past Wardenship of Lord Neill of Bladen.

Introduction

Lord Denning famously observed in 1974 of the treaty then constituting the European Union that:

But when we come to matters with a European element, the treaty is like an incoming tide. It flows into the estuaries and up the rivers. It cannot be held back. Parliament has decreed that the treaty is henceforward to be part of our law. It is equal in force to any statute. The governing provision is s 2(1) of the European Communities Act 1972. The statute . . . is expressed in forthright terms which are absolute and all-embracing. Any rights or obligations created by the treaty are to be given legal effect in England without more ado. Any remedies or procedures provided by the treaty are to be made available here without being open to question. In future, in transactions which cross the frontiers, we must no longer speak or think of English law as something on its own. We must speak and think of Community law, of Community rights and obligations, and we must give effect to them. This means a great effort for the lawyers. We have to learn a new system. The treaty, with the regulations and directives, covers many volumes. The case law is contained in hundreds of reported cases both in the European Court of Justice . . . We must get down to it.[1]

The same sort of point could today be made about human rights law as interpreted by the European Court of Human Rights in Strasbourg. It re-interprets rights guaranteed by the European Convention on Human Rights (the 'Convention') and renders decisions which, as critics point out, often go far beyond what was envisaged when the Convention was signed in 1950.

Flooding was sadly very topical in the winter of 2014. It is a graphic image that Lord Denning created. But there was no hint of fear or of being overwhelmed.

---

[1] *H P Bulmer Ltd and another v J Bollinger SA and others* [1974] 2 All ER 1226 at 1232–3. A few years later, however, Lord Denning MR compared the doctrine of direct effect to flooding above the high water mark. He said: 'All this shows that the flowing tide of Community law is coming in fast. It has not stopped at high-water mark. It has broken the dykes and the banks. It has submerged the surrounding land. So much so that we have to learn to become amphibious if we wish to keep our heads above water' (*Shields v E Coomes (Holdings) Ltd* [1979] 1 All ER 456 at 462).

Simply an injunction that 'we have to learn a new system' and that 'we must get down to it'. I intend to do both those things in this paper.

More particularly, my aim in this paper is to stand back and look at the architecture of the European legal scene as it has developed and stands in 2014. By European legal scene, I mean the principal national courts in Europe and their relationship with the supranational courts in the European Court of Human Rights (the 'Strasbourg Court') and the Court of Justice of the European Union (the 'Luxembourg Court'). I shall talk mainly about Strasbourg, but I shall refer also to Luxembourg. I call them 'supranational' courts as these courts are not merely transnational, that is, courts which transcend a state's boundaries, but they are also in themselves international organizations under which contracting states have agreed to share in the decision-making.

I do not propose to argue for or against membership of the European Union or being a contracting party to the Convention: those are political questions. Judges have to give effect to the law as it stands and I will assume that the law will remain as it stands simply because that is what we have to implement. But, in my professional capacity, I have obtained some important insights into the role of the supranational courts which I want to share. Out of court, I fulfil, under the Lord Chief Justice's overall direction, the work of Head of International Judicial Relations for England and Wales. This paper, however, represents—for better or worse—my own thoughts based on my own experience, and I do not express any views in an official or representative capacity.

I have a few more points to make by way of introduction before I come to my main theme. It is my view—just as it was Lord Denning's—that we have much to learn by looking at some foreign systems of law in any event. By looking abroad we can in my view learn to do a better job at home. The courts used to take it for granted that advocates would, where appropriate, cite foreign texts. This happened, for example, in *Hadley v Baxendale*,[2] which is the leading authority on the measure of damages in contract.

In that case, the iron shaft of the plaintiff's flour mill broke and the plaintiffs consigned it to the defendant carrier for delivery to the repairer. The carrier delayed unreasonably so that the plaintiffs lost profits while their mill was shut, but they had not told the carrier that that would happen. It was held that they could not recover damages for these profits. The decision establishes that the damages should be such as may 'fairly and reasonably be considered either arising naturally, i.e., according to the usual course of things' from the breach of contract or 'such as may reasonably be supposed to have been in the contemplation of both parties, at the time they made the contract, as the probable result of the breach of it' (per Alderson B, giving the judgment of the court). It is noteworthy that in the course of the argument Parke B interposed to say that the sensible rule appeared to be that which had been laid down in France and which was indeed the *Code Civil*, which he proceeded to quote in translation. There was a discussion of the American

---

[2] (1854) 9 Ex 341.

authorities and counsel submitted that the English courts should follow those decisions. There is nothing to suggest that the use of comparative law in *Hadley v Baxendale* was exceptional. On the contrary, it seems a perfectly natural part of the argument in the case. It leads one to believe that in the 19th century and possibly earlier it was commonplace for the English courts to look for inspiration to systems overseas.

With the burden of work we may have lost a little of that inquiring mind when it comes to foreign law. We need in my view to find out what we can about other systems in order to strengthen our own law, and we need to be able to promote the value of our common law among others so that it inspires transnational law.

The Luxembourg Court's primary responsibility is to give interpretations of the European Treaties and EU legislation. EU law has primacy over domestic law in areas of competence conferred by member states on the EU.[3]

EU law is made binding in English law by s 2 of the European Communities Act 1972, to which Lord Denning referred. On the face of it, as he said, it is absolute. American lawyers would say it was the equivalent of the supremacy clause in the US constitution which governs the relationship between the states and the federal government.[4]

The function of the Strasbourg Court is authoritatively to interpret the European Convention on Human Rights. It hears cases mainly on individual petitions from persons within the territory of the contracting states. There are 47 contracting states which are parties to the Council of Europe as opposed to 27 members of the European Union. The protection provided by Strasbourg stretches from Ireland in the west to Vladivostok in the east. Its rulings affect about 800 million people.

The Convention is given effect in English law by the Human Rights Act 1998.[5] The principal provision for my purposes is s 2(1):

(1) A court . . . determining a question which has arisen in connection with a Convention right must take into account any—

(a) judgment, decision, declaration or advisory opinion of the European Court of Human Rights . . .

This obligation is far less 'muscular' than s 2 of the European Communities Act 1972. It had to be. One of the reasons why the Human Rights Act refers to 'tak[ing] account' of Strasbourg jurisprudence is that, unlike the European Communities Act, the Human Rights Act does not provide for the wholesale incorporation of Strasbourg case law: it merely enables effect to be given to Convention

---

[3] See, for example, *R v Secretary of State for Transport ex parte Factortame Ltd* [1991] 1 AC 603.

[4] 'This Constitution, and the Laws of the United States which shall be made in pursuance thereof; and all treaties made, or which shall be made, under the authority of the United States, shall be the supreme law of the land; and the judges in every state shall be bound thereby, anything in the constitution or laws of any state to the contrary notwithstanding.' US Constitution, article 6(2).

[5] The Convention rights incorporated by the Human Rights Act 1998 and the principal provisions of that Act are set out in the Appendix, together with Arts 1 and 13 of the Convention which were not incorporated by that Act.

rights when they do not conflict with the clearly expressed will of Parliament or when they did not conflict with primary legislation from Parliament.[6]

The Convention has an important place in the world. Since the Convention was signed, many national constitutions have included rights in terms of those set out in the Convention, including constitutions of countries outside Europe. That gives you some idea of the global importance of the Convention.

No one can doubt the enormous achievements of the Strasbourg Court in interpreting the Convention rights.[7] The Convention has helped to change the culture in many European countries. For example, in the United Kingdom, the Political Parties, Elections and Referendums Act 2000 brought the laws on campaign funding for non-party campaigners up to date after the Strasbourg Court held in *Bowman v UK*[8] that the United Kingdom had violated freedom of expression by limiting such funding to £5.

A remarkable book of essays has been published about the first decade of implementation in Russia.[9] You may think this is just propaganda, but it is unexpected to find President Valery Zorkin, the President of the Constitutional Court in the Russian Federation describing the steps that have been taken by his court to give effect to Strasbourg jurisprudence. He explains, for instance, how '[by] referring, in its [reasons], to the Convention, to its provisions and their interpretation by [the Strasbourg Court], the Constitutional Court implants them directly into the "tissue" of the Russian legal system'. Russia is not known for its participation in dialogue about human rights. Things may be moving even there.

I must immediately get one issue out of the way. The Strasbourg and Luxembourg Courts, like any other court, do not always get it right. In his Essex lecture, Lord Dyson MR powerfully explained how the Strasbourg Court had effectively reversed its earlier case law on Art 1 of the Convention (which states that the Convention applies to persons within the jurisdiction of the contracting states). In the result, contracting states have increasingly been held responsible for acts which occur outside their own territory but where they have control over others.[10] Shortly before that speech, the Strasbourg Court delivered another decision on the same subject in which it suggested that, in the light of developments in international law,

---

[6] See, generally, Human Rights Act 1998, ss 3 and 4, and see *Ghaidan v Godin-Mendoza* [2004] UKHL 30, [2004] 2 AC 557. The Human Rights Act 1998 preserves Parliamentary sovereignty. In the opinion of the Joint Committee of the House of Lords and the House of Commons on the Draft Voting Eligibility (Prisoners) Bill, Parliamentary sovereignty is not an argument against giving effect to a Strasbourg judgment. Parliament remains sovereign but that sovereignty resides in Parliament's power to withdraw from the Convention (HL paper 103 HC 924 16 December 2013 at pp 64–5).

[7] See, generally, *The Conscience of Europe, 50 years of the European Court of Human Rights* (Strasbourg, 2010), ch 13.

[8] (Application No 24839/94) (1998) 26 EHRR 1, 4 BHRC 25.

[9] Olga Chernishove and Mikhail Lobov (eds), *Russia and the European Court of Human Rights: a Decade of Change*, essays in honour of Anatoly Kovler, judge of the European Court of Human Rights in 1999–2012 (Wolf Legal Publishers, 2014), 27–38.

[10] *The Extraterritorial Application of the European Convention on Human Rights: Now on a Firmer Footing but is it a Sound One?* 30 January 2014, <http://www.judiciary.gov.uk/wp-content/uploads/JCO/Documents/Speeches/lord-dyson-speech-extraterritorial-reach-echr-300114.pdf>.

it might in the future have to consider whether sovereign immunity in civil proceedings concerning torture was compatible with the Convention.[11]

Some may question whether the Strasbourg Court has taken a wrong turn in relation to extraterritoriality. One of the consequences of this developing case law is that, even where the Geneva Conventions apply to the contracting state's acts, it may be additionally responsible under the Convention for acts outside its own territory. As I said in *Al-Jedda v Secretary of State*,[12] before the latest developments in Strasbourg:

If courts hold states liable in damages when they comply with resolutions of the UN designed to secure international peace and security, the likelihood is that states will be less ready to assist the UN achieve its role in this regard, and this would be detrimental to the long-term interests of the states . . . It is thus not correct to say that the executive had unfettered powers of internment. A decision of the executive in breach of [the Fourth Geneva Convention of 1949] can be remedied in this jurisdiction through the processes of judicial review, and a breach may also constitute a criminal offence over which the United Kingdom courts would have universal jurisdiction under the Geneva Conventions Act 1957.

I took the view, therefore, that the Convention jurisprudence on detentions should not bind contracting states in areas already policed by the Geneva Conventions. Peace-keeping troops often are drawn from various countries, many of whom will not be parties to the Convention. Strasbourg jurisprudence may create practical difficulties for joint operations between Convention and non-Convention states in the future, which is not in anyone's interest. If I am right in this, Strasbourg jurisprudence may impede, not promote, international humanitarian law.

Let me give you an example of the Strasbourg Court demonstrably taking the wrong path. In *Osman v UK*,[13] the Strasbourg Court held that the decision of an English court that a public authority did not owe a duty of care to a victim of its negligence was effectively to give that part of the state an immunity and that was contrary to the right of access to court in Art 6 of the Convention. But the duty of care is a fundamental step in the reasoning whereby liability in negligence is imposed under English law. English law is very unlike civil law in this respect. In civil law systems, liability is often imposed on a public authority for its incompetence although the compensation awarded will tend to be lower than in England and Wales. I was appointed an ad hoc judge of the Strasbourg Court for a case from England which raised the identical issue: *Z v UK*.[14] The important point for

---

[11] *Jones v UK* (Application Nos 3456/06 and 40528/06), where the applicant complained of a violation of Art 6 of the Convention because his proceedings for damages for torture in the English court against a foreign state had been struck out on the grounds of sovereign immunity: *Jones v Saudi Arabia* [2006] UKHL 26, [2007] 1 AC 270. The Grand Chamber held that a state did not violate Art 6 of the Convention by granting immunity to officials of a foreign sovereign state alleged to have been involved in acts of torture but that, in view of developments in international law, contracting states needed to keep the matter under review (at para 215).

[12] [2010] EWCA Civ 758, [2011] QB 773.

[13] Application No 87/9997/871/1083 [1998] 5 BHRC 293.

[14] Application No 29392/95 [2001] 2 FCR 246.

present purposes is that the Strasbourg Court took careful note of the criticisms that were made of its decision in *Osman*. It reconsidered its earlier decision and accepted that the determination of the English court that a public authority did not owe a duty of care was simply part of the process whereby substantive national law was applied. This decision demonstrated a very important characteristic of Strasbourg case law—its *plasticity*, its genuine desire to respond to the needs of the contracting states' legal systems, in other words its *receptivity* of the need for change. *Receptivity* is the Strasbourg Court's coping strategy, and we would do well to remember this. The *plasticity* of Strasbourg case law is a cause to celebrate. The Strasbourg Court absorbs ideas from the legal systems of contracting states and it is capable of adapting itself when need arises. *Plasticity* is a point I shall come back to at the end of this paper.

A unique feature of the Convention system is that the judgments of the Strasbourg Court are implemented by a peaceful process. The Universal Declaration of Human Rights, for instance, has no similar process. Decisions of the Strasbourg Court are implemented through the Committee of Ministers of the Council of Europe. That means that, if there is a violation by one contracting state, other countries represented on the Committee of Ministers may expect to receive reports from it as to when the violation will be remedied and it will apply pressure to see that it is done. The process is the same for all the contracting states.

What the Convention, therefore, gives is *the collective right to intervene* in the internal affairs of another sovereign state via the Committee of Ministers of the Council of Europe.

Ought this intrusive process of implementation to be a matter of concern to a country like the United Kingdom? The figures alone would suggest not. In 2013, for instance, out of 1,652 applications against the United Kingdom, Strasbourg gave only eight judgments holding that the United Kingdom had violated the Convention, as opposed to 28 against France.[15]

Strasbourg's dynamic interpretation of the Convention is known as the 'living instrument' theory. Lord Phillips described this in his lecture in Oxford.[16] It means that in determining the scope of a right Strasbourg has regard to changing conditions. It laid down the principle in *Tyrer v UK*[17] when it declared that birching was inhuman and degrading treatment contrary to Art 3 of the Convention even though that would not have been thought to be the position when the Convention was signed in 1950. In terms of principle (though probably not the scale), this does not differ from the dynamic way in which our own courts tend to interpret open-textured legislation.

But there are concerns about Strasbourg's living instrument theory. What sometimes upsets people is the unpredictability of the dynamic interpretation:

---

[15] *The ECHR in Facts and Figures 2013*, issued by the European Court on Human Rights.
[16] 'The Elastic Jurisdiction of the European Court of Human Rights', Oxford, 12 February 2014.
[17] [1978] EHRR 1.

Strasbourg has brought within the Convention large areas of activity which would not have been considered to involve human rights in the past, such as night flights at Heathrow, which were held to fall within Art 8. Later in this paper I shall consider steps which would meet some of the criticisms that have been made of the living instrument theory.

On the ground, English judges are now very accustomed to deciding cases with many different systems of law. One can start at the level of devolution and deal with Welsh or Scottish or Northern Irish legislation. Then there is Westminster legislation, then there is legislation at the level of the European Union and the jurisprudence of the Court of Justice of the European Union. In the very same case you may have all these levels of law and in addition an issue as to human rights. The stratification of law reflects that in certain fields there are now many levels of governance today in Europe. I have in another place described this as 'multi-level judging'.

With that introduction, I want to turn to look at the architecture of the European legal scene with particular reference to the complications created by the presence of the two European supranational courts.

Architecture of the current European legal order

Both the Luxembourg and Strasbourg Courts are products of post-Second World War Europe. The Holocaust and the massive violations of human rights in Germany and other European countries that had taken place during the War and the years preceding it led the political leaders to realize that there had to be some way of intervening in a country's internal affairs when human rights violations occurred. This was the background against which the Council of Europe was set up and its main showpiece, the Convention, was signed.

The Council of Europe and the European Union are regional organizations empowered to perform certain tasks that the contracting states which are parties would formerly have made decisions about separately and individually. If we are going to understand the new European legal scene and the relationship between national and supranational courts, we have to recognize that the formation of these regional organizations of states represents a seismic shift away from the conventional notion of the nation state. It may seem obvious but, by grouping together, the states involved have agreed to work together in particular spheres. This necessarily has implications for the legal scene. It has inevitably been a step into a new world and into the unknown.

An interlinked world

Another major change in international affairs is that today we live in an interlinked world. If, for instance, Romania were to mistreat its Roma population, the Roma people might leave Romania in large numbers and seek to come to (say) France or the United Kingdom.[18] Likewise if there is political unrest in (say) Ukraine, and the authorities react in a way which does not respect the right of democratic protest or the human rights of the protesters, not only the people of Ukraine but investment in Ukraine may suffer and as a result the loss of confidence may spill over and affect foreign investment in a number of other related areas of Europe. That would be bad for trade and bad for the economy of the United Kingdom and Europe. No doubt many other examples could be given.

Some states will recognize that we do now live in an interlinked world, and they will therefore take the view that it is to their advantage to be parties to organizations such as the Council of Europe in order to have some influence over the internal affairs of another state. In the case of the membership of the Council of Europe, that influence is through the European Convention on Human Rights: visionaries like Churchill saw that this was a way of obtaining real and lasting peace in Europe. There is both a gaining and a loss of control: a gaining of power with the other member states to intervene in the internal affairs of another sovereign state, and at the same time a loss of control—those other member states may seek to intervene in one's own internal affairs and there is no control over decision-making. So the price of membership of a regional organization with its own judicial system is a certain inevitable loss of control over the formation of law by the supranational court. Each state is simply one of 47 member states and can only exercise a limited amount of influence.

Nation states are bound to respond differently to the major structural changes that have taken place in Europe, including the institution of the supranational courts.

How different courts have reacted to the role of the European supranational courts

It is inevitable and to be expected that there are tensions in this situation. There are now many countries which have experienced difficulties with the decisions of the Strasbourg Court. We are not alone in having the type of episode that occurred in *Z v UK*.

As I have said, different states may react in different ways to this dilemma. At one end of the scale will be those who either never join, or who react by withdrawing from the supranational systems which create additional complexity for the domestic system. By withdrawing from supranational systems, states simply have their own national law again. That would mean the end of the complex multi-level judging which our courts and others do today. That is the decision for the democratic

---

[18] There is considerable evidence of discrimination against the Roma throughout Europe. For example, according to figures published by the *Financial Times* on 25 February 2014 only approximately 1% of the Roma population in Greece receive the educational advantages received by 85% of the rest of the population. According to the same report, there are some 12–13m Roma in Europe, mainly in Romania, Bulgaria, and Hungary.

legislature of that member state to take, having weighed up the pluses and minuses and worked out what is in the national interest.

At the other end of the scale are those states that have no difficulty in participating. There are probably very few of those.

Many of the contracting states to the Convention are, however, positioned at various points along the scale. They have elected to be parties to the Convention, but have sought to accommodate the supranational system more closely to the national paradigm.

The best known example is Germany. I start with its approach towards the Luxembourg Court. In its famous *Solange I* ruling[19] in 1974, the German Federal Constitutional Court (FCC) held that it had the right to review the compatibility of EU law with the German constitution (known as the Basic Law), as long as the European Union does not have a catalogue of fundamental rights equivalent to rights guaranteed by the Basic Law. In its 1986 *Solange II* decision, impressed by the developing Luxembourg case law, the FCC modified its position.[20] It stated that, in the sphere of competence of the European Union, a standard of protection of fundamental rights had arisen that had to be deemed equal in substance to that provided by the Basic Law. The FCC further held that it would no longer review secondary EU law on the basis of the fundamental rights of the Basic Law, as long as the European Union generally ensured an efficient protection of fundamental rights against the authorities of the European Union deemed equal in substance to the protection of fundamental rights inalienably required by the Basic Law.

In one case,[21] the FCC considered aspects of the European Stability Mechanism (ESM) adopted by Eurozone countries in February 2012. It held that it could examine whether the authority of the European Central Bank under the ESM to purchase bonds of member states on the market was within the powers conferred by the EU treaties, and in addition whether the ESM was compatible with the Basic Law. It has announced that it has formed the view that there was more than one possible interpretation and that it proposes to request Luxembourg for a preliminary ruling on that matter. It also made it clear that a finding that the authority was outside the powers conferred by the EU treaties would lead to breaches of the Basic Law. This is a stark position in which the Luxembourg Court and the FCC might find themselves at odds. We shall have to see what is decided in Luxembourg.

The FCC initially adopted a similar position in relation to Strasbourg jurisprudence. However, in *M v Germany*,[22] a case concerning detention of prisoners after they had served their sentence (preventive detention) on the grounds that they were still a danger to the public, the FCC decided that the detention violated the Basic Law because the Strasbourg Court had held that such detention violated Arts 5 and 7 of the Convention and that should be taken into account, even though

---

[19] BVerfGE 37, 271.   [20] BVerfGE 73, 339.
[21] See Press Release No.9/2014 issued by the FCC on 7 February 2014.
[22] BVerfGE 128, 326. This was particularly significant because normally the first decision would have been a bar to any further proceedings regarding the same statutory provisions. In its judgment, the FCC approved the setting up of a new system of detention for dangerous persons and held that this new system was not in violation of the Convention.

Convention jurisprudence is of a lower status in German law than the Basic Law. Significantly, the FCC reversed an earlier decision that held that preventive detention was constitutional.

Another example is the approach of the Conseil d'Etat in France in relation to Luxembourg's decisions. In *Arcelor*,[23] the question arose whether an EU directive was consistent with the constitutional right of equality in the French constitution. The Conseil d'Etat formed the view that the EU principle of equality provided for equivalent protection but it referred to the Luxembourg Court the question whether the directive in question complied with the EU principle. The Luxembourg Court held that the directive complied with the EU principle of equality.[24] The Conseil d'Etat would not have enforced the EU measure unless it afforded equivalent protection to that available under domestic law.

Likewise, the Constitutional Tribunal of Poland has held that the Polish constitution has primacy over any other law, including EU measures, though both it and the Luxembourg Court would owe reciprocal obligations to avoid any conflict.[25]

I could give other examples. In short, a number of countries have laid down a marker that there will be a protected sphere in which the writ of Luxembourg or Strasbourg will not run. This is all a long way from s 2 of the European Communities Act 1972, which as construed by Lord Denning gives EU law absolute effect in the United Kingdom. EU law has been developed so that, if domestic law conflicts with EU law, the court must disapply it.[26]

The supranational courts may not particularly like the approach taken by courts such as the FCC, but, ironically, they take just the same approach when faced with challenges to their own boundaries, as I will now explain.

Kadi I[27] concerns the EU's implementation of the sanctions regime established by the UN Security Council. The nub of the Luxembourg Court's decision was that, even though the European Union is bound to respect international law and the UN Charter indirectly, given that the member states are subject to those sources of law, EU acts cannot infringe the European Union's own fundamental rights. The critical paragraph of the judgment specifies that international obligations:

[c]annot, however, be understood to authorise any derogation from the principles of liberty, democracy and respect for human rights and fundamental freedoms enshrined in article 6(1) EU as a foundation of the Union.[28]

---

[23] Conseil d'Etat: Decision No 287110 of 8 February 2007, *Société Arcelor Atlantique et Lorraine and others.*
[24] Case C-127/07.
[25] Case SK 45/09 of the Constitutional Tribunal of Poland, 16 November 2011.
[26] See n 6.
[27] *P Kadi and Al Barakaat International Foundation v Council and Commission* (Joined Cases C-402/05 P and C-415/05) [2008] ECR I-6351, [2010] All ER (EC) 1105.
[28] Paragraph 303.

The relevant regulation was found to breach those fundamental rights standards, as it did not provide any means for Mr Kadi to know the basis under which he was placed on the sanctions list. His victory was a pyrrhic one as the Luxembourg Court delayed its annulment order so that a replacement Regulation could be adopted.[29]

Strasbourg has also retained a role even where other systems of protection exist. We have seen this in relation to the United Nations, as in *Al-Jedda*. In addition, where an applicant contends that an EU measure violates a Convention right, the Strasbourg Court does not relinquish the field to the Luxembourg Court but applies a rebuttable presumption that EU law provides equivalent protection for Convention rights.[30]

Where does the United Kingdom stand on this? We are contracting parties to the Convention and a member of the European Union. Have our courts similarly policed the boundaries between their field of operation and that of the supra-national courts?

UK approach to the supranational courts: the 'mirror' principle

UK jurisprudence has taken its own course. After all, unlike, for instance, Germany, we have no higher constitutional law which is to be protected in priority to Convention rights. Indeed, as we have seen, s 2 of the European Communities Act 1972 has the effect that EU law is seamlessly absorbed into our domestic law. The Human Rights Act 1998 is different in its approach to the Convention because it provides that judges will 'take into account' Strasbourg jurisprudence. In the light of this, our courts have adopted what Baroness Hale has called 'the mirror principle', which means that English law will apply and reflect the clear and constant jurisprudence of Strasbourg, save in special cases.[31]

I do not propose to allow myself to be drawn into a discussion of whether this reading of the Human Rights Act 1998 is the right one or, as Lord Judge, formerly Lord Chief Justice of England and Wales,[32] has suggested, the wrong one, on the basis that the courts are only bound to 'take into account' Strasbourg jurisprudence. Nor do I intend to be drawn into the argument over whether our courts should go further and speak on questions on which the Strasbourg Court has not yet spoken. These are questions which I or others may have shortly to decide in our judicial capacity and we must wait to hear the arguments.

The effect of the mirror principle is that the courts must follow Strasbourg jurisprudence without exercising their own scrutiny save at a relatively minimal

---

[29] *Kadi II* concerned Mr Kadi's challenges to the decision to place him on the sanctions list: Joined Cases C-584/10 P, C-593/10 P and C-595/10 P, [2014] All ER (EC) 123.
[30] *Bosphorus Hava Yollari Turizm v Ireland* (Application No 45036/98) (2006) 42 EHRR 1.
[31] Baroness Hale, 'Argentoratum locutum: Is Strasbourg or the Supreme Court supreme?' [2012] HRLR 12.
[32] *Constitutional change: unfinished business* <http://www.ucl.ac.uk/constitution-unit/constitution-unit-news/constitution-unit/research/judicial-independence/lordjudgelecture041213/>.

level. The original formulation of this principle came in a case known as *Ullah*.[33] It is to be found in a judgment of Lord Bingham, one of the greatest judges of the United Kingdom in the twentieth century. It has been the subject of some refining in the highest court. The most recent statement is in the judgment of Lord Sumption in *R (Chester) v Secretary of State for Justice*:[34]

The courts have for many years interpreted statutes and developed the common law so as to achieve consistency between the domestic law of the United Kingdom and its international obligations, so far as they are free to do so. In enacting the 1998 Act, Parliament must be taken to have been aware that effect would be given to the Act in accordance with this long-standing principle. A decision of the European Court of Human Rights is more than an opinion about the meaning of the convention. It is an adjudication by the tribunal which the United Kingdom has by treaty agreed should give definitive rulings on the subject. The courts are therefore bound to treat them as the authoritative expositions of the convention which the convention intends them to be, unless it is apparent that it has misunderstood or overlooked some significant feature of English law or practice which may, when properly explained, lead to the decision being reviewed by the Strasbourg court.

Thus the adoption of the mirror principle amounts to a decision not to develop the UK's own jurisprudence on human rights. On this basis, it can be said to be ahead of its time. If the *Ullah* principle had been accepted by all the contracting states, it would have led to an integrated legal order in Europe but Europe as presently constituted would not accept that.

Some might observe that there is something odd about a supranational system of law in which one country implements Strasbourg case law by having courts which protect the constitutional identity of the nation state while others implement it in way that starts from a position of full compliance from which only a limited number of exceptions are available. But the fact is that the English courts have come to this particular issue only recently with the Human Rights Act 1998. They are slowly working their way towards a solution. The correct view is, as I see it, that the attitude of the English courts to Strasbourg jurisprudence is still developing. In due course it may well come to provide the United Kingdom with just as much protection as that available in other contracting states.

Some suggest that, if the mirror principle is set aside, English courts will somehow be liberated altogether from Strasbourg jurisprudence, and that England and Wales will be free to develop their own rights jurisprudence. I would rather doubt that. What tends to happen in practice is that, if a party claims that their human rights have been infringed, they point to some Strasbourg case law. Since the English courts were not able to give effect to Convention rights from the start in 1950, we are still playing 'catch-up'. Strasbourg jurisprudence would thus be likely to play an important role even if we did not have the mirror principle.

---

[33] *R (Ullah) v Special Adjudicator* [2004] UKHL 26, [2004] 2 AC 323.
[34] [2014] UKSC 63, [2014] 3 WLR 1076 at [121].

Metaphors for this new inter-judicial relationship: pyramid or mobile?

In a recent speech, Professor Dr Andreas Voßkuhle, the President of the FCC, discussed the question whether the relationship between the supranational and national courts was that of pyramid or a suspended, free-flowing mobile.[35] He concluded that the relationship was more like the latter: that there is no duty on national courts of strict obedience where the constitutional identity of the member state is jeopardized. He points out that the parts of the mobiles are linked together by strings and that those strings must not become entangled. I find this a very compelling metaphor but I would suggest that it must not be taken too far. The analogy with the mobile could suggest that the courts are open to influence and are blown by the winds. The fact is that domestic courts often have an important role to protect the constitutional identity of the domestic system in the supranational sphere. This is particularly so if the margin of appreciation (or, as it is called in EU law, subsidiarity) which they have been allowed by the Luxembourg and Strasbourg Courts is exceeded.

I would also compare the position in some respects to that of an ill-fitting jigsaw. I prefer this metaphor because it conveys the idea of two or more pieces jostling to occupy the same space from different directions. The supranational court and the national court are seeking to occupy the same legal space but approach it from very different angles. Thus, for example, the Luxembourg Court may be concerned about the impact of integration on the single market. The national court may be concerned with compatibility of an EU measure with the national constitution.

Our national courts are in a pyramid—High Court, Court of Appeal, and Supreme Court. The position is similar in Scotland and Northern Ireland. What the analogies with a mobile and jigsaw show is that it is wrong to assume that, just because our national courts exist in a pyramidal system, so do our courts in relation to the supranational courts. The supranational courts have their own spheres of operation. Those spheres are limited: they do not cover the huge range of matters which national judicial systems cover. So on no basis is the relationship between national courts and European courts one that could be described as pyramidal.

Checks and balances, not democratic deficit

I am now going to develop some ideas about how the system of supranational courts might be improved. The protection of a state's constitutional identity cannot solely be achieved at the level of the state. It must also be appropriately protected in the supranational court itself.

---

[35] European Court of Human Rights, *Dialogue between Judges 2014*, p 19.

A criticism that people tend to make about the Strasbourg Court is that there is a 'democratic deficit': they say that the decisions made by a state's elected legislators, or by its constitution or constitutional court, can in effect be overturned by a court which is an unelected body and whose decisions cannot be appealed to any other body. In a sense, it is a fool's errand to seek a democratic system when assessing a supranational court. In the case of a supranational court, states, which give up a certain measure of control over their own affairs, need to establish something else: they need to establish that there are checks and balances in the system or that there are *accountability mechanisms* which, as far as possible, ensure a proper balance in the relationships.

Do these checks and balances exist or can they be created? My answer is yes, this can and is being done in at least three ways: internal working methods, brakes on implementation, and constant renewal of the relationship between supranational courts and national courts.

Supranational court's own working methods

I shall have space only to deal with the Strasbourg Court: a similar exercise could be conducted for the Luxembourg Court. The following features can be identified:

(1) *Transparency*: The Strasbourg Court maintains much information on its website and holds hearings in public. It also publishes an annual report and holds an open meeting at the start of its legal year.

(2) *Role of the national judge*: In any case concerning a contracting state, its national judge will always participate in the decision. This is an important means of helping to ensure that the Strasbourg Court is properly informed about the position in the nation state.

(3) *Implementation*: Decisions are reported to the Committee of Ministers of the Council of Europe, who oversee implementation.

(4) *Precedent*: The Strasbourg Court does not regard itself as always bound by precedent. This helps give Strasbourg jurisprudence its plasticity.

(5) *Guarantee of quality of judgments*: One of the ways this is achieved is by a rigorous process of electing judges. Strasbourg judges have to be elected by the Parliamentary Assembly from national lists.[36] There is always room for improvement here. There is a panel to advise the Parliamentary Assembly on the candidates before it. This panel system may not work very well at the moment but it is new. The Parliamentary Assembly of the Council of Europe should give the highest priority to electing as judges the persons who are the best qualified for the role. In addition, contracting states need to be encouraged to ensure that they nominate candidates who are well

---

[36] Thus, unusually, Strasbourg judges are not simply appointed by the governments of the contracting states.

qualified and suited for election, and that they have systems for selection designed to bring forward a diverse range of the ablest candidates.

(6) *Margin of appreciation*:[37] This is the term used to describe the recognition by Strasbourg that the democratic authorities in any particular contracting state are best able to decide on measures in a particular area. It is, therefore, a mechanism which is used to mark out the boundaries between contracting states and Strasbourg. It is one of the Strasbourg Court's coping strategies: if the case involves a sensitive matter on which the views of contracting states tend to differ, the Strasbourg Court allows a 'margin of appreciation', which means that it will leave it to the contracting state to make the final decision. The decision to allow a margin of appreciation can be very controversial: if the Strasbourg Court declares that an act is within the margin of appreciation, it may be accused of failing to ensure compliance with the Convention. Conversely, if it fails to declare a margin of appreciation, it may be said to have interfered with national sovereignty. The decision is therefore a tricky one for it.

(7) *Consensus*: The Strasbourg Court may use consensus among European countries to narrow the margin of appreciation allowed to a member state or to enable it to interpret the Convention rights more dynamically. The use of consensus is somewhat like the use of state law by the US Supreme Court—Brandeis J famously referred to the states' laws as 'laboratories of democracy'. He said: 'A state may, if it choose, serve as a laboratory, and try novel social and economic experiments without risk to the rest of society.'[38] They could experiment with new ideas, giving new rights to their citizens, and in due course the Supreme Court would consider whether those ideas were in fact also reflected in rights in the US Constitution.[39]

(8) *Subsidiarity in implementation*: Both EU law and Strasbourg case law depend on national courts to apply their decisions in future cases. It is very important that the national courts have responsibility for implementation because it is at that stage that the ill-fitting edges of a supranational court's decision and domestic law can be made to work together.

(9) *Right of individual petition*: A key feature of the Convention system is that an individual may petition the Strasbourg Court over violations of Convention rights. This ensures that they have a right of immediate access to Strasbourg and, in an appropriate case, to a remedy under the Convention. I should say a word here about the proposition that human rights are universal in abstraction but national in application. This proposition, which has been very powerfully advanced by Lord Hoffmann[40] in particular, is used as an

---

[37] In EU law, the equivalent mechanism is subsidiarity.
[38] See *New State Ice v Liebmann*, 285 US 262, 311 (1932) (Brandeis J, dissenting).
[39] The US experience, for instance with abortion rights, has been that if there is no consensus there may be a long rearguard action testing the limits of what has been decided by those who do not agree with the case law.
[40] 'The Universality of Human Rights' (2009) LQR 416.

argument for not permitting the right of individual petition so that the Strasbourg Court would never make a decision in a particular case: that would be left to the contracting state. I do not myself think that this argument is correct. There can be acceptable differences of opinion as to whether something constitutes a violation of human rights: for example, on the extent to which the state may be involved in religion without violating an individual's Convention right to manifest his religion. Some states adopt a strict approach of *laïcité*: ie no intervention by the state in religious affairs. There are other contracting states, like the United Kingdom, where the Head of State is also head of the established Church in one of the constituent parts of the United Kingdom. No-one would seriously argue that there cannot be a cultural difference of that kind in the way a state is organized. However, there is also a large measure of agreement on basic rights: the disagreement is more at the level of the proportionality of, and justification for, differences. In that situation, the societal choice of the contracting state should be respected and the restriction is tested against well-established standards of proportionality. This is not inconsistent with the important right of individual petition.

Brakes on national implementation

Having discussed the internal working methods of the supranational court, I now turn to make some observations and proposals about the important subject of how their decisions, which may be very controversial in some states, are to be implemented. A certain amount of leeway in implementation freedom is inherent in the Convention.[41]

There can be variations in the speed of implementation. When Strasbourg case law requires to be implemented by the national court, the latter decides how to develop its own law and makes appropriate decisions about the period of time over which changes are to be made.

Importantly, national courts can disagree with the Strasbourg Court and require it to think again. There are now several instances where the UK courts have done this. The national courts may not succeed in persuading the Strasbourg Court to change its mind, but as in *Z v UK* there have been cases where it has been shown that the Strasbourg Court has unfortunately drawn the wrong conclusions about national law. Parliament may also enter into a dialogue with Strasbourg, as has happened with prisoner voting.

We should never reach the stage where there is complete disagreement between the Strasbourg Court and the contracting state but there may be long delays in implementation.

---

[41] See generally N Bratza, 'The Relationship between the UK courts and Strasbourg' [2011] EHRLR 505.

Constant renewal of the relationship between national and European legal orders by formal and informal dialogue

I have already referred to the formal dialogue that goes on when a national court disagrees with a decision of a supranational court but we also need informal dialogue—a conversation between the leading European courts and the supranational courts.

Judges have, therefore, engaged in a considerable amount of dialogue with the Strasbourg Court, that is informal meetings in which we each exchange views on general issues. It is a very important form of contact. In a recent speech the former president of the European Court of Human Rights, Nicholas Bratza, said that the United Kingdom was one of the countries which had the most effective dialogue with Strasbourg.[42]

But there is another important form of dialogue: the formal dialogue between the Court and the contracting states through the Interlaken, or Brighton, process. The contracting states began a process of formulating reform proposals at a High Level Conference on the future of the Strasbourg Court in Interlaken in 2010. There was particular concern over the size of its backlog, which has now greatly reduced. The process is continuing and has led to a number of administrative changes and to new Protocols. There have been a number of conferences since including one at Brighton in 2012. The process has been very successful. I have some further suggestions to make.

Before I do that, there is a word of explanation needed about judicial accountability. A principal badge of judicial accountability in national courts is that judges show restraint in their decision-making and do not venture into those areas which should be left to national Parliaments. For the Strasbourg Court, there is a constant tension between its international obligation to interpret the Convention and national sovereignty. One of the difficulties for Strasbourg is that it is difficult for it to know whether it has gone outside that area of restraint. I think it would help in that regard if there was the ability to use a new form of judgment, which I will call a 'provisional judgment'. This is not a challenge to Strasbourg's independence but rather an attempt, as its jurisprudence matures and reaches more deeply into the legal systems of contracting states, to link it up more effectively with contracting states.

There are various ways in which provisional judgments can be used. Under one version, if the decision would significantly develop its jurisprudence, the Strasbourg Court would not issue a binding decision but only a provisional decision. So, if it proposed to declare for the first time, say, that there was a right of access to court, it would first issue a provisional judgment. In that provisional judgment it would indicate how it proposed to interpret the Convention but give national courts the opportunity, and a generous period of time, to express their view on the practicality of this development.

---

42 Miriam Rothschild and John Foster Memorial Lecture, London, 2013.

Another situation is where a provisional judgment will simply indicate that Strasburg's current view, was that unless there was a change in circumstances, it would decide, in an appropriate case, in say three years' time that a new interpretation would be given to a certain right. Contracting states would be able to intervene in the proceedings when the point next arose for final decision and file submissions for Strasbourg's consideration. National courts would be able to express their views in their judgments, so promoting a dialogue between national courts, on the one hand, and Strasbourg on the other. National courts might even consider each other's approach, which could be mutually instructive. Strasbourg might then confirm its provisional judgment or it may decide not to do so or, more likely, to do so with adjustments that meet, so far as appropriate, the points raised by the national courts or contracting states.

There are yet other cases in which a provisional judgment might be used. It could save a lot of friction if they were used where Strasbourg was minded to draw conclusions about the legislative procedure or domestic laws in a contracting state. I will give two examples. First, the majority judgment in *Hirst v UK*,[43] decided in 2005, on prisoner voting criticized Parliament for having no substantive debate on prisoner voting. That criticism is only valid if it means that Parliament had not considered the matter. The majority judgment refers to a working party on electoral reform which considered whether prisoners should have the right to vote. It did not give the date of its report. In fact the report was completed in 1999,[44] not in the Victorian era but just six years before *Hirst*. It was a cross-party working party. The Chair was a minister of state. The majority do not mention that the report was laid before Parliament and the Representation of the People Act 2000 was explicitly drafted to give effect to its recommendations.[45] The point was that the report dealt with prisoner voting and that Parliament had the opportunity to debate the matter had it wished to do so. A provisional judgment would have enabled these details to be flushed out before the judgment was finalized. With a proper explanation, it might have been seen that the criticism did not reflect the reality of how Parliamentary business is conducted.

Another example is *Vinter v UK*,[46] in which the Strasbourg Court held that it was contrary to Art 3 of the Convention[47] for the UK to have a category of prisoners serving whole life terms (a highly charged subject in national debate) with no prospect of release unless they were suffering from a terminal illness and were near to death. However, as the Court of Appeal presided over by the Lord Chief Justice, recently pointed out, there was a material error in the Strasbourg Court's understanding of our domestic law because it did not appreciate that there was really no doubt but that the Secretary of State would have to review the sentence of even a person with a whole life sentence if there would otherwise be

---

[43] Application No 74025/01 (2005) 19 BHRC 546.

[44] Report of the Working Party on Electoral Procedures, chaired by the Parliamentary Under-Secretary of State for Northern Ireland, Mr George Howarth MP, presented to Parliament on 19 October 1999 (Deb, 1999 WA 435 19.10.99).

[45] See the Explanatory Notes on the Bill, published by Parliament.

[46] Application No 66069/09 (2013) 34 BHRC 605.

[47] This prohibits inhuman or degrading treatment or punishment.

a breach of Art 3 of the Convention.[48] So the Strasbourg Court's reasoning in *Vinter* was thoroughly undermined. The Court of Appeal, therefore, held that it should not take any account of the Strasbourg Court's decision.

The provisional judgment would not prevent the Strasbourg Court from dealing with the cases already filed, or before it, on a different basis from that set out in the provisional judgment.

Is there any prospect of the Strasbourg Court taking this idea on board? I feel sure it would consider it. I have already described the plasticity of Strasbourg jurisprudence and its ability to embrace new ideas. It is a resourceful court. It has already developed new forms of judgment, such as the 'pilot' judgment.[49] It has already agreed that in future all cases involving departures from its existing case law should be relinquished to the Grand Chamber.[50] This should both ensure greater consistency but also enable the cases that might be suitable for a provisional judgment procedure to be more easily identified. The Strasbourg Court has also accepted the principle of the non-binding judgment in Protocol 16, which lays down a new procedure for non-binding advisory judgments but has not yet come into force. I am hopeful, therefore, that the idea of provisional judgments can be injected into the Brighton process and that the Strasbourg Court will consider it and experiment with the idea. The provisional judgment would go a long way to meeting some of the most serious criticisms of the Convention.

To my mind the idea of a provisional judgment is consistent with the notion that the relationship between national and supranational courts is not as, currently assumed, a strictly hierarchical one. As we saw earlier, in many respects, it is more like a mobile or an ill-fitting jigsaw. A provisional judgment process would lead to a more balanced relationship between contracting states and the Strasbourg Court because contracting states would have had an opportunity to contribute to the process. The procedure currently gives them a right to intervene in any case but with nearly a 1,000 judgments being issued in a year it is impossible for them to do so in practice without a provisional judgment.

There are other ideas that could be injected into the Brighton process. At all events we must keep the process alive.

Relationship with the Luxembourg Court

It is an aspect of sovereignty that the state is entitled to reach a view as to the limits of the powers which it has delegated to another international body. The

---

[48] *Re Attorney General's Reference No 69 of 2013, R v McCloughlin, R v Newell* [2014] EWCA Crim 188, [2014] WLR(D) 82.

[49] Where there are serial cases involving the same violation, Strasbourg selects a 'pilot' case and gives a judgment which decides what remedies are called for in the individual case and also how the problem should be dealt with more generally by the country concerned. Pending the outcome of the pilot state's reaction, all the other comparable cases are put on hold: *Broniowski v Poland* (Application No 31443/96) (2005) 43 EHRR 1.

[50] *The Interlaken Process and the Court* (2013), 11, published by the European Court of Human Rights. The reform process is variously called the Interlaken process and the Brighton process.

international body may disagree and may have the final word, but there is nothing to stop the national court from expressing a view. As I have explained, there are a number of leading courts in Europe which have laid down a marker, and who have not simply treated EU laws as having in all respects immediate and automatic effect, as the United Kingdom has done.

The FCC and other courts have already developed mechanisms which enable them to uphold their own state's constitution or constitutional identity in the face of challenge from the European Union. In 2004, I wrote an article suggesting in effect that, if it was thought right, something similar could be done in the United Kingdom.[51] Nothing has yet been done. To my mind it is still an option and would help to put us on a par with countries like Germany. I envisaged that Parliament would give the courts jurisdiction to determine for the purposes of English law whether an EU measure goes beyond the powers which the United Kingdom has agreed to confer on the European Union. Their decision might be of some weight in the European Union. Parliament could also give the courts jurisdiction to determine whether any proposed EU measure threatens the United Kingdom's fundamental rights or constitutional principles. It ought not to be an obstacle that we do not have a written constitution. Jurisdiction along these lines might provide some reassurance to the citizens of this country if it is decided that the United Kingdom's future is to remain in the European Union.

The Supreme Court has taken some tentative steps in the same direction in its 2014 decision on *HS2*.[52] It considered the position if a relevant EU directive had required the courts to consider the adequacy of information placed before Parliament. This might have infringed Art 9 of the Bill of Rights. Lord Reed held that it would be for the UK courts, and not Luxembourg, to determine if there was a conflict between EU law and a constitutional principle of the UK.[53] I respectfully agree with that view. It is consistent with the decisions of the FCC and the Conseil d'Etat.

The key question is, however, how such a question should be resolved. On that point, Lord Neuberger and Lord Mance, with whom the other Justices of the Supreme Court agreed, considered it arguable that Parliament had not authorized the abrogation of certain fundamental principles laid down by statute or the common law.[54]

Some seeds have, therefore, been sown and we shall have to see if they bear fruit. Nothing, however, has been said about determining whether an EU measure, which did not involve a violation of constitutional principle or fundamental right, fell outside the terms of any powers conferred by the United Kingdom on the European Union or any of its institutions. As I have explained, my paper in 2004 extended to encouraging discussion and resolution of this issue too.

---

[51] 'Jurisdiction of the New United Kingdom Supreme Court' [2004] PL 699. (Reproduced at Chapter 19.)

[52] *R (Buckinghamshire County Council) v Secretary of State for Transport* [2014] UKSC 3, [2014] 1 WLR 324.

[53] At [79].   [54] At [204] to [208].

Summary: Community of courts or Bowling Alone?

In this paper, I have made the following points:

(1) The question whether the United Kingdom should remain a party to the European Convention on Human Rights or a member of the European Union is a question for Parliament. I assume for the purposes of this paper that the present legal position continues.

(2) There is a complex and sophisticated European legal order.

(3) Different national courts, for example the German Federal Constitutional Court and the French Conseil d'Etat, have reacted in a range of ways to the new European supranational courts in Luxembourg and Strasbourg.

(4) It would be wrong to assume that, because national courts are hierarchical, that the same is true of the relationship between national courts and supranational courts.

(5) In some respects, the relationship is like that of a suspended, free-flowing mobile, or an ill-fitting jigsaw.

(6) States should look for checks and balances in the relationship, not democratic mechanisms.

(7) I propose that the Strasbourg Court should consider issuing judgments which are provisional only in the first instance when it significantly develops the law so that the national courts and contracting states can contribute to the process. This idea could be considered in the current Brighton reform process.

(8) I also propose that courts be given more powers to determine whether EU law is inconsistent with fundamental rights or constitutional principles of English law or whether EU measures exceed for English law purposes the powers conferred by the United Kingdom on EU institutions.

(9) There are other ways to strengthen the relationship with both supranational courts, especially through dialogue.

The development on the European legal scene might usefully be compared with the idea in Robert Putnam's book, *Bowling Alone*.[55] In this book, Putnam analysed the fragmentation in American society by analysing the growth in the social phenomenon of people who went to bowling alleys alone to bowl by themselves.

That for many years has been how European courts have done their work. However, they are now rapidly becoming a community of courts and working together to produce a new European legal order in which all the domestic legal orders take part. They are no longer *bowling alone* but bowling with each other.

---

[55] R Putnam, *Bowling Alone: The Collapse and Revival of American Community* (Simon & Schuster, 2000).

The UK can be a 'big player' in the world legal scene because of the quality of its legal system and law schools, but in my view the courts have to be prepared to be more receptive towards other systems of law for this to be done most effectively.

The role of judges today can include stepping beyond their national shores and finding out what is happening in the highest courts of their own region in the world and in the supranational courts whose jurisprudence applies to them. Judges need to establish networks with judges in different jurisdictions—to understand those legal systems and take inspiration from them, like Parke B in *Hadley v Baxendale*.

What can we do in the future to help this complex non-hierarchical legal scene evolve into the future? In my view we need to pursue many forms of dialogue. Tensions are inevitable in a complex system with ill-fitting jigsaw pieces. What tends to happen is that there is a tension over some quite minor issue but it is seen as having much wider significance and so becomes a source of great attention and public debate. In the case of the Strasbourg Court, we need to continue the successful Brighton reform process. We need to keep the process going and inject new ideas into it.

With the idea of provisional judgments, and the new powers I have suggested for our national courts in relation to EU law, my aim has been to show that there is more we can do to perfect the burgeoning relationship between our domestic courts and the supranational courts in Europe.

Epilogue

This collection of papers is dealing with live subject matter. The new legal orders referred to in the title of this Volume are not yet fully built.

There can be few occasions in legal history when judges have given lectures questioning so fundamentally some international instrument which Parliament has incorporated into domestic law as they have in recent times.[1] Certainly in the United Kingdom, courts usually interpret an enactment purposefully, so that it complies with the international instrument as interpreted by the court set up for that purpose. This was no doubt behind the famous speech of Lord Bingham in *R (Ullah) v Special Adjudicator*,[2] which stated that English law should in general follow Strasbourg jurisprudence 'no more, but certainly no less'. But judges have not merely questioned the decisions of the two supranational courts. In some cases they have gone further and challenged their right to decide issues. By contrast, I have examined the way in which the supranational courts decide cases and I have suggested improvements, such as the introduction of provisional judgments.

Why are human rights law and EU law openly criticized? Does the legal debate simply mirror the intense controversy in society as to whether the United Kingdom should remain a party to the Convention and whether it should continue to be a member of the European Union? I have said in the Introduction that judges do not express views on party political matters. The decisions on being a party to the Convention and membership of the European Union clearly involve wide political, social, and economic factors and not simply the legal considerations on which judges would be competent to speak. On the other hand, all courts have to be sensitive to major controversy of this kind. In deciding any case, courts have to take account of what is acceptable from many angles, and one of those angles is public opinion, if there is evidence of it.

Thus the Supreme Court of the United States often declines to take a case or to decide an issue until there has been sufficient experience of it, often in the form of cases decided across the United States, in order that it has a good view of the

---

[1] See Lord Hoffmann, 'The Universality of Human Rights', Judicial Studies Board Annual Lecture 19 March 2009; Lord Sumption, 'The Limits of the Law', 27th Aslan Shah Lecture, Kuala Lumpur, 20 November 2013; Lord Justice Laws, 'Lecture III: The Common Law and Europe', Hamlyn Lectures 2013, 27 November 2013; Lord Judge, 'Constitutional change: unfinished business' <http://www.ucl.ac.uk/constitution-unit/constitution-unit-news/constitution-unit/research/judicial-independence/lordjudgelecture041213/>.

[2] [2004] UKHL 26, [2004] AC 323.

spectrum of legal and public opinion on a matter on which the population is deeply divided. It is in general open to the Supreme Court of the United Kingdom to decline to take an appeal in the same circumstances. It has very wide power to decline to take appeals.

By contrast, the Luxembourg Court has very limited power to refuse to accept a request from a national court for a ruling on EU law. The Strasbourg Court likewise has in general power to reject an application only if it is manifestly not well founded. Both the Luxembourg Court and the Strasbourg Court may therefore have to take cases before they are ready to do so, and that may mean that their reasoning is obscure or over-condensed because they have not had sufficient experience of that issue or because they are not ready to give a final answer.

The debate between national and supranational courts has brought out into the open an aspect of judging that was previously not to the fore, namely that the judgments of courts, whether they are national or supranational courts, have to be acceptable in numerous senses of that term. Courts do not operate in a vacuum. They must factor into their consideration the attitude of other institutions in society. Therefore perhaps one of the problems for the supranational courts is that they do not enjoy the relationship with the institutions of civil society that national courts do. That relationship is fundamental to relatively trouble-free decision-making.

If that is the source of the problem, then there is an opportunity here for national courts to make a real contribution to the processes of decision-making in supranational courts by offering their views on the issues that face supranational courts. That would be another use for dialogue. National courts and supranational courts can conduct their dialogue informally through regular meetings or formally through their judgments.[3] But there could be other ways in future of providing this dialogue. There could be new institutions, composed of senior judges from the national courts or other institutions, to provide supranational courts with essential feedback. Supranational courts could be given power to call for the views of national courts. National courts could combine to set up study groups to produce submissions for the supranational courts. Such submissions would inevitably carry considerable weight.

This development would usefully throw new light on the function of judges in national courts in relation to supranational courts. That those judges do have such a function is clear. But, to perform any function, they must have the willingness and ability to speak the legal language of other jurisdictions.

Such developments in the relationship between national and supranational courts provide yet another reason for judges to adopt an international perspective on their work and to be alive to solutions to legal issues in other jurisdictions.

---

[3] In the case of the Strasbourg Court, an additional opportunity for dialogue through judgments would also be provided by Protocol 16, but this has not yet been signed or ratified by the United Kingdom.

The road since the coming into force of the Human Rights Act 1998 has been steep. Looking back, it has often been the case, as TS Eliot said,[4] that we had the experience but missed the meaning. I hope this Volume has demonstrated that we are now well on the way to finding the meaning of the developing new legal orders in Europe.

---

[4] *The Dry Salvages.*

Selected Provisions of the Human Rights Act 1998 and of the European Convention on Human Rights

Human Rights Act 1998

1 The Convention Rights

(1) In this Act 'the Convention rights' means the rights and fundamental freedoms set out in—

    (a) Articles 2 to 12 and 14 of the Convention,

    (b) Articles 1 to 3 of the First Protocol, and

    (c) Article 1 of the Thirteenth Protocol, as read with Articles 16 to 18 of the Convention.

(2) Those Articles are to have effect for the purposes of this Act subject to any designated derogation or reservation (as to which see sections 14 and 15).

(3) The Articles are set out in Schedule 1 . . .

2 Interpretation of Convention rights

(1) A court or tribunal determining a question which has arisen in connection with a Convention right must take into account any—

    (a) judgment, decision, declaration or advisory opinion of the European Court of Human Rights,

    (b) opinion of the Commission given in a report adopted under Article 31 of the Convention,

    (c) decision of the Commission in connection with Article 26 or 27(2) of the Convention, or

    (d) decision of the Committee of Ministers taken under Article 46 of the Convention,

whenever made or given, so far as, in the opinion of the court or tribunal, it is relevant to the proceedings in which that question has arisen . . .

3 Interpretation of legislation

(1) So far as it is possible to do so, primary legislation and subordinate legislation must be read and given effect in a way which is compatible with the Convention rights.

(2) This section—

    (a) applies to primary legislation and subordinate legislation whenever enacted;

    (b) does not affect the validity, continuing operation or enforcement of any incompatible primary legislation; and

(c) does not affect the validity, continuing operation or enforcement of any incompatible subordinate legislation if (disregarding any possibility of revocation) primary legislation prevents removal of the incompatibility.

4 *Declaration of incompatibility*

(1) Subsection (2) applies in any proceedings in which a court determines whether a provision of primary legislation is compatible with a Convention right.

(2) If the court is satisfied that the provision is incompatible with a Convention right, it may make a declaration of that incompatibility.

(3) Subsection (4) applies in any proceedings in which a court determines whether a provision of subordinate legislation, made in the exercise of a power conferred by primary legislation, is compatible with a Convention right.

(4) If the court is satisfied—
   (a) that the provision is incompatible with a Convention right, and
   (b) that (disregarding any possibility of revocation) the primary legislation concerned prevents removal of the incompatibility, it may make a declaration of that incompatibility.

(5) In this section 'court' means—
   (a) the Supreme Court;
   (b) the Judicial Committee of the Privy Council;
   (c) the Court Martial Appeal Court;
   (d) in Scotland, the High Court of Justiciary sitting otherwise than as a trial court or the Court of Session;
   (e) in England and Wales or Northern Ireland, the High Court or the Court of Appeal;
   (f) the Court of Protection, in any matter being dealt with by the President of the Family Division, the Chancellor of the High Court or a puisne judge of the High Court.

(6) A declaration under this section ('a declaration of incompatibility')—
   (a) does not affect the validity, continuing operation or enforcement of the provision in respect of which it is given; and
   (b) is not binding on the parties to the proceedings in which it is made.
   . . .

6 *Acts of public authorities*

(1) It is unlawful for a public authority to act in a way which is incompatible with a Convention right.

(2) Subsection (1) does not apply to an act if—
   (a) as the result of one or more provisions of primary legislation, the authority could not have acted differently; or
   (b) in the case of one or more provisions of, or made under, primary legislation which cannot be read or given effect in a way which is compatible with the Convention rights, the authority was acting so as to give effect to or enforce those provisions.

(3) In this section 'public authority' includes—
   (a) a court or tribunal, and

    (b) any person certain of whose functions are functions of a public nature, but does not include either House of Parliament or a person exercising functions in connection with proceedings in Parliament.

(4) ...

(5) In relation to a particular act, a person is not a public authority by virtue only of subsection (3)(b) if the nature of the act is private.

(6) 'An act' includes a failure to act but does not include a failure to—

    (a) introduce in, or lay before, Parliament a proposal for legislation; or

    (b) make any primary legislation or remedial order.

7 *Proceedings*

(1) A person who claims that a public authority has acted (or proposes to act) in a way which is made unlawful by section 6(1) may—

    (a) bring proceedings against the authority under this Act in the appropriate court or tribunal, or

    (b) rely on the Convention right or rights concerned in any legal proceedings, but only if he is (or would be) a victim of the unlawful act.

(2) In subsection (1)(a) 'appropriate court or tribunal' means such court or tribunal as may be determined in accordance with rules; and proceedings against an authority include a counterclaim or similar proceeding.

(3) If the proceedings are brought on an application for judicial review, the applicant is to be taken to have a sufficient interest in relation to the unlawful act only if he is, or would be, a victim of that act.

   ...

(5) Proceedings under subsection (1)(a) must be brought before the end of—

    (a) the period of one year beginning with the date on which the act complained of took place; or

    (b) such longer period as the court or tribunal considers equitable having regard to all the circumstances, but that is subject to any rule imposing a stricter time limit in relation to the procedure in question.

(6) In subsection (1)(b) 'legal proceedings' includes—

    (a) proceedings brought by or at the instigation of a public authority; and

    (b) an appeal against the decision of a court or tribunal.

(7) For the purposes of this section, a person is a victim of an unlawful act only if he would be a victim for the purposes of Article 34 of the Convention if proceedings were brought in the European Court of Human Rights in respect of that act.

(8) Nothing in this Act creates a criminal offence.

(9) In this section 'rules' means—

    (a) in relation to proceedings before a court or tribunal outside Scotland, rules made by the Lord Chancellor or the Secretary of State for the purposes of this section or rules of court, ...

(10) In making rules, regard must be had to section 9.

(11) The Minister who has power to make rules in relation to a particular tribunal may, to the extent he considers it necessary to ensure that the tribunal can provide an appropriate remedy in relation to an act (or proposed act) of a public authority which is (or would be) unlawful as a result of section 6(1), by order add to—

    (a) the relief or remedies which the tribunal may grant; or

    (b) the grounds on which it may grant any of them.

(12) An order made under subsection (11) may contain such incidental, supplemental, consequential or transitional provision as the Minister making it considers appropriate.

...

8 *Judicial remedies*

(1) In relation to any act (or proposed act) of a public authority which the court finds is (or would be) unlawful, it may grant such relief or remedy, or make such order, within its powers as it considers just and appropriate.

(2) But damages may be awarded only by a court which has power to award damages, or to order the payment of compensation, in civil proceedings.

(3) No award of damages is to be made unless, taking account of all the circumstances of the case, including—

(a) any other relief or remedy granted, or order made, in relation to the act in question by that or any other court), and

(b) the consequences of any decision (of that or any other court) in respect of that act, the court is satisfied that the award is necessary to afford just satisfaction to the person in whose favour it is made.

(4) In determining—

(a) whether to award damages, or

(b) the amount of an award,

the court must take into account the principles applied by the European Court of Human Rights in relation to the award of compensation under Article 41 of the Convention.

(5) A public authority against which damages are awarded is to be treated—

...

(b) for the purposes of the Civil Liability (Contribution) Act 1978 as liable in respect of damage suffered by the person to whom the award is made.

(6) In this section—

'court' includes a tribunal;

'damages' means damages for an unlawful act of a public authority; and

'unlawful' means unlawful under section 6(1).

12 *Freedom of expression*

(1) This section applies if a court is considering whether to grant any relief which, if granted, might affect the exercise of the Convention right to freedom of expression.

(2) If the person against whom the application for relief is made ('the respondent') is neither present nor represented, no such relief is to be granted unless the court is satisfied—

(a) that the applicant has taken all practicable steps to notify the respondent; or

(b) that there are compelling reasons why the respondent should not be notified.

(3) No such relief is to be granted so as to restrain publication before trial unless the court is satisfied that the applicant is likely to establish that publication should not be allowed.

(4) The court must have particular regard to the importance of the Convention right to freedom of expression and, where the proceedings relate to material which the respondent claims, or which appears to the court, to be journalistic, literary or artistic material (or to conduct connected with such material), to—

(a) the extent to which—

(i) the material has, or is about to, become available to the public; or

(ii) it is, or would be, in the public interest for the material to be published;

(b) any relevant privacy code.

(5) In this section—

'court' includes a tribunal; and

'relief' includes any remedy or order (other than in criminal proceedings).

Schedule 1

Part I: The Convention Rights and Freedoms

Article 2: Right to life

1. Everyone's right to life shall be protected by law. No one shall be deprived of his life intentionally save in the execution of a sentence of a court following his conviction of a crime for which this penalty is provided by law.

2. Deprivation of life shall not be regarded as inflicted in contravention of this Article when it results from the use of force which is no more than absolutely necessary:

   (a) in defence of any person from unlawful violence;

   (b) in order to effect a lawful arrest or to prevent the escape of a person lawfully detained;

   (c) in action lawfully taken for the purpose of quelling a riot or insurrection.

Article 3: Prohibition of torture

No one shall be subjected to torture or to inhuman or degrading treatment or punishment.

Article 4: Prohibition of slavery and forced labour

1. No one shall be held in slavery or servitude.

2. No one shall be required to perform forced or compulsory labour.

3. For the purpose of this Article the term 'forced or compulsory labour' shall not include:

   (a) any work required to be done in the ordinary course of detention imposed according to the provisions of Article 5 of this Convention or during conditional release from such detention;

   (b) any service of a military character or, in case of conscientious objectors in countries where they are recognised, service exacted instead of compulsory military service;

   (c) any service exacted in case of an emergency or calamity threatening the life or well-being of the community;

   (d) any work or service which forms part of normal civic obligations.

Article 5: Right to liberty and security

1. Everyone has the right to liberty and security of person. No one shall be deprived of his liberty save in the following cases and in accordance with a procedure prescribed by law:

   (a) the lawful detention of a person after conviction by a competent court;

   (b) the lawful arrest or detention of a person for non-compliance with the lawful order of a court or in order to secure the fulfilment of any obligation prescribed by law;

(c) the lawful arrest or detention of a person effected for the purpose of bringing him before the competent legal authority on reasonable suspicion of having committed an offence or when it is reasonably considered necessary to prevent his committing an offence or fleeing after having done so;

(d) the detention of a minor by lawful order for the purpose of educational supervision or his lawful detention for the purpose of bringing him before the competent legal authority;

(e) the lawful detention of persons for the prevention of the spreading of infectious diseases, of persons of unsound mind, alcoholics or drug addicts or vagrants;

(f) the lawful arrest or detention of a person to prevent his effecting an unauthorised entry into the country or of a person against whom action is being taken with a view to deportation or extradition.

2. Everyone who is arrested shall be informed promptly, in a language which he understands, of the reasons for his arrest and of any charge against him.

3. Everyone arrested or detained in accordance with the provisions of paragraph 1(c) of this Article shall be brought promptly before a judge or other officer authorised by law to exercise judicial power and shall be entitled to trial within a reasonable time or to release pending trial. Release may be conditioned by guarantees to appear for trial.

4. Everyone who is deprived of his liberty by arrest or detention shall be entitled to take proceedings by which the lawfulness of his detention shall be decided speedily by a court and his release ordered if the detention is not lawful.

5. Everyone who has been the victim of arrest or detention in contravention of the provisions of this Article shall have an enforceable right to compensation.

Article 6: Right to a fair trial

1. In the determination of his civil rights and obligations or of any criminal charge against him, everyone is entitled to a fair and public hearing within a reasonable time by an independent and impartial tribunal established by law. Judgment shall be pronounced publicly but the press and public may be excluded from all or part of the trial in the interest of morals, public order or national security in a democratic society, where the interests of juveniles or the protection of the private life of the parties so require, or to the extent strictly necessary in the opinion of the court in special circumstances where publicity would prejudice the interests of justice.

2. Everyone charged with a criminal offence shall be presumed innocent until proved guilty according to law.

3. Everyone charged with a criminal offence has the following minimum rights:

(a) to be informed promptly, in a language which he understands and in detail, of the nature and cause of the accusation against him;

(b) to have adequate time and facilities for the preparation of his defence;

(c) to defend himself in person or through legal assistance of his own choosing or, if he has not sufficient means to pay for legal assistance, to be given it free when the interests of justice so require;

(d) to examine or have examined witnesses against him and to obtain the attendance and examination of witnesses on his behalf under the same conditions as witnesses against him;

(e) to have the free assistance of an interpreter if he cannot understand or speak the language used in court.

Article 7: No punishment without law

1. No one shall be held guilty of any criminal offence on account of any act or omission which did not constitute a criminal offence under national or international law at the time when it was committed. Nor shall a heavier penalty be imposed than the one that was applicable at the time the criminal offence was committed.
2. This Article shall not prejudice the trial and punishment of any person for any act or omission which, at the time when it was committed, was criminal according to the general principles of law recognised by civilised nations.

Article 8: Right to respect for private and family life

1. Everyone has the right to respect for his private and family life, his home and his correspondence.
2. There shall be no interference by a public authority with the exercise of this right except such as is in accordance with the law and is necessary in a democratic society in the interests of national security, public safety or the economic well-being of the country, for the prevention of disorder or crime, for the protection of health or morals, or for the protection of the rights and freedoms of others.

Article 9: Freedom of thought, conscience and religion

1. Everyone has the right to freedom of thought, conscience and religion; this right includes freedom to change his religion or belief and freedom, either alone or in community with others and in public or private, to manifest his religion or belief, in worship, teaching, practice and observance.
2. Freedom to manifest one's religion or beliefs shall be subject only to such limitations as are prescribed by law and are necessary in a democratic society in the interests of public safety, for the protection of public order, health or morals, or for the protection of the rights and freedoms of others.

Article 10: Freedom of expression

1. Everyone has the right to freedom of expression. This right shall include freedom to hold opinions and to receive and impart information and ideas without interference by public authority and regardless of frontiers. This Article shall not prevent States from requiring the licensing of broadcasting, television or cinema enterprises.
2. The exercise of these freedoms, since it carries with it duties and responsibilities, may be subject to such formalities, conditions, restrictions or penalties as are prescribed by law and are necessary in a democratic society, in the interests of national security, territorial integrity or public safety, for the prevention of disorder or crime, for the protection of health or morals, for the protection of the reputation or rights of others, for preventing the disclosure of information received in confidence, or for maintaining the authority and impartiality of the judiciary.

Article 11: Freedom of assembly and association

1. Everyone has the right to freedom of peaceful assembly and to freedom of association with others, including the right to form and to join trade unions for the protection of his interests.
2. No restrictions shall be placed on the exercise of these rights other than such as are prescribed by law and are necessary in a democratic society in the interests of national

security or public safety, for the prevention of disorder or crime, for the protection of health or morals or for the protection of the rights and freedoms of others. This Article shall not prevent the imposition of lawful restrictions on the exercise of these rights by members of the armed forces, of the police or of the administration of the State.

Article 12: Right to marry

Men and women of marriageable age have the right to marry and to found a family, according to the national laws governing the exercise of this right.

Article 14: Prohibition of discrimination

The enjoyment of the rights and freedoms set forth in this Convention shall be secured without discrimination on any ground such as sex, race, colour, language, religion, political or other opinion, national or social origin, association with a national minority, property, birth or other status.

Article 16: Restrictions on political activity of aliens

Nothing in Articles 10, 11 and 14 shall be regarded as preventing the High Contracting Parties from imposing restrictions on the political activity of aliens.

Article 17: Prohibition of abuse of rights

Nothing in this Convention may be interpreted as implying for any State, group or person any right to engage in any activity or perform any act aimed at the destruction of any of the rights and freedoms set forth herein or at their limitation to a greater extent than is provided for in the Convention.

Article 18: Limitation on use of restrictions on rights

The restrictions permitted under this Convention to the said rights and freedoms shall not be applied for any purpose other than those for which they have been prescribed.

Part II: The First Protocol ·

Article 1: Protection of property

Every natural or legal person is entitled to the peaceful enjoyment of his possessions. No one shall be deprived of his possessions except in the public interest and subject to the conditions provided for by law and by the general principles of international law.

The preceding provisions shall not, however, in any way impair the right of a State to enforce such laws as it deems necessary to control the use of property in accordance with the general interest or to secure the payment of taxes or other contributions or penalties.

Article 2: Right to education

No person shall be denied the right to education. In the exercise of any functions which it assumes in relation to education and to teaching, the State shall respect the right of parents to ensure such education and teaching in conformity with their own religious and philosophical convictions.

Article 3: Right to free elections

The High Contracting Parties undertake to hold free elections at reasonable intervals by secret ballot, under conditions which will ensure the free expression of the opinion of the people in the choice of the legislature.

Part III: Article 1 of the Thirteenth Protocol

Abolition of the Death Penalty

The death penalty shall be abolished. No one shall be condemned to such penalty or executed.

Articles 1 and 13 of the Convention (not included in Human Rights Act 1998, Schedule 1)

Article 1: Obligation to respect human rights

The High Contracting Parties shall secure to everyone within their jurisdiction the rights and freedoms defined in Section 1 of this Convention.

Article 13: Right to an effective remedy

Everyone whose rights and freedoms as set forth in this Convention are violated shall have an effective remedy before a national authority notwithstanding that the violation has been committed by persons acting in an official capacity.

Note: the legislation shown here is as in force at 1 September 2014.

Glossary

Appellate Committee of the House of Lords Most senior appeal court of the United Kingdom which was replaced by the Supreme Court of the United Kingdom set up by the Constitutional Reform Act 2005 with effect from 1 October 2009.

Convention The European Convention for the Protection of Human Rights and Fundamental Freedoms 1950 (usually referred to as the European Convention on Human Rights) and the Protocols in force. The Articles applicable in England and Wales are set out in Schedule 1 to the Human Rights Act 1998. (See Appendix.)

Convention rights Rights guaranteed by the Convention.

EU Treaties The treaties constituting the European Union.

German Federal Constitutional Court The Federal Constitutional Court of Germany.

Lisbon Treaty Treaty signed on 13 December 2007 and coming into force on 1 December 2009 which amended the Maastricht Treaty (renamed the Treaty on European Union (TEU)) and the Rome Treaty (renamed the Treaty on the Functioning of the European Union (TFEU)) and establishes the constitutional basis of what is now the European Union.

Luxembourg Court The Court of Justice of the European Union (CJEU), which sits in Luxembourg or its predecessor the European Court of Justice (or ECJ).

Luxembourg jurisprudence Case law of the Luxembourg Court.

Margin of appreciation Margin of discretion or corridor within which the Strasbourg Court permits a national body to choose between acceptable options for a rule which engages Convention rights.

Privy Council Judicial Committee of the Privy Council which hears appeals from members of the Commonwealth whose constitutions provide for such appeals and other territories, and certain other appeals.

Strasbourg Court The European Court of Human Rights, which sits in Strasbourg.

Strasbourg jurisprudence Case law of the Strasbourg Court.

Subsidiarity Principle whereby the European Union leaves it to the member states to take action on any particular matter, now governed by Art 5 TEU. Also used in relation to Strasbourg to refer to the doctrine of the margin of appreciation.

TEU Treaty on European Union, formerly the Maastricht Treaty.

TFEU Treaty on the Functioning of the European Union, formerly the Rome Treaty.

General Index

comparative law (*cont.*)
  treaty interpretation 294–8
  US Supreme Court 261–2
constitutional law
  national courts 2, 283–4
  supranational courts 2–4, 283–4
  variety of systems 131–2
constitutional order
  importance 256
  judicial role 256
control orders
  anti-terrorism measures 136, 153, 169, 182
  closed material 194
  deprivation of liberty 194
  derogation from Convention rights 192–4
  duration 191
  fair procedure 193
  function 191
  hearings 193
  non-derogating orders 192
  particular risk 191
  restrictions on movement 192–4
  terrorist suspects 191, 193, 197, 200
Council for Civil Service Unions v Minister for
  the Civil Service (1985) 56
Council of Europe
  Directorate of Human Rights 19
  establishment 17
  Human Rights Commissioner 19
  human rights protection 11, 237, 280, 301,
    304–6, 312
  treaty implementation 19
Court of Justice of the European Union
  (Luxembourg Court)
  admissibility of cases 322
  authoritative rulings 279
  balancing of rights 61
  case load 284
  delegation to national court 62
  enforcement of judgments 280
  EU law compliance 84
  flexibility 61–3
  free movement provisions 61
  function 279, 284
  fundamental rights protection 61–2, 84, 275
  intensity of review 63
  judicial restraint 61
  least intrusive means of interference 61
  legitimate aim 61
  manifestly inappropriate test 61–2
  national security measures 61, 94
  nature of decision-maker 63
  necessity test 61–2, 94
  policy decisions 63, 94
  precautionary principle 63
  preliminary reference procedure 76, 238,
    279–80, 322
  proportionality principle 61–3, 84 *see also*
    proportionality principle

public health measures 61, 94
public policy 62
subject matter of decision 63
subsidiarity principle 76–7, 81–2 *see also*
  subsidiarity principle
suitability test 61–2
treaty interpretation 279, 284, 294, 301
Criminal Justice Council 128

data protection
  privacy issues 212
De Freitas v Permanent Minister of Agriculture,
  Fisheries, Land and Housing (1999) 73
declarations of incompatibility
  Convention rights 25, 32, 100, 104, 106–8,
    119, 135–6, 176, 267
defamation
  privacy issues 211–12
democracy
  democratic deficit 312
  human rights protection 30, 36, 40
  institutions of democracy 36–7, 40
deportation
  deportation orders 150, 155
  inhuman and degrading treatment 177–8
  national security 177
  terrorist suspects 155, 177–8
  third countries 152
detention
  arbitrary detention 45
  ECtHR jurisprudence 303, 307
  Guantanamo Bay detainees, 146, 149,
    161–3, 173, 185–7
  indefinite detention 33, 45, 133, 136,
    145, 182
  preventative detention 33–4, 150, 159–60
  terrorist suspects 145–6, 159–60, 166–8,
    173, 178, 181–2, 197, 200
devolution
  accountability 81
  balancing of interests 126
  constitutional arrangements 80
  control of devolved institutions 81
  decentralization 81
  devolved powers, 78, 80–1, 125–6
  judicial role 126
  location of state power 80
  reserved powers 126
  statutory interpretation 125–6
  UK domestic legal order 78, 80–1
discrimination
  ECHR protection 120, 131, 150, 152,
    154, 282
  terrorist suspects 181, 183–5
Doherty v Birmingham City Council (2008) 288
Douglas v Hello Ltd (2000) 226
dynamic model of interpretation
  declarations of incompatibility 119
  development 112–13

Names Index